PRECIOUS VICTIMS

ABOUT THE AUTHORS

Don W Weber is a prosecutor and attorney in Madison County, Illinois, and was the prosecutor in the Paula Sims case. Charles Bosworth Jr is an award-winning investigative reporter for the *St Louis Post-Dispatch*, and has covered the Paula Sims case since 1986, with exclusive access to the key players involved on both sides.

PRECIOUS VICTIMS

Don W Weber and
Charles Bosworth Jr

This edition published in 2006 by
Virgin Books Ltd
Thames Wharf Studios
Rainville Road
London
W6 9HA

Published by Virgin Publishing in 1998

First published in Great Britain in 1992 by True Crime

First published in the USA by Signet, an imprint of New
American Library, a division of Penguin Books USA Inc.

A catalogue record for this book is available
from the British Library.

ISBN 0 8636 9598 1
ISBN 978 0 8636 9598 8

Typeset by TW Typesetting,Plymouth, Devon
Printed in the UK by CPI Bookmarque, Croydon, CR0 4TD

*To the prosecutors, the police, and the press,
and their search for the truth.*

Prologue

April 29, 1989

Sheriff Frank Yocom shifted his formidable girth behind the steering wheel of his unmarked police car without taking his eyes off the back door of the tavern, half a block away in the midnight darkness. He hated stakeouts, and he already had been sitting there for an hour and a half, waiting for a drug buy that may or may not come off. It wasn't even in the Jersey County sheriff's jurisdiction. But he had been asked for help by the police chief in tiny Grafton. Drug deals at the new tavern had become a persistent problem, and a bust by the police would let the mayor yank the liquor license and close down the place.

So Yocom sat and waited. If the two informants made the buy inside, the police would nail the dealers when they stepped out of the back door. It should be fairly routine; the stakeout certainly had been routinely boring.

But the quiet was broken by the surprising message over the police radio from the sheriff's dispatcher at headquarters in Jerseyville. The sheriff had an urgent call from the police in Alton, some fifteen miles away in neighboring Madison County, and the dispatcher didn't want to relay the message over the radio. Yocom fired up the engine and drove down the street to a small grocery store where he could use the telephone without alerting anyone. He called the emergency number for the Alton police and got a message from the dispatcher that sent a shudder through him.

"I'll be right there," the sheriff said as he hung up the phone.

It was fortunate that there was little traffic at midnight on the Great River Road, the scenic stretch of highway that runs along the Mississippi River for the fifteen miles between Grafton and Alton. Yocom thought he must be setting a land-speed record as he gunned his car down the highway, his mind lost in thoughts of what was awaiting him in Alton. The police there had called for Yocom's assistance with an investigation into a reported kidnapping. A woman named Paula Sims had told the police that a masked gunman had stolen her infant daughter from the family's home.

What a horrible crime—every parent's nightmare. A kidnapping is a tough crime for a cop to solve, and one that happens much less frequently than most people would believe.

Almost always, the sheriff knew, these cases turned out to be something other than a kidnapping. One of the parents, perhaps divorced or estranged, had taken the baby; maybe a baby-sitter or even the grandparents were responsible. Rarely do the police encounter a genuine kidnapping.

But Sheriff Frank Yocom already knew this case would be something else again. As shocking as a kidnapping would be, this had to be a million times worse, and more foreboding. After all, this was Paula Sims reporting the disappearance of a baby girl.

And for Paula Sims, this would be the second time.

The second time in three years that an infant daughter had disappeared from the Sims house. The second time that the police had received a panicked call in the night and had descended on the Sims house.

Yocom shook his head. Could this be happening again? How could it happen again? Another baby girl gone? It couldn't be.

The sheriff still lived with his memories of the first case, in June 1986 when the family lived near Brighton in Jersey County. Those events never seemed far from his thoughts, and the nagging frustration from that case never was far below the surface. The worn file marked "Loralei Sims" always sat on the table by his desk, and he still clung to the hope that the case that had reached inside and touched him the most deeply in sixteen years of police work would yet be solved.

But here he was, being pulled into a new Sims case—roaring down the highway toward a new Sims case. The Simses lived in Alton now, not even in his county. So it really was someone else's responsibility. But he had been called for assistance, and he knew there was no chance he could stay away.

My God, he thought. *How can this be?*

Chapter 1

June 17, 1986

The midday heat shimmered off the farm fields that covered the landscape around Brighton, and the humidity made the air seem even more oppressive. Muggy, as the natives called it. The temperature climbed to ninety-seven degrees that day, unusually hot for mid-June in southwestern Illinois. But after sunset the air cooled and a soft breeze blew away the day's heat.

The windows were open to catch some of the breeze that night at the home of Don and Minnie Gray on Cotter Road. They lived a mile west of the Brighton city limits, but the quiet that surrounded them and the nearby farm fields made it seem farther than that from the town of 2,400. The houses were spaced well apart out there, giving everyone room for gardens or orchards.

As they always did, the Grays—who were in their early fifties and looked like everyone's favorite aunt and uncle—were watching the ten o'clock news on Channel 2 that Tuesday night. They already had changed into their pajamas and soon would be turning in. Don Gray, still recovering from a hernia operation, had just gone back to work the week before in the office of a small manufacturing plant. When the weather forecast was over about 10:20, he closed the front door and headed for bed.

As he always did, he stopped in the kitchen for a glass of water. As he sipped, he gazed through the open window over the sink. Off to the right, he could see down his neighbors' long driveway, all the way to their house that sat in the amber glow from their dusk-to-dawn yard light. At the back edge of the light, he could just see the trees in the thick woods that began where the hill fell off sharply into a ravine just behind the house.

Nothing stirred; there wasn't a sound in the warm night air.

Minnie Gray picked up a magazine and was flipping through the pages when she wondered if she had locked the basement door. She called to Don to go down and check. It was the last normal moment the Grays would share for a long time.

The woman's voice from outside the living room window was shrill, and it frightened Minnie as it pierced the quiet.

"Let me in! Let me in!"

Minnie squinted through the peephole in the door, but couldn't see anyone. She stepped toward the window and yelled defensively, "Who is it? What do you want?"

The reply from outside was urgent, and a shock.

"It's Paula. Let me in!"

Minnie pulled opened the front door, and her young neighbor, Paula Sims, stumbled in. She was crying almost hysterically, a look of horror across her face.

'Help me! Help me! They stole my baby! They stole my baby!"

Minnie nearly shrieked back, "Who did? What happened?"

Paula was shaking and seemed unable to breathe. She bent over and propped her hands against her knees. Minnie guided her into one of the matching easy chairs just inside the living room door.

Paula's words tumbled out in a voice edged with a slight twang that betrayed her upbringing in rural Missouri.

"I was watching the news downstairs when a man with a mask and a gun came in and told me to lay on the floor for ten minutes or he would kill me. So I did. When I heard him leave, I started to run after him and I saw that he had taken my baby out of her bassinet. She was gone. I ran outside and I saw a shadow running down the driveway and I heard footsteps in the gravel. I chased him out to the road. But I couldn't see him. He was gone."

Don Gray had been checking the basement door when he heard the commotion upstairs. Must be some kids fooling around on the porch. He was shocked to find his neighbor, the new mother, sitting in his living room, telling this horrible story to Minnie. Paula Sims's face was contorted and she seemed nearly hysterical. But oddly, it didn't look like she was really crying.

The twenty-seven-year-old woman was dressed as the Grays had become accustomed to seeing her over the two years since she and her husband, Robert, had moved into the house at the end of the long driveway next door. Blue jeans, a T-shirt, and thongs. Her long, wavy, almost-red hair was parted in the middle and hung well below her shoulders.

"We have to call the police," Don urged. As he reached for the phone, Paula sobbed, "I have to call Rob! I have to call Rob!"

Minnie promised they would call him as soon as they alerted the police. But Paula bolted for the door.

"I have to get the number. I don't remember his number at work." She was out of the door before Minnie could stop her.

Don already was dialing the number for the Jersey County Sheriff's Department when Minnie yelled to him that she was going with Paula. Minnie ran into her bedroom, pulled on a blouse and some jeans, and then she was out the door, too. She was worried for Paula's safety, afraid that the kidnapper or his accomplices could still be out there, hiding in the dark. If they had taken Baby Loralei—Paula's beautiful, red-haired little girl—what other horrible things were they capable of doing?

"Lord, what am I getting into?" Minnie wondered as she crossed her yard and started down the Simses' driveway. It didn't matter; Paula needed help. Minnie had become very fond of Paula over the last two years. Paula had started visiting her regularly for those comfortable and enjoyable little chats. Minnie had raised two sons, and it was nice to have a younger woman as a friend. Neither had a job outside of the home, and they would talk for hours about all sorts of things—families, husbands, recipes, and children. Paula often sought, and seemed to appreciate, Minnie's advice.

Minnie had not had much contact with Robert Sims. He was a shift worker, and he slept and worked odd hours. Still, he seemed friendly, and even hauled some railroad ties in his pickup truck for the Grays when Don built a retaining wall.

Minnie remembered the day Paula had come to announce that she was pregnant. She didn't need to speak; Minnie had known by the look on Paula's face. They had talked so often after that about the coming of the baby. Minnie enjoyed sharing in the first-time mother's worries and joys.

Paula had turned to Minnie when the doctor suggested inducing labor because the baby was late. Paula had worried about the effect on her baby, and Minnie had assured her the doctors wouldn't do anything dangerous. With that support from her friend, Paula seemed less frightened.

She had called Minnie from Alton Memorial Hospital to tell her of Loralei Marie Sims's birth at 6:03 P.M. on June 5. Paula had been so excited, so happy. Minnie went to see Loralei the day after Paula brought her home. Minnie took a little lavender dress as a present, and arrived as Paula was feeding the baby in the basement family room.

In a poignant moment, Paula had looked up and said, "Isn't she pretty? I guess this is what life is really all about." The simple joy in that remark had brought tears to Minnie's eyes. She had cuddled the little girl while Paula straightened up the bassinet. Paula told her Loralei slept well and was no problem at all.

But now Loralei was gone, the victim of some bizarre kidnapping that had shattered the serenity of a soft summer evening.

It was a long run down the loose gravel in the Simses' driveway—every bit of 120 yards north from the road to the house. Minnie was surprised she had made it as well as she did in the dark. She slowed when she reached the Simses' porch, taking care not to stumble up that ridiculous step in the middle of the porch. The step was so awkward that even people who knew it was there could stumble over it in broad daylight.

As she reached the door, Minnie could see Paula standing in the dining room, already on the phone and crying again, "They stole the baby. They stole the baby." Minnie called, "Paula, it's me," and stepped in.

Paula hung up the phone. "I just told Rob," she said. "He's on his way home."

The Simses' big female collie, Shadow, slipped out of the door as Minnie opened it and ignored Minnie's pleas to return. Paula darted past Minnie. As she pulled Shadow back into the house, Paula said, "I just lost my baby. I can't lose you, too."

Minnie remembered that Paula once had said that Shadow heard everything and always warned her when anyone was outside. Minnie asked where the dog had been when the kidnapper had struck, and Paula said she must have been in one of the other rooms in the basement.

Minnie wondered aloud how the kidnapper had gotten into the house. Paula shrugged and shook her head. She pointed to the screen door and said she had locked it before she went downstairs to the family room with the baby. Minnie stepped to the door and saw a small rip in the screen near the handle. "This is how he got in," Minnie said.

Paula looked stricken. "Oh, Lord. I didn't know anyone would do that. I thought I was safe."

The stairway to the family room was a quick left turn just inside the front door. Paula took Minnie downstairs and pointed out the easy chair where she had been sitting. She had been watching the Channel 2 news, too, and the weather was on when she saw the kidnapper coming down the stairs. He ordered her to lie on the floor; she hoped he would ransack the house and leave. After what could have been as long as five minutes, she heard him go out the front door. She got up and ran toward the stairs, and saw that Loralei was missing from the bassinet.

To Minnie's surprise, Paula went back upstairs to search the house again for the baby. Minnie lingered for a moment, and looked at the bassinet. The blanket was folded back perfectly. Minnie resisted the urge to touch the mattress and check for warmth.

Paula seemed very nervous and upset, and was talking louder than usual. She kept putting her hands up to her face and saying, "They stole my baby. We have to get her back." She rambled on about what a good father Rob was and the plans they had made for the daughter they loved so much. Paula even said, "I've got to warm Loralei's bottle," and then answered herself by saying, "No, that won't do any good."

Minnie tried to reassure Paula, but it was no use. As the minutes ticked by, Paula even began to worry about her husband. "Rob should be here. I just know something happened to him."

About twelve miles away, at the Jefferson Smurfit plant in Alton, shift supervisor Richard Combs took the call from Paula Sims about 10:30 P.M. She was so upset that he had trouble understanding her. It took several minutes to get her calmed down enough for him to realize she was saying that someone had stolen her baby. He immediately sent word for Robert Sims to be called to the telephone from his laborer's job at the paper-manufacturing plant. Robert arrived in three minutes and Combs handed him the phone. Robert also seemed to struggle to understand his wife. Then he said, "You're kidding. You're not kidding—I can tell. I'll be right home."

He turned to Combs. "Damn. You're not gonna' believe this. Someone just took my baby." He slammed down the receiver and dashed out of the room.

About fifteen minutes later, Robert Sims was pounding on the door at the home of a friend, Dave Heistand, in Godfrey, an unincorporated area between Alton and Brighton. As Heistand opened the door, Robert collapsed on the living room floor.

He was nearly hysterical. "I can't drive any farther. You've got to help me. Someone stole my baby." All the way home, as Heistand drover faster than he ever had, Robert was crying and sobbing, "Why has this happened to me? Who has done this?"

Heistand had known the Simses for several years, and this was a Robert he had never seen before. Robert Sims had always been a calm, almost unemotional man.

Robert was thirty-four, slim and five-foot-nine. His beard and hair were a mixture of gray and brown. His dark eyes seemed large and piercing, perhaps more noticeable because of the odd arching of his eyebrows that seemed to convey a constant expression of surprise. He was so soft-spoken that it sometimes was hard to hear him, and his words came slowly and deliberately.

This night, in Heistand's car, there was a very different Robert Sims.

The night shift at the sheriff's department had been uneventful until Deputy John Hazelwood took a call at 10:27 P.M. from Don Gray reporting a kidnapping. The deputy told the caller that he would radio the Brighton city police for help and would get a deputy there as soon as possible. Gray promised to stand at the Simses' driveway with a flashlight to mark the house amid the darkness of the farm fields along Cotter Road.

Hazelwood dashed to a car and sped away. He radioed the Illinois State Police on their emergency radio network, called ISPERN. Relaying the information he had been given, Hazelwood asked for an emergency bulletin over the network to all police cars in the area.

He arrived at the Simses' just after Brighton Patrolman Chris White and Don Stewart, a village trustee who liked to ride along on patrol. They had heard Hazelwood's call and were at the house in two or three minutes.

They were met at the driveway by Don Gray, who had pulled on a pair of pants over his pajamas and was standing in the road waving a flashlight. He pointed toward the Simses' house and hopped into the backseat. Patrolman White drove down the long driveway and pulled up to the two-car garage on the end of the house. White and Stewart hustled inside, leaving Don Gray outside to wonder what in God's name was happening.

While Minnie Gray showed White the basement crime scene, Don Stewart started the first official interview with Paula Sims. She was sitting at the dining room table. She seemed almost incoherent and kept her hands over her face most of the time. She kept repeating, "Someone stole my baby. Please get my baby back."

Her description of the kidnapper was sparse, other than the details of a man about six feet tall, wearing dark clothing and a mask. He had a medium build and a deep voice. She couldn't describe the handgun.

As Deputy Hazelwood entered the house, he noticed

the four-inch, L-shaped tear in the screen door near the handle. When he spoke to the victim, she was so incoherent she couldn't answer his questions.

"Mrs. Sims, I know you're upset." Hazelwood used his most sympathetic voice. "But what we really need now is information. If we're going to get your baby back, we have to have some information about what happened."

Paula struggled to tell him the story, stopping often to gasp for breath.

Hazelwood went back out to his car to radio the state police that he had nothing new for the bulletin.

Someone asked Paula if she wanted her parents called. But she insisted that no one notify them yet. Her mother was very nervous and might not be able to take the shock.

Sheriff Frank Yocom had turned in early that night, but he and his wife, Carol, weren't asleep yet when the telephone rang at 10:27 P.M. The dispatcher was on the line with the news that a baby had been kidnapped from a home near Brighton. Within minutes, Yocom was driving south toward the scene eight miles away. He heard the ISPERN broadcast on the radio.

He had investigated several abductions before, but this was the first time he had been called on an infant kidnapping. He was anxious to get to the scene and find out what had happened. Surely it would turn out to be something else.

Yocom was a well-liked sheriff serving his fourth four-year term, a Republican in a rural Republican county. He had a soft-spoken demeanor and a ready smile, but he could shift immediately into a serious tone when it was necessary. His generally avuncular style was accompanied by a huge abdomen that protruded well over his hidden belt buckle. He could have been a sheriff in any small county, anywhere.

He pulled into the Simses' driveway about 11:00 P.M. and was met in the yard by Hazelwood. The deputy motioned toward the young woman standing near the porch and identified her as the mother of the victim. Hazelwood had asked everyone to step into the yard so another deputy could make a pass through the house to look for evidence.

Yocom walked over and introduced himself to Paula Sims. She was crying, but it was an odd sort of crying, unlike anything else he had ever heard.

In a fatherly tone, Yocom told her, "I know you've been over this with the other officers, but I'd like you to tell me what happened." After she ran through the story, Yocom began probing for more details.

"Do you know what kind of gun it was?"

"Just a gun."

"Was it brown or black or silver-colored?"

"I think it was black-colored."

"Was it a revolver?"

Paula looked puzzled. She obviously didn't know what a revolver was.

"It was just a gun."

"Could you identify his voice?"

"It was just an ordinary voice."

"Did he have gloves on?"

"I don't remember. Wait. I think he did have gloves on."

It wasn't much, Yocom thought, but it was a start. After all, this young woman had just been the victim of a horrible crime. Maybe she could give them more information when she had settled down a little later.

The sheriff had started to confer with some of the other officers when a car raced into the yard and skidded to a stop near the porch. A bearded man jumped out of the passenger's side, leaving the car door hanging open, and ran toward the house.

"I'm Robert Sims," he shouted to a deputy.

Robert hurried over to Paula and put his arm around her shoulders. She dropped her head onto his shoulder and began to sob. "Somebody stole our baby, Rob. They took Loralei."

He asked softly, "What happened, Paula?"

Yocom watched closely as Paula told her husband what had happened. It seemed an awkward moment for the couple, and Yocom was surprised that Mr. Sims never hugged his distraught wife.

They walked over to the porch, and Paula sat down on

a bench at a picnic table. She buried her face in a towel and began to cry. Someone asked if Robert's father should be notified. In a flash of anger, Paula jerked down the towel and spat out, "No, definitely not. He wasn't interested in being a grandfather. He didn't even want to come to the hospital. We're not calling him."

A few minutes later, Paula looked up and said, "Rob, I'm so sorry I disappointed you."

He answered quietly, "You didn't disappoint me."

"Yes, I did. You were disappointed when Loralei was a girl, and I disappointed you because I didn't stop the man from taking her."

Robert noticed that people were listening. He leaned down and whispered in her ear, and she didn't say any more.

If this was a real kidnapping, Sheriff Yocom knew he needed help and he needed it fast. He could get extra manpower and expertise from the Division of Criminal Investigation—the Illinois State Police detective group known as the DCI. Like a state-level FBI, the DCI could muster a crushing response of manpower and technical assistance from its crime laboratory in a short time, and the agents were well respected by the local police. Yocom would call for Captain Philip A. Kocis, the DCI zone commander stationed at the district headquarters in Collinsville, about forty miles south in Madison County.

And the state police also could bring in their canine units. Yocom had seen the dogs work many times, tracking the energetic, if overly optimistic, runaways from the state's youth correctional center at nearby Pere Marquette State Park. Yocom had watched the dogs track those kids through the woods, almost always sniffing them out. The sheriff knew Trooper Mike Donovan was the best canine officer he had ever seen.

Yocom used his car radio to call the state police headquarters and put in his requests for help. The state police said all of their canine units were in training at the state capitol in Springfield, some fifty miles to the northeast. It would be a while before they could be dispatched to Brighton. Yocom made some more checks over the radio, and got a promise of a quick response from a canine unit from the city of Wood River, about fifteen miles south into Madison County.

The sheriff walked back into the house and heard Robert Sims on the telephone. He had called Paula's parents, Orville and Nylene Blew, who lived about fifteen miles away in Cottage Hills, near Wood River. He was talking to his father-in-law.

"Are you sitting down? You're not going to believe this. Someone stole Loralei. That's right."

Five minutes later, the telephone rang. Orville Blew called back to confirm that it was Robert who had called. Orville said the Blews were on their way.

When Yocom went back outside, Robert followed him and when the men were alone, Robert demanded to know what was being done. The sheriff was put off by the tone, but he knew the young man must be feeling immense fear and pressure.

"Have you called the FBI?"

"Not yet. There's no jurisdiction for them yet."

"Have you set up roadblocks?"

"I don't think they'd do any good right now, Mr. Sims."

"Have you notified the airport?"

"What airport?"

"Lambert in St. Louis."

"No."

"Are you going to have dogs here?"

"Yes."

"Where are they?"

"They'll be here, Mr. Sims. You know, it takes a little while to get everything going and to get the people here. The state police dogs are in Springfield and they'll be here as soon as they can. We've got everything in the works and everything is under control."

Yocom was a bit offended by the exchange. He understood Robert Sims's concern, but getting in the sheriff's face wouldn't get the investigation under way any faster. There was little else that could be done at the moment, and Yocom realized that might seem strange to the Simses. The bulletin had been sent out over ISPERN, and the dogs and DCI agents were on the way. With such sparse information about a suspect or a vehicle, there was little else to do but wait.

Deputy Hazelwood had begun to draw more information from Robert. He remembered that a light blue Ford Falcon had been parked by the pond next to the Simses' house when he left for work about 8:30 that night. He had stopped and told the man in the car that he couldn't fish there.

Robert also recounted an angry exchange three days earlier, on Saturday, with a man driving a dingy green pickup truck. The stranger had come to the Simses' door to ask about fishing in the pond. He was upset when Robert told him it was not allowed. The man had driven his truck through the front yard on the way out, obviously in retaliation for being turned away.

Robert remembered another thing. A nurse at the hospital where Loralei was born had commented that she would like to "steal that baby."

"I'm sure she was just joking," he added, almost embarrassed to bring it up.

And Robert told Hazelwood that the Simses had received a number of harassing telephone calls to their unlisted number since they brought Loralei home from the hospital. When Robert would answer, no one would speak, and the caller would hang up.

They had brought Loralei home on Sunday, June 8. Robert stressed that she had not been out of the house since then. That didn't seem like an important detail, but it would play a role in another enigma in the case a week later.

Robert said they had lived in the house for more than two years. They were happy there, and got along well with each other. They liked to camp and had bought all-terrain vehicles to ride together. That image would become clearer for Hazelwood in a most memorable way during a subsequent search of the house.

Before long, Orville and Nylene Blew arrived with their son, Dennis. Although he was thirty years old, he still lived with his parents. He had suffered severe seizures since he had had the measles when he was three, and he was unable to live alone. Yocom noticed that Dennis, a tall, husky man, spent the rest of the night sitting at the picnic table outside.

Yocom also noticed that a hefty blonde woman had wheeled in about that time. One of the deputies told Yocom she was Linda Condray, Robert Sims's sister. She lived near the Blews in Cottage Hills.

The sheriff finally got the call he had been waiting for. His police radio crackled with a transmission from Phil Kocis, who already was en route to the scene. Yocom was relieved; he knew it was a little unusual for a captain to respond in person.

Shortly after midnight, the canine unit from Wood River arrived. At Yocom's direction, Patrolman Ralph Timmons led his dog on a search around the driveway for a scent leading toward the road. That was the kidnapper's direction of flight, according to Paula. Not long after Timmons arrived, Trooper Mike Donovan and his dog pulled in. Trooper James Buysse arrived with his dog just after 12:30 A.M., and Yocom thought things might start to happen.

Hazelwood noticed a van from KSDK-TV, Channel 5 News in St. Louis, parked on the road by the driveway. He was amazed they were on the scene already. It was the first sign that the Paula Sims story would draw intense coverage by the media.

Phil Kocis was awakened about midnight by the call from headquarters in Springfield. He followed that with a call to the duty agent, and directed him to send detectives to the scene immediately. Kocis started to go back to sleep, but a bureaucratic alarm went off in his head. Just the month before, headquarters had been upset because DCI had not included the state's new "I SEARCH" program in an investigation into the disappearance of a teenaged girl who later was found raped and murdered. I SEARCH was a favorite project of the chief inspector, designed to coordinate efforts to look for missing children. The name was an acronym for the labored title of Illinois State Enforcement Agencies to Recover Children. Kocis decided he had better be informed on this case so he could bring in I SEARCH as soon as possible.

He swung his feet out of bed as he mumbled, "I'd

better go to the scene.'' Anyway, he thought, this would be the first baby kidnapping case he had worked in his sixteen years as a cop.

Kocis was a trim man with neatly combed, graying hair who usually appeared in one of his trademark natty wool sport coats. His strengths were organization and quick decisions in the middle of an investigation.

After the twenty-minute drive to Brighton, Kocis turned on Cotter Road just as Hazelwood and Yocom were taking a young man into custody in the parking lot of an abandoned service station on the corner. Kocis pulled into the lot and walked over to Yocom. The sheriff gave him a briefing on Paula Sims's report, and Kocis thought, ''My God, what a terrible thing.''

Yocom also told Kocis that the man they were arresting had pulled into the Simses' driveway and then sped off as Hazelwood approached the car. Hazelwood had chased him down and noticed he was wearing a black T-shirt and blue jeans. He would turn out to be just a nosy passerby.

Kocis followed Yocom to the Simses' house. Robert and Paula were in the basement, and Kocis took a moment for a quick tour of the house. It was being photographed and processed by Dee Heil, a DCI crime scene technician responsible for finding and preserving evidence. Kocis noticed nothing unusual, except that there was nothing out of place in the house that would mark it as a crime scene.

The DCI duty agent that week was Jimmie Bivens, one of the most respected officers in the area. He was a tall, rangy man with natural cop instincts that had been honed to a fine point after twenty-nine years as a state trooper and detective. After Kocis called, Bivens started to shrug off the case and assign it to one of the other agents. But kidnappings were rare; he decided to drop by the scene. The I SEARCH situation also flashed through his mind.

Bivens arrived at the Simses' shortly after 1:00 A.M. and found Kocis and Yocom in the front yard. Bivens and the sheriff had met before, but they didn't know each other well. Bivens got the quick version of Paula Sims's story and what the police were doing. The three men decided that Bivens would coordinate the investigation outside, leaving Yocom and Kocis to deal with the Simses and later, it was expected, the media.

Robert came off the porch and approached Jimmie Bivens immediately. As soon as he could get Bivens alone, he began asking about the FBI and roadblocks, and offering other suggestions. He got the same responses from Bivens he had received earlier from the sheriff. But he persisted in following Bivens around, and soon the cop felt his new sidekick could get in the way.

"Why don't you go back over there with your wife," Bivens suggested firmly. "She needs you more than I do. If you want to do something, make a list of areas we can search." His tone left little room for argument, and effectively conveyed the thought running through his mind: *That's enough of this, buddy*.

Jim Bivens was a loner when he was working. He preferred to be off to one side, taking in the scene and letting the situation soak in slowly so he could sort it out. He didn't need a shadow, even if it was a concerned father.

About 1:50 A.M., the three officers decided it was time to get every bit of information possible from the Simses. Yocom hoped Paula had settled down a bit by now, so he asked her to join the officers in the basement to go over the events in detail.

But to the sheriff's disappointment, the still-trembling woman was unable to offer anything new. Bivens dug for more.

"Did you hear any other sounds when you chased him to the road, like his feet slapping on the asphalt?"

"I can't remember."

"Did your dog bark when the guy came in?"

"No."

"Your house is immaculate. How come nothing is disturbed?"

"I guess he never touched anything. He just took my baby."

She couldn't offer any suggestions as to why someone would do this to them; they had no enemies.

Yocom fished for a motive. "Do you or Robert use drugs?" he asked bluntly.

Paula was just as candid, and admitted that they

smoked a little marijuana now and then. But it was purely recreational, she swore, and neither of them sold drugs.

Phil Kocis tried his hand. "Are you cheating on your husband? Or is he cheating on you?"

"No." Her answer was unemotional, and she didn't seem to resent the question.

As they talked, Kocis noticed the unmistakable screech of the screen door at the top of the basement stairs as the police officers went in and out of the house.

Eeeeeerrrr . . . . . SLAM!!
Eeeeeerrrr . . . . . SLAM!!
Eeeeeerrrr . . . . . SLAM!!

Kocis whispered to Yocom, "Go up and close that screen door as quietly as you can."

eeeerrrr!

eeeerrrr!

Even with the sheriff trying to muffle the sounds, they were like a burglar alarm in Kocis's ears. Hadn't she heard them before she saw the kidnapper?

"No," Paula shook her head.

"It's pretty loud. Why do you think you didn't hear it?"

"I don't know."

Paula had begun to cry more and more as the interview progressed and the officers pressed harder for answers. By 2:20 A.M., she seemed so distraught that Bivens ended the interview.

Robert Sims was next. The first bit of information that surprised Yocom was the young husband's revelation of a previous marriage. Robert's first wife was from Maine, and they had met and married while he was stationed there in the Navy. She had gone back there after their marriage ended and he hadn't heard from her for years.

He and Paula had been married for about five years. They had waited a long time to have children and were thrilled with Loralei's birth. He had taken some vacation time so he could be there to help after they brought Loralei home from the hospital. He had just returned to work the Thursday night before the kidnapping.

He hold them he had received another hang-up phone call about 4:30 P.M., just six hours before the kidnapping. He had left for work about 8:30, a little earlier than usual, so he could stop at the Toy Chest toy store on the Beltline in Alton and return a mobile crib toy they had received as a gift for Loralei. He had then gone down the street to two other discount stores, Target and Venture, to buy a garden tool and a flashlight that was on sale. They were out of the tools. The flashlight also was out of stock, but he had the rain check from the store right here.

Quite a memory, Frank Yocom thought as Robert recounted the call from Paula and his stop for help on the way home.

Robert mentioned his workshop in the garage. He talked about his woodworking projects, and how he tinkered with an old car.

The sheriff was struck by the almost irritating monotony of Robert's slow, soft voice, and the odd boredom of interviewing this father of a kidnapping victim.

But Phil Kocis had a much harsher reaction. He had disliked Robert Sims on sight; he just was the kind of man who brought out that reaction in the captain. And Kocis gave his suspicion free reign while Robert was talking. Was he just so careful and thoughtful about what he said, or could he be on drugs?

Kocis also was put off by Robert's long discussion of his woodworking shop. Wasn't he going to ask about the investigation? Kocis finally reined him in.

"Tell me about a fight at work or something. Tell me something above a motive for this."

There was nothing to tell, Robert said.

Bivens had written out the basics of Robert's statement. He asked him to sign it if it was accurate. He signed "Robert E. Sims" on all four pages, and Bivens and Yocom signed as witnesses. Bivens timed it at 3:15 A.M.

Yocom was glad that was over.

Bivens had been pleased to see his old buddy Mike Donovan and his dog, Judd, roaming the yard. Bivens knew Judd's reputation for finding bodies. But by 3:00 A.M., Donovan and the other canine officers had drawn a blank. There was no scent from a kidnapper and no scent from a corpse. Donovan's dog had been interested briefly in something at the edge of the pond. But he hadn't followed through with it, so it probably wasn't anything.

More dogs would be called in after daylight, the three top cops decided. There was a lot of ground that had not been covered, and it would be easier after the sun had come up.

Kocis added that I SEARCH involvement would mean almost unlimited resources, and it was agreed to ask for the maximum on three fronts. They could use an airplane equipped with a heat-seeking camera to search the terrain around the house for body heat. A boat with sonar could check for objects in the pond next door. And divers could scour the murky bottom.

With more dogs and the high-tech gear, it would be an all-out assault.

Firing up that kind of investigation in the middle of the night can take some time, all the cops knew. It would be a while before even the basic points could be covered and even a preliminary judgement could be rendered about what was going on. But already, some things didn't feel right, and each cop had some doubts gnawing inside.

Sheriff Frank Yocom was sure that this rural area near a small town was an unlikely spot for this strange kind of kidnapping. And surely Paula would have seen the fleeing kidnapper under the yard light in the driveway, or at least heard the getaway car. But most of all, it rubbed Yocom wrong to believe that a new mother would lie down on the floor and pay so little attention to the gunman standing over her precious daughter.

Yocom's early hope that Paula Sims might come up with something more useful as the night drew on had faded. Her answers during the last interview hadn't been any more lucid than before, and that made him uncomfortable.

And Yocom was bothered by the lack of scents anywhere for the police dogs to find.

That didn't bother Bivens or Kocis too much. But Bivens had other problems with what he had seen and heard so far. He wasn't ready to buy that rip in the screen door. It was too small, almost like someone didn't want to do any more damage than necessary. And that bassinet, still made up perfectly after little Loralei was pulled so ruthlessly from its warmth.

Paula's account of the kidnapping was bizarre, and Bivens was uncomfortable with the way she told it—almost as if she were in a trance or reading from a script. There was some sniffling and crying, and just enough details to offer some credibility. But it wasn't right.

And Bivens was concerned because the Simses had not slipped into either of the two reactions that would have been normal. They never surrendered to the emotion, never ranted in that gut-wrenching combination of anger, fear, and grief. On the other end of the scale, they never withdrew into the sanctuary of their own thoughts, pulling back from the world outside. They should have done one or the other.

Bivens stepped outside, alone for a few minutes. He stood in the driveway in the dark and listened. Nothing but quiet—deep, still quiet.

"It's so quiet, I could hear a cricket fart. And no one heard this kidnapper or this hysterical mother chasing him down this gravel driveway?"

Phil Kocis kept thinking about the way Paula acted during the interview, especially the way she cried. She seemed to cry at the right times, but Kocis hadn't been able to see the tears.

"She's doing what she wants me to think is crying. But where are the tears?" he wondered.

It wasn't long until all those doubts bubbled to the surface. Yocom and Kocis joined Bivens outside, and they huddled near a patrol car. Bivens's hands were stuffed into his pants pockets and he was staring at the ground.

"Something's not right," he muttered.

Yocom nodded. "Something doesn't add up here. It doesn't fit."

Kocis was shaking his head. "They're not acting right. Not like this is a kidnapping. And there's nothing even close to a motive."

They exchanged knowing glances.

The Grays went home about 2:00 A.M. There wasn't much more they could do at Paula's. Her family was there, and the place was crawling with cops. Don Gray went right to bed. It had been a long night for a man recuperating from surgery.

But Minnie Gray knew she would never be able to sleep. She sat down in the living room to ponder the events of the last three and a half hours, and to shed a few tears. It didn't seem real. Surely that sweet baby wasn't really gone.

Minnie went over Paula's story again and again. There was nothing to prove that it hadn't happened, but none of it made much sense. The more she thought about it, the more contradictions she found. But the alternative made Minnie shudder. The Paula Sims who Minnie knew was a gentle, loving young woman who had anticipated her first child's birth eagerly and had been so happy with her new daughter. All those hours talking, over all that time. Could that same woman somehow be involved in some unspeakable deed?

It was a long night for Minnie Gray.

Chapter 2

The investigation into Loralei's disappearance would reveal only bits and pieces about the strange lives of her parents. Some of it was vaguely interesting to the police. But little of it seemed very useful to the investigation. It wasn't evidence, and it didn't even seem to offer an explanation, let alone a motive, for what had happened. But this mother's biography was a perplexing story.

Paula Marie Blew was born into what easily could have been a happy, normal family living the middle-class version of the American dream in the Midwest. Instead, the family seemed destined to struggle under the weight of omnipresent tragedy.

The strife began before Paula was born on May 21, 1959, the last child of Orville and Nylene Blew of Freeman, Missouri. They already had two sons—Dennis, born in 1955, and Randy, born the next year. Dennis had been struck with a severe seizure disorder after a bout with the measles when he was three years old. He was left with disabling seizures that struck without warning, toppling him dangerously to the floor. He could not be left unattended. His classmates could be cruel with their teasing, especially to a young boy whose mind not only was clear but was sharp and hungered for knowledge. He was well read and had a striking grasp of current events and politics.

When Paula was in the second grade, her family moved to La Plata, in Northeastern Missouri. It was a quiet farming town of 1,400, some two hundred miles northwest of St. Louis. Orville Blew was employed by the Amoco Oil Company, and he had been transferred to La Plata to work on the pipeline that cut through that part of the state.

Paula was a relatively normal child, though somewhat shy. To neighbors of the Blews, she was the pleasant tomboy playing outside the family home on Bates Street. She loved to bake and often brought plates of cookies to a man who lived nearby.

To her best friends as a youngster, such as Robin Veatch, Paula was "an ordinary, ornery kid." She could be moody, and often just wanted to be alone. Paula, Robin, and some of their girlfriends amused themselves by shoplifting little items from the local stores—candy and other kid stuff, just to see if they could get away with it.

Paula's interests leaned toward athletics, such as basketball and swimming at the lake just outside of town; she excelled in both of those activities. Paula and Robin also loved to ride their motorized minibikes. Paula was tougher than most girls, and not afraid of anyone. She never hesitated to stand up for herself or something she believed in. To some, it seemed to go beyond just the courage of her convictions. She became known as "a good scrapper," ready to challenge anyone—boy or girl—to fight if they offended her. She impressed one boyfriend as a girl who wouldn't "take any shit off anybody."

Paula didn't seem to be interested in typical "girlish stuff." She didn't join the other girls for a soda after school to act silly and giggle about boys. She was more interested in the newest minibikes coming out, and her conversation ran more toward the number of 'cc's' in the bikes' engines than which girl had insulted which other girl.

Paula also never expressed much of an interest in children. In fact, Paula chose to make extra money by mowing lawns rather than by babysitting.

Paula was close to both of her brothers, but in ways as different as the boys themselves. She was protective of Dennis, and very attentive. She often could be seen in the evenings escorting him on a walk or taking him to the movies. With her reputation for being tough and unafraid, no one made fun of Dennis when his sister was around.

But Paula idolized Randy, who grew into one of the most handsome and popular boys in town. Indeed, he seemed to have an almost charismatic effect on other people, especially the other students who looked to him as something of a natural leader. He dated often, and even girls a few years younger than him "thought the world of him."

As the big brother, Randy teased his little sister mercilessly. But he also took the time for some one-on-one basketball with her. Except for the color of their hair—Paula's was auburn, Randy's dark brown—they even looked very much alike.

Paula loved being with Randy and his friends. As she entered her teen years, she began spending her time with them, running with the older crowd. Her other friends, such as Robin, pulled away. Paula began to build a reputation like the crowd she ran with—rougher, faster, rowdier. There were rumors of drinking and marijuana use, maybe even stronger drugs.

Robin knew Paula was experimenting with marijuana and alcohol. But she chalked it up to the influence of the older kids, especially the boys Paula was dating.

Paula never was in trouble at school. The teachers and administrators knew her as a fairly bright student, often friendly, but sometimes almost sour. School officials heard the rumors of the alcohol and marijuana use, but there was never any official confirmation.

She played on the girls' softball team, but really shined as a standout basketball player. It was during the basketball games that some noticed Paula's temper when she became angry over a call by a referee or the actions of another player.

One of Paula's boyfriends was Randy's best friend. Their dating included smoking marijuana regularly, but no other drugs were involved. She impressed him as not being "a real truthful person, and not above telling a lie."

That impression also struck the mother of one of Paula's girlfriends. The woman thought Paula was someone who would "lie to your face."

Another boyfriend was brutally frank in his comments to the police fifteen years later. He said he had begun dating Paula when she was a fifteen-year-old freshman in high school, and she already was taking birth-control pills. He claimed to have had a sexual relationship with Paula while they dated for about two years.

He told the police that she liked to "party and get high," and that she was drinking and using marijuana regularly by the time she was a freshman. He had joined her in both activities before and after school almost daily. He said their drug use expanded to LSD when they could get it, and she occasionally had stolen and taken some of the pills prescribed for her brother's condition.

The man claimed that he had visited Paula shortly after she had moved to Illinois, spending several days at the Blews' home while Orville and Nylene were out of town. He and Paula partied in that area, as well as in nearby St. Louis. Paula provided the marijuana and LSD, apparently having established her own source near her new home, he alleged.

That boyfriend went on to spend time in prison on convictions of selling drugs and carrying a concealed weapon.

It may have been Paula's choice of him as a boyfriend that figured in one of the Blews' tragedies—one from which the family may never have recovered.

On April 10, 1976, Randy borrowed a friend's car (some reports said without permission) and took Paula for a drive. He may have wanted to talk to Paula about her boyfriend; Randy didn't like him.

They were speeding along a road on the western edge of town when Randy lost control of his car, crashing it head-on into another car and then ricocheting off a tree. Randy's skull was crushed; he was dead at nineteen. Paula, then sixteen, was sitting beside him. She suffered severe facial injuries and was hospitalized. But she was able to attend her brother's funeral.

The report on the accident by the Missouri Highway Patrol said Randy Blew was intoxicated at the time of the crash, and it listed "drinking and drugs" as contributing factors.

Paula was never the same after the crash. She had always been quiet and a loner. But she withdrew even more after Randy died beside her. She was quieter and much less aggressive.

To some, Paula never seemed happy again, as if she held herself responsible for the crash. Was she nurturing the seeds that would grow into a sister who couldn't forgive herself?

Even her parents noticed the change. While still in the hospital, Paula told her mother she was mad over Randy's death. The Blews watched Paula become quieter and more withdrawn. She seemed to have fewer friends, just one or two at a time. Nylene knew that Paula was hurt deeply, even though she was the kind who rarely allowed herself any outward display of emotion. Paula would do no crying for Randy in the presence of others.

Years later, the kind of rumor that can thrive in a small town surfaced about Randy and Paula. According to an FBI report, a trooper with the highway patrol who participated in the investigation of the fatal crash said he had been told at the scene by a police officer from La Plata that he had found the brother and sister committing a sex act in Randy's parked car one night.

The FBI tried to confirm that report. If Paula had suffered some kind of sexual abuse or trauma as a girl, even in a consensual sexual relationship with her brother, it could provide some clue to a psychological injury that could affect her in unpredictable ways as an adult. But the agents never heard another word to support the story. They interviewed every current and former policeman who worked in La Plata in 1975 and 1976, and no one claimed any knowledge of the incident.

Bill Bullock probably knew Orville Blew and his family as well as anyone in La Plata, and better than most. Bill and Orville worked together on the pipeline every day for more than 10 years, and had known each other for some time before that. Bullock had watched his friend care for his family, and had watched the children grow up. He had watched one of them lowered into his grave.

Bullock would be retired before the name of Paula Sims came back to haunt La Plata, and he never would be able to reconcile the family he had known in the past with the people he was reading about in the news.

But one thing was certain in his mind. The Blews were better people than the publicity about them allowed, and he thought the beating they were taking in the press was a dirty shame. There never was a fair account of their "positive side," he thought.

Bill liked Orville, all the way around. Orville was a good man, a good worker, a good provider for his family, and a good friend.

Nylene was almost as outgoing and friendly as her hus-

band. But she was more "hyper," and the tragedies the
family suffered aggravated her tendency to become extremely nervous under stress. Randy's death had a devastating effect on her. One of the reasons the Blews
moved from La Plata may have been because Nylene
would not stay away from Randy's grave.

Orville and Nylene were married in 1954, when Orville was 25 and Nylene was 28, and lived in Freeman,
near their home towns in northeastern Missouri. Orville
was a "pipeliner"—a skilled laborer maintaining the
pipeline for Amoco and running the machinery that kept
it operating. He was transferred to La Plata with his wife
and three children in May 1966.

To Bill Bullock, there wasn't a better, more dedicated
family man than Orville Blew. Bullock never saw Orville
Blew do anything his friend thought would be detrimen-
tal to the Blew children. Orville attended all of his
daughter's basketball games, cheering loudly and proudly.
He had been thrilled with her athletic achievements.

Orville's love for all of his children was unconditional.
In fact, Orville and Nylene were so supportive of their
children that they generally blamed the school if one of
them got into some trouble. The Blews seemed very de-
fensive and protective of the kids. But to Bill Bullock, that
was a trait he never saw manifested in a negative way.

Bullock respected the Blews for their care of Dennis,
whose condition was so difficult and exhausting to deal
with that many parents would have institutionalized him.
But the Blews wouldn't consider it.

Bullock saw a "wild streak" in Randy that included a
temper and a tendency to want to experience the changes
that were part of society in the mid-1970s. Randy was a
live wire, and he drank a little beer. But Bullock never
saw Randy drunk, and he never knew for sure that he
was using marijuana or other drugs, despite the rumors.
Even though many people in town later would remember
Randy and Paula as part of the faster crowd, Bullock
never knew Paula to drink, and the siblings were good
kids who were home at night, not out running the streets.

Bullock saw firsthand the grief brought to the family
by Randy's death; it was Bullock who drove the Blews to

hearing that Orville had gone to the crash scene after hearing only that Paula had been in an accident. When he arrived, he found Paula and was jubilant that she was not seriously injured. Then he asked whose body was under the sheet, only to learn it was his son's.

The Blews moved from La Plata a month after Randy's death. Orville transferred to a job at Amoco's refinery in Wood River, Illinois, just across the Mississippi River from St. Louis. He became a deliveryman, the person who keeps track of the oil moving through the pipeline and the locations to which it is shipped.

They settled into a comfortable ranch house in Cottage Hills, an unincorporated area sandwiched between several small communities near the refinery.

Paula finished her senior year at Civic Memorial High School in nearby Bethalto. She lettered in girls' softball, but she didn't play basketball anymore. She had quit after Randy died. She graduated without much fanfare in 1977; the yearbook, the *Spectator,* listed her name, but there was no picture. Many of her classmates had no recollection of her years later, when her name hit the news and sent them scurrying back to their yearbooks. Even the girls' softball coach could not remember her.

But she made some close friends. One of them was June Bland, who lived a block and a half from the Blews' new home. She met Paula when they were assigned to the same homeroom at school in August. They started talking the first day, hit it off, and became inseparable for the next two years.

June knew a very different Paula from the one remembered in La Plata years later. The Paula in Bethalto was a very caring person who wouldn't do anything to hurt anyone. She loved animals. And she really wanted to have kids, especially girls. The two friends often talked about that. When a song by Queen, "Loralei," came out in 1978 or 1979, Paula decided that would be the name of her first daughter.

June's new friend showed no sign of aggression or any interest in fighting, and June never knew her to lie. June knew Paula was a good basketball player, and felt it was a shame that she didn't seek a college scholarship.

But one part of the new girl remained unchanged. Paula was haunted by her brother's death. June once accompanied the Blews on a visit to La Plata, and Paula took her on a route commemorating the tragedy. They visited the spot along the road where the accident happened, and then went to the cemetery. Even though the Blews were Baptists, Paula had bought a small concrete statue of the Virgin Mary and she placed it on Randy's grave.

Paula confided to June that Randy's death had been devastating emotionally. Randy had been her best friend; indeed, the siblings had been like two peas in a pod. When Randy died, so too did Paula's desire to party. The loss had made her realize there was more to life than that.

Still, June and Paula often smoked marijuana together, a habit that lasted for more than a decade. But June had never seen Paula take a drink or get too high on pot to function. Paula knew her limit and would not exceed it, June learned.

Paula seemed to keep her emotional guard up at all times, a trait June attributed to a desire not to repeat the pain of losing Randy. Paula seemed to deal with people from a position of "not quite." She was friendly, but not quite outgoing. She would speak if someone spoke to her, but she wasn't quite willing to start a conversation. She seemed nice, but she kept to herself and minded her own business.

After graduation, June and Paula decided to become computer operators. They attended Lewis and Clark Community College in nearby Godfrey for a year together, but they never finished the program.

June married and started a family. Paula rarely dated.

She went to work as a cashier at the National Food Store on Godfrey Road in Godfrey in 1978. Even there, Paula remained distant from the people around her; quiet and a loner—there were those words again. To some, she had seemed standoffish and weird. She was not friendly with the customers as the other employees were. She never discussed her social life, and was so withdrawn that others who worked by her side for five years couldn't even think of anything to say about her years later.

But even at the store, there were flashes of a hostile and threatening Paula Blew. One cashier was convinced that Paula had slashed her tires with a knife she was known to carry the night after she and Paula had quarreled at work.

Another worker once accused Paula of stealing some money from her purse. And another saw Paula get angry with a customer over a seemingly trivial thing, and blow up at the janitor because the Pepsi machine wasn't stocked.

It was an unsettling portrait of a quiet young woman, with violent flashes of temper.

Paula and June sometimes went to parties at the home of June's cousin in Alton. A friend of the cousins's occasionally brought along a young man named Robert Sims, known as Rob. He was a laborer at a paper-manufacturing plant in Alton.

He called the cousin in 1979 or 1980 and invited her to a rock concert. She suggested, fatefully, that he call June's friend, Paula, and invite her. He did, and Paula accepted.

Robert and Paula were married on May 2, 1981, less than three weeks before Paula's twenty-second birthday and less than three weeks after Robert's twenty-ninth. Neither of them attended a church, so a friend recommended a Baptist minister who performed the ceremony. He knew nothing of the personalities of the bride and groom, but he sensed that "the sincerity of getting married and really loving each other was there."

The newlyweds rented a small house near Cottage Hills and seemed to settle well into married life. June and Paula still talked to each other on the telephone sometimes, but they didn't visit each other much.

Not everything was smooth sailing for the Simses, however. Paula's job at the National Food Store ended in December 1983. Someone told the store manager that Paula was discounting—ringing up amounts on groceries for friends that were lower than the marked prices. He used a hidden camera to watch Paula as she rang $200 worth of groceries for $50 for another employee. The manager later called her at home and told her she was fired.

A month later, Robert and Paula bought the house in Brighton. It wasn't long until Paula told June that they were planning to start a family, now that they had bought their house and their financial affairs were in order. Sometime later, June got a call from an ecstatic Paula with the news that she was pregnant with her first child.

Chapter 3

Sometime before daylight on Wednesday, June 18, three weary cops drove into Jerseyville and flopped down in the office of Sheriff Frank Yocom. He had suggested that they get away from the Sims house for a while to collect their thoughts, get some coffee, and use the telephone to line up the activities for the day.

Frank's first call was to his wife. He gave her a brief account of the night's bizarre activities, and added the comment that she knew was coming: "Don't look for me until you see me. I don't have any idea when I'll be home."

The cops' conversation that gray morning about what they faced was not upbeat. With some sixty years of experience between them, it wasn't much of a leap to a couple of painful, and perhaps cynical, conclusions. All three of them held the belief that Loralei Marie Sims was dead; her short life probably ended well before the police were called. The queer kidnapping story from Paula Sims didn't hold up under close scrutiny, and her behavior was too off-center to be explained innocently as emotional stress. Robert Sim's behavior had left a bad taste with the three cops, and he bore watching, too.

But they had no clue on a motive or on who the killer was, and they certainly had no physical evidence. Frank Yocom was determined to investigate every possible angle provided by the Simses, almost as if there were no doubt about their kidnapping story. Despite his serious suspicions about the Simses, he was trying to give them the benefit of the doubt.

The cops were running on instinct and experience, and they agreed that they had two good shots at breaking this case. The first was to crack someone who knew the awful secret. Jimmie Bivens suggested leaning on Paula harder that day in another interview to get a signed statement. Maybe she would crack. After that, they could move on to the others who might know something. Everyone agreed with that approach.

The second hope was to find the body, which the officers agreed, again, probably was concealed somewhere on the Sims property. To give themselves time to go over every inch of the area, they needed to stay in control of the scene, around the clock, as long as possible. To assist in that pursuit, Bivens called state police headquarters in Springfield and asked for more canine units, especially Donovan and Judd. Donovan had said Judd hated the "find dead" command to search for a corpse, but he was good at it. And at this point, the cops were sure that was the right direction for the investigation.

The sergeant in charge of the training session said Donovan and his dog were too tired; other dog teams would be assigned. Bivens's temper flared and he demanded that Donovan return, even if he brought a different dog. At least Donovan knew which areas had been searched before.

But the sergeant flexed his authority. He would send other dogs, but not Judd and not Donovan.

Bivens slammed down the telephone. That wasn't the way he had hoped things would start this morning.

Kocis called state police inspector Jeremy D. Margolis, the benefactor of the I SEARCH program. Margolis told him to spare nothing in the investigation, and immediately approved the requests for an airplane and divers from the State Police Underwater Rescue and Recovery Team.

With a quick call to the Illinois Department of Conservation, Kocis arranged for a boat equipped with sonar. Anything hidden in the depths of that small pond would be found with the sonar waves and the divers probing the bottom.

About 6:00 A.M., Yocum called State's Attorney Lee Plummer, the county prosecutor, and gave him a rundown on what was shaping up as a real puzzle. Plummer also agreed with the sheriff's request for a court order to install a tap on the Simses' phone, presumably to record ransom calls from a kidnapper and to check on the hang-up calls reported by the couple.

Yocom turned to Bivens. "What about the FBI? I'd really like to see if they could find out if anybody has had anything like this anywhere else in the country. The feds would be the ones to know. And they could help us on a lot of the other out-of-state checks we need to make."

Bivens grimaced and sighed. "They're not one of my favorite groups, but I guess we could use them. Yeah, go ahead."

Yocom called the FBI office in the satellite federal courthouse in Alton and left an urgent message.

Yocum looked up. "Okay, where do we go from here?"

Kocis suggested keeping the men's responsibilities as they were, so no ground would be covered twice. With Yocom's assent, Bivens would oversee the investigative details while Kocis and the sheriff handled the family and the media. The three men seemed to work well together. Even though Kocis and Bivens were not close, and had very different styles and personalities, they knew they could count on each other to do their jobs.

There still was a significant amount of work to do around the Simses' property, and everyone who knew anything about the Simses needed to be interviewed. There even was some discussion about calling in psychics. But the men knew this kind of case would draw the psychics anyway, and inviting them in was a dubious tactic at best.

Shortly after dawn, the three cops were back at the Sims place to get things under way. And Jimmie Bivens soon had his second encounter with a member of the Sims family. Robert's sister, Linda Condray, confronted Bivens in the yard and, in no uncertain terms, let him know that she was upset by the implication that the police considered Robert and Paula suspects.

"I want to know how you can think that. They loved that baby. I know. I was at the hospital when that baby was born and I've been around them since then and I've seen how they acted with her."

Bivens lowered his chin and looked down at her the way a bull looks at the matador.

"Look, lady. The family isn't running this investigation. We are. Now, the best thing you can do is stay out of the way and let us do our jobs. We're here to do a thorough investigation so we don't have to come back later. Understand?"

Linda Condray glared at him briefly, and then stalked back to the house.

The DCI assault began early. By 8:20 A.M., the residents of the three houses closest to the Simses had been interviewed, and reported that they had seen or heard nothing unusual Tuesday night.

At Alton Memorial Hospital, Agents Diana Sievers and Nick Bowman went after everyone who worked in the maternity ward during the three days Paula Sims was there with Loralei—twelve registered nurses, three nurses' aides, one licensed practical nurse, and two doctors. Most of them had few memories of the Simses, other than to recall them as a quiet couple who had a healthy little girl with red hair and a pretty name.

But three of the nurses remembered that Robert had scrutinized the birth certificate more than any father they had seen before. One said he had seemed "overly concerned" with it.

Paula's gynecologist, who delivered Loralei, said everything had been normal. He had observed no distress by the mother, and the parents seemed to have a stable relationship. The attending pediatrician said she had noted nothing unusual with the baby.

One of the R.N.s in the nursery said she had commented to Paula, "I want to take that baby home." But that was a typical comment all nurses in the maternity ward had made at one time or another about some cute newborn. It hardly qualified as a kidnapping threat.

The first noteworthy interview came later, when Sievers and Bowman talked to Paula's hospital roommate. Julie Fry of Jerseyville, whom Yocom had known all her life, remembered awakening to the sounds of Paula Sims crying on the other side of the curtain between the beds. Paula was on the telephone to her husband, Mrs. Fry believed, and said, "I'm sorry we had a little girl." Paula also had said something about her husband being upset because they had wanted a boy.

But, other than that, Mrs. Fry said Paula and her husband had seemed very pleased about their baby's birth.

That much emphasis on having a male baby, and that kind of emotional response to a girl, struck the agents as a little unusual, but hardly enough to qualify as a motive.

Bowman and Sievers were surprised later when more support for the male-preference idea popped up from an unexpected source. The couple apparently the closest to the Simses, Dave and Linda Heistand, recalled that the Simses had said they wanted a boy. Dave Heistand asked Robert after Loralei's birth if he was disappointed. But Robert said no, he was happy with a healthy child.

Linda Heistand also told the agents that Paula had quit drinking alcohol and had nearly quit smoking while she was pregnant. When the Heistands visited the Simses after Loralei was born, the baby seemed healthy and happy, and there was no hint of problems between the new parents. But Paula had mentioned being upset by a nurse's comment that someone might steal the baby.

Linda Heistand also related that Paula called her several times during the past few days and said Loralei had been "very fussy lately" between 9:00 and 10:00 P.M. Linda told her the baby probably just needed "a good burp."

Everything else in the Simses' stories that could be checked had, indeed, checked out—from the Grays to Robert's account of his stops on the way to work the night before.

While the agents were on the streets, the efforts at the Sims house intensified. The cops even pulled the trash bags from the two barrels inside the house and checked the contents for dirty diapers; the ones they found seemed fresh enough not to raise any more suspicions. No one would fully appreciate that insignificant action for several years.

Two more state police dogs arrived about 8:30 A.M., but found nothing within a half-mile radius of the Sims house. This time, they had been looking for the scent of a body, not some mysterious intruder.

Yocom and the others weren't surprised, but they were

disappointed. And Bivens still was angry, convinced the sergeant's refusal to send Donovan back had screwed up the search.

Thirty minutes after the dogs began, the police airplane started flying circles over the house to see if the infrared camera mounted on the wing picked up any signs of body heat in the nearby woods or farm fields. The plane circled at 1,000 feet for two hours, covering a one-mile area with the house in the center. There wasn't a blip on the monitor.

The boat with a sonar unit arrived about midmorning and began sweeping the pond with sound waves. While the boat was circling the pond, three divers from the state police underwater team began their slow, cumbersome search. Several hours would be needed to cover the two or three acres of muck under the pond's calm surface. They would have to feel their way along the bottom because the water in such places always was too murky to see through.

As the divers were pulling on their wetsuits at the water's edge, Bivens noticed Paula and some other family members standing on the front porch, looking repeatedly at the pond. Those glances bothered Bivens—one of those itches that cops get. He even wondered if they were telegraphing the location of the baby's body.

He decided it would be better to get Paula and the others out of sight of the pond. He didn't relish the scene that could erupt if that tiny body were dragged from the water under the family's watchful eyes. He asked DCI Sergeant Wayne Watson to suggest to Paula that this would be a good time to go the sheriff's office with Yocom and Bivens to give them a written statement.

Her answer made the hair on the back of Watson's neck stand up.

"No, no. I want to be here when they bring her body up," Paula protested. But then she flinched and her face tightened. It was obvious to Watson that she knew she had made a mistake. She nervously corrected herself.

"No, that's not what I mean," she said slowly. "I mean, my baby is alive, and I want to be here when they bring her onto the porch."

The look on her face sent Watson quickly to his car to

write down what she had said. He reported immediately to Yocom, Kocis, and Bivens, and told them he was convinced Paula had killed Loralei and hidden the body on the property. He urged them to keep searching around the house.

"From the look on her face, I know that body's here," he said.

Another strange comment from Paula; another cop's hunch.

Her remark didn't seem so incriminating to Kocis. Bivens didn't know if it was significant, but he didn't like the sound of it. But Frank Yocom thought it, at least, was more confirmation of his suspicions, and perhaps meant the search of the property was on target. It seemed a bright spot in a situation growing steadily more dismal.

The cops also realized that Watson was in the best position to interpret what had happened. They knew sometimes it was the way the words were said, or the look on the person's face, that made something like that so powerful and decisive.

Watson was undeterred when nothing was found in the pond. He said her comment could have been less specific than it sounded, referring to bringing the body "up" from wherever it had been hidden. His view would turn out to be prophetic.

But something else was bothering Bivens. Despite Robert's persistent interference, Linda Condray's curt remarks, and the unblinking supervision by Paula at the pond, no one had offered to join the search. Not Robert. Not Paula. Not a single relative. That wasn't right. The parents and family should be leading the search, and staying with it long after weary police officers took a break. Jimmie Bivens would be out there if his baby were missing.

The Sims case had hit the news. Television stations in St. Louis, only twenty-five miles to the south, were running reports throughout the day. TV crews and newspaper reporters had arrived en mass, standing in the road at the end of the Simses' driveway. As the sun beat down and the heat radiated off that blistering blacktop, the reporters began to wilt. Suit coats came off and ties were pulled loose. The vigil had begun.

The press corps sprang to life when police cars arrived or departed. Only Yocum and Kocis were authorized to comment, and what they were offering was unsatisfying for the hungry mob. In addition to the local newspapers like the Alton *Telegraph*, reporters had arrived from the Madison County bureaus of the St. Louis *Post-Dispatch* and the St. Louis *Globe-Democrat*. But the *Globe* would cease publication because of financial problems before the Sims case had run its course.

Kocis was not releasing many details of the case. He believed the best course was to give the reporters as little information as possible. The public stayed informed to some degree, but only the detectives really knew the details. That kept the investigation under control, and minimized the kook calls, especially from those with a penchant for phony confessions.

He released only the basics of Paula's account, and said the police were following every lead. He acknowledged that they had no motive yet, and that the FBI was assisting with out-of-state leads. He explained about the airplane, the boat, and the divers, and said I SEARCH was helping coordinate all the agencies that dealt with child abuse or abductions.

As family members made their way to or from the house, they too had to run the media gauntlet.

Paula's father, Orville Blew, told the *Post-Dispatch* that he couldn't imagine who would have stolen his first grandchild. "Somebody's got to be sick to do something like that, or have no feelings at all. It must be somebody in the market for selling babies, or maybe somebody who lost theirs and wants another one."

Robert's uncle, Delmar Loveall, offered that Robert and Paula had wanted a baby for a long time. "He's very much in love with Paula, and they've been very anxious to start a family."

Linda Condray, who ran a photography studio with her husband, Herb, announced they were having 200 fliers with Loralei's picture printed for distribution to area businesses. She said Robert and Paula were emotionally drained, and were fighting hard to hold up under the pressure. They were too upset to make any public statements yet.

Linda and Herb would become regulars with the press corps over the next few days, and Linda's presence would be even more important in a few years.

Prosecutor Lee Plummer arrived that morning with the court order for the phone tap, and it was installed by the DCI's electronics expert.

Plummer had been state's attorney for ten years. He was a short, thick man with a heavy black moustache and mop of curly hair that he kept longer than usual for an elected official in a conservative place like Jersey County.

After he was introduced to the Simses, and took a look at the rip in the screen and the rest of the house, he agreed with the cops' assessments. He went along on a detailed search of the house and, as everyone, was struck by the compulsive neatness.

In Loralei's nursery, he had the feeling that it was "too much baby." He had three kids of his own, but the way the room was decorated and equipped made him uncomfortable. There were too many blankets and clothes and supplies, all lined up in rows and perfect stacks. And Bivens thought later that he had noticed that the baby's room had been decorated mostly for a boy, with a blue theme.

But it was Robert's workshop that overwhelmed Plummer and the others. Every tool was placed carefully in order. All the screwdrivers were hung by descending size and the wrenches were lined up exactly right. And he had many duplicate tools, including expensive power tools. He had complete sets of woodworking tools and mechanical tools, which also struck Plummer as odd. Usually a man leaned toward woodworking or mechanical work, but seldom did one man have all the tools for both endeavors.

Plummer took a look at the step in the middle of the front porch. *No way*, he thought. *No stranger bolted across that porch in the dark, running for his life with the baby he had just kidnapped, without falling on his face.*

At 11:40 A.M., Paula sat down at the desk in the sheriff's small office with Yocom, Bivens, and Kocis for another interview. Bivens wrote out her version of the events as she spoke. She was unshakable. The cops took turns suggesting that she knew more than she was telling. She simply denied it, and insisted she was telling the whole truth.

As before, Paula grew more emotional as the interview went on. But near the end, Yocom thought her weeping was different—coming from so deep inside. Part whimper, part cry. Like she was feeling sorry for herself, perhaps. But it was unlike anything he had ever heard. It was unique to Paula Sims, and Frank never would find the words to describe it.

After an hour and fifteen minutes, Bivens handed her the statement and explained that she could make any changes she felt were appropriate. She made some insignificant alterations, such as scratching in "front" where Bivens had written "back storm door." She initialed each change with PMS, which some of the more sarcastic observers would have fun with later when they joked about Paula's "premenstrual syndrome." Then she signed all four pages.

The cops were left with a statement painfully simple and direct. It ran in one long paragraph:

I went downstairs around 10 p.m. with the baby to watch the television news. I usually watch the 10 o'clock news on Channel 2. I had fed the baby and she was asleep in the bassinet near the foot of the stairs. I was sitting in my easy chair near the baby. I think the weather was on. The next thing I know [sic], I saw a man on the steps. I didn't hear a thing. The man was white, wearing a dark ski mask pulled over his head. It had eye and mouth holes. His shirt was a dark T-shirt. He was wearing gloves and had a handgun. He stuck his arm out, pointed the gun at me and said, "Get on the floor. Stay there ten minutes or I'll kill you." I laid down on the floor. My head was pointed towards the back door away from the baby. I thought, "What is he doing here? The door is locked." He had a gun in his right hand. I didn't rec-

ognize the voice. It didn't appear too young or too old.
The man didn't say a word after that. I didn't hear a
thing, not even the baby crying. I heard the front screen
door close. I got up right away, started running up the
stairs and as I passed the bassinet, I noticed she, the baby,
was gone. I ran out of the door after the man. I couldn't
see him, a car or anything. I could hear what I thought
was someone running on the driveway gravel as I was
running towards the main road. I ran all the way to the
end of the lane. I thought I would see a car or something,
but didn't. I then ran to my neighbors', the Grays' house,
to have them call the police. I was going to have them
call my husband at work, but didn't have his number, so
I went back to our house to get the number.

Paula added that Loralei was wearing a white dispos-
able diaper, a white T-shirt, and white booties trimmed
in pink.

As Yocom listened to Paula's statement, he tried in
vain to identify what he felt inside. Later, he described
it as emptiness.

After the interview failed to jar anything loose, the
men decided they would ask the Simses to undergo lie
detector tests. They would present it as standard procedure, an investigative tool to eliminate the parents as suspects. Bivens wanted Clinton Cook of the state police to
administer the polygraphs. He was the best in the state,
and you could count on a valid reading.

Cook would be standing by before the idea was proposed to the Simses. If they agreed, they could be
whisked in front of Cook before they changed their
minds.

The last order of business that day was the roadblock.
From 8:00 to 10:30 P.M., the police stopped every driver
on Cotter Road. The agents interviewed thirty-one people, but no one had seen anything the night before.

Frank Yocom and the others had set up a command
center at the Brighton Police Department in a spare room
graciously provided by Chief Jerome Woolridge. The
cops spent most of the night there writing reports and
turning things over and over in their minds, looking for

that something they felt had to be missing. About dawn on Thursday, the nineteenth, Yocom took another drive past the Sims house on the way back to his office in Jerseyville. He was startled to see Robert and Paula Sims walking along the road in front of the Grays' house. They were holding hands, just walking along the side of the road.

What are they doing out here at 6:30 in the morning, Frank wondered. It struck him as odd, just out of place. He didn't look at them as he drove by.

On the trip back to his office, Frank felt a deep uneasiness, unlike anything he remembered in any other case. What the hell could the cops do next? How could they break this thing? Could they break it? He returned a few calls from the office before the bottom fell out. His throat hurt and his voice was raspy. And he was dead tired—tired in a way he hadn't felt in a long time. It was time for some sleep. He drove home and called his wife Carol at her office to tell her there was nothing new on the "Lone Ranger," as he had started to call that elusive kidnapper.

He showered and shaved, and crawled into bed for the first time since 10:30 P.M. Tuesday, June 17. But he still couldn't clear the case from his head. He couldn't shake it off, and it took much longer than it should have to drift off to sleep. When he awoke sometime after noon, the case was back in his mind before his eyes were open. He rolled out of bed and drove back to Cotter Road.

It was old-fashioned police work that day, following up slim leads and trying to nail down other facts. Even though the cops had their own suspicions, they followed up every possible lead.

Yocum and Bivens concentrated on tracking down the fisherman in the green pickup truck. When they found him, he confirmed the exchange of words over fishing in the pond. But he checked out, and clearly was not a suspect. There was some satisfaction in that for Frank—proving Robert Sims was wrong. It felt good when the sheriff told Robert the man had been found and eliminated from suspicion.

To the FBI fell the task of checking into Paula's background, and a less than flattering portrait of her emerged from her former coworkers at the National Foods Store in Godfrey. "Weird, strange, and standoffish" were the nicest words applied to the former Paula Marie Blew, and the manager explained Paula's firing.

The agents also learned of her brother's death and the siblings' reputations for drinking and smoking pot.

For the media, the news of the day came when Robert and Paula stepped into their driveway to make their first public appearance. Robert, dressed in bib overalls, with Paula weeping on his shoulder, somberly issued an appeal to the public for help in finding Loralei. He told reporters that his daughter had been planned and anxiously awaited, and her disappearance was almost more than they could bear.

"They could have stolen anything I own. They could have burned my house down. They could have fired me or sent me to war again. But nothing can compare to this tragedy."

Robert's allusion to a war record was dutifully reported by the media, and it wasn't until much later that reporters learned his time in the navy had been spent mostly in Maine. He never served in Vietnam, although one of Paula's friends told the police later that Paula had said Robert was having nightmares from his Vietnam experiences. A curious lie for no apparent reason.

Paula, dressed in jeans and a T-shirt, did not look at the reporters. She kept her head securely against Robert's shoulder. "I just want my baby back," she whimpered through her tears.

Robert expressed anger at a television reporter who had suggested on the air that the police were looking into the possibility that the kidnapping report was false. It was the first public comment on the unthinkable.

"I can't believe people would start that bullshit," Robert snapped. "If they're looking for sensationalism, they should go somewhere else," he said.

It was a brief appearance, but the media loved it. They had waited for two days for some word from the anxious parents, and now they had it. Quotes and pictures for the front page, and fresh tape for the news at five, six and ten.

It also was announced that I SEARCH was distributing

7,000 fliers bearing Loralei's picture and information on the case. They carried a headline of "Have You Seen This Missing Child?" over Loralei's picture and the telephone numbers for tips. An I SEARCH coordinator was assigned to work with the police.

Except for the Simses' brief appearance, news coverage was starting to slow down. Reporters began making the rounds in Brighton, collecting the predictable comments from the residents about being shocked and frightened by the abduction in their small, quiet town. Most of them said they were watching their children more closely. Some suggested Loralei had been stolen to be sold on the "black market."

Friday morning, Yocom and Bivens walked into the Simses' dining room and asked if they would be willing to take polygraphs. Bivens explained, "It would remove any doubt from yourselves."

Paula looked at Robert. He said calmly, "We want to cooperate. We'll do anything to help you get our baby back."

They were driven to Yocom's office in separate cars, and arrangements already had been made to be sure they did not speak to each other between the tests. Lee Plummer was there, in case something broke.

A psychologist was sent in by state police headquarters, even though none of the officers wanted him there. Bivens told him he could stay, but he wasn't allowed to say anything if the Simses were interviewed after the tests.

Paula insisted that her mother go along, and Nylene Blew rode next to her in the backseat of the car. Mrs. Blew agreed to Biven's request that she stay in the waiting room.

Paula was escorted into the conference room where Cook had set up. Robert was kept strategically in another room at the other end of the building, and Nylene Blew sat outside Yocom's office.

Cook asked some general questions with known answers, such as their names, to test Paula's responses. Then he asked four questions on which he would base his conclusions. Three questions would be the same for

Paula and Robert. But the first question was designed to fit their specific roles in the case.

The first question to Paula was, "On Tuesday evening, June 17, 1986, did an unknown white male display a pistol in your home and steal your baby, Loralei Sims?"

Paula answered yes.

The next three questions would be the same for both of them.

"Do you know where your baby is now?"

"Did you dispose of, sell, and/or give your baby away?"

"Have you falsified or withheld any information to police regarding this investigation?"

Paula responded no to each of them. As the machine measured her breathing, heart rate, pulse, and respiration, the needles scribbling on the paper told Cook she was lying—blatantly.

Cook told her there were indications that she was being deceptive, and he asked the questions again. He got the same answers, and the same scribbling from the machine.

Cook went to Yocom's office with the response the cops had expected.

"She's being deceptive, but she's not coming off her story."

Bivens asked, "How sure are you?"

"Positive. It's all wrong," was Cook's resolute answer.

"There you go," Yocom said.

Cook returned to ask Paula the questions once more, with the same results.

Paula was delivered to Yocom's office and greeted by the battery of investigators and the psychologist. They stalled for a few minutes to give Cook time to get Robert into the polygraph room. They wanted to be sure any outburst from Paula didn't alert her husband.

Before Bivens closed the door, he quietly told a deputy not to allow anyone in, especially Paula's mother.

Yocom's office was small. His desk was against the left wall, and just far enough from the back wall to leave room for a bookcase and a chair. Bivens sat behind the desk, and the sheriff took a seat in the corner to the right of the desk. Paula sat at the end of the desk. Kocis was sitting behind her left shoulder, and the psychologist was sitting farther behind her.

Bivens informed Paula she had failed the polygraph. Her response was simple.

"I don't know why I did. I don't care. It was the truth. I probably was just nervous."

Bivens countered that nerves wouldn't have caused her to show deception on every question. Now was the time to tell them the truth, Bivens urged.

Paula began to cry. But to Bivens, it was the same act. The crocodile tears flowed, and then she snapped back for the next question.

"I've told you the truth over and over again," she insisted.

Bivens offered her an out.

"Look, Paula. If it was an accident, we can work with you. If you accidentally dropped her or something, tell us. It's not too late now."

"That didn't happen," she insisted through more tears.

Yocom nearly pleaded with her.

"Paula, the state's attorney is here. If you hit her in a rage, not really knowing what you were doing, tell us now. If you did something, anything, we can work with it. Mr. Plummer is here to help us straighten this thing out and get it off your shoulders. You can't carry this around the rest of your life."

"No, I'm telling you the truth."

Kocis suggested that the baby had died from natural causes.

"Paula, look. Maybe it was sudden infant death syndrome, or she smothered somehow. Maybe she choked on some food. Anything like that."

"No," she said again softly.

Bivens suggested that maybe their big dog had climbed into the bassinet and laid on Loralei.

Paula was irritated. "No, no. The dog was never near the baby."

Bivens decided to throw her another emotional anchor.

"Look, Paula. Maybe Robert did something. Maybe it was an accident. Maybe he dropped her and she died, or maybe he dropped her into some water. We can handle that, too, if you'll tell us what happened.''

''No! No!'' she protested more loudly.

Bivens knew that he had pushed her past the point when an innocent person would lose patience with these damned cops. She was past the point where an innocent parent would scream, ''Stop it! I didn't do this and I'm not taking any more of this. Stop worrying about me and find the guy who took my baby.''

But she never did that. She sat there and took it. To Bivens, that was part of a guilty profile.

So he dropped the next one on her.

''Paula, you know Loralei's dead. We know Loralei's dead. She's out there somewhere. Help us find your baby and give her a Christian burial.''

Paula's head was sinking lower between her hunched shoulders. Her hands were folded in her lap, and she was crying again.

But it looked real this time. It was real emotion, and Bivens wondered what was behind it. Was she crying for her lost baby? Was she crying in guilt, out of genuine regret for what had taken that young life? Could she be crying because her husband had done something terrible? Or were the tears a crack in that facade, and she was afraid her unbelievable story was about to sink her?

Whatever was behind it, it was real and it was something the three policemen hadn't seen before.

Yocom and Bivens exchanged quick glances. They were feeling the same thing in their bellies. They might be close to breaking her. Without Robert there, she had lost some of that strength.

Yocom turned up the volume. ''Your story just doesn't add up, Paula.'' His voice was rising, the sympathy gone and the harsh edge of anger creeping in. When he said, ''Let's go over it all again,'' it sounded like a threat.

She began to cry louder, and her head seemed to sink even lower.

But, like something out of a bad movie, there was a knock on the door and Nylene Blew angrily pushed in and glared at the cops. ''What are you doing to her? That's enough. She can't take any more of this. You've done enough. Come on, Paula.''

With her mother there, Paula snapped back. Nylene pulled her out of the office, leaving the three cops sitting there in disbelief. Defeat snatched from the jaws of victory.

Bivens followed them out. He asked to speak to Nylene, and offered to have an officer take Paula home. Nylene agreed and stepped back into the office. Bivens was gentle and friendly, and offered a strategic apology.

"Mrs. Blew, Paula flunked the polygraph test and we were just trying to get more information from her. If we're going to find out what happened to your granddaughter, we need as much information as possible. We have to know from Paula what really happened. I'm sorry if it sounded like we got too rough on her."

After the women left, the cops realized that probably was their last shot at Paula. For Yocum and Bivens, it was a big disappointment. They had been so close to bringing her down; the "what if" would haunt them forever.

But Kocis wasn't so sure Paula had been faltering. After her first answer to flunking the lie box, he had doubted that they could shake her. She was just too strong, too hard.

Bivens asked the deputy how Nylene had slipped past him. He shook his head apologetically. He had just left for a second, to go to the bathroom.

Jimmie Bivens thought, "It figures."

Down the hall, Cook was getting an instant replay with Robert's polygraph. The first question for him had been, "On Tuesday evening, June 17, 1986, was your baby, Loralei Sims, alive and in your home when you left for work?" Robert answered yes, and then gave three no answers to the other questions.

Cook went back to Yocum's office and told them Robert had flunked every question, too; they weren't surprised.

After Robert sat down in Yocum's office, Bivens came on a little stronger. But Robert remained calm and steadfast. He listened to the cops' questions and suggestions that he knew more than he was telling. But he softly denied the allegations.

"No, I've told you the truth," he said triumphantly.

That afternoon, Robert's brother-in-law, Herb Condray, announced to the *Post-Dispatch* that Robert and Paula voluntarily had taken polygraph tests and had passed them. In Saturday morning's newspaper, Herb was quoted as saying, "They've been absolutely cleared on this now. They've been put through the third degree for three days. Taking the polygraph was awfully rough on them. If you've ever been through anything like this, it's hell. But we know the police have to check out every possibility. Now we hope the police can find the baby."

Frank Yocum was sitting in his office that morning when a deputy stuck his head in the doorway. "Hey, Sheriff. Did you see what Herb Condray said in the *Post* this morning?"

Yocom hadn't read the paper yet, so the deputy told him. He couldn't believe it. It was a flat-out lie, and Yocom felt the anger swelling. He called Bivens at home immediately, and he was just as astounded. "You gotta' be kiddin' me. Herb said that?"

They didn't like it, but they decided the best course at the time was to leave it alone. Yocom called Plummer, and he agreed that it would be better at this point not to make it an issue.

Nylene Blew was interviewed later that day by agents from the FBI and DCI. She and her husband had seen their granddaughter last on Monday, June 9, at Paula's house. Everything had seemed fine, and Paula had called every day after that and mentioned how good the baby was.

Nylene said she had been disappointed, however, when Paula had canceled plans for a family get-together to celebrate Father's Day on June 15 at the Blews'. It would have been Robert's first as a father, and Orville's first as a grandfather. But Paula had called a few days before that and said Robert did not want to bring Loralei for fear there would be too many people spreading too many germs, and the baby would get sick. Nylene thought Robert was "overly protective" of the baby, even requiring everyone to wash their hands before they picked her up.

Nylene said she had cried, but Paula had not seemed

too upset. Paula had promised to bring the baby to visit her grandparents that very evening, June 20.

FBI Agent Jim Quick explained that the polygraph failures by Paula and Robert were not borderline, but indicated they had answered "completely and totally falsely."

Nylene responded that she did not believe polygraphs were very accurate because she had seen a television show about them. There was no way her daughter or Robert had anything to do with their daughter's disappearance. But Nylene said she could never bring up the test results with Paula, because it would make her daughter "hate her."

Bivens spent most of the weekend at home, writing reports. But Frank Yocom drove out to the Sims house on Saturday and Sunday. He wasn't sure what he expected to find, but he did it anyway. Carol accompanied him on Saturday; she had wanted to see the house. No one was home either time, and Yocom assumed the owners were visiting their relatives to get away for a while. On Sunday, he walked through the yard and looked around. It seemed peaceful enough on a warm summer morning. What the hell had happened here?

Yocom was beginning to feel the pressure. It was a horrible crime in his county, and it was his job to solve it. His department was fielding dozens of calls from concerned citizens who wanted it solved. Most of them were young mothers whose voices carried their fear. Was a maniac kidnapper on the loose in peaceful Jersey County? Were the kids at risk in their own yards?

Frank Yocom had to give them an answer. But his hopes were fading, and deep pessimism was setting in. He was glad Bivens continued to be so gung ho on the case, so convinced it would be solved.

On Monday, June 23, it was back to the legwork. The DCI interviewed Robert's father, Troy W. Sims, a retired teacher who lived in Alton. There were distinct similarities between the Sims men, especially the soft, slow speech pattern. Troy Sims knew almost nothing about the case firsthand; he and his son were not really close. Robert had told him their only guesses on a motive were to replace a child some other couple had lost, or to sell her.

Mr. Sims believed the couple had waited to have children because Robert was worried that the seizures afflicting Paula's brother could be passed to their children. They must have forgotten those fears because they had been thrilled with Loralei's birth, Mr. Sims said. He visited his granddaughter once at the hospital.

He described Robert as pretty much of a loner as a child. He had not taken to college as his two brothers had, and got a job as a loan collector. Robert had said it was dangerous, and he had made quite a few enemies trying to collect from blacks in Alton; Mr. Sims considered his son prejudiced against blacks, and said Robert could have a temper on occasion. But Mr. Sims was sure Robert and Paula had nothing to do with their daughter's disappearance.

It had been a bad time for Troy Sims. His wife, Wilma, had died eight months ago without knowing that Robert's wife was pregnant. He had lost a sister-in-law two months ago, and a cousin last month. And now his granddaughter had been stolen.

The Simses' plight had begun to draw a considerable amount of community support. A reward fund had grown to $14,000 with contributions from Robert's employer, the Jefferson Smurfit Corp.; the company where Paula's father had worked for 30 years before retiring, Amoco Oil Co.; and other businesses, such as the First National Bank of Brighton.

Two of Paula's friends from high school, Rhonda Scott and June Gibson, were making and selling pink bows for one dollar to add to the reward fund. The bows were to be worn until Loralei was found and returned home safe, the women said. They had daughters of their own, and couldn't imagine what they would do if something happened to them.

Monday afternoon, Robert and Paula, wearing pink bows and carrying pictures of their daughter, appeared before the television cameras again in front of the house. Robert announced that he and his wife had passed the polygraph tests "with flying colors." Now, he hoped, the police could concentrate on finding the real perpetrators. Paula sobbed on her husband's shoulder.

When the cops learned of Robert's comment, they couldn't believe their ears. Bivens shook his head and mumbled, "That son of a bitch."

Frank Yocom's anger over Herb Condray's comment still was percolating, and this boiled it over. He was astonished that Robert would say something so stupid, and so damned brazen.

"We have to refute that," he fumed.

Kocis explained that regulations barred him from making any comment on polygraph tests. He couldn't confirm or deny that the Simses even had taken them, let alone what the results had been.

"But that doesn't mean you can't say something," Kocis told Yocom. So Yocom was ready with a succinct little response when the reporters arrived later for his reaction to Robert's claim.

"Hell, no, I won't confirm that," Yocom boomed angrily.

Bivens was elated that Robert finally had done something stupid. Until then, everything had been so calculated. This "in your face" lie by Robert, almost daring the cops to contradict him, could be a break.

The police gathered early that evening at the Brighton police station for a brainstorming session. Everyone was sure they knew who was responsible for Loralei's disappearance. So why had the case stalled? Plummer warned that the Simses soon would stop cooperating. They seemed to him to be getting more indignant, almost hostile. Bivens noted that Robert had stopped calling regularly to see if anything was new.

As Kocis listened, he realized everyone was feeling the same frustration. Their comments all masked thoughts of, *This is starting to make us mad. Here we have this red-haired girl and her dingbat husband, and we can't break the case.*

Finally, it was decided to make one more big push. Robert and Paula would be brought to the Brighton police station the next day for some gloves-off interrogation, probably for the last time.

FBI Agent Jim Quick suggested that he and Agent Dale Schuler take on Robert. "We haven't had a shot at him yet. Let us hit him with everything we've got."

Kocis and Bivens suggested bringing in women agents to interview Paula, since she probably never would co-operate with the men who had been leaning on her so hard all along; she might confide in women. The two best women agents in the DCI were Diana Sievers and Debra Morgan. They were smart, expert interviewers, and they worked well together. Bivens had ridden with Morgan for six years and he knew how capable she was.

And while the Simses were being interviewed, the police would make one more top-to-bottom search of the house and grounds, using Mike Donovan's dog again.

"Let's wrap this thing up," Bivens said.

Tuesday, June 24, was a week after Loralei Marie Sims was reported missing.

Bright and early, Yocom and Bivens took their friendliest smiles and softest voices to Robert and Paula, politely suggested searching the house again and talking to them at the police station while that was being done. Bivens offered Robert a chance to meet with the FBI. He looked apprehensive, so Bivens challenged him. "You've wanted them in the case all along. Now's your chance to tell them something that will get them involved."

Slowly, Robert nodded. He had risen to the challenge.

Paula would meet with two women. "We thought you might have felt uncomfortable talking to men," Bivens suggested. Paula looked at Rob for a signal. It wasn't perceptible to the cops, but it must have been there. "Okay," she answered.

After the Simses were driven off in a police car, the teams moved in and Donovan unloaded Judd. The dog was sent on a general search of the house, looking for anything, including drugs.

The police checked every drawer, every cabinet, every nook and cranny. Nothing useful turned up. But the drawers in the nightstand next to the couple's waterbed gave up two bizarre collections.

Plummer was amazed at the library of detective magazines—the tawdry issues with a cover shot of a man in a sexually threatening pose over a woman whose blouse spilled open. Plummer wondered if Robert's reading habits had influenced his dealings with the police, thinking perhaps that he knew how to handle them. But the second collection in the drawer was astounding. There, in about fifteen Polaroid pictures, was a very pregnant and very naked Paula Sims in a variety of poses progressing through the stages of pregnancy. There she was posing provocatively on the all-terrain vehicle. Here she was in the bathtub. One cop quipped to a companion who hadn't seen the photos yet, "It ain't a pretty sight."

When Plummer spotted a canister on top of the refrigerator in the kitchen, he remembered Paula's admission to smoking marijuana, and he laughed, "Aha. There's the stash." Judd bounded onto the counter, sniffed the canister, and barked.

Inside was a little marijuana residue, along with some cigarette papers and "roach" clips for holding a marijuana cigarette. Plummer laughed again. Just enough residue to be obvious, and not enough for a criminal charge. Another little game with the cops?

The house had been turned upside down and nothing had been found. They moved outside.

At the police station, FBI Agents Quick and Schuler were hammering Robert. He had told his story in painstaking detail, from the important events to the tiniest bits of useless information. He suggested that the kidnapper needed money, and planned to sell Loralei.

The agents flatly rejected it all. Abductions for money like that never happened at homes; they happened in shopping centers and other public places. That didn't shake Robert. He didn't have any enemies. He didn't have any gambling debts. He had never had a drug problem or a mental problem. He didn't have a lot of money, but his father-in-law always loaned him money if he needed it.

And Robert added firmly that he believed his wife. Quick and Schuler pounced on that. Her story was "totally unbelievable." The agents stated bluntly that they thought he and Paula were responsible for Loralei's disappearance. Robert denied it again. And he volunteered that Loralei had not died accidentally or naturally, causing him and Paula to panic, hide the body, and concoct the kidnapper story.

Why had he and Paula failed the polygraphs so miserably? Because they were nervous. Besides, Robert added, he didn't believe lie detector tests were 100 percent accurate anyway. Even so, the agents said, the chances of Robert and Paula both failing the same questions, in the same manner, when they were both innocent, were astronomical. The feds pressed Robert on his lie about passing the tests. He shrugged it off. His relatives had told the press they had passed, and he felt he had to say something. Other than that, he and Paula had been completely honest.

On the other side of the building, three women sat at a table in the corner of a small gymnasium the police had used as their command center. Paula Sims looked blankly at the agents; Morgan was across the table and Sievers sat next to Paula. The officers started out nice enough, telling Paula they just wanted to go over her story again to get more information.

Paula gave them a brief history of her life. It was obvious to the agents that Randy's death still hurt. She told them about Dennis, and added that she was the only child in her family who could produce grandchildren for her parents. That seemed important to her, and she seemed to feel she had let them down over Loralei.

Paula seemed sad and sullen. She told them the story of Loralei's abduction again. She said that she had seen a "shadowy figure" running down the driveway, a point that would be important years later.

Debby Morgan, a petite redhead, leaned forward from across the table. Her voice quiet, but firm and accusatory.

"Come on, Paula. Nobody's going to believe this story. The whole town thinks you're lying. No masked guy comes into a house and takes a baby."

Paula started crying. "That's what happened. I keep telling you, all of you. That's what happened," she said defensively.

The agents stayed after her, pushing her on the absurdity of her story. She began to slump down in her chair, and then she leaned forward onto the table and put her head down on her arms. The agents could hear her crying as their accusations rained down on her.

Sievers, a husky blonde with the ability to call almost anyone "Hon' " and make it sound comfortable, patted Paula on the arm.

"Paula, we all know your baby is dead. Tell us what really happened."

Paula was crying from deep inside, and her head seemed to sink lower. She seemed to slip into a trance for a few moments, but then she sprung back up and stunned the agents by pounding her fist on the table and nearly shouting, "My baby is not dead. I know it. I know she's alive."

It was a flash of power the agents hadn't expected. There had been nothing to suggest she was capable of that kind of force. All Morgan had seen of Paula Sims was the sobbing woman on television. But now she was facing them down and fighting back.

Sievers drew Robert into the fray. Maybe he had done something to the baby, and Paula was covering up for him. She denied it, and the suggestion obviously angered her.

Morgan leaned in again. "Paula, come on. Nobody believes this story. Today's the day. Let's get it right today."

Paula dropped her head down on her arms. But then she reared back up and pounded the table again, as if someone were pulling her strings. This time, she screamed at the agents, "She's not dead!"

The door opened and the woman from I SEARCH barged in. "How many more fliers do you think we'll need?" she asked, holding up a sheet of paper. Sievers and Morgan couldn't believe it. Didn't she know better than to walk into the middle of an interview to pursue a kidnapping story rejected by the investigators some time ago? They angrily waved her out of the room, and both of them had fleeting thoughts about a summary execution.

But the interruption didn't slow the agents' momentum, and they returned to the attack. They offered Paula several ways out. It could have been a natural death or an accident. Whatever had happened, they could help her if she would tell them the truth.

"Your baby's dead, Paula," Sievers said softly. "Help us find your baby."

Morgan added, "We need to have a Christian burial for your baby, Paula. You want that. You know you do. Think about your parents."

Paula's head fell back onto her arms and she was almost moaning. The agents looked across the table at each other. A lot of people had confessed to these two women, and they knew the signs. They flashed each other a quick "thumbs up."

But Paula reared back again, screaming her denials as she slammed her fist onto the table. Now she was furious. Morgan remembered Bivens saying Robert seemed to have some strange power over Paula. Could they be seeing the manifestation of that? It was almost as if Paula were ready to confess, but drew into her shell to await some telepathic transfer of strength from Robert. It was eerie, and the women almost felt the presence of the bearded man with the strange eyes.

Sievers wasn't slowing down, and she waded into Paula again in a louder voice.

"Paula, you know you're lying."

Morgan added a new sense of outrage to her voice.

"We know you're lying. Paula, the lie is up."

Paula had slipped down in her chair again, and Morgan sensed anew that the break was within their grasp.

But this time, Paula stood up abruptly and screamed at the agents, "I'm sick of you accusing me of doing something to my baby. I've told you the truth and you won't believe me. I'm not talking to you anymore."

Paula whirled around, threw open the door, and ran down the hallway. Morgan and Sievers looked at each other in shock. Their faces said it all: *We blew it.*

They chased Paula into the hallway and saw her dart directly into the room where Robert was being interviewed. Morgan hadn't known which room Robert was in, and Paula couldn't have either. Was it that same mind-connection that had pulled Paula back from the brink repeatedly in their interview?

Paula's tearful entrance brought an end to the interview with Robert, although Quick and Schuler already knew they had played out their hands. Paula was crying loudly as Robert comforted her.

The reporters had assembled outside the station. Word had spread that the police might have an announcement, and it was expected that they would repudiate in detail Robert's claim of passing the lie detector tests.

But the journalists were surprised when Robert and Paula were escorted out of the police station and walked through the media gauntlet. It was obvious that a change had come over Paula Sims. She wasn't the pathetic, sobbing mother they had seen all week. Her face had a harsh cast to it. Her eyes were narrowed and her jaw was set in defiance. There were no tears.

One reporter whispered to a colleague, "God, she looks mad."

It was the debut of a stony, icy look that Paula Sims would present to the world from that day forward and which would become a tragic symbol of the Sims case.

Chapter 4

Robert Sims's father once described his son as having led "a rather sheltered life." A more apt description may have been that he seemed to have lived his life in the shadows, in deliberate anonymity that was broken only when events slipped beyond his control.

In the cliché of retrospectives, Robert Sims grew up in what seemed to be a normal family living a normal life. He was born to Troy and Wilma Sims on April 20, 1952, in Carbondale, Illinois, a small town notable as the location of the primary campus of Southern Illinois University. The Simses lived in nearby Marion, another small town notable for a campus of sorts—the maximum-security federal penitentiary that replaced Alcatraz as the home for the worst actors in the federal prison system.

Robert had two older brothers and a younger sister. An older sister died less than a day after she was born prematurely. His father was a schoolteacher and moved the family to Alton in 1958 to teach elementary classes and music in the public schools. The family bought a house at 3521 Hoover Drive, where the widowed Troy Sims lives today in retirement.

The neighbors remember the Sims kids as being fairly quiet and staying mostly in their own yard. Robert preferred working with tools and building models to activities such as sports. His father said he was well behaved.

In high school, Robert was a B and C student, although he dropped to Ds in physics and geometry. He graduated smack in the middle of his class in 1970, ranked 350th out of 706 students. He played the tuba in the marching band and was in the chorus.

His older brothers went on to college and somewhat

related professional careers, one as a doctor at an Army medical center and the other as a medical illustrator. Their sister, Linda Condray, is a professional photographer, and lives near Robert, who was called "Rob" by his family.

He went to work as a loan collector for the credit union operated by the Laclede Steel Co. in Alton in July 1970, just after high school graduation. In September, he started classes at the campus of Southern Illinois University at Edwardsville, near Alton. He dropped out during his fourth quarter.

Troy Sims said his son seemed to enjoy working with his hands more than pursuing academic activities.

Robert enlisted in the navy in October 1972. Although he would later tell Paula that he was having flashbacks and nightmares from his service in Vietnam, Robert actually served most of his three-year tour at the naval air station at Brunswick, Maine. He reached the rank of yeoman third class.

Although his military records carry no disciplinary action, the navy was strangely uninterested in his continued service. He was classified as ineligible for reenlistment "due to his negative attitude toward the Navy."

While in Maine, Robert met Brunswick resident Martha B. Smith, known as "Martie." She was seventeen and he was twenty-one when they were married on July 5, 1974. She returned to Alton with him when he left the navy in August 1975.

Robert went back to his job as a loan collector at the credit union. But his coworkers, mostly women, saw significant changes in him. He was moody and dissatisfied with his salary. It was obvious that he didn't like taking orders from women, including his immediate supervisor. She thought he was having trouble taking orders because he had been a supervisor in the navy.

One coworker believed Robert's apparent trouble dealing with women as authority figures stemmed from a problematic relationship with his mother when he was living at home; Robert had mentioned that.

His supervisor called Robert just plain "weird," a description that seemed to be the general consensus of all of his coworkers. But the real problems began in 1976 when a woman whose desk was next to Robert's—and who graciously had referred Robert and Martie to an apartment in Alton just down the street from hers—became the victim of a series of strange incidents. Her sandwich would be smashed before lunch, or a soft drink would have been poured into her desk drawer. The tricks eventually moved to her car, and someone eventually spray-painted an obscenity on the front door. The next day, she received a letter in the mail that had a picture of a nude woman glued on it. The breasts and genital area had been clipped out and, in the style of all B-movie ransom notes, cut-out letters were glued to the page warning, "This could happen to you."

She received hang-up calls at home for several weeks. After she turned to the police, the telephone company installed a trap on her line that would register the number from which all calls were placed. Three days later, two hang-up calls were traced—to the home telephone of Robert Sims.

When the Alton police investigated, Martie Sims took the rap. She said she had found the telephone number on a piece of paper on her husband's dresser, and had called it twice. She had hung up without speaking. She was charged with disorderly conduct, but the charge was dismissed later. Robert never was charged.

The victim told the police she believed Robert had talked his wife into admitting something she hadn't done. The woman was convinced Robert had made the calls.

The credit union manager gave Robert a choice between quitting or being fired; he quit.

Years later, Martie Sims confessed again, this time to the FBI. The calls had been her way of expressing her anger because Robert had invited the woman to their home for dinner, and because of the problems she and Robert had at work. Martie Sims wasn't sure if the calls had been her idea, or her husband's. But it wouldn't have made any difference; she would have adopted the plan if he had proposed it because of her immaturity and her resentment of the woman.

Martie Sims didn't remember whether Robert had made any of the calls. But he had been present when she did, and he hadn't discouraged her until he learned about the phone trap. She had made a few more calls, foolishly believing that they couldn't be traced if she wasn't on the line too long.

But she rejected suggestions that she had taken the blame for Robert. In fact, she told the FBI that Robert lacked the charisma to command that kind of loyalty from a woman. The FBI report on the interview was bluntly eloquent: "She simply does not envision him as commanding that type of response in a woman."

Robert had personality problems at his next job, too. He stayed only eighteen months at the credit union at the Olin Corporation, a manufacturing plant in adjacent East Alton.

He moved on to the job as a laborer at the Jefferson Smurfit plant; it had been known for years as the Alton Boxboard Company until it was bought out. Over the years, Robert developed a reputation among some coworkers as a chronic complainer whose written grievances always were unfounded.

One coworker described Robert as being "very quick to anger," and told of Robert harassing a black woman who worked with him. He had put a used condom and a cockroach in her sandwich.

Robert and Martie also had problems. She told the police later that Robert was too domineering. She had returned to Maine when Robert filed a petition for divorce in Madison County Circuit Court in Edwardsville in June 1978. His grounds were "extreme and repeated mental cruelty." His attorney was Donald E. Groshong of Alton, who would become even more important to Robert Sims and his second wife.

Little is known about the next few years in Robert's life. He had a brush with the law in November 1979. He was charged with misdemeanor shoplifting after leaving a Central Hardware store in Alton with two screwdrivers and a chain for a chain saw. He was spotted by a woman security guard as he slipped the items in the pocket of his overalls. She confronted him outside the front door, but he walked away and left in a truck driven by a friend. Robert was arrested when a patrol car stopped the truck a short time later. He pleaded guilty, and was fined $100 and court costs of $15.

After Robert and Paula Blew were married in May 1981, they rented the house on Fosterburg Road, and then bought a house in Alton on a contract for deed. They lived there less than two years, and got their money back after complaining that the condition of the house had been misrepresented.

Robert and Paula bought all-terrain vehicles, and liked to spend their spare time camping in Missouri and riding the ATVs through the countryside.

Meanwhile, they decided to move out of the city. They didn't like living in town. It would be better to be out in the clean air, and the peace and quiet. In January 1984, they bought a ranch house outside of Brighton. It sat well back on a deep, wooded lot. There was a 120-yard gravel driveway—so long it seemed more like a private lane—that ran south from the house to Cotter Road, a two-lane country blacktop that cut through the sparsely populated area.

The Simses' lot abutted a picturesque little pond. Behind the house to the northwest, dense woods provided maximum privacy for the walk-out basement and sliding-glass doors.

Robert and Paula thought it would be a great place to raise children.

Chapter 5

The police walked out of the Sims house sometime after noon, ending the fruitless search inside. This was their last chance, and Yocom and Bivens agreed to run another search around the yard, just in case. They still were standing in front of the house when Robert and Paula returned from their interviews, accompanied by Paula's father and Robert's sister. The family went into the house without any conversation with the police.

Mike Donovan had told Yocom how Judd had once tracked a man who had been missing for days in the woods in Pike County; Judd found the man's body hanging in a tree. The story was on Yocom's mind as he watched Judd begin his search near the Gray's property to the west. The dog worked around to the north and soon was behind the Sims house. On a shared hunch, Yocom and Bivens asked Donovan if any of the dogs had covered the steep hillside in the woods just behind the house. It was northeast of the house, and the area closest to the sliding-glass doors from the Simses' walk-out basement. And the complete, opposite direction from the way Paula Sims said the kidnapper had fled.

Donovan wasn't sure if the dogs had been over that ground. The underbrush was thick and it would have been easy to go around.

Robert was standing just outside the sliding doors, watching the search with Lee Plummer. When the search moved toward the woods, Robert turned to Plummer with some advice.

"I wouldn't go down in those woods. They're full of poison ivy. I haven't been down there in years. If you go down there, I wouldn't stay very long."

The comments struck Plummer as strange and obvious. Robert didn't want them in the woods.

Plummer responded casually, "I don't think dogs get poison ivy." Robert retreated into the house.

Donovan took Judd's leash off and gave him the command to "find dead." The dog wandered down the hillside, weaving his way carefully through the brush.

About a hundred feet down the slope, the dog crouched down and crept carefully over to a spot near the base of a small tree. He froze. Donovan and the others, watching from the edge of the woods above, saw the dog react. Donovan announced excitedly, "He's hit. He's found it. He's found the body."

Donovan cautioned everyone to stay back as he hurried down the hill and tied Judd to a nearby tree. The trooper dropped onto his hands and knees to squint through the thicket. He was startled by what appeared to be parts of a small skeleton. He pushed the brush back to get a better look, and decided he was looking at the skull and attached spinal column of something very small. Possibly a small animal, but more likely the remains of a little girl who lived for a very short time in that house just above the woods.

Frank Yocom and Jimmie Bivens had run down the steep hill, and were looking over Donovan's shoulder as he turned back and asked, "Is it human?"

Bivens looked at the tiny skull. "I don't think so."

Donovan looked again, and nodded his conviction that it was indeed the object of their search. "That dog doesn't lie. It's human."

Yocom could feel his heart pounding as he got down on all fours to examine the discovery. He leaned in and sniffed; the odor was unmistakable. He was struck by the tiny size of the remains and their odd, brownish color. On the back of the skull, he could see a pathetic scrap of skin and faint, red hair. He thought of the photo of Loralei—and her pretty red hair.

As he stood up, he turned his head away from the others. The tears were welling up in his eyes, and he felt nearly overwhelmed by the emotional impact of the discovery—the sorrow, the pity, and then the anger. My God, that little body had to have been rotting in the

woods the whole time. Or was it even worse, even more unthinkable? Had she been dumped here alive and left to die?

Bivens too was feeling that flash of anger. He looked
back up the hill, back up the 150 feet to the Sims house.
Those sons of bitches, he thought. He was angry over
that baby's fate, and he was insulted about being sent off
on that wild-goose chase down the driveway to the south
while the body was in the woods to the north. Surely the
location of the body destroyed forever the kidnapper
story, and even the Simses would have to admit that.

Phil Kocis still was at the Brighton police station when
Bivens called with the news. Kocis was shocked that the
body had been so close to the house, but he was mad, too.

"How the hell could we have missed it?"

As he drove back to the house, he asked himself a
simple question: *Why would some kidnapper grab the
baby, run to the back of the house, pitch the baby down
the hill, and then run off again?* Not only was that a
preposterous scenario, but it destroyed the only possible
motives—ransom or baby selling.

He realized, too, that the location of the body locked
Paula into an indefensible story about the masked gunman carrying the baby and running down the driveway
with Paula just seconds behind. If the body was in the
woods, didn't that disprove Paula's story and, logically,
prove she did it? Even if that were proof, it still left
unanswered the question of motive. Why had she done
something so bizarre?

Dee Heil, the crime scene tech, had been at the house
to help with the search. He looked at the remains and
advised Bivens to call in Mark Johnsey, another crime
scene technician uniquely trained for this job. Johnsey
carried the additional certification of forensic anthropologist, making him qualified to identify and analyze skeletal remains. He was the only one in the state with that
dual certification. It made him the best man for the painstaking search for the rest of the remains, the identification of what was found, and the difficult task of
interpreting what the physiological evidence meant to this
investigation. Now it was an apparent homicide.

Bivens put in a call for Johnsey while Heil used yellow

tape to mark off the location of the body until Johnsey arrived.

Yocom and Bivens realized that they had not seen the clothes Paula said Loralei had been wearing when she disappeared. Could there be a shallow grave nearby, too?

The twelve officers at the scene were pulled in for a shoulder-to-shoulder search around the remains. They walked the entire hillside looking for any scraps of clothing or any suggestion of a grave. In the most careful search of a wooded area any of them had ever seen, they turned up nothing.

Yocom looked at Bivens, and nodded toward the house. "Let's go in and break the news." As they walked up the hill, Yocom wondered how he would make the announcement. What could he say, and what would the Simses' reactions mean to the case? Would it be heartbreaking news of death, or shock that a secret was out? Amid the jumble of thoughts, Frank couldn't even put together an idea of what to say.

He soon found himself facing the family. Robert and Paula were sitting at the table with Orville Blew and Linda Condray. Yocom swallowed and felt his words rumble up from deep inside. His voice trembled as he spoke.

"We think we found your daughter," he said softly.

Robert brightened, as if he were reacting to good news, and asked "Where is she?"

Yocom answered, "No. We found her down in the woods."

Robert asked again, "Is she all right?"

"We found the skeletal remains of what we believe to be a human infant," Yocom said.

Robert and Paula looked stunned. Paula sobbed and put her head down on the table. Yocom was surprised again by the reaction; still no deep, genuine emotion. *I'm sadder than they are,* he thought, and it made him angry again.

Bivens fixed his gaze on Robert and still saw no sign of a bereaved father.

There were no questions from the parents. No request to see the body, no query as to when they could bury their little girl.

The tiny skull and spinal column already had been taken to Jersey Community Hospital to be X-rayed, and the radiologist had confirmed them to be human remains. Yocom got the news as he was getting ready to drive into Brighton and announce the grim discovery to the press. But what did this really mean? There was so little left of the body. Could they even establish an identity? He was sure they would fail to find a cause of death. Where did they go from here? He still couldn't sort out his thoughts, and the pain of the discovery seemed to be growing.

He was shaking as he drove into town; he had faced the press many times, but he felt strangely nervous now. He had never made an announcement that seemed as tough as this one. He had been to a lot of doors in the night, bringing too many heartbreaking words to too many grieving parents—a son or daughter killed in a wreck, most often. Death was no stranger. He had held his first wife, Rebecca, in his arms in 1975 as her life surrendered to the cancer she had fought for seven years. But this duty today was taking a different toll on him. He still didn't know what he would say; his thoughts wouldn't leave the image of that little body in the woods.

The reporters had gathered inside the police station in Brighton, still expecting a stinging denial of Robert's polygraph claim. They knew that could signal the start of some tense charges and countercharges between the cops and parents, finally bringing into the open the suspicions that had been brewing, but were so difficult to get out under the circumstances.

As Yocom stepped into the station lobby, the press surrounded him, backing him into the corner. But what they heard was stunning, as the sheriff glumly disclosed the discovery of what was believed to be the remains of Loralei Marie Sims. His voice still was subdued as he gave a few details in response to a jumble of questions. He did decide to release the whole truth about the Simses and the polygraphs. He offered bluntly, "They were not in fact truthful on the polygraph. The polygraph examiner concluded that they did falsify their answers to all the questions."

The reporters buzzed with more questions. Had the polygraphs and discovery of the body changed the direction of the investigation?

Frank was careful about assessing the impact on the

case. ''Nothing has really changed as far as the investigation is concerned. We will continue the investigation and we are hopeful we will be able to put the persons responsible where they belong.''

But the reporters knew that, for the first time, the police were casting the same doubt on this story of a frightening, bizarre kidnapping that most of the people in the streets had been expressing for days.

Mark Johnsey pulled up at the house late that afternoon. After one look through the dense underbrush at the few tiny bones, he knew it would be a long, slow, delicate process. Bivens ordered troopers posted at the scene around the clock.

Johnsey and a trooper carefully pulled away as much of the larger pieces of brush as they could without disturbing the soil near the remains. Johnsey dropped to his hands and knees and began the back-breaking process of sifting through every loose leaf and twig. Each minuscule shoot had to be examined to be positive it had not come from a little hand or foot.

As he found bones or pieces of bones, he wrapped them in plastic, stuck a wire marked with an orange pennant through the plastic, and stabbed the wire into the ground where the bones had been.

The bones were stained dark brown from body fluids that drained away during the rapid decomposition in the intense heat. The coloring made the bones even harder to discern from the twigs and sticks lying about in the natural clutter on the floor of the woods. When all of the loose matter had been removed, Johnsey began pulling out each blade of grass by hand, one or two at a time, as he crawled along squinting at every bit he picked up.

He gave up about dark, delaying the rest of the work until the next day.

Frank Yocom sat with Carol for a long talk that night; he needed to let out some of the thoughts in his mind that were too personal to share with anyone else. At least, one of the big questions was answered. For the first time in a week, Frank slept well that night.

* * *

Johnsey returned on Wednesday, June 25, to continue the meticulous process. By the time he was done, he had found more than fifty bones scattered over an area twenty-nine feet long and twelve feet wide on the steep hillside above a ravine. The scene was strikingly peculiar—a bald patch of earth amid the thicket of the woods, dotted by dozens of little orange pennants.

In addition to the skull and vertebral column, the anthropologist identified parts of the jaw, right arm, right leg, rib cage, and the hands and feet. Some of the bones had small bits of tissue or hair attached, but not enough for any significant forensic evaluation. The left arm and leg were missing.

Johnsey's analysis was that he had the partial remains of a human infant who had been within the first month of birth, had weighed six to eight pounds, and had been twenty to twenty-eight inches long.

His secondary conclusion was chilling, but scientifically unmistakable. Some small animal, probably a raccoon, had been eating on the body and had dragged the remains downhill, strewing them about in the process. There were no chew marks on the bones, and the ground was too covered by leaves and brush to find animal tracks. But the other evidence at the scene and the condition of the body made the heartbreaking truth inescapable.

Bivens was repulsed by the thought of what had happened to the tiny body. He wondered how anyone could have remained in that house, knowing that tiny body was rotting in the woods nearby. That takes some hard bark, he thought.

Johnsey took the remains to the crime lab in Fairview Heights for further study. After a last look around about 1:15 P.M., the police drove down the lane and left the Simses' property for the last time.

Frank Yocom was the last man out.

Gage Sherwood was sitting in his law office in Bethalto, a small village near Alton, when his receptionist buzzed and told him Herb Condray was on the line. Sherwood and his partner had inherited Herb when the firm's founder took an appointment as a federal magistrate some years before. Herb hung around the office, served some process papers and subpoenas, and did a little investigating for the firm. His work as a photographer had come in handy a few time.

Herb told Sherwood that he had some relatives who were in trouble. An hour later, Sherwood—a stocky, compact man with a graying beard—was sitting at the dining room table in the home of Robert and Paula Sims. They told him their stories and complained that the police had refused to believe them. They had been accused repeatedly of killing their baby and hiding her body. Sherwood knew of the case, of course, and he agreed to represent them.

His first official act was to inform the authorities that their free trips to the Simses' well were over. He called Yocom and explained that all further communications with the family were to be made through their attorney.

Yocom knew that was it. There would be no more chances at Paula or Robert.

And Bivens knew that solving the case now would require some new physical evidence or a break from some family member who couldn't live with what was going on anymore. In this case, Bivens thought, surely someone would "come in" on the guilty party. He couldn't believe that the in-laws on either side of the family would stand behind someone they knew had committed such a deed, especially if it wasn't their blood relative. Someone had to know.

Later that morning, Robert and Paula Sims packed up and drove away with Paula's father. They would begin a long stay with the Blews, and never spent another night at the secluded home in Brighton. The house quietly went up for sale, and the Simses returned only to move their belongings after it sold.

Robert Sims explained that he and Paula moved out because of "pressure from the media."

The case still held some surprise for the cops. Agents Sievers and Morgan were sent to Jack's Hallmark Card Shop in Jerseyville to talk to a clerk named Gisella Rasp. She had reported talking to Paula Sims when she was in the shop with Loralei on Saturday, June 14. Being in the card shop didn't seem like a big deal. But Robert and Paula had stressed that they never had taken Loralei out of the house. They even had canceled the Father's Day celebration at the Blews' to keep the baby home.

Mrs. Rasp was an immigrant, and her thick accent made her German origin unmistakable. She told Sievers and Morgan that she had noticed a woman carrying a tiny baby in the shop early that Saturday. As the woman was leaving, Mrs. Rasp had asked about the baby, and was told it was a girl named Loralei. She had been pleasantly surprised to hear such a Germanic name. She described the baby's hair as bright red; Loralei's eyes were open, and she was not crying.

Mrs. Rasp was jolted a few days later when she saw the parents of a kidnapped baby on the television news. She recognized the mother as the woman who had been in the store earlier. A couple of days after that, she recognized the Loralei she had seen as the same one whose pictures appeared on fliers brought into the store.

The report puzzled the agents. Why would Paula have lied about taking the baby to the card shop?

They were accompanied by Lee Plummer when they went to the Blews to ask Paula about Mrs. Rasp's story. Orville Blew answered the door, and announced gruffly that he, Paula, and Robert wouldn't talk to anyone. Then he looked at the women agents.

"If you're Morgan and Sievers, you can get your asses off my porch." The door slammed abruptly.

Mark Johnsey spent several days studying the bones he had collected on the hillside. He prepared a diagram of a skeleton to mark each bone that had been found and each one that was missing.

Yocom arranged to have the autopsy performed by Dr. George Gantner, the medical examiner for the city of St. Louis and a nationally known pathologist. The sheriff figured Dr. Gantner would have the most resources to try to identify the pitiful remains as Loralei's and establish a cause of death. That would be essential if someone were to be charged in the baby's killing.

Gantner had spent several days studying the bones when he told the *Post-Dispatch* on July 11 that there was no way an autopsy would identify the remains or set a cause of death. The body was too young to determine the sex, but Gantner called it "a reasonable assumption" that the bones were those of the missing Sims baby. The most pathologists could hope for was to use bone marrow to match blood types between the remains and Paula. If the blood type didn't match, he said, "It would be the case of the century."

Yocom and Plummer decided to pull out all the stops to identify the body. In talks with FBI experts in Washington, Yocom learned that a new kind of testing, using genetic factors in the blood, was being performed at two laboratories in the United States. One was in Phoenix; the other was in Atlanta. The diligent sheriff called both to discuss his needs, and decided on Dr. Moses S. Schanfield at Allo Type Genetic Testing, Inc. in Atlanta.

The doctor explained that the markers used in the testing were called "immunoglobulin allotypes." They occurred in blood and body fluids such as bone marrow. A series of factors and subclasses of those factors would be tested in samples from the two sources. The common factors in the two samples could be used to establish a genetic likelihood that the sources were parent and child. If all the markers were present, that certainty could be as high as 99.1 percent.

Dr. Schanfield said the percentage commonly accepted to establish parentage was 95 percent, and the forensic rule for establishing a medical fact was the same as the burden of proof in a criminal case—beyond a reasonable doubt.

A lot of the biological details escaped the sheriff's grasp. But he knew these tests could provide the scientific link that was mandatory if criminal charges ever were to be filed.

Sherwood agreed to provide a blood sample from Paula. Yocom took a nurse to Sherwood's office, expecting it to be an uncomfortable reunion. He was surprised at how uncomfortable it was. Neither Paula nor Robert even looked at him, and no one spoke a word. They just sat there with solemn looks on their faces.

On August 19, Jimmie Bivens flew to Atlanta, where he delivered a small box with some of the remains and Paula's blood samples to Allo labs. Ten days later, a report from Dr. Schanfield arrived. Yocom scanned quickly through two pages of scientific garble before he reached the conclusion on the third page. He held his breath as he read that the factors were compatible with Paula Sims being the mother of the infant. A factor called "Km type" that was found in both samples occurs in one in six white females in Illinois.

The last sentence read, "The likelihood of finding two unrelated white individuals with this phenotype is approximately 2.8 percent versus 100 percent if they are mother and child."

Yocom knew that meant the tests had established a 97.2 percent certainty that the body was Paula's daughter, Loralei Marie Sims. That was well over the 95 percent that Dr. Schanfield had said would fly in court as a positive identification.

Yocom was thrilled. But his bubble burst when he called Sherwood. The attorney was unimpressed.

"That means there's a 3 percent chance that this is not Loralei. That's unacceptable. We want something more than that. I think the tests can do better if that really is Loralei's body. If they can do more, we want it done before we make any final decisions."

Yocom made a desperate call back to Dr. Schanfield, who confirmed that there were more tests that could be run. The days passed slowly while Yocom waited again; the results came back in less than two weeks. Frank was elated as he read the conclusion of a 99.75 percent certainty that the body in the woods had been Loralei.

"You can't get any closer than that," he thought.

The next day, September 19, Sherwood announced that Robert and Paula had accepted the test conclusions, and would bury the remains as their daughter.

"There's nothing more that can be done," Sherwood said. But he rejected the insistence by the sheriff and the prosecutor that the Simses remained suspects. "It's over and done with as far as we're concerned."

He said the Simses had been shaken badly by the final test results and their own decision to accept the remains as their daughter.

"There's an obvious, very keen sense of depression. The one thing that they feared came true," said Sherwood.

The words rang hollow to the cops.

The case had become nearly an obsession for Frank Yocom. He had prayed that the results of the blood tests

would shake up the Simses enough to jar something loose.
Maybe providing that the body was Loralei's would rattle
someone in the family, touch something in someone's
heart, and they would decide to make things right for that
baby. His hopes were dim, but he refused to give up.

More than three months after her death, Loralei's remains were buried in a private service September 27 at
the Woodland Hill Cemetery in East Alton.

The day before the funeral, Robert Sims held the only
exclusive interview he ever granted a reporter. Sherwood
had known the reporter covering the Sims case for the
Post-Dispatch, Charles Bosworth, Jr., for years. Sherwood relayed Bosworth's request for an interview with
Robert, adding that he thought Bosworth would be fair
and, if Robert felt like making a statement to the public,
this was the best way. Robert agreed.

They met in Sherwood's office. Robert described—in
that soft-spoken, cautious, and contemplative style—the
emotional devastation he and his wife had suffered over
their daughter's death. He could not say that they had
accepted fully that their daughter was dead and the body
they would bury was hers.

"As much as possible, we have. But it's hard to say
100 percent positive that it's her. We're going along with
the findings. But I can't say, down in my heart, that I
absolutely know it's her. I don't believe she was murdered. I can't imagine anybody in the world . . . There's
just no reason for it."

Sherwood would not let Robert discuss details of the
case. But Robert spoke repeatedly of the "abductor."
Robert still hoped that the man would be caught. But he
acknowledged, regretfully, that most people had rejected
the stories told by him and Paula. He seemed perplexed
by the unwillingness of the police and the public to believe their accounts, and in their innocence.

"What I can't believe is how little support we've got
from the world in general. We've been condemned."

He and Paula were keeping their sanity, "but just
barely." They had gone to the funeral home the day before to select a coffin, but Loralei's death still hadn't
seemed real.

Robert slumped slightly in an armchair, with his legs crossed. His chin rested in the palm of his left hand, and his right arm was folded across his waist. He looked off in the distance most of the time, but occasionally he would look directly into Bosworth's face. The look could be penetrating from those hazel eyes, but it was hard to find in them any clue as to the thoughts behind them.

Bosworth asked if Robert believed things would get better for him and Paula. Robert paused for a long time, and then sighed. "Yeah, it'll get better. I guess the true peace will never be reached until they find the guy that did this. But it'll get better."

Asked if he and Paula hoped to have more children, Robert looked stricken. He stared off to the side and said in a whisper, "I don't know."

Then, as he had while standing in his driveway on June 19, he issued an appeal to the public for support and understanding.

"I just wish you could put down the magic words to make people believe in us again. That hurts more than anything right now. What's done is done, until they find the guy. But to have everybody condemning you . . ."

As Bosworth left, Robert shook his hand and said, "Thank you. Be fair with us."

Lee Plummer had a prosecutor's decision to make. Every cop on the case was convinced that Paula Sims was responsible for Loralei's death and had lied brazenly with the elaborate kidnapping story. They all shared suspicions that Robert Sims was involved somehow. But as state's attorney, Plummer had to go by the law, and he couldn't issue a criminal charge because everyone thought they knew who was responsible. He needed hard evidence, and he had precious little here.

Plummer had his own speculations, too. The whole plan had seemed so neat and tidy that Plummer thought he knew who had been the architect. It was convenient that Robert had a rock-solid alibi at work, wasn't it? But there had been major blunders. The body should have been dropped into the river or buried deep in the middle of nowhere. And the rip in the screen door was wrong—too small, too neat.

But none of that was evidence to support a murder charge.

What he did have was a decent circumstantial case against Paula on felony charges of obstructing justice, concealing a homicidal death, and giving false evidence. But convictions on those counts probably would lead to probation for Paula. A judge would consider Paula's lack of a criminal record and the practically absurd thought she ever would commit such a crime again.

No one in their right mind would believe that this could happen again.

Worse yet, convicting Paula on such lesser charges might prohibit an attempt later to charge her with murder; that could be ruled double jeopardy. So Plummer decided to wait and see if evidence to support a murder charge was found.

Yocom, Bivens, and Kocis—the trio that at times had seemed joined at the hip—agreed completely with Plummer's appraisal. The Sims case had been the most frustrating experience of their careers. But they knew how to face the facts.

The prosecutor and the cops also shared the view expressed in the popular, not to mention sardonic, comment, "We'll find out what really happened after the divorce."

After Loralei was buried, the news coverage faded. But Plummer was preparing to impanel a grand jury for an eighteen-month term on March 12, 1987, and he and Yocom decided to subpoena Robert and Paula, just to see if anything would shake loose. And it would serve as a reminder to the Simses that the authorities still were watching.

Bivens gladly agreed to serve the subpoenas. By now, Robert and Paula had been living for two months in a house they bought at 1053 Washington Avenue in Alton. When Bivens pulled up in front, Robert was standing in the driveway. He seemed surprised, but not hostile, as Bivens walked up.

He grinned. "Hi ya', Bob. How ya' doin'?"

"I'm fine. How are you, Jim?"

They exchanged a few pleasantries about how long it

had been. Just a couple old friends chit-chatting, Bivens laughed to himself.

"I've got some subpoenas for you and Paula for the Jersey County grand jury on the twelfth. They want to get some information on the case. Is Paula home?"

"She's inside. I'll give it to her."

The famous Sims cool was engaged and intact. No reaction. Just a flat, "Okay. We'll talk to our lawyer about it. Thanks."

On March 12, Robert and Paula slipped quietly into the old sandstone courthouse in Jerseyville with Sherwood at their sides. Only the reporter from the *Post-Dispatch* was there. Sherwood filed a motion to quash the subpoenas, but it was denied by Circuit judge Claude Davis.

Before Bivens and Yocom testified, Plummer explained to the grand jurors that this session was for information only. They would not be asked to take any action.

Robert and Paula were called into the grand jury room separately. Each one stayed less than two minutes, just long enough to take their attorney's advice, and to take the Fifth. They had no comment for a reporter.

Robert and Paula wore the faces the public would see many times over the next few years. Robert's almost relaxed look seemed to carry no particular message. His gaze was fixed off in the distance, making no eye contact with anyone who was watching him. There would be times when some of the more jaded observers claimed to detect a hint of amusement in his eyes, as if he took some degree of pleasure in facing the world—especially the police and prosecutors—and coming out on top, untouchable by the sheer force of his intellect and will.

But Paula's emotionless, blank face was disturbing. Anyone looking for something to identify could read in that countenance the hardness of a mother capable of snuffing the life from her child and dumping the naked little body in the woods behind the house. If Paula had erected an impenetrable facade to protect herself from the prying eyes of the public, she also had taken on the burden of that stone face.

When June 17, 1987 came around, there were a few newspaper stories commemorating the first anniversary of the

Loralei Marie Sims case. Robert and Paula had no comment. Yocom reiterated his belief that the case would be solved someday, and he vowed to keep it open until then.

Minnie Gray, who asked that she not be named in the papers, said she was haunted by the memories of that night and she had been unable to visit her new neighbors in the Sims house; it was like there was some sort of cloud hanging over the place. "I still find myself looking back there and wondering what happened." Minnie didn't know it, but the "haunted house effect" was common in unsolved crimes, and it would last for four years in this case.

In Brighton, Loralei's death still was a topic of conversation.

Nylene Blew told the *Post-Dispatch* of a year that could be described only in words such as "nightmare and horrible." Her granddaughter's death and its aftermath had nearly destroyed Paula and Robert. "Paula called me on the fifth of June, Loralei's first birthday. She was so upset about it. She was crying, and saying we would have been having a birthday party. I pray every day that there will be an answer. There has to be an answer."

But Robert's father, Troy Sims, said he believed the couple was starting to emerge from the "traumatic year."

"They're changing their way of life and looking forward now."

On Tuesday, September 8, Jersey County coroner Paul D. Schroeder closed the book on the case. A brief, low-key inquest was held, and Frank Yocom was the only witness before the six coroner's jurors. Schroeder read the inconclusive results of the autopsy.

The jurors deliberated about twenty minutes before returning a verdict: the cause and mode of death of Loralei Marie Sims was undetermined. They added a statement to the verdict form that said the baby "came to her death by means and circumstances which were unable to be determined by the investigation and testing."

At Woodland Hill Cemetery, the tiny grave remained unmarked.

Chapter 6

Even the most intriguing stories fade quickly from the public's attention, and the Sims case was no exception. News coverage died out, and even private comments among the cops and reporters became rare. By the end of 1987, hardly anyone mentioned the Sims case anymore.

Sheriff Frank Yocom's attention was demanded elsewhere; something always was buzzing in a small sheriff's department. Captain Philip Kocis had new cases crossing his desk daily. Agent Jimmie Bivens retired on December 31, 1987, and opened a private investigating firm. State's Attorney Lee Plummer decided that twelve years in office were enough and did not seek reelection in November 1988. He was succeeded by Richard J. Ringhausen, a young lawyer who inherited an open file on a case that had left a score of more experienced authorities baffled.

Few people knew when Robert and Paula moved permanently into Madison County in January 1987. They bought a house in Alton, barely ten miles south of Brighton, but across the line into the larger and more urban Madison County. Alton is a town of 34,000 along the Mississippi; its streets stagger up the hillsides from the riverfront, where the old downtown retains some of the picturesque buildings that were there when Abraham Lincoln and Stephen Douglas conducted a debate in the square. The city is just a few miles upstream from the impressive skyline of St. Louis.

The Simses' new home was a white frame house at 1053 Washington Avenue. It wasn't a house that would attract much attention from the passing traffic. It was simple, a two-story rectangle decorated only by a front porch with columns supporting the roof. The column on the left bore the address, the black numbers 1-0-5-3 running vertically down the post. The house sat next to the East Middle School, and hundreds of school kids passed the yard every day.

More than two years later, however, the little house would be one of the most famous in the area, immediately recognizable by anyone who watched television or read the newspapers as the scene of a new, and equally bizarre, Sims case. One evening it would host a most curious event, compared sarcastically to a circus, and it would draw a rowdy crowd likened to a lynch mob.

Washington Avenue is an unusual street, lined with mostly older homes and looking every bit like a typical residential street in any older, Midwestern city. But it is wider than most streets, marking its service as a major east–west artery connecting the older downtown along the riverfront to the busier, new commercial district on the Beltline, as most people called the Homer Adams Parkway. That four-lane route strikes an arc along the eastern and northern edges of the city, and every known fast-food restaurant and discount store has sprung up along its shoulders. It has attracted the only major shopping center on the north end of the Metro East area—Alton Square.

So Washington Avenue became a busy link between the old and the new. Most of the residents never saw the new owners of the house at 1053, however, and the few that did got no more than a reserved nod or a quick hello from the young husband. Some thought they recognized the couple from the news almost a year before, but no one got close enough to ask. They never saw the couple out in the yard, wandering about the property as most new owners would do.

It wasn't long before a five-foot, chain-link fence went up around the small front yard. It was a strange sight, so much higher than normal. Only a row of barbed wire wound around the top would have made it more like the prison fence it evoked. The sidewalk that led from the front porch toward the street hit a dead end at the new fence, leading nowhere and inviting no one in. There was no front gate, although the driveway was open and ran along the north side of the house.

The fence was the first clue that something was amiss. It was the first hint that the owners had become obsessive, maybe even paranoid, about their security and their privacy.

But the evidence mounted; Robert Sims soon erected a redwood privacy fence from the south side of the house to the property line, blocking the view of the yard from the street. "Too many nosy people watching you all the time," he would say. He installed a dusk-to-dawn yard light on the back of the house, just like the one he had put on the pole in the driveway in Brighton—the one that should have illuminated a fleeing kidnapper.

The couple put up heavy new blinds, Robert said, "so no one could stand at the windows and look in." The dining room window was covered with a special film so the daylight could shine in, but the view from the outside remained blocked.

The back door, with the large pane of glass on top, was replaced with a steel security door with no window. The door was equipped with a heavy dead-bolt lock that always was thrown.

When a man broke into a house down the street and robbed an old woman, Robert would say later, he loaded a pistol and put it on top of the antique cabinet in the dining room. He claimed that he had shown Paula how to use it, and told her it always would be within reach.

The Simses lived a strange, reclusive existence then, hiding from the celebrity that had been bestowed on them in a most unwelcome way. They often left town to shop, crossing the Lewis and Clark Bridge to the expanse of commercial areas in north St. Louis County. There they had a better chance of passing without the occasional second glance or the more obvious stares of recognition that intruded into their private world.

Eventually, it seemed to the Simses, the people had begun to forget. A second child was planned and, in June 1987, they learned Paula was pregnant. A sonogram later convinced the doctor that the child would be a boy. The Simses had wanted a boy to carry on the family name, and they both were very happy.

The Simses probably assumed that there were at least

a few people keeping tabs on them. They certainly were right.

Frank Yocom hadn't forgotten. An Alton policeman who lived near the Simses kept watch on them, and Yocom usually got the word as soon as anything happened. He knew all about the fences and the yard light. When he was in Alton, perhaps to visit someone in the hospital, Yocom automatically drove by the house for a look. He never noticed anything significant and never saw Robert or Paula. But he had to do it, like the teenaged boy cruising past the home of the girl he watched from afar. She didn't even know he was out there, but somehow he felt better just doing it, just being on that street.

Quite a few of the policemen in Alton were aware of the Simses' presence, as were some of the DCI agents. It was the subject of some typically dark humor among the cynical cops. The agents often would provoke Alton Detective Sergeant Anthony Ventimiglia with warnings that the next Sims baby case would be the city's problem. "You get the next one," they would tell him. It was, of course, only a joke, not a prediction. That thought never seriously entered anyone's head.

But Yocom and some of the others knew when the Simses' second child was born on February 1, 1988. The boy was named Randall Troy, after Paula's ill-fated and still-mourned brother, and Robert's father.

No one ever saw the little boy outside the house. There were no walks by proud parents pushing a stroller. There was no baby crawling through the grass, nor a giggling toddler discovering the wonders in a handful of dirt. Little Randy wasn't heard making engine noises while he steered a toy truck through a sandbox. Dirt and sand would have been against Robert's rules, it would be learned later.

Yocom and the others heard rumors that another little girl had been born to the Simses in early 1989. But they wouldn't know that for a fact until a cool spring evening a little later.

Chapter 7

Alton Patrolman Bob Eichen had been a cop for about ten months on Saturday, April 29, 1989. The 30-year-old rookie had come on duty at 11:00 P.M., and was hoping for a nice, quiet Saturday night. But that wasn't to be; not even close.

He had been out in the patrol car for only a few minutes when a radio dispatch sent him to 1053 Washington Avenue to answer a call on a reported child abduction. Even rookies know that bona fide child abductions are rare. So it was likely that this was really something else. Probably just another goofy Saturday night domestic beef.

Eichen slowed down as he entered the 1000 block of Washington, straining his eyes to look for house numbers. He drove past the East Middle School on his right. Ten-fifty-three had to be pretty close now. As he looked past the school, he could see a man standing on the sidewalk of the house next door. He looked at his watch; 11:27 P.M. He looked up again to see the man waving his arms frantically. This bearded guy was wearing bib overalls and no shirt, hopping and waving his arms like he was doing some kind of crazy jumping-jacks. This must be the place.

As he pulled up to the curb, the man hurried over to the driver's window and began nearly babbling. "We've got to set up roadblocks. They've taken my daughter. They took my other daughter." The man seemed almost incoherent.

"Who did it?" Eichen asked.

"I don't know."

"Did you get a description?"

The man pointed back up the driveway, past the high

chain-link fence that surrounded the front yard. A woman was standing farther back in the driveway by the house.

"They took her from my wife. They knocked her out and took our baby."

Eichen pulled the car into the driveway and stopped near the woman. She was slim and rather tall, wearing slacks and a short-sleeved blouse. As he climbed out of the car, the woman ran toward him. She was nearly hysterical, but didn't really seem to be crying.

"You've got to set up roadblocks," she said. "They took my baby."

From the way they acted, Eichen thought his first guess had been right. *They're nuts or on something, and this really isn't a baby abduction. The kid is probably in the house or something.*

"Did you see a car?"

"No."

"Did you see the offender?"

"Yes, but I can't remember much. He was wearing dark clothes and a mask. He had a gun."

The woman looked toward an apartment building to the east of her house and pointed to a lighted window.

"That man's lights are on. He probably saw what happened," she said.

As Eichen was talking to the woman, Patrolman Richard Gillespie arrived with his police dog. Eichen asked Gillespie to stay with the couple while Eichen checked with the neighbor. The man in the apartment hadn't seen anything, however, and Eichen guided the couple into the house to continue the interview. Gillespie took his dog on a tour of the yard to see if he could pick up a scent.

The couple walked around the back of their house with Eichen following them. They climbed a few stairs, crossed a small porch, and walked through the back door into the kitchen.

The man turned to the officer and said slowly, "I'm Robert Sims. This is my wife, Paula."

The names meant nothing to Eichen.

He asked the woman to tell him what had happened. As she spoke, he watched her and her husband's actions. They were nervous, but something didn't seem right. It was just too, too—*alien* was the word that popped into his mind. It was too alien from the way he would be reacting.

Eichen tried not to think of his three little sons, and how he would be if one of them had just been kidnapped. As a cop, he usually tried not to put himself in the other person's place and make a judgment based on what his own emotional response might have been under those circumstances. He knew that people reacted differently to stress, and he didn't want to jump to the wrong conclusion about something someone else was experiencing.

But he looked at the man and the woman, and the father in him thought, *This isn't right. Man, I'd be out of my mind.*

Paula told Eichen that she had been taking out a bag of trash about 10:30 P.M. and, as she stepped off the stairs from the back porch, she saw a man standing near the driveway to the west, about ten feet from her. He was wearing a dark ski mask and holding a pistol. He pointed the gun at her and told her, "Get back in the house." She turned and walked across the porch and through the back door into the kitchen. Just as she stepped into the kitchen, the gunman struck her on the back of the head. She didn't remember anything else until her husband had awakened her when he returned from work at 11:12 P.M.

Robert picked up the story there. He had found his wife lying face-down, unconscious on the kitchen floor, just inside the back door. He had been unable to rouse her at first, and then had run into the dining room to discover that their baby, Heather, was missing. She wasn't in her bassinet or her infant seat. He returned to Paula again, shaking her, calling her name and asking repeatedly, "Where's Heather? Where's Heather, Paula? Where's Heather?" Paula finally came around, and said Heather should be in her bassinet. He had told her the baby was missing, and they had run upstairs to check on their fifteen-month-old son, Randy. He was fine, sleeping soundly. Then they called the police.

That's it? Eichen thought.

"Do you remember anything else? Any details about the man or what he said that would help us?"

Robert and Paula shook their heads.

"Usually, either you're rich and someone wants ransom, or someone hates you so much that they do this to hurt you," Eichen said. "Why would someone do this to you?"

They shrugged. "We have no idea," Robert mumbled.

Paula Sims looked intensely at Eichen.

"This happened to us before," she said slowly. "When we lived in Brighton. Someone took our other baby girl then, too."

Then it clicked. It hit Eichen like a lightning bolt. When he realized who was telling him about another daughter being abducted, he was almost embarrassed that his first thought was no more profound than *Oh, wow.*

Everything that happened from that point on took on new importance. Eichen knew that what he got from these people in these first few minutes could be more important than anything else he would do as a cop.

He pressed Paula for a description of the kidnapper. But she had little to offer—dark clothes, a mask, a gun. *She doesn't have a clue,* Eichen thought.

He urged her to think about the man. Anything would help. But Paula was able to say only that the man was wearing a dark ski mask and dark clothes, and was carrying a pistol. Every time he asked for more information, Eichen got "I don't know."

She was unable to say what had been used to hit her in the back of the head, or whether it had just been a punch from a hand.

Eichen was able to get more information only by asking questions that suggested answers. "Was the man about my height?" Yes. "Was he about my weight?" Yes. "Did his gun look like my gun?" Yes.

Eichen stood there for a moment, amazed that the only description he had was the one he had suggested. It could fit him or dozens of other men he knew.

As he questioned her, he was struck by the way she turned her emotions off and on. In between the questions, she would seem nearly hysterical and the tears would flow. When he asked a question, she would turn off the tears, stop and think for a while, and then offer her answer. Eichen could almost see the wheels turning as she thought over each answer before speaking.

No, he thought, *she shouldn't have to think about these*

*answers like that. This just happened. She shouldn't have
to take so long.* After each answer, as if she felt obligated
to be hysterical, she would begin to cry again.

Gillespie came in with the news that the dog had turned
up nothing in the yard or driveway. He asked the Simses
to tell their stories again. As the cops listened, they
glanced back and forth at each other. They both knew
they should be getting more information from the victim
of such an attack and kidnapping. The looks the men
exchanged agreed: *This is bogus.*

They decided to do nothing more until a ranking officer or a detective arrived to take charge of the scene.
Eichen hoped that the tension of just sitting there in silence might push one of the Simses into saying something that would give the police some clue as to what was
really going on.

Paula's only remark wasn't incriminating, but it certainly was curious. She looked up at Robert and said
softly, "My son's all right. That's all that matters." Robert looked down at his lap, and just nodded his head
slowly.

Eichen was taken aback. Paula knew the police could
hear her. What kind of thing was that to say at a time
like this? Her infant daughter had been kidnapped, and
the only thing that mattered was that her son was safe?

Eichen thought Robert seemed to do little to comfort
Paula. Usually the husband would have his arms around
his wife, striking the "protective man" pose. He would
be caressing her and patting her. He would promise that
he would move Heaven and Hell to see that their baby
was found. But the most Robert offered was putting his
hand on Paula's shoulder a time or two. That was the
only gesture of comfort he gave his distraught wife.

Within a few minutes, Sergeant Terry Lane arrived
with Patrolman Morey Fraser. Eichen gave them a brief
account of what he had learned, and told Lane that he
felt uncomfortable about the whole thing. Eichen also
noted the woman had not complained at all about any
pain from the blow to the head.

Sergeant Lane asked Paula if they could examine her
for injuries. Eichen stepped behind her and pushed her hair
aside. Nothing. Not a mark. Eichen looked at her face

and elbows. Nothing there, either. If she had fallen forward, unconscious from a blow that knocked her out for forty-five minutes, and had struck the tile floor, there would have been some marks somewhere.

On orders from Lane, Eichen called the station and told Lieutenant Allen Tuetken, the shift commander, to call out the detectives. Then Eichen left the house and walked to the street, relieved to be out of that house. He sat down in his car and began to write his report.

Inside, Robert had made a telephone call to his sister, Linda Condray. Fraser heard him say Heather had been kidnapped. And then Robert added that he needed to call their lawyer. That was odd. This man's daughter was kidnapped a little while ago, and he's worried about calling his lawyer?

Sergeant Rick McCain was thirty-three and had been a cop in Alton for ten years when he was promoted to chief of detectives on April 27, 1989, by the new police chief, Dennis Downey. It was the chance McCain had been waiting for. Being a policeman was in his blood; his father, Clarence McCain, had been the assistant chief in nearby Collinsville, Illinois, for years before he retired. Rick McCain even looked and talked like a cop. Tall and lean, with a thick dark moustache that curled down just slightly over the corners of his mouth. He had a deep voice that could be authoritative and confident.

He had met with the men who would be in his squad and had told them he wanted the best detectives in the region. Like Rick, they were young and eager and hungry, and he thought they were the best cops on the force. They were to wear suits all the time. They would be sharp and tough and proud. Solving cases wouldn't be just a job; it would be a matter of pride.

Sergeant Tony Ventimiglia was coming back to detectives as Rick's assistant chief the next week. He had been there before and had handled a lot of homicides. He was finishing up a little stint on patrol, a reminder that he had backed the wrong candidate for mayor in the recent election.

But McCain's ideas for the squad got a quick test before the men even got on the job. On April 27, the day

McCain's appointment was announced, a two-year-old girl named Terria Graves was hospitalized with critical injuries apparently inflicted in a beating by her mother's boyfriend. Word from the hospital was that she probably wouldn't make it.

McCain and Detective David Hayes were finishing a seminar that day on "the medical and legal effects of death investigations," sponsored by the St. Louis University School of Medicine. When they returned to the office that afternoon, McCain discovered that little had been done on the Graves case by the detectives who would be leaving the squad at the end of the week. McCain was forced to throw his new authority around a little sooner than he hoped, and he ordered several detectives into action. He was angry, and he wasn't too gentle about what he said or how he said it.

The boyfriend, Randall Gater, was brought in for questioning by Sergeant Bud Pyatt and by Hayes. Gater began by suggesting that Terria had been injured accidentally, perhaps falling and hitting her head on the vacuum cleaner. But he finally admitted that he had beaten her because she wouldn't stop crying. When she kept crying, he had shaken her until she was silent.

Little Terria died the next day from shaken baby syndrome. The violent shaking had battered her brain. Based on Gater's admissions, murder charges were issued by the state's attorney.

So in his first two days as the new detective chief, McCain and his men had broken a child-murder case with a confession. They felt pretty good, and McCain thought his judgment about this group had been right. He was proud of that first outing.

On Saturday, April 29, McCain had just started undressing for bed about 11:30 P.M. when the phone rang. It was Lieutenant Tuetken.

"Rick, do you remember that case in 1986 where the couple in Brighton named Sims told the police their baby girl was kidnapped?"

"Yeah, I do. Why?"

"Well, the same family is reporting that another baby girl has been kidnapped."

McCain wondered what that had to do with detectives in Alton. "Do they still live in Jersey County?"

"No, Rick. They live over on Washington now. We've got patrolmen at the scene already and they wanted me to call you guys out."

Tuetken's words sunk in. The same Simses. A different daughter. This time, in Alton.

"Oh, shit," Rick said. "Okay. I'll get right over there. Mick Dooley's on call tonight. Call him at home and tell him to meet me there."

McCain put on a suit. He wanted the Simses to know up front that this wouldn't be a replay of 1986. They weren't dealing with a small county sheriff's department this time.

He remembered the first case pretty well. He recalled sitting on the couch with his wife watching a television news report in the early days of the case. He told her then that the parents had done it; that was obvious to him just from the news.

It was a ten-minute drive to the Simses' from Rick's house; he arrived a little before midnight. Gillespie and his dog were being assisted by a dog with Deputy Russ Gentry from the Madison County Sheriff's Department. The two canine units were scouring the Simses' property and the wooded area behind their house. Two bloodhounds and another German shepherd would be brought in later, but none of the five dogs would find a single scent.

The officers from Alton couldn't know it yet, but the story of the kidnapping given by Robert and Paula, and the subsequent search for Heather, already had begun to show striking similarities to the frustrating ordeal their police colleagues had experienced in the death of Loralei Marie Sims in 1986.

McCain met Eichen in front of the house and told him not to let anyone onto the property without McCain's approval. Rick went around the back of the house and walked in through the kitchen door.

Paula and Robert Sims were standing in the kitchen. Rick's first thought was that they looked like a couple of country bumpkins. Robert was standing there in his bib overalls and a plaid shirt. Paula was just plainlooking—

not unattractive, but just so plain. They were very simple, unremarkable people, with a remarkable story to tell.

Then he realized that they weren't crying and didn't even appear to be upset. That wasn't right. No one could be that calm in the middle of this. Rick knew anyone looking at them at that moment would know something wasn't right. But he was determined to give them the benefit of the doubt. Who knows? Some sicko just might have kidnapped their baby.

While Rick was introducing himself to them, Detective Mick Dooley came in. McCain was glad to see him. They had worked together for a long time, and there seemed to be a special sort of telepathy between them. "Vibes," they called it. All they had to do was make eye contact and they knew what the other one was thinking and what he would do or say next.

Dooley was wearing a suit. He was a muscular, clean-cut man who wore his black hair in a flat-top and carried himself with a slight swagger. He easily could have passed for a marine officer. He had been a policeman for six years.

Robert began to tell the new arrivals what had happened. McCain and Dooley immediately were put off by the slow, boring tone of Robert's narration. Dooley thought he had talked to people who were more excited about the theft of a bicycle, and he was struck by two things. The first was that this guy had done this before. He knew how to tell the story so that there was little room for the police to probe. And Dooley thought that if this baby really were missing she probably was with the grandparents or some other relative. In these cases, that always was what had happened.

McCain and Dooley exchanged a few looks while Robert was talking. The message was clear; neither cop was buying this.

When Robert had finished, they asked Paula to tell her story. It was the same scripted, monotone delivery, as if she were reading it. But she obviously was more uncomfortable than Robert had been.

She told them she had been watching the 10 o'clock news and, toward the middle or end of the program, she had started straightening up a little around the house. She decided to take out the trash that contained some soiled diapers from Heather's bout with diarrhea. She didn't want Robert to come home from work to those smelly diapers. She took the trash bag outside and set it at the bottom of the porch stairs. Sometimes she would leave the trash there and, when Robert would arrive home from work, he would take it to the trash cans on the other side of the house.

She was volunteering little bits of information like that before the police had a chance to ask, Dooley thought. It struck him as a practiced, programmed effort to make the story seem complete and believable, and to give the police as little to question as possible.

Paula said she had put the bag down and, as she looked up, she saw the man standing near the driveway. He pointed the pistol at her and ordered her into the house. She didn't scream or say anything; she just turned and walked back into the house. As she entered the kitchen, he struck her on the back of the head, knocking her out.

Here was McCain's first opening for a question on a detail.

"Did he hit you with the gun?"

"No, I think it was with his hand, like this," she said, her hand cutting through the air like a karate chop.

That was what McCain had hoped for. That meant the man, who odds-on was right handed, would have to switch hands with the gun to hit her with his empty hand. That would have been awkward and clumsy at best, and an unlikely move for someone to make. It was a detail that didn't make sense. *This is the first crack in the bedrock of the story*, McCain thought.

The next thing Paula remembered was being roused by her husband, hearing him asking repeatedly, "Where's Heather?" That would have been about 11:15.

McCain and Dooley looked at each other again. She had been knocked out for about forty-five minutes. That must have been one hell of a blow.

Dooley was watching Paula's body language for signs that she was lying—tapping her foot or wiggling her leg. He waited to see if she would pat her hand on her thigh, or if her lip would quiver. He watched to see if she looked to the right while she was formulating an answer. Since the right side of the brain handles abstract thinking in right-handed people, they usually will look to the right while they are trying to make up a lie.

But she gave nothing away. She was reading this off a script, so she didn't have to make up lies, he thought. When she was asked something that hadn't been covered by the script, she just said she didn't know. That's a pretty good way to keep the story straight.

Even her answers to McCain's series of simple, basic questions about the kidnapper seemed vague enough to be harmless. She never had seen him before and didn't know if he was black or white. She didn't recognize his voice; there had been nothing distinctive about it.

McCain and Dooley couldn't know it then, but those answers would come crashing down on Paula later when she departed from the script at a crucial moment.

Dooley looked around the kitchen and the rest of the house he could see from there. It was immaculate and everything was in order. The rug in front of the kitchen door, where Paula said she had taken a nosedive, was perfectly straight. Either no one had fallen unconscious across that rug, or someone had stopped in the middle of all of this, leaned over, and straightened it.

As she talked, Paula occasionally reached up and rubbed the back of her neck. McCain asked if she was in pain from the blow. "No, I'm all right," she said.

He asked if they could look at her head. She leaned forward, and Dooley pushed her hair back. Nothing more than some redness where her hand had been, and the redness was even shaped like her fingers. He looked up at Rick and shook his head slightly.

If she hadn't been injured by a blow that supposedly knocked her out for three-quarters of an hour, Rick wanted documented proof for later. He struck a very concerned pose and softened his voice.

"Mrs. Sims, I think you ought to go to the hospital and let a doctor take a look at you. It could be important to the case later. If we can prosecute this guy for attacking you, we'll need medical reports to support the charges."

Dooley quickly volunteered. "Come on, I'll drive you

to the hospital.'' He thought how great it would be if she broke down and confessed on the short ride of eight blocks to Alton Memorial Hospital.

"No, I'm all right," Paula said more emphatically. "It's not that bad, really. I want to stay here in case you find something out."

But Dooley was already walking her toward the door. "It may not feel like much now, but you're still in shock. This could be a delayed-reaction thing. You might really feel it later."

She still was balking, but McCain was urging her on. "Don't worry. Your husband will be here. We'll let you know if anything happens."

Dooley was leading her toward the door like a used car salesman steering a customer toward the lemon he wanted to unload. He was walking toward the door as he talked, and she had to follow.

"Come on, we won't be gone long."

Paula glanced at Robert. "Okay," she said.

After they left, McCain phoned Lieutenant Tuetken and told him to call out Dave Hayes, Sergeant Pyatt, and Sergeant Richard Wells. McCain also wanted Ventimiglia and Chris Sullivan, even though they weren't due to return to detectives until the beginning of the week.

Tony Ventimiglia knew the Simses had moved to Washington Avenue; he lived barely three blocks away. DCI Agent Jimmie Bivens had alerted him when the Simses moved to Alton. And when the word had spread that Paula was pregnant with Randy, DCI Lieutenant Larry Trent had jokingly told Ventimiglia that the next Sims baby case would be the city's, not the state's.

"You better just sit by the door, because it's going to happen again. You're next," Trent had laughed.

Ventimiglia remembered thinking then, *That's silly. They'd never do it again.*

So Tuetken's call about a new kidnapping report from the Simses was a shock. Ventimiglia asked, "You mean over on Washington? That's ridiculous. I can't believe they did it again."

He pulled some blue jeans around his beefy middle and slipped on a nylon jacket. He was from the old school, and hadn't quite shifted gears into McCain's suit-and-tie program.

But Dave Hayes arrived in a suit. He was slim and the shortest of the new squad members. With his short hair, neat moustache, and business suits, he could have passed for a certified public accountant. He remembered the Sims case from 1986, and he was surprised to find out they lived in Alton now. *My God,* he had thought, *if they have another baby girl missing, there will be pandemonium over there.*

He arrived at 12:30 A.M., just minutes after Dooley had left with Paula. Hayes noticed a sign on the back door asking visitors to take off their shoes before entering, and wondered if McCain had put it up to preserve the crime scene. Hayes knocked on the door and was just about to slip off his shoes when McCain opened the door. It wasn't his sign, so Hayes could leave his shoes on.

A bearded man Hayes assumed was Robert Sims was sitting calmly on a couch in the dining room leaning forward with his elbows on his knees. *Where's all the excitement,* Hayes wondered. He looked around. Nothing in the house appeared to be disturbed. Something's wrong here, he thought. Major wrong.

Hayes photographed every detail in the house that he thought might be important, and then stepped outside to begin the exterior shots. The first thing he noticed was the brightness of the huge light mounted on the wall above the back porch. It illuminated the entire area behind the house. *Hell, you could read by this,* he thought. There's no way Paula couldn't have seen well enough to have more details about a kidnapper.

Chris Sullivan arrived shortly after Hayes. Sullivan probably was the only cop there who couldn't appreciate the tragic irony in what had happened. He had moved to Alton from Clinton, Iowa, in January 1987, several months after Loralei's death had ceased to be big news. It would be hours into the investigation before he would learn of the 1986 case and comprehend the shock being felt by his colleagues.

But even without knowing the background, Sullivan immediately doubted the kidnapping story in Heather's disappearance. He had never heard of anyone being knocked out for forty-five minutes. And the orderly condition of the house belied it as the home of a six-week-old baby. He knew. His son, Chris, had been born the week before Heather, in the same wing of the same hospital. The Sullivans had checked out two days before the Simses had checked in. He knew that there should be diapers stacked here and there, and other baby items sitting around that seemed like clutter until they were needed in a hurry.

But not here. Everything was perfect. Even the bassinet where Heather had been sleeping looked like it had just been made.

McCain also was trying to assign some meaning to the incredible orderliness. He had never seen a house where everything was so neat and tidy. No, it went beyond that. It seemed compulsively neat and tidy, as if the residents had been expecting a lot of company that night. Was it staged for the cops' benefit? That didn't make sense. A staged crime scene usually included carefully overturned furniture and the contents of the proper number of dresser drawers appropriately strewn around to approximate a burglar's hurried rummaging.

But here, even the normal clutter of a lived-in house was absent. And more importantly, there was nothing that McCain, as a father, expected to see as evidence that children lived there. No toys, no mess, not a single thing out of place.

But what really nagged him was that baby blanket folded over the edge of the bassinet. At the very place where Heather supposedly had been sleeping when she was so ruthlessly wrenched from her family, at the point where she had been snatched so cruelly from her peaceful security, that damned blanket was draped over the edge in perfect folds. Undisturbed. Unwrinkled. Perfect. Just as if someone had placed it there with great care, and just like the rest of this house. It didn't fit, and it wasn't right.

With Hayes outside, McCain and Robert were alone. Robert was sitting on the couch and McCain was standing nearby. McCain explained that there would be more detectives arriving soon and, in addition to taking pictures of everything, they would be conducting a very thorough search of the house and property, peeking into cupboards and peering into closets. McCain asked Robert if he had any objection if the police needed to take some items from the house as evidence. Robert calmly said he understood, and that was fine.

McCain also asked that the Simses refrain from making any comments to the press, so no vital information would be leaked. Robert agreed not to speak to reporters, and asked in return that Rick allow a photograph of Heather to be broadcast on television in case someone saw her later with the kidnapper.

Robert handed him a small color picture of a beautiful blonde baby surrounded by pink blankets. McCain looked at Robert as he handed over the photo. No reaction, no emotion. McCain thought how most fathers would have reacted to giving a policeman a picture of their kidnapped daughter. Surely that had to be a painful, heartbreaking act, and McCain wondered how many men could have held back the tears.

McCain also had been surprised that Robert hadn't asked any questions about what was being done to look for the kidnapper and Heather. He was being friendly and cooperative, but he wasn't asking the right questions.

When Robert did ask a question, it was just as surprising as those he hadn't asked. He looked up and asked calmly, "Sergeant McCain, do I need an attorney?"

"Robert, what would you need an attorney for? We're here to investigate a kidnapping case. You've reported this as a kidnapping, and until I find out otherwise, that's how we're working it."

Robert's eyes narrowed. "Well, do you know about what happened in Jersey County?"

McCain nodded, "Yes, I do."

"Well, Sheriff Yocom up there never did believe us on that case. I don't know why he was like that. But I didn't appreciate the way he handled that case or how he dealt with us. I wasn't very happy with any of it. And I'm not real crazy about Sheriff Yocom."

McCain countered that he had developed a high regard for Yocom while working with him while Rick was an undercover drug agent for the regional drug task force called the Metropolitan Enforcement Group of South-western Illinois. Rick decided that this was a chance to gain Robert's confidence, even if it meant he had to seem to criticize Frank Yocom.

"This is not the Jersey County Sheriff's Department on this case, Robert. This is the Alton Police Department. If this is a kidnapping, we'll find out who did it and we'll solve it as a kidnapping. If it's not, Robert, we'll find that out, too. If you want a lawyer, that's up to you. You can call a lawyer if you want to. I don't know why you need one. If it's a kidnapping, you will have no need for a lawyer, if what you're telling me is the truth."

Robert didn't blink. "Okay. I just want to be sure we'll be treated fair."

"You will be. We're doing this with an open mind. We're not closed to anything. But if this is a homicide, Robert, you won't get away with it. I'll tell you that right now."

Robert nodded passively.

A few minutes later, McCain decided to prod Robert a little, just to let him know this kidnapping story wasn't too believable, and to give him an opportunity to come clean on it right then.

"Robert, you know, you've got to admit that this case is kind of suspicious. This is twice now that you've lost baby girls like this. Have you ever considered that maybe your wife is doing this? If you're gone when it happens, like you said, maybe it's your wife."

Robert nodded. "Yes, I have considered that. But I have to trust my wife. I think she's a good woman and she's good to the kids. But I have considered what you're saying."

Tony Ventimiglia had reached the scene a few minutes after Hayes and Sullivan, sometime just after 12:30 A.M. From outside, he radioed Rick, or "Mac," as he usually called him. They met at the end of the Simses' driveway and, before either of them spoke, they began shaking their heads in unison.

Ventimiglia assumed Rick could read his mind. "I can't believe this is happening. I can't believe they're doing this again."

McCain kept shaking his head.

"I know. I can't believe this, either. Wait until you talk to them. I've never seen anything like this. These people aren't even upset. They're the calmest people I've ever seen."

McCain told Ventimiglia that it would be his case, and he would be in charge of the scene as soon as McCain left to go back to the station to coordinate things from there.

Ventimiglia walked over to Eichen. Years on the job had taught the sergeant that the first cops on the scene often have the best perspective and information. Eichen told him what the Simses had said and how they had acted.

This ain't even original, Ventimiglia thought. *They're even using the same old story. And Robert isn't even trying to act upset.*

Ventimiglia thought of his three-year-old son.

I'd be bouncing off the walls. You'd have to sedate me just to talk to me, he thought.

McCain took Ventimiglia behind the house and recounted Paula's story. Ventimiglia looked up at the yard light glowing so brightly off the back of the house, and then looked back at McCain.

"Are you sure they said it happened here, Mac? Are you sure they didn't say the front of the house? This light must be three million candle power. You can read back here."

"Yeah, I know."

As Rick continued his narrative, his partner kept looking at him in disbelief. Rick knew that look. Finally, he said, "Hey, look. I'm just telling you what the woman said."

"These people must think we're stupid if they think we're going to believe this," Ventimiglia replied.

The pair walked back into the house and Rick introduced Ventimiglia to Robert to get a brief account of what had happened. After hearing Robert's story, one word ran through Ventimiglia's mind: *Bullshit.*

Before McCain headed back to the station, he and Ventimiglia decided to call in some bloodhounds to search the area.

Ventimiglia sent Sullivan and Pyatt out on a neighborhood canvass, giving them the unenviable job of waking up everyone within a block or so and asking them if they had seen or heard anything that might be related to a kidnapping.

Sergeant Wells had arrived in the crime scene van and went to work dusting everything in the kitchen for fingerprints.

At the police line out front, Linda Condray had arrived and was insisting that she be allowed into the house. Eichen and Fraser explained that Sergeant McCain had said she was not to be admitted until later.

"But I'm family. I'm Mr. Sims's sister," she kept insisting.

Fraser finally threatened to arrest her if she continued to interfere. He suggested she should return to her parked car across the street if she wanted to wait. Some time later, Robert came out and spoke briefly with her. But she was not allowed into the house, and finally drove away about 3:00 A.M.

While Ventimiglia and the other officers were searching the house, Robert placed a call to Paula's parents at the home of Orville's sister near Kansas City, Missouri. Robert had told McCain that the Blews were away for the weekend. Their trip to Peculiar, Missouri would become a major point in the case later, playing a morbid role in a plot twist that would make the circumstances of Heather's death and disappearance absolutely chilling. In more ways than one.

It was 2:00 A.M. when Orville was awakened and called to the phone. The voice on the other end of the line was soft, and so deliberate.

"Orville, this is Rob. You're not going to believe this, but Heather's gone. She's been kidnapped."

Orville was dumbfounded. "I just can't believe it. I'll call you back."

He hung up. Had it really been Rob? The caller's voice had sounded strange. Maybe it wasn't him. *Please, God. Let it be some horrible, sick joke.*

Orville dialed his daughter's phone number. Robert

answered, and the sad grandfather's worst fears were
confirmed.

Without waiting to be asked, Orville unexpectedly told
Robert that the Blews would return home as soon as possible to be with him and Paula.

"We'll start back in the morning," Orville said.

Orville's decision to return would be fateful in ways
no one would understand for months.

Mick Dooley was being extra careful to make Paula as
comfortable as possible on the way to the hospital. He
still hoped she might confess soon if things broke right.
For the first time in his life, he was in exactly the position
he had always wanted to be as a detective working on a
major case. But he also was a little unsure of just how to
handle her. Technically, she was the victim. But he knew
that she was looking like a good prospect for the "suspect" role, too. If he questioned her now, did he have
to read her rights to her? He decided it might be best to
wait.

As they pulled away from the curb in front of the
house, Paula startled Dooley with her first words.

"I just knew this was going to happen because Robert
told me about the lady down the street who got broken
into and tied up. That's why he put a gun on the cabinet
in the dining room."

Dooley wondered if she was planning to use that case
as an excuse, and he decided to head her off. Even though
no arrest had been made in the other case, he knew one
was expected soon.

"No, we took care of that. That was her nephew and
we already arrested him. That doesn't have anything to
do with this."

She seemed surprised. "Oh, I didn't read that in the
newspaper."

That seemed to deflate her, as if she had hoped to use
that as an explanation in Heather's disappearance.

As Dooley watched, Paula seemed to be hitting what
he thought of as "the pain barrier."

She began to rub the back of her neck with one hand.
Soon, she had both hands on her neck, and then she
pulled her knees up and began to rock back and forth

and moan. It reminded Dooley of a little kid trying to get out of going to school by getting sicker and sicker the closer it got to time to leave. When they reached the hospital, Paula was nearly in a fetal position.

Dooley walked around to her door. She was still rolled up in a ball, so he opened the door, reached in, and got her by the arm to help her out. Supporting her by one arm as they walked toward the hospital entrance, he thought it was like walking with his grandmother. He was sure that if he had let go of her arm, she would have crumpled to the ground.

Quite an act, Dooley thought. It had been two hours after she claimed she had been attacked, and she had talked to half a dozen cops without any symptoms. But just before she was to see a doctor, suddenly she was in great pain.

Just inside the hospital doors, Dooley grabbed a wheelchair and slid it under Paula, who nearly collapsed into the seat. Dooley identified himself to the reception-ist and told her he had a woman with a head injury who needed treatment. Paula was wheeled into a small ex-amining room to await treatment at 12:30 A.M.

Janet Harkey was one of the emergency room nurses that night. Five minutes after Paula Sims arrived, Janet examined her and took a history to give to the doctor. Paula was crying as she told the nurse that a man had knocked her unconscious and kidnapped her baby. She complained of a headache and a stiff neck. Nurse Harkey also jotted down in her notes that the patient seemed pale. Her vital signs were normal. Some redness was noted on her neck, but there were no bumps, bruises, or lacerations that would accompany a blow that had ren-dered a patient unconscious. The nurse wrote that the patient exhibited a full range of motion to her head, neck, and shoulders. She seemed oriented to time, place, and person, and showed none of the usual confusion or dis-orientation that usually followed a head injury and a pe-riod of unconsciousness.

The emergency room was busy that night. Paula's lack of significant symptoms meant she was in line behind more serious cases. And that meant Dooley had to cool his heels, too.

He decided to call McCain at the Simses' house and discuss the question of medical tests for Paula. If she were released after a brief medical examination, that may not be enough to substantiate charges later that Paula had never been struck on the head, had never been unconscious and, therefore, had never been the victim of a kidnapping.

Dooley told McCain that he thought X-rays and drug tests were the minimum, but even a CAT scan could be justified to prove she had not suffered a head injury. The last thing he wanted was for Paula to be able to argue later that she really had been injured and more tests would have proved that. But Dooley didn't think he had the authority to order a series of expensive tests.

"You know she's not hurt and they're going to release her as soon as they look at her. What do you want on her?"

McCain dropped it back in Dooley's lap. "Anything you can get. What can you talk her into? Whatever you think we need, get it."

Dooley laughed. "Is the city going to pay for this?"

McCain laughed, too. He realized that their inexperience as detectives in charge was showing. They had talked earlier about sparing no expense on major cases once they were in charge. But this was the real thing now, and they hadn't even had time to begin checking on such procedures.

McCain authorized any tests Dooley wanted. "If the worst happens, I'll pay for it myself," Rick said.

"What do you want me to do with her when we're done here?"

"We're going to have to interview her and her husband, so bring her on down to the station from the hospital. I'll arrange it with her husband so that you can take her back when we're finished with her and bring him down after that."

"She's not going to want to do that," Dooley said.

Rick chuckled. He knew Dooley could talk just about anybody into just about anything. "Aw, you can get her to do it."

Dooley hung up. "Great. Now it's all up to me."

The first clue of how much attention this new Sims

case would draw came as word spread through the emergency room that THE Paula Sims, whose baby died in 1986, was there, and was claiming a second kidnapping. Nurses and other hospital staff members began wandering by for a look.

Dooley decided that was a good time to ask Paula to sign a standard release form to give the police access to her medical records. To his surprise, she balked, saying she didn't like to sign anything until her attorney had seen it. Dooley explained that the form was standard procedure that allowed the cops to get her medical records. They couldn't charge the bad guy with assaulting her if they didn't have her records.

Dooley tensed up. If she hesitated to sign this form, they'd really have a hard time getting her to sign a confession later. He kept cajoling until she agreed. But he had to get another copy and have her sign both of them so she could keep one. And before she signed, she read the whole form. Dooley shook his head. It was the first time he had ever seen anybody read that form.

At 1:38 A.M., Nurse Harkey was checking Paula again when Dr. Duk C. Kim, a Korean immigrant, came in. He looked at the back of her head and neck, and checked her reflexes. He saw the redness on her neck, but noted no other visible trauma. He questioned Paula briefly, but she complained of nothing that indicated any serious injury. In fact, he could find nothing that supported her claim of being struck and knocked out for forty-five minutes.

Dr. Kim told the nurse to give the patient some Tylenol for her headache, an ice pack to take home, and the printed sheet of standard instructions for anyone who had suffered a head injury.

Then he told the nurse to discharge the patient. Dooley took Dr. Kim aside and explained that the police department wanted drug tests and X-rays on the patient. The doctor said such steps weren't necessary.

"But we want them," was Dooley's emphatic response. The doctor shrugged and ordered the tests.

While the X-rays and blood tests were underway, Dooley went back to the telephone. Six years ago, he had worked at the same plant where Robert Sims was employed. It was the Alton Boxboard then. Now it was known as the Jefferson Smurfit Corporation. He called and spoke to the supervisor, who confirmed that Robert's time card showed that he had clocked out at his regular quitting time the night before.

At 2:34 A.M., Paula was still sitting in the examining room, rubbing her neck and rocking. Dr. Kim walked in and told her she could leave. Dooley watched as Paula effortlessly hopped off the table and walked away. She looked at Dooley and asked, "Well, what's next?"

It's a miracle. She's been miraculously cured, Dooley marveled to himself.

As they walked through the hospital lobby, Dooley explained the interview plan and said they were going straight to the police station. She balked again; she wanted to talk to her husband. She thought she should go home to be with him and their son, and to be there if something happened. But Dooley explained that it already had been cleared with her husband, and he would stay with Randy until she got home. Dooley had covered the bases, anticipating her objections. Paula reluctantly agreed.

On the drive to the station, she seemed amazingly relaxed. She would hold the ice pack to her neck occasionally, but she didn't complain about pain.

She hadn't said anything about Heather since they left the house two hours ago. She hadn't even asked about the investigation. She seemed so unconcerned that Dooley was startled when she suddenly announced in the car, "All I want is Heather found." He wondered if it was too cynical for him to think that her comment was an afterthought. It had been said as if the thought had struck her, "Oh, yeah, I guess I should bring this up," a realization that it might seem strange if she didn't mention the supposed focus of all of this—her missing baby.

With that out of the way, Paula made some light conversation. She said she had watched a television news story about the discovery of a pin in a jar of Heinz baby food, and had been concerned because she used that brand. What could be more normal than a new mother worrying about such a thing?

She began chattering about Randy, and how much fun

it was since he was getting a little older. He was walking well now, and was getting into everything. Dooley told her he had a son almost the same age as Randy, and he certainly knew what she was talking about. He still was trying to appear sympathetic, laying the groundwork for a cooperative interview at the station.

The news of this incredible, second Sims case had begun to spread to other police agencies. Yocom already was rocketing to Alton from the stakeout in Grafton. Lieutenant Larry Trent, the assistant zone commander of the DCI, had been called at home by a state police patrol sergeant, and he relayed the news about 1:00 A.M. to Captain Phil Kocis.

"Phil, are you awake?"

"I am now. What's up?"

"Let me tell you a story you've already heard before. But I'm not kidding. Paula Sims says she's had another baby girl kidnapped from her home."

"No. The same damned story? No, I don't believe it. Are you sure she just didn't lose a baby and there's some miscommunication here?"

"No, it's the same story."

Trent and Kocis agreed to meet immediately at the Alton police station to offer any assistance they could provide.

Jimmie Bivens, the third member of the 1986 police triumvirate, had retired four months earlier. He got the word at home from his daughter-in-law, Linda Bivens, who was a state trooper married to Jim's son, also a state trooper. She had seen a television news report about Heather's disappearance and knew her father-in-law would want to know. When Jimmie Bivens hung up, he turned to his wife and said, "It doesn't surprise me a bit. I'm shocked that they would do it again, but it doesn't surprise me one damned bit."

Trent had been in charge of special operations in 1986 and wasn't involved in the Loralei case. But he had discused the case a million times with Kocis and the other agents who worked it.

And he had something of a personal connection with Paula and her family—they attended the same church as

Trent, the First Baptist Church of Rosewood Heights. Trent's mother knew Nylene Blew, and had mentioned in 1986 that Nylene was excited because her daughter was pregnant with their first grandchild. Larry Trent even had seen the pregnant Paula in church a few times.

After Loralei died, Nylene and Paula stayed away from church for some time. Nylene came back first and, a few months later, Paula returned to sit quietly with her mother in the back. Trent had harbored the secret hope that Paula might confess to their pastor and agree to call Trent in to take a statement. He even had made the pastor aware that he was available if that ever happened. But eventually he surrendered that hope and quit paying attention to whether Paula was there.

On the drive to the Alton police station that night, Trent was wondering what the police could do this time. They knew who did it, but how could they break that pair—especially Paula? She knew the program. She'd seen the movie before. Hell, she had been the star of the movie. Trent was worried about how to approach the case, but he couldn't wait to get started.

When he was buzzed through the door into the detective section at Alton, Yocom already was there. The sheriff was shaking his head as he said softly, "I just don't believe it."

Kocis took a drive by 1053 Washington on the way in, just to get a look at the scene. He talked briefly to a patrolman in front of the house. "Do you believe this?" the patrolman asked with a grimace.

When Kocis walked into the detective section a few minutes later, he exchanged the same look of disbelief and shock with Trent and Yocom. For all three men, it was one of those moments that can't be described adequately to others. How do you explain how you feel in the middle of this kind of situation? To Trent, it was the kind of look people exchanged after Bobby Kennedy was shot. How could another Kennedy have been shot? It couldn't be real.

Trent thought that even the Alton police, faced with the challenge of investigating this new mystery, couldn't fully appreciate the jolt of "déjà vu" from being in the middle of it again. They hadn't gone face to face yet with Robert and Paula, and come away with nothing.

When Kocis and Trent had a minute alone, Kocis turned to his partner with an ironic half smile, and mused aloud.

''You know, I can see this happening again. Knowing Paula, I can see it happening again. But to tell the same story. I can almost picture this. Paula saying, 'Honey, it happened again.' And Robert saying, 'Okay, what are we going to do?' And Paula saying, 'Well, let's tell them the same story.' And Robert saying, '*Oh, no*. We can't tell them the same story. Let's tell them something else. We *can't* tell them the *same* story.' And Paula saying, 'Well, yeah, it worked last time. Why couldn't we tell them the same story? We'll just change it a little this time.' ''

In church the next morning, a friend commented to Trent that he looked tired. Trent explained why, and the news that another infant daughter of Paula Sims had disappeared spread through the congregation like wildfire.

McCain got back to the police station about one o'clock and was met by Yocom, Kocis, and the others. It was a relief to realize how much assistance and support he would have. And McCain was especially glad to see Kocis and Trent. There were few cops around McCain respected as much as Kocis, and Rick always had been impressed by the DCI. He had only met Kocis a time or two, but he regarded him as a real professional. In fact, McCain felt complimented when Kocis walked over and called him by name.

''Rick, if there's anything we can do, just say the word. We're not here to interfere. This is your case. I want you to understand that. But we'll do anything you want us to. We'll help you with the background. We'll get you manpower. Whatever you want. But you better grab your butt with both hands because the press is really going to come at you now.''

Just two days into his new job, McCain felt pretty raw as he looked at what could become the biggest crime in Alton since an angry mob shot down newspaper editor Elijah P. Lovejoy. Rick felt better having Kocis in his corner.

The subject of conducting surveillance on the Simses came up immediately and Kocis offered to provide the manpower if McCain wanted to set it up. But everyone agreed that the baby already was dead and the body had been disposed of, perhaps in the Mississippi River that flowed past Alton's western boundary. Sitting on Robert and Paula was of little use. It also could anger them, halting their cooperation before the investigation could get off the ground. Surveillance was ruled out.

State's Attorney William R. Haine had turned up the volume on his answering machine before he went to bed at his home in Alton. When the call from Police Chief Dennis Downey came in about 2:00 A.M., Haine heard the message. He got up and made the call immediately. Downey asked Haine if he remembered the Sims case from Jersey County.

"Yeah, I do," Haine said.

"Well, they moved to Alton some time ago."

"I didn't know that."

"Yeah, and we have another one."

"You mean another abduction?" Haine asked. His voice rose, carrying the shock at the suggestion that such a thing could happen again, and this time in his county.

"Yeah, another Lone Ranger," Downey said.

Haine offered every assistance necessary from the prosecutor's office, warning Downey that this would be "a media extravaganza" and a tough case all the way around. Haine referred Downey to either of his top felony assistants, Don Weber or Bob Trone.

"Wait. Trone lives pretty far away. Maybe you should call Weber or Randy Massey," Haine said.

Don Weber was sound asleep when the telephone rang with Downey's call about 3:00 A.M. Don's wife, Virginia, was used to getting calls for her husband from the police at that hour, and they often really weren't that important. She picked up the phone, and asked what the call was about. Downey asked her if she remembered the woman from Brighton who had claimed that her daughter had been kidnapped. Virginia said she did.

"Well, she's down here at the police station now and she's telling us the same story about another daughter."

Don heard Virginia's response, which was to quote one of her favorite lines from the movie, *Sleuth*.

"Surely not two times running," she said in disbelief. She handed the phone to her husband as he tried to shake the sleep from his head.

"What's up?" Don asked in a cavalier tone he would realize later was remarkably inappropriate.

"We have a case down here that's going to be a public relations nightmare." Downey sounded exasperated, tired, and very tense. He asked if Weber remembered the Sims case from before.

"No, not really. Maybe, vaguely. Why?"

"Well, it just happened again."

He said Haine had told the police to notify Weber and get any advice. The chief gave Weber a brief description of what the police had learned so far, and told him they were planning to interview Robert and Paula Sims at the station soon.

Weber told him, "Be sure you get as much information as you can from them now, because eventually they're going to quit talking to you and call a lawyer. This kind of case usually has to be solved in the first twenty-four hours or it may never be solved."

After Weber hung up, Virginia wanted to discuss what had happened. She remembered many of the details from the 1986 case well and was curious about what had happened this time. But Don shrugged it off and rolled over. He just wanted to go back to sleep. The fact that he had just been drawn into the biggest case of his career didn't enter his mind.

Chapter 8

Even when he was just twelve years old, the part of Don Weber's soul that was a meat-eating prosecutor was trying to get out. Summer afternoons, when other boys were playing baseball or riding their bikes, were spent in mock trials in the Weber family's basement in Collinsville, Illinois. Prosecutor Don squared off against his older brother, Phil, who always was the defense attorney. There would be bombastic legal arguments and dramatic closing statements. But the young prosecutor usually lost to his older adversary.

It would not be that way years later. Don Weber would become one of the most successful, and certainly one of the most aggressive, prosecutors who ever walked into a courtroom in Madison County. And he would prosecute a series of the most bizarre and shocking crimes the county ever would see.

His entry into politics as a conservative Republican was inevitable, too. Weber's grandfather, John Weber, had been president of the town's school board in the 1930s. Don's father, Norman, had followed course, and was elected city commissioner in 1955 in a come-from-behind, dark-horse victory in a town ruled by Democrats. One of Don Weber's earliest political memories was waiting for the final count in the crowded, smokey office of the Collinsville *Herald,* where election results were tabulated in an atmosphere of political grass-roots suspense. The seven-year-old had stood there, holding his father's hand and looking up at the man who seemed so tall then. Norman Weber had run behind in the returns all evening. But when the last precinct came in, it swept him to victory amid a noisy celebration that riveted the winner's young son.

After two terms as commissioner, Norman moved up in 1963 to a term as mayor. His four years there were marked by the Weber characteristics of conservative politics delivered in blunt and outspoken style.

Despite the lower-court sessions in the Weber basement, Don had decided to become an engineer. After graduating from high school in 1967, he attended the University of Illinois at Champaign-Urbana and was two years into the program when he realized that engineering wasn't for him. He decided to go to law school, as his brother Philip had. Don then could combine his interests and become a patent attorney. After graduating from the U of I, he enrolled in the John Marshall Law School in Chicago, where he was on the Law Review. He transferred to the St. Louis University School of Law in his second year.

While a senior in law school in 1973, Weber took a part-time job with the office of State's Attorney Nicholas G. Byron in Madison County, even though Byron was a Democrat. Don was assigned to work in the juvenile division. A young lawyer who had left the state's attorney's office, Donald E. Groshong of Alton, was a defense attorney representing many of the juveniles. It was across the trial table there that the two Dons first met, and it would be the beginning of a close and long-lasting friendship. Neither of the young men could know that they would face each other one day in the most celebrated criminal trial in Madison County's history.

The fledgling prosecutor handled fifty or sixty cases, running the gamut from burglaries to assaults to murder. His first real exposure to Groshong's methods in the courtroom came in a murder case in Alton. Groshong's sixteen-year-old client had shot an acquaintance in what had started as a minor dispute. Groshong stunned the court with a surprising move at the first hearing, a preliminary session at which a judge routinely would order the juvenile held in detention pending trial. Groshong announced that the youth was ready to plead guilty to the juvenile level of a murder charge. Weber recognized the offer as an attempt to prevent the prosecution from certifying the young defendant for trial as an adult, as allowed by state law under certain circumstances. If certified, the offender could face adult-level penalties, including hard prison time.

Groshong's plea offer was unprecedented, and Weber decided to counter innovation with innovation. His response was equally surprising, and it showed the young prosecutor's love of combat. He threatened to dismiss the charge to prevent Groshong's ploy, and then to reinstate it later. The judge refused to take any action then and, after weeks of arguing, Weber and Groshong struck a deal. The defendant was certified as an adult, entered a guilty plea to murder, and was sentenced to a juvenile facility because he was still under seventeen. Round One in a long match was a draw.

It was then that Weber realized Groshong was a formidable and very crafty legal gamesman. That was something Weber could appreciate and respect.

Weber stayed in the prosecutor's office after he graduated. He began a climb through the trial ranks as a prosecutor and developed the kind of aggressive stance that became his trademark and earned him a nickname among some defense attorneys—Mad Dog Weber. In 1976, he moved up to the felony division and began dealing with the worst the county had to offer—armed robbers, burglars, thieves, rapists, and some of the most vicious murderers in the United States.

The case that first brought Don Weber into the glare of publicity was the brutal gang-rape of two high school girls by nine young men in 1976. The victims and the rapists were from the nearby St. Louis area in Missouri, but they had crossed the Mississippi River into Madison County to commit the crime at a well-hidden spot along the river. The girls, both seventeen, had just met some of the boys and had agreed to go to a party with them. Instead, the boys picked up some of their friends and took the girls to the isolated crime scene. They were raped sadistically and repeatedly and were forced to commit a variety of disgusting acts. When the rapists left their victims behind three hours later, one of the men also left something else on the scene—his wallet.

Weber had worked on the case with another young prosecutor, Stephanie Robbins. She got the assignment when three of the rapists went to trial together, and We-

ber sat in with her. But the case ended in a hung jury.
When the three defendants sauntered out of the courtroom, Weber watched them sneer over their shoulders at
the two crying victims. It sent such a pulse of anger and
disgust through Weber that it became one of the motivating images in his career. Those infuriatingly smug and
taunting looks on those creeps' faces reaffirmed Don's
decision to be a prosecutor. He wanted the ability to make
things like that right. It was a drive that all good young
prosecutors had to find. They could make more money
in corporate law. But being the state's attorney, literally
representing the people of the state when they have been
violated or abused or injured, was something that becomes ingrained in prosecutors.

Weber took the case to trial again and, applying what
he had been learning from other prosecutors and trial
attorneys like Robert Trone and Phil Weber, Don threw
himself into the case. It was the first application of some
of the techniques Weber would use with such success
later. He participated in the investigation, looking for
ways to answer the unanswered questions. He sent the
cops back time and again for more information. He
worked with the victims and witnesses until he knew their
stories inside out.

At the next trial, it was Weber's turn to relish the results; the jury convicted on all counts. That time, it was
Weber who could glare victoriously at those same three
creeps. The other four defendants pleaded guilty; all
seven rapists were given sentences of four to six years in
prison.

One of the first murder cases Don worked was with
Robert E. Lee Trone, whose years as an assistant state's
attorney had earned him the reputation as "the dean of
prosecutors in Southern Illinois." With his rough-hewn,
country looks, the lanky lawyer reflected his origins in
rural Schuyler County, near Abraham Lincoln's home in
Salem. But Trone was a shrewd and skilled prosecutor
known for building strong cases and presenting them
masterfully to a jury.

In this case, Trone and Weber were faced with proving
that a factory worker named George Hanei had poisoned
his father by giving him what Don called "tasty pastries"

laced with thallium, a metallic toxin used in rat poison. Hanei already was suspected in the death of a seventy-seven-year-old neighbor woman in 1971. But the police were unable to prove that he had poisoned her in an unsuccessful attempt to inherit her property. Hanei also was suspected when a potential witness in that case became ill after eating some doughnuts someone had left on his porch in 1972. He survived, but a medical test suggested by Trone and Weber found thallium traces.

Hanei got greedy and trotted out the bakery goods once too often. In 1976, his eighty-three-year-old father, Herman, died after eating doughnuts delivered by his son. George Hanei produced a will making him the sole beneficiary of his father's estate of farmland and cash, cutting out his siblings.

It was during this case that Weber began to perfect two theories—one legal and the other deductive—that would serve him in many of the cases he handled later.

The first was the use of the "doctrine of other crimes." Under state law, other crimes a person may have committed could not be used as evidence in a separate case unless they fell under one of several exceptions. One was if a connecting "modus operandi"—a method of operating—could be established. Weber wrote a brief proving to the judge that Hanei had been linked to several deaths involving the use of poisoned pastries, and that such a unique connection was enough to justify using evidence from all the similar cases. A judge agreed, and the evidence of Hanei's involvement in the other death was allowed in the trial in Herman Hanei's death.

The other theory Weber developed was that any crime could be solved if an investigator could break the code used by the criminal. Each criminal leaves clues, sometimes purposefully, that can be used to solve the crime if interpreted properly. To do that, Weber knew he had to get inside the criminal's head, to think like him and to understand what he meant by his words and deeds.

Weber used that idea successfully in the George Hanei case, figuring out how Hanei had managed to get his father to eat the one poisoned goodie from the plate of five doughnuts. He had simply turned it into a game. Herman Hanei got first choice, and he picked a safe doughnut. Son George took another safe one. When Herman took a third safe one, George ate the last untainted one. Finally, George simply pushed the plate toward his father, saying in effect, ''Here, Dad, you take the last one.''

Trone took the case to trial and won a conviction; Hanei still is serving his forty-to-eighty–year sentence.

While enjoying his growing success as a prosecutor, Weber's political interests were emerging. He decided to follow in his father's footsteps and run for city commissioner in Collinsville in 1979. It turned out to be a fateful decision. Don was elected, and promptly fired by Byron, who argued that the offices of prosecutor and municipal official were incompatible. Weber opened a private practice in Collinsville.

As one of the few Republican officeholders in the largely Democratic area, Weber was approached in 1980 to run as a delegate committed to Ronald Reagan at the national convention. Weber was flattered and agreed. And since Byron had fired him, canceling all bets in Weber's mind, he decided to run against his former boss for state's attorney, mostly to boost his candidacy for delegate.

Weber had no opposition in the Republican primary election that March. Byron defeated two opponents in the Democratic primary—Dick Allen, a lawyer from Granite City, and William R. Haine of Alton, a lawyer who already served as a member of the county board. The strange twists of time would see all four men in that election eventually serve as state's attorney.

Don campaigned hard in the fall, focusing on his record of convictions, and everything broke his way. Byron conducted a lackluster campaign, Reagan won in a landslide, and Don slipped into office with a margin of 632 votes out of 96,000. He became the first Republican to win a countywide office in twelve years, and only the second Republican prosecutor since the 1940s.

The style and flourish that would become the hallmark of the Weber administration emerged quickly. He plunged into criminal cases with relish, and with an aggressiveness that quickly divided observers. Some found his candor and frank comments refreshing; others found them improper, if not just damned irritating.

But the press seemed to love it. Headlines touting Weber's latest adventure in crime fighting began appearing regularly, spurred by Don's very quotable language describing some very bizarre and intriguing crimes. The mostly favorable press, and an uninterrupted string of convictions, angered defense attorneys and Democrats whose dislike of Weber had begun to grow into a hatred.

Within four months of taking office, Weber kept his campaign promise to restore the death penalty in Madison County. After a one-month trial, a jury ordered death for one of the worst multiple killers who ever walked the streets in Madison and St. Clair Counties. Girvies Davis, a twenty-two-year-old man who already had been sentenced to death for one of three murder convictions in St. Clair County, was given a second death-sentence for killing an eighty-three-year-old, nearly blind widow in her home in Madison County. For Weber, the case became personal. The victim, Esther Sepmeyer, was the grandmother of one of Don's best friends in high school.

In September 1982, Weber won his second death-sentence case and learned an important lesson about the element of timing as evidence. Larry Joe Adams of Alton was charged with executing pharmacist Eugene Ponder during an armed robbery at his store. The case was entirely circumstantial, but Weber was able to tie Adams to the killing with the time on a receipt from a cash register that established the last known time when Ponder was alive. Weber matched that to the time when Adams was seen in the store and played it off against the times when Adams was seen by other witnesses later. With the timing locked in, Weber proved that Adams was at the scene when Ponder was so ruthlessly executed.

In 1982, what seemed then to be the most dramatic case of Weber's career was brought to him in shambles by two of the people he was closest to—Agent Dennis Kuba of the DCI, and Pamala Klein, director of the Rape and Sexual Abuse Care Center at Southern Illinois University at Edwardsville. They had spent weeks investigating allegations that a teacher in Weber's hometown had molested a number of twelve- and thirteen-year-old girls. After the teacher was indicted for molesting nine of the girls, a judge ordered him tried first on the allegations from only one of them. But Weber used the doctrine of other crimes again to introduce evidence that the teacher had molested four other girls the same way. The teacher was convicted.

In the middle of that case, Weber finally got the break he was looking for in a murder that had haunted him since he was an assistant prosecutor in 1978. The body of Karla Brown, a twenty-two-year-old college student, had been found dunked head-first in a ten-gallon bucket of water in the basement of a house she had moved into the day before. Her hands were tied behind her back and she was nude from the waist down. She had been beaten and strangled by a sock tied around her neck.

Weber was able to reopen the case based on the results of work by Alva Busch, an evidence specialist for the Illinois State Police, who sent some photographs of the victim's body to an expert on forensic dentistry and computer enhancement of photographs. The expert said the victim had suffered a bite mark to her collarbone that had been overlooked before. Weber also called in a forensic dentist who testified in the trial of serial killer Ted Bundy, who was executed in Florida. Bite-mark evidence was crucial to that case.

Weber had Karla Brown's body exhumed, and a new autopsy was performed by Dr. Mary Case, the chief deputy in the St. Louis medical examiner's office. The mutual respect that developed between Dr. Case and Weber during that investigation would be an important factor in the Paula Sims case years later.

The investigation also initiated Weber into the FBI's use of psychological profiles to look for killers. The bureau's expert reviewed the evidence in the Karla Brown case and produced a profile with striking detail of a loser with a scruffy beard—a young man who probably drove a beat-up foreign car, such as a Volkswagen. The FBI suggested an upbeat campaign of hype in the media to put pressure on the suspect amid announcements of a new investigation. The idea was to rattle the killer into making mistakes, and it worked. John Prante, an unemployed barge worker who drove an old red Volkswagen was charged, and the experts said his teeth could have made the bite on Karla Brown's neck. He was convicted and sentenced to 75 years in prison.

Karla Brown's sister made Weber an embroidered wall hanging that read, "You can lie through your teeth, but your teeth don't lie. John Prante, July 15, 1983." The border of the plaque was a design of rectangles and triangles in the pattern of the bite mark. It still hangs on Weber's office wall.

The bashings Weber had taken over the years paled against what happened in 1984. It was then that Weber turned to his old friend, Don Groshong, for help. Groshong's stature as a defense lawyer had continued to grow, and he added a few flourishes along the way. He noticeably favored actor Alan Alda, and was known for dressing in double-breasted suits set off by bright, flowered ties. He drove a classic Rolls-Royce, and spent his free time on his beautiful sailboat.

So the defender was well known when Weber brought him into a court battle as some of Weber's opponents tried to wrest from his control a grand jury investigation into political corruption. A judge finally agreed with Groshong's arguments that Weber had done nothing improper. And the grand jury continued its investigation into repeated allegations that James Barton, the county's Democratic supervisor of assessments, had allowed reductions in property tax assessments as political favors, costing the county treasury hundreds of thousands of dollars in lost revenue. Barton, who was called a "bag man" for contributions to Democratic powers, later was convicted of bribery in one case, and pleaded guilty to conspiracy and official misconduct in another. He lost his job and served a six-month jail sentence.

The long-running controversy was costly to Weber politically. In November of 1984, after a bitter campaign, Weber lost his bid for reelection to Democrat Dick Allen by 1,365 votes out of more than 103,000. It was a surprising and disappointing loss. Weber feared it was a rejection of everything he had stood for and an affirmation of the criticism he had suffered. He was disgusted that the voters would choose a man with no experience as a prosecutor and a philosophy on crime that belonged on the defense side of the table.

Weber went back to his original plan and became a patent attorney. But he kept in shape as a prosecutor as a special assistant to Jersey County State's Attorney Lee Plummer, winning a conviction in a complicated embezzlement case against a secretary in a real estate office. Weber also notched another win in a murder, but for the first time, it was on the defense side. He won an acquittal for a man in a stabbing during a fight at a tavern. DCI Agent Jimmie Bivens, the investigating officer, took the verdict pretty hard.

In January 1988, Weber was appointed interim state's attorney to fill a vacancy in Ford County, Illinois, the same county made famous in a series of commercials about Chevrolet trucks. He served until the next December.

During that period, he decided to run again in Madison County. Weber thought Dick Allen had been a dismal failure as a prosecutor and it was apparent that the police, courts, and public agreed. Weber discussed the situation with Bill Haine, one of the Democrats who had run against Nick Byron in the primary in 1980. The two men agreed that they would run in hopes that one of them would knock off Allen. Haine wrestled the endorsement of the county Democratic Central Committee away from Allen, and then overwhelmed him in the primary in March. Weber won the Republican nomination without opposition, but lost his enthusiasm for the race. He withdrew, leaving Haine unopposed. Weber figured it wouldn't be long before Haine realized that he needed an experienced felony prosecutor on the staff.

He was right. The call from Haine came in March 1989, and Weber agreed to start work the next month. So in April, Weber was back on the case, to the delight of the police and the chagrin of the Democratic political machine. He had no inkling that the biggest case of his career, and in Madison County history, was just a few days off. It was about to test everything he had learned as a prosecutor, and pit him against his old friend Groshong under the glare of unprecedented publicity.

Chapter 9

Mick Dooley could see that Paula was becoming increasingly apprehensive about the interview by the time they reached the police station about 3:00 A.M. He still was straining to be friendly, treating her as the victim and doing everything he wouldn't do if he were about to grill a suspect. He even asked if she would like a soda, and then delivered the Pepsi she requested. She said it was the only kind she drank.

He seated her at a table in the squad room, and then slipped out to talk to McCain. Dooley whispered that Paula seemed pretty shaky, and he was afraid she would walk out if they pushed her very hard. McCain agreed that taking it easy with her appeared to be the best approach. They would get her story first and then bring in Robert. McCain was confident that the combined interviewing skills of the two detectives would bring out the truth once the Simses were interviewed separately.

But the officers also knew they probably would get only one shot at these people. Robert and Paula had been in this situation before. They had been interviewed under almost identical circumstances and they had been pressured by good cops before. And they had held up.

Yocom had agreed with that assessment and, in fact, had decided to stay well out of view when Robert and Paula came in. He didn't want the Simses' dislike for him getting in Alton's way.

McCain and Dooley even decided that, to be extra careful on this case, they would depart from their standard procedure and tape record the interview rather than make lengthy notes and put together a report from them later. That way, when the Simses inevitably got an attorney, there could be no questions about what was said or whether the statement had been voluntary.

McCain pulled a tape recorder from the storage cabinet and he and Dooley went back to the room where Paula was waiting. McCain sat down next to her; Dooley stood across the table from her and leaned forward, resting his weight on his knuckles and towering over the woman.

"Paula, Sergeant McCain and I want to talk to you about what has happened. We have some questions—"

Paula broke into tears.

Dooley hadn't meant to seem quite so intimidating. "No, wait a minute, Paula. You don't understand. We're not accusing you of doing anything. This is standard procedure. We just need to find out as much as we can about what happened."

Rick joined in. "Paula, you're the victim in this case. You're the only person who saw anything. You've reported a kidnapping and you're the only person who saw the kidnapper. We can't investigate a kidnapping unless you tell us everything you can. But you're free to leave at any time you desire to and, if you want an attorney, you can call anyone you want to. But we don't believe an attorney is going to be necessary. We're just going to be asking you questions about this kidnapper."

Paula stopped crying, and looked up. "All right."

She put the ice pack on her neck again, and it looked like she was ready.

Rick told her they would be taping the interview. Paula looked a little apprehensive again. But he explained that it was being done only so they didn't have to take notes while they talked to her. He turned on the recorder, checked to make sure the cassette spools were turning, and clearly stated the time and parties involved. And they were off and running.

Paula recounted Heather's birth on March 18 at Alton Memorial Hospital; she had been a good baby, fussing recently only because of a touch of diarrhea. The Simses had taken her to the doctor the Saturday before to be sure she was all right.

Paula told them the same story of the kidnapping, but added more details about what happened before the at-

tack. She had put both of the children to bed between
9:30 and 10:00 P.M.; Randy in his bedroom upstairs, and
Heather, wearing a white sleeper with a bunny pattern,
in her bassinet on the table in the dining room. The room
had been converted to a temporary bedroom for Paula
and Heather. Paula had delivered by caesarian section
and had been told by the doctor to avoid climbing stairs.
Robert, on swing shifts, slept upstairs so the baby
wouldn't disturb him when she cried.

After the children were in bed, Paula straightened up
around the house for a while, and then watched the news
on television. The story about the pin in the baby food
that she had mentioned earlier to Dooley had been on
that program. She later decided to take out the trash because of the smelly diapers.

Paula was unable to give them any new bit of description about the kidnapper. She didn't know whether his
clothes were black, blue, or green. She puzzled the police by describing his shirt as being like a T-shirt, but
with long sleeves. He wore gloves and a ski mask.

Dooley and McCain zeroed in on the mask. Surely she
had been able to get a good look at it.

Paula put together the thumbs and forefingers of both
hands to make a large circle, and then held the circle up
to her mouth to show the size of the hole in the mask.

Bingo, McCain thought. He and Dooley leaned forward in their chairs, both of them sensing what might
come next.

"Paula, think real carefully about this," McCain said.
"You must have seen what race he was. Think about it,
Paula. Think about it real hard. You must have seen his
skin around the holes for the mouth and the eyes."

Dooley added, "Close your eyes and try to visualize
it." He was pointing at her face, making circles with his
forefinger to approximate the size of the eye holes.

Suddenly the holes slammed shut.

"No, they weren't that big," Paula said quickly. She
seemed startled; she back-peddled so fast her interroga-
tors could tell she thought she had stumbled.

"I couldn't see what race he was. They weren't that
big."

McCain and Dooley would laugh later that they could

hear those holes snapping shut, and Dooley had been lucky not to lose the tip of his finger when those openings closed up so quickly.

And, instead of Paula returning to the boring recitation from the script, she gave them another piece of useful information. Dropping the edge of one hand into the palm of the other, she said she had been hit with a "karate-type blow." That could be important later when the issue of her injuries, or lack of injuries, came up. McCain had her repeat the description several times so she could not dispute it later. Each time, she chopped her hand down into her palm.

Paula, and even the cops, had no idea that the karate chop she was describing would indeed be a serious blow in this case.

She was unable to offer any motive for either of the kidnappings. She and Robert had no enemies and, since Loralei was abducted, Paula seldom went out or took Randy out in public for fear this would happen to him, too.

The cops asked about drug involvement. Paula admitted some occasional marijuana use, but she said she hadn't smoked any for at least ten days. She was careful to minimize it; she and Robert didn't keep it in the house, and she used it only when someone else offered her a hit.

McCain decided to be blunt, and see how she reacted.

"Paula, you understand that I have to ask you this question. With the case like this that happened to you before, it all can look a little suspicious. So I wouldn't be doing my job if I didn't ask you this. Paula, did you kill your daughter?"

There was no reaction—only a flat "No."

After an interview lasting more than an hour, McCain and Dooley had very little to show for it but dulled senses. They had run out of things to ask and couldn't think of any more stalling tactics to give the guys at the scene more time.

Dooley wondered how you could have a boring conversation with a mother who had just had her baby kidnapped. And he wondered why she had put up with it for so long, willing to drone on about any subject the police raised. Why hadn't she put a screaming end to the relentless questions and angrily ordered them to go out and find her daughter? That was the way a mother would act if her baby had been stolen.

McCain, too, had watched Paula closely. She was nervous, but not nearly emotional enough for a mother plunged into this horrible nightmare for a second time. He would have been a hell of a lot more upset if one of his daughters were missing. He'd never sit still that long while one of his kids was out there somewhere.

He also was bothered by the fact that the only spark she had shown, the only sign of life, was when she talked about Randy. Then she was just like a typical mother talking about her child. She would chat happily about how he was walking and starting to talk. But when the questioning turned back to Heather, Paula turned back to the flat, cold monotone.

The interview ended about 4:00 A.M. It wasn't until then that Dooley learned that Yocom had stood on a box outside the room, listening through an air vent as Paula told her story. Yocom knew Paula so well that he could visualize her face as she talked—the same cold look he had seen so many times three years ago.

Yocom approached Dooley as he came out of the room. "Guy, this is bull."

Dooley smiled. "Yeah, I know."

After Dooley left with Paula, McCain called Robert and told him Paula was on her way home. He asked Robert to return with Dooley for an interview. Robert balked, but McCain told him that getting the information was essential to solving the case. Surely that was what Robert Sims wanted.

"Okay," Robert said.

Chris Sullivan was searching the dining room when Paula walked in and sat down on the couch. She lit up a cigarette, crossed her legs and leaned back. He watched for some sign of emotional wear under the strain of another daughter's kidnapping and another intrusive assault from suspicious police. Some tears, something.

Nothing. *This doesn't even mean enough to her to put on a show for us,* he thought. *She's not even going to act upset.*

The house had been searched top to bottom and back again while Paula was gone, and the police still were rooting around. Ventimiglia had each room searched repeatedly, with the officers taking turns, one cop after the other, looking for any clues. The idea was to eliminate the house as the location of the body.

By now, all of the detectives at the scene were assuming that Heather was dead. There was, perhaps, a 10 percent chance that she was alive. With 1986 in mind, they would conduct an intensive search of the woods near the house after daylight in case Heather had been left out there. But they were sure she was dead.

McCain knew his men did not believe the Simses' story. But the policeman in each of them wanted to eliminate every possibility before reaching a conclusion. *This is not a case we want to be wrong on,* McCain thought.

The plan by then was to stall as long as possible, drawing out the search to stay at the house. The longer the police were there, the better the chance that something would happen or someone would say something that would help in the investigation.

Closets were searched and drawers were rechecked. The police looked under all the beds and opened the cabinets. As they do in all searches, they looked in the refrigerator. They can't really explain why they do it; they just do. Nothing significant was seen, of course, and the irony of checking there in this case couldn't be appreciated at the time.

Robert had asked the police to stay away from Randy's room, to avoid waking him so early. But every other room in the house was explored thoroughly.

The drawers in the frame under Robert's and Paula's waterbed were pulled out, and Hayes found some magazines. A copy of the *National Enquirer* with a front-page story about satanic sacrifices caught the cops' attention, as did the huge poster of Janis Joplin hanging on the wall. What a bizarre juxtaposition for this drug-dead rock singer to stare back from the wall in this home.

Even though the police felt the house had been prepared thoroughly for their visit, Hayes carefully photographed everything. That included the handwritten messages on a calendar in the kitchen that all the officers were convinced had been left for them to find. The notes on the pages for March and April read, "We love Randy and sweet Heather, Heather Lee Sims is beautiful, and Thank God for Heather Lee."

Hayes and the other officers had discussed the fact that there were no pictures of either of the Simses' daughters on the walls, just some nice shots of bright-eyed, red-haired little Randy. No mementos of their lost daughter, Loralei, and no new celebrations of their new daughter, Heather.

In later searches, McCain would be struck by the total lack of decorations or anything else that would indicate the presence of a baby girl in the house. Randy's room was beautifully decorated with oak furniture, wall hangings, and Mickey Mouse wallpaper. But the other bedroom, which Rick expected to be decorated as the nursery for a baby girl, was unused. There was no sign anywhere that a little girl had lived in that house.

As the father of four daughters, that nagged at McCain's guts.

Ventimiglia started to videotape the inside of the house, but the battery in the camera failed almost immediately. He and McCain made a note to be sure nothing like that ever happened again. Hayes had to call his brother after daylight and borrow his video camera to complete the taping.

During the search, Robert asked Ventimiglia how many officers were on the case and what they would do next. He wanted to know when Paula would be back. He jotted down some notes on a yellow pad as Ventimiglia answered.

For a while, Robert followed him around the house, watching every move the sergeant made. So he could join in the search without the vigilant eye of a potential suspect over his shoulder, Ventimiglia finally started passing Robert off to other officers for a few minutes.

When Ventimiglia got a chance to look at Robert's basement workshop, he quickly concluded that this was the domain of an obsessive-compulsive personality. Everything was excessively ordered. All the tools were lined up perfectly. The drawers in the workbench were lined with shop towels, and the odd nuts, bolts, and washers were separated in little containers. The Allen wrenches and screwdrivers were evenly spaced, lined up according to size and placed at right angles with the edge of the bench.

Ventimiglia knew he had a touch of that syndrome. He liked things in their place, nice and neat. But he had never seen anything like this, and wouldn't have believed it if someone had described it to him. *This is nuts,* he thought.

Sullivan noticed that stacks of plastic crates in the basement contained collections of magazines, including a number of detective magazines. Not only were the various magazines filed alphabetically, but the issues of each magazine were in chronological order.

During a search later on, Dooley noticed that the library of videotapes about Randy that was kept by Robert was equally compulsive in its order. Each tape was titled in red marker, something such as "Randy's First Steps" or "Randy's First Birthday," with the amount of tape used listed in black marker. And each tape would contain only that one scene; the rest of each tape would be blank. Dooley was amazed. Robert couldn't even stand to have more than one episode on each tape.

It was then that Dooley decided to mess with Robert's mind a bit and leave a cryptic little message behind in the workshop. He went through the drawers methodically, switching the occasional tool here or turning something the wrong way there. He knew that would drive Robert crazy until he got everything restored to order. Just Dooley's way of saying, "We know who you are, pal."

While the others turned the house upside down, Sergeant Wells covered nearly everything in the kitchen with black fingerprinting dust, something that surely would irritate the fastidious residents. Ventimiglia thought Wells must have spent hours dusting the refrigerator, where he lifted a few prints. A kitchen mop, which theoretically could have been used to clean up a murder scene, was seized.

But Wells also noticed something about the two tables sitting side by side in the dining room and holding the bassinet, infant "pumpkin" seat and an assortment of baby-care items. The tables were covered with a fine layer of what was either dust or baby powder. Leaning down for a better look, Wells could see that the layer was undisturbed. If a kidnapper had touched anything on that table, he would have left some marks in the dust. To check, Wells ran his finger across a small part of the table. The trail in the dust was unmistakable.

Outside, Hayes confiscated the Simses' trash, which had been set out in white plastic bags. He couldn't have guessed, not in his wildest dreams, the import those trash bags would have later on in this case. At the time, Hayes only wanted to check Paula's story that the trash she was setting out contained soiled and foul-smelling diapers from Heather's diarrhea.

Back at the station later, Hayes would be pleasantly surprised to discover that the odor of the bag's contents was not nearly as offensive as Paula had suggested. Hayes gingerly removed fifteen diapers from the bag—eight in the small size worn by Heather and seven medium-sized ones worn by Randy. But only one of the small ones was soiled by diarrhea, and it had been at the bottom of the bag. That didn't seem right.

Hayes had expected there to be twice as many diapers for Heather as Randy. Infants seemed to go through them a lot faster, especially when they had diarrhea. So the almost even numbers of the two sizes didn't seem right, either.

Paula's story about the trash bag and its contents didn't work. The bag hadn't been full of dirty, smelly diapers, and the only soiled one had been put into the bag first. And the small number of small diapers could imply that Heather hadn't been around there for some time before the police were called.

Just after daylight, Hayes made a startling discovery in the Simses' nightstand. He didn't know it, but it actually was a rediscovery of something found in the same drawer three years earlier by another policeman in Brighton. Hayes was startled by Polaroid photographs of the naked and pregnant Paula. Something new had been added, however, and this time there were a couple of nude shots of Robert. Hayes was astounded and amused. He took them discreetly to Ventimiglia, who grimaced, called them "gross and perverted," and ordered them put back where they were found.

While Dooley was ferrying the Simses to and from the station, McCain took the tape recorder into the detectives' room to play some of Paula's statement for Yocom, Kocis, and the others. But to McCain's horror, the tape was blank; nothing but static when he hit the "play" button. Right there, in front of his colleagues and peers, the new chief of detectives felt like he had just dropped his pants.

He found out later that the tape recorder he had used required a separate microphone. *How could he have been so stupid?* McCain thought. Besides being embarrassed and furious with himself, he was hoping the blunder would not come back to haunt the investigation later. But, of course, it did.

He wouldn't make that mistake when Robert came in. This time, the microphone would be attached and the recorder would be recording.

Dooley delivered Robert to the station about 4:30 A.M. When he checked in with McCain, he learned about the blank tape. Dooley looked up and succinctly expressed everyone's reaction: "Aw, shit."

During the interview, Robert was the same cool character the cops had seen at the house. Relaxed, calm, collected. He gave them the basics about his family and he listed Loralei Marie Sims as one of his children.

McCain was a little surprised. "And Loralei is deceased now? Is that correct?"

Robert said quietly, "I don't know."

"Okay. Do you believe her to be deceased?"

Robert paused for a few seconds and said, "Not 100 percent sure."

McCain asked Robert to recount the activities leading up to the baby's disappearance. Robert told a story that sounded like nothing so much as an average day in the life of an average family. Only a few details gave away the true nature of that family's background, such as Robert's mention that the Simses had been "paranoid" for the last three years, keeping almost all the shades in the house pulled all the time, the dead bolt on the door locked at all times, and the answering machine on all the time to screen harassing calls.

But Robert also mentioned one thing that tipped the police to a peculiarity they would concentrate on later. Robert mentioned that sign on the Simses' door telling everyone who entered to remove their shoes. Robert explained flatly, "Because I don't like my children crawling around in somebody's dirt."

Only later would they learn that the shoes-off requirement was one of a list of regulations that came to be known among the cops and prosecutors as "Robert's Rules of Order"—another manifestation of this man's curious obsessions.

Robert told the detectives he had gone to work on the afternoon shift as normal that day. His shift passed without incident, and he returned home expecting to find everything normal. But he had noticed the trash bag by the steps, and thought that was strange because he usually took out the trash. And then he discovered the unlocked dead bolt on the back door. Paula always kept the door locked.

When he opened the door, he found Paula face down on the kitchen floor. Had she fallen? Was she dead? He reached down and touched her hand. It was warm, reassuring him somewhat. He shook and called her name, but was unable to rouse her.

"And it just hit me," he said. He described his scramble into the dining room to discover that Heather was missing. He returned to Paula, shaking her harder for two or three minutes until she came around. He kept asking, "Where's Heather, Paula? Where's Heather?" Although still a bit groggy, she told him Heather should be in her bassinet. He told her Heather was not there, and that was when Paula first mumbled something about a man with a mask and gun who had walked up to her about 10:30.

Robert bolted down the hall and up the winding stairs to check on Randy as Paula followed him. Their son was safe and asleep.

"I said, 'Thank the Lord,' " Robert added.

He and Paula went back downstairs and searched again for Heather, making several passes through all the rooms.

Robert's voice dropped to a whisper. "And I said, 'This can't be happening again.' "

McCain said, "Referring to the first time you had a similar incident with your daughter, Loralei?"

Robert's voice was even softer. "Yes. And I believe I said to Paula, 'What'll we do?' She said, 'We got to call the police.' "

After Robert made the call, he said, they searched the house again, even going into the basement and checking the other bedrooms upstairs.

He said he had little chance to get a description of the kidnapper from Paula before the police arrived. But he noted that Paula didn't even know whether the man was black or white. It was another clue that wouldn't seem important for months.

McCain shifted the focus to drugs and alcohol. Robert said they would drink a beer occasionally, and that they smoked marijuana. He said the last time they had used pot was two to four days ago.

Robert's interview was finished about 5:20 A.M. Nothing new, nothing different from Paula's story, and even more routine.

But he handled himself well. He had stuck to the basics and never suggested that he had seen or done anything questionable. The only time he let himself be pulled close to the danger zone was when he verified that Paula had been unconscious on the floor when he got home. He had deftly avoided anything else that could incriminate him.

He's a pretty smart guy, McCain thought. *He's got his old lady taking the heat no matter what, and the only way he could get burned is by her. He's just repeating what Paula told him.*

It also struck McCain that Robert seemed to perk up, just as Paula had, when the conversation turned to Randy. His tone returned to dull and scripted, however, as soon as Heather and her disappearance were discussed.

Both of the Simses had seemed prepared for the interviews with the police. Robert might have been a little cockier about it than Paula had been, feeling perhaps that he had defeated the police three years ago and would do it again. But it was obvious to McCain and Dooley that they were faced with two people who would be difficult to shake, even if their stories were pure fabrications.

Robert and Paula had laid across their bed to get a little rest sometime before dawn, while the search in their house continued. But Randy awoke before 7:00 A.M., forcing the Simses into the start of a new and different day—Sunday, April 30. As Robert and Paula fed Randy his breakfast in the kitchen, Ventimiglia watched the scene with amazed disdain. Hours after their infant daughter disappeared, Robert and Paula were laughing and cooing with Randy as if nothing had happened. It was an "Ozzie and Harriet" breakfast scene, just an all-American family enjoying time together in the room where Paula claimed to have been so brutally attacked hours before, and only a few feet from the place where Heather had been snatched from her bed.

It's like she never existed, Ventimiglia thought.

Sometime after 8:00 A.M., Linda Condray arrived at the house to bring Robert some pictures she had taken recently of Heather, in case he needed to distribute them to the media or use them to print up fliers, as they had done in 1986.

While Linda was there, Robert told Paula to go over to her parents' home in Cottage Hills. "You can't be of any use here," he said. Paula loaded Randy and some personal effects into the Simses' brown Chevrolet station wagon and drove off. It was to be a fateful trip.

Ventimiglia suggested to Robert that he should leave, too, while the police made one last pass through the house with some of the dogs. But Robert said he would stay.

Ventimiglia told the detectives to open all the windows to air out the house and remove the scents from all the people who had been there over the last twelve hours. Then he closed it up again and brought two bloodhounds and a German shepherd through to see if they could pick up the scent from the baby, just in case the body had been hidden there so well that the police had missed it. No luck again.

Hayes had decided to check out a hunch. He knew that the road from the rear of Jefferson Smurfit to the Berm

Highway, which runs along the Alton riverfront, was isolated and covered by underbrush. There were many
places along the road where a body could be stashed.
Hayes changed into some jeans and met Wells at the road
about 9:00 A.M. They walked the one-mile route for an
hour, but saw nothing.

By the time he got back to the Sims house about 11:00 A.M.,
the operation there was winding down. Ventimiglia had
run out of stalling tactics and had called off the search.
After everyone packed up, he took one last walk through
the house just to make sure he hadn't overlooked something obvious. He shook his head again in sheer frustration, and walked out.

The detectives assembled next door in the parking lot
behind the East Middle School. Chief Downey and Alton
Mayor Edward Voumard arrived with a supply of coffee
and doughnuts, and pledges that the detectives would
have whatever they needed to make this case. It was a
new experience for the cops. None of them had ever been
treated this way by a chief or a mayor, and they appreciated the gesture.

Just before the cops pulled away, the first TV news
crew arrived and got a shot of Ventimiglia and Hayes
waking up the school driveway. The assault by the media
had begun.

McCain was greeted at the station by a fistful of messages from reporters and others asking him to call, and
a list of complaints from the patrol division about all the
calls jamming the switchboard. He had expected the case
to generate a lot of interest from the three major television stations in St. Louis and the local newspapers. But
he was getting calls from newspapers he hadn't heard of,
radio stations and television stations from outside the
area, and national wire services.

He decided the only way to handle the crunch was with
a press conference that afternoon. One nerve-wracking
moment in front of the media and the cameras, and it
would be over. He told the dispatcher to inform the reporters that he would meet with them at three o'clock.
He dashed home, showered and changed clothes, and
came back to face the cameras.

He prepared by jotting down some notes on index cards, hoping to disclose only the right details while still being informative and professional. He would keep it simple and straightforward. Issue a statement, take a couple of questions, and shut it down. It worked for the president.

The conference was held in the city council chambers on the floor above the police department at City Hall. McCain was shocked when he walked in and was confronted by more than a dozen reporters and cameramen assembled in the room. He was more nervous than he had expected as he read the basics from his notes.

He wasn't prepared for the intensity of the reporter's questions. They asked repeatedly if the Simses were considered suspects. Each time McCain refused to call the couple suspects, the reporters would bore in on the similarities and the almost astronomical chances that two such kidnappings could strike the same family, three years apart, in different cities, resulting in the disappearance of infant daughters.

McCain said several times, "Considering the similarity in the cases, we cannot rule out any possibility. This has been reported as a kidnapping and, right now, we're treating this as a kidnapping."

The reporters hammered him for specifics and asked if the Simses had taken polygraph tests, an obvious reference to the tests they flunked in 1986. On question after question, McCain explained that he couldn't comment.

When he had finished, he felt like a human sacrifice offered up by the police department to satisfy the press. He felt battered by the reporters' insistence that he answer questions in the terms they wanted. And he was frustrated that they had asked questions over and over again after he had said he couldn't answer them.

Later, when he watched himself on television, he thought he had looked stupid reading from notes. He wouldn't do that again. From then on, he would just wing it.

Reporters and TV crews fanned out through Alton that Sunday and swarmed over Washington Avenue. No one answered the knocks at 1053. Neighbors were interviewed over and over; they explained that the Simses were quiet and kept to themselves, and remembered how the tall, chain-link fence had gone up around the front yard. The television crews snapped up the easy man-on-the-street bits, getting the expected responses of shock and surprise.

The calls were made to the Condrays, who had been so vocal in 1986. Herb was more reserved this time. "We have not heard a thing. We have been told to send all inquiries to the police."

While McCain was facing the press, the other detectives were figuring out what they had and deciding what else they had to do. Ventimiglia was putting together lead cards, so that each angle to be checked would be listed and could be marked later with the results. Sullivan and Pyatt were conducting another neighborhood canvass.

Sunday night, the police set up a roadblock in front of the Simses' house, just as was done in 1986. And with the same results. Of dozens of drivers stopped, only four had been on the street the night before, and they had seen nothing suspicious.

The new Sims baby disappearance was the lead story on television that night and front-page news in the next day's newspapers across the two-state region. The media's skepticism was apparent. The similarities between the two cases were played prominently, described as "chilling, striking, haunting, or amazing." Robert and Paula were recalled as suspects in Loralei's death, and the press reminded the readers that the parents had flunked lie-detectors tests then.

But it was just a taste of the coverage to come.

Chapter 10

The detectives hit the ground running Monday morning, usually shadowed by television news crews recording their every move. Hayes and Dooley were sent to the offices of the Simses' doctors at the Alton Medical Group to confirm the diarrhea report and get copies of the family's medical records. But even that became difficult when the clinic's administrator said he would need a subpoena to produce records. Not unreasonable, Hayes thought.

On Tuesday, he and Dooley returned with the subpoena. But the administrator told them he had consulted with the clinic's attorney, and would not honor the subpoena. Hayes was incensed; he had plenty to do without being yanked around by some office manager. State's Attorney Bill Haine immediately issued a search warrant and, on Wednesday, Hayes and Dooley went to the clinic a third time. They were accompanied by a furious McCain, Ventimiglia, Assistant Prosecutor Randy Massey, and a parking lot full of reporters who had caravanned along behind the police.

Hayes handed the search warrant to the administrator, and McCain asked to speak to him privately. Barely controlling his outrage, McCain explained that everyone else in this investigation had been cooperative, and his detectives had plenty to do without jumping through hoops to get a few records.

And then McCain added, "I'm going to confiscate every record you have in this office if I don't have everything I want in five minutes." The documents were delivered promptly.

As McCain walked out of the administrator's office, the other detectives nodded approvingly. McCain was

genuinely angry, but he also knew how important it was
to back up his men.

The records supported the Simses' story that Heather
had suffered from diarrhea and had been examined by a
pediatrician on April 22. They were of little value beyond
that.

Despite his experience with the press on Sunday,
McCain had been nearly astounded by the growing number of reporters clustered outside the police station Monday. McCain realized this would be a much bigger case
than he had imagined. Crews from television stations
parked their logo-covered vans all over the street in front
of the station—especially in the no-parking zones.

City Hall sits on the steep side of one of the many hills in
downtown Alton, lending something of a San Francisco
aura. A few blocks below the building, the Mississippi
River flows by picturesquely, slowed by the huge concrete dam. But the pitched angle of the streets seemed to
make the scene even more incongruous as reporters
milled around on the slopes and cameramen lugged the
equipment up the inclines.

As interest in the case grew, TV stations sent in their
huge microwave trucks to transmit live reports by satellite. The trucks began parking on the roof of a small
parking garage across from the police station, their huge
transmission antennas rising into the air. Camera crews
and reporters set up their tripods at various locations
around the intersection, drawing crowds of curious onlookers who had never seen anything like this before.

By Monday afternoon, McCain had collected nearly
200 messages from reporters across the country asking
for details. He decided to hold daily press conferences
as the only hope of reducing the load on the department's
emergency switchboard.

The DCI had returned in force Monday, with Wayne
Watson, now a lieutenant, accompanying Trent and the
others. Watson was perhaps the first person convinced
absolutely of Paula's guilt in 1986 because of her slip of
the tongue by the pond. That comment, and the look on
her face, had haunted him ever since.

He had known McCain for some time, and their wives

had worked together at a doctor's office. Watson offered McCain a somewhat unusual perspective on dealing with Robert and Paula. Watson was convinced that the Simses were under tremendous family pressure to maintain their innocence. Watson remembered Paula stressing that she was the only one capable of giving her parents grand-children. Under that kind of pressure, it would be almost impossible for her to admit that she had killed those grandchildren, Watson believed.

McCain and the other detectives spent most of Monday checking out leads and fielding calls. Some calls were from the number of psychics who always offered their unsolicited assistance. Most of the "impressions" were too vague to be of any use, and they soon became a nuisance for the cops. Since Alton is on the riverfront, tips that Heather's body would be found near water and something green, or near a road, were of little help. To cut the tension, Dooley and some of the others occasion-ally would ask one of the volunteer psychics for tips on lottery numbers.

But one psychic from St. Louis came to Alton and told reporters he had "a feeling" that there was some freshly turned earth in the woods off Indiana Street near the river. McCain sent Hayes, and he found a patch of just-turned soil and a foul odor in that area. But as he dug, all he found was raw sewage.

One call that came in early that morning was different. Edward Werner, a funeral home operator and former deputy county coroner from Granite City, told Hayes that he had just seen a television news report about Heather's disappearance.

"My daughter, Stephanie, was Paula Sims's roommate in March when that baby that was kidnapped was born. Paula told her how her first baby was kidnapped in 1986. But the story she told about 1986 was the same way she said this baby was kidnapped Saturday night."

Hayes wasn't sure he had heard Werner right. But if he had, it meant that Paula had told the blow-to-the-head story six weeks before it happened. He asked if he had heard correctly.

"Yes, that's what I'm telling you. That's why I called."

Hayes asked Werner to hold on, and went to tell Ventimiglia.

"You got to hear this, Tony. You won't believe what this guy is saying."

As Hayes repeated the story, Tony's eyes got wider and wider.

"Get an appointment made with her right now."

Werner said he would have Stephanie call the police as soon as possible. She called back later that day and made an appointment for a week later, Monday, May 8.

Sergeant Wells also checked out one of his hunches that morning, with some help from Ralph Baahlmann, Jr., the county's chief deputy coroner. Wells asked Ralph to cut through the red tape and see if there were any state records indicating that Paula Sims had other children who had died. Baahlmann, who had keen investigative instincts of his own, pulled a few strings with state officials in Illinois and Missouri. They checked the birth records for the last four or five years under the names of Paula Marie Blew and Paula Marie Sims. The only records that popped up were those for the three known children. But everyone he asked knew about the case and was anxious to help.

And that last name, Blew, rang a bell with Baahlmann. He soon realized that he knew her parents through his work with Compassionate Friends, a support group for grieving parents who had lost children to violence or accidents. Orville and Nylene Blew were on the board of directors of a local chapter.

It struck Ralph that the family's grief over Paula's brother, Randy—and Paula's feeling of responsibility for the crash—could have destroyed her self-esteem. She could have been so traumatized by his death, and the years of her parents dwelling on it, that she started to believe that all daughters did was cause grief and harm to their families. She had lived, and her brother had died. But it was the dead brother who concerned her parents most. Ralph urged the police to look for clues in that psychological milieu.

A few hours later, Dooley drove over to the Simses' house to pick up copies of Heather's footprints and Robert's divorce decree from his first marriage. Robert went into the basement to get the documents while Dooley waited in the kitchen. His close proximity to the Sims refrigerator went unnoticed. Robert returned within minutes and handed the papers to Dooley.

Robert looked deeply into his eyes, and said softly, "Be careful with Heather's prints, because that's all that I've got now, man."

Dooley nodded.

Monday's press conference offered little news for the media. By then, however, Hayes and Dooley had begun stationing themselves in the rear of the council chambers to help McCain during the questioning. If Rick was asked something he wasn't sure about, he would glance at Hayes and Dooley for a sign.

Asked about leads, McCain said simply, "I think it's fair to say we don't have anything solid."

But behind the scenes, McCain was working on a new approach that he ultimately would believe had led to the big break. McCain called FBI headquarters in Quantico, Virginia, to ask the bureau's experts to develop a psychological profile on a person who would commit such a crime. McCain was referred to Tom Salp, a specialist in psychological criminology.

After McCain described the case, Salp said a psychological profile would not be of much use because the parents were so obviously the suspects. Instead, Salp offered McCain a series of suggestions about how to apply pressure to the suspects through the media in ways that could force them to make a fatal mistake. Salp told McCain to tell reporters that the police were confident of solving the case and were pursuing useful evidence. The flow of information to the press should remain constant, so the story would remain big news. The more confident the police seemed, and the more hype the case got in the news, the more pressure the suspects would feel. That could force them to do something else to try to cover their tracks, something that might be a big enough mistake to crack the case.

Then Salp gave Rick a curious phrase and told him to read it to the press, but not to elaborate on it.

McCain called Bill Haine and told him about the advice from the FBI and the plan to use the press to apply psychological tactics. Haine said that was an interesting idea, and that he had no problem playing the case broadly for the media as long as the cops released valid information that didn't harm the investigation.

Haine also said he was assigning the case to Don Weber, and would talk to him about the FBI's advice. McCain was glad the case was going to Weber, who was considered by most cops to be a tough prosecutor willing to take risks and back up the police.

Weber was picking a jury in a rape trial that day. The case was the first he had prosecuted in a couple of years, and the first in Madison County since he left office as state's attorney almost five years earlier. He had been on Haine's staff barely ten days.

At lunch, Haine told him about the conversation with McCain. Weber didn't hesitate.

"If McCain's talking to the FBI psychological profile people, tell him to do exactly what they say. I know it works. That's how we solved the Karla Brown case. Those guys are great; they're incredible. If they're saying to hype the case in the media, tell him to do it. That could be a small problem later, but as long as they're giving out correct information, we'll be okay. Tell McCain to do exactly what they tell him to do and to say exactly what they tell him to say."

Haine said he and Randy Massey were going to Alton that evening to check on the investigation, and he invited Don along.

Weber was glad to get the Sims case, but he knew it would be a while before he had time to get involved very deeply. He expected a verdict in the rape case by midweek, and he would be leaving town immediately after that to drive his parents to their new home in Virginia. Don's father was ill, and his mother had decided to move closer to her relatives in the East. Don knew it was going to be a tough week.

He met Haine and Massey at the police station about 6:00 P.M. The prosecutors were buzzed through the security door into the detectives' room. Weber looked around but recognized few of the cops. A lot of faces had changed. He had never met McCain, and he knew

Ventimiglia only slightly. The rest of the detectives seemed awfully young and inexperienced, although very eager.

Don was impressed with the talent that had assembled in the room. Yocom was there with his file from 1986. Kocis and Trent were there, two of the cops Weber respected the most. Diana Sievers was there. And when Weber saw his old friend, Jimmie Bivens, the importance of the case began to dawn on him. If a hard-as-nails veteran like Bivens was willing to come out, even though he was retired, this must be some case.

He got a quick synopsis of the Loralei case from Sievers. And he decided to sit back and absorb the incredible exchange of information buzzing through the air. Across the long, narrow room used by McCain and Ventimiglia as their office, small groups of cops had broken off and were deep in discussion about a dizzying myriad of angles, from the most obvious facts to the most subtle nuances. The sheriff and state agents who had worked so hard in 1986 were imparting their best recollections, impressions, and advice to those confronted by the new case.

Fascinating images emerged.

The sincerity of Frank Yocom. It was obvious no one cared more about the Sims cases than he did. He was willing to do anything, talk to anyone to help. He didn't want to get in the way, but he was there to do anything that was asked of him.

The cool professionalism of Phil Kocis. His mind had filed the facts and details of the last investigation, and he could organize them instantly into a meaningful presentation for a fellow investigator. He was backed by the resources of the DCI, and had put them at the disposal of the Alton Police Department.

The intensity of Diana Sievers. She was doing everything she could to impart to the Alton cops what they were up against with Robert and, especially, Paula Sims. Sievers's eyes flashed as she described interviewing Paula three years ago, and Weber could feel the frustration when she talked about being so close to a confession, only to have it slip away. She would clench her fists in front of her or reach out to the person across from her as she tried to emphasize a point, as she struggled to make sure her ideas got through.

The anger of Jimmie Bivens. For a cop, watching someone get away with murder is the most frustrating feeling in the world. That futility obviously had turned to anger in Jimmie Bivens. When he talked about Paula and Robert, his language turned the air blue. If there were any way for him to help get them this time, he would do it. He had opened a successful private investigating company since he had retired, but for now, solving this second Sims case was the most important thing on his agenda.

The cops were passing around pictures of Loralei and Heather. *What beautiful little girls,* Weber thought. *How could anyone do this to them?* How many times that night did he hear someone say it was a shame that this had happened to a second Sims girl?

Someone suggested that the police go after Robert and Paula again in interviews and try to get them to crack. Sievers shook that off, saying Paula could be incredibly tough. Sievers and Debra Morgan had taken Paula to the edge in 1986, but they hadn't been able to get her to take that last step. Sievers was sure Paula wouldn't break under interrogation unless something dramatic happened before that.

Massey said several times that he thought conducting surveillance on the Simses could be valuable. He was unaware that the police already had decided against it for the time being. Massey thought additional evidence might be gained by watching everyone in the family and waiting for a misstep. When he asked McCain about it directly, Massey understood McCain to say that it was being handled by the DCI. McCain had meant only that the DCI would do it if they all agreed later that it was a good idea.

Weber also called surveillance impractical. Massey realized that he had been overruled.

At one point, Massey turned to Haine and said, "I'll bet that body's frozen somewhere."

Haine wrinkled his face. "Frozen? That's strange. Why would you think that?"

"Because there are lots of meat lockers in the area

around Brighton. That would be an easy place to hide that body. And freezing it would be a way to try to confuse the time of death."

Haine passed the idea along to Weber, who dismissed it out of hand. "No, that's crazy."

All the officers there that night had been struck by the obvious—two Sims daughters were gone, but the son was unharmed. Was there something there that should be, or even could be, probed? What was it about baby girls the Simses disliked, or about boys that they revered? No one had any answers.

But as the man who would take this case to trial, if it ever got that far, Weber filed that gender dichotomy for future reference.

From what Weber heard, he concluded that Heather's body never would be found. The discovery of Loralei's body had cast serious doubt on Paula's story, and that mistake wouldn't be repeated. The new story already had been altered to eliminate some problems from the first time; hence, the knockout blow that avoided the "Which way did he go?" questions. No, that body probably had been weighted with rocks and dropped in the river days ago.

The three prosecutors thought the atmosphere among the Alton cops was a kind of organized confusion. They didn't see a real direction to the investigation. Randy Massey viewed it as mostly reactive, waiting for something to happen and then trying to take advantage of it. Weber agreed. He would like to have seen more attempts being made to find evidence and, especially, ways to contradict the Simses' statements.

But Weber was impressed by McCain's attitude. He was open to advice and recommendations from everyone, and that was reflected in the way his men were dealing with the other cops who had come to help. They were anxious to soak up everything they could about the Simses from the cops who already knew them so well. It was a mark of McCain's leadership, Weber thought.

With that rape trial the next morning, Don decided not to stay too late at Alton. He asked if anyone wanted to go for a beer. When he got no takers, he decided to head for home. He intended to drive past the Simses' house, but he couldn't find this average little house plopped down in some average little neighborhood in an average little town in middle America that had just become national news. He drove around for a few minutes before giving up and heading for home outside the small town of Carpenter, some ten miles away.

On the drive, Don reflected on the talent working the case, the intensity of the feelings of the cops, and the incredible set of facts.

This is going to be some case, he thought. Even with the series of bizarre cases he'd handled, he wondered how any case could be more remarkable or challenging than this Sims mess.

It already was clear to him that the key to a successful prosecution, if the case remained circumstantial, was putting the two crimes together in front of a jury. Reaching back to his experience in the Hanei poison doughnut case, Don knew that it would be vital that the jury see the whole picture—Loralei's death in 1986 tied directly and identically to Heather's three years later.

Weber was glad the FBI psychological profile was in use already. It had been uncanny how accurate the feds had been with their predictions in the Karla Brown case.

This could be some case, he thought.

At Tuesday's press conference, McCain said the police still held out hope that Heather would be found alive, and the case was still being investigated as a kidnapping. Again, he refused to call the Simses suspects, or to eliminate them as suspects. The canvasses of the Simses' neighborhood had failed to find anyone who had seen a kidnapper. "But that doesn't mean there wasn't one," he added unenthusiastically.

But then he surprised the reporters by announcing that he had a statement to read from the FBI's National Center for the Analysis of Violent Crime. McCain said the FBI predicted that guilt would drive the person responsible for the crime to "suffer severe anxiety as time passes, and that anxiety will manifest itself in behavior that the subject will be unable to control."

The reporters seemed stunned. What did that mean? They asked for more. Could McCain explain the statement or elaborate on what kind of behavior he was referring to? Could he say how the police might become aware of such uncontrollable behavior? Could he explain why he had released that part of the statement?

McCain would not discuss it further. Although the reporters obviously were uncertain about the statement and what it meant, they dutifully reported it in their stories and on television.

Everything connected to Heather's disappearance had run in such dramatic parallels to Loralei's death that the police decided to play that angle out. Larry Trent suggested another search of the woods where Loralei's body had been found. He was convinced Heather's body would be found, and leaving it at the same place as Loralei's might have been some kind of logical, if perverted, thing to do. To Trent, it seemed that Paula's Christian upbringing might force her to leave Heather's body where it could be found and buried. And that would give Paula a chance to grieve, get some more attention, and, perhaps, some sympathy.

The police called in State Trooper Michael Donovan and Judd, the dog that had found Loralei's body. On Tuesday, Ventimiglia and Donovan drove to the small house outside of Brighton. But this time, Judd found nothing.

The dog also searched the woods behind the Simses' house in Alton and behind the school next door, and a wooded area where a caller claimed to have seen a woman resembling Paula Sims acting strangely on Friday night. The caller said the woman had stood and gazed into the woods for a few minutes before turning and running down the street. But no scent was found anywhere.

That morning, Hayes took a flight in a state police airplane so he could take aerial photographs and videotapes of the area around the Simses' house. McCain wanted an aerial photograph to map out the terrain.

Another bothersome angle the police were checking was the persistent rumor of overtones of satanic worship and rituals. The detectives got a number of calls from people suggesting that the dates on which the Sims girls had disappeared were holidays on the satanic calendar, perhaps calling for the sacrifice of virgin females. Yocom remembered that there had been similar rumors in 1986, but nothing had been found to support them.

The detectives checked several books on satanism and discovered that almost any day of the year could be a satanic holiday. An expert on satanic worship with the St. Louis County Police Department came over and talked to McCain, but saw nothing to support the idea in this case.

The police also were checking reports that some kind of witches convocation had been held near Kansas City over the weekend, and perhaps that was why the Blews had gone there. The police later debunked that, too.

Weber had checked the satanic angle with DCI Agent Dennis Kuba, an expert on the occult in crime investigations. He told Weber that satanic markings or mutilation of the bodies would accompany such sacrifices, and a number of other factors that appeared to be absent in this case would be needed.

McCain had heard several times that the new owners of the Simses' house near Brighton had found satanic symbols and other items behind a wall torn down during remodeling. Rick was surprised when the owner of the house called because he had heard the same rumor so many times. He told Rick nothing of the sort had happened, and asked that the press be told that. At the next news conference, McCain made that announcement when a television reporter who seemed preoccupied with the satanic angle asked again.

Wednesday, May 3, started out cool and rainy, and with little promise for the police. The detectives were following up more unlikely leads, and Sergeant Pyatt interviewed Robert's father, Troy Sims, at his home in Alton. Mr. Sims said he was convinced that a professional kidnapper was behind these attacks, and that the babies were being sold on the black market. He said Paula was incapable of harming her children, calling her the quietest, most obedient and mousy housewife he had ever seen. In fact, he said, Paula was overprotective of her children because she was afraid something might happen to them.

Orville and Nylene Blew were interviewed at their home by Dooley. They said they had no idea why someone would do this again. Robert and Paula were good parents, and could not have done anything wrong. The Blews confirmed Paula's statement that they had last seen their granddaughter in a visit to the Simses' house the Thursday night before she disappeared. Everything had seemed fine then. Nylene said that nothing notable had been said during a couple of telephone conversations with Paula on Friday. The Blews had left town early Saturday to drive to Orville's sister's home in Peculiar, Missouri, where they received the phone call early Sunday from Robert. Orville's sister and her husband, Donna and Thomas Ewigman, had driven back to Alton with them later that morning.

Paula had not told them much more than the basic story when they got home that afternoon. She and Randy had spent the night at the Blews' home on Sunday, but went back home Monday.

At one point during the day, Hayes and Dooley decided to have some fun with the press. They picked up a couple of empty boxes and threw them into the trunk. When they wheeled up in front of the police station later, they made a big production out of carrying them inside. A reporter asked what was in the boxes, and both cops muttered, "No comment."

The joke was complete later when tape of Hayes and Dooley carrying the boxes was used on television and a reporter announced that the detectives had collected more unknown evidence in the Sims case.

During the next several days, the detectives would be forced to play similar games with the reporters just to keep some of the cops' work discreet. If a detective needed to go somewhere and didn't want the press to follow, several detectives would leave at the same time, all going in different directions. It was fun watching the reporters go crazy trying to decide which cop car to follow.

Trent called Ventimiglia Wednesday morning to see if there was any interest in surveillance on the Simses in light of the psychological efforts being used to force a mistake. Ventimiglia and McCain agreed that the time could be right to start watching Robert and Paula, as well as the homes of the Blews and Condrays.

Ventimiglia told Trent, "If you've got the manpower, go ahead and set it up. But they'll probably be watching for it."

Trent and Watson knew it would take a while to line up enough agents. At least two cars would be needed on each of the three locations. Another two roving cars would be needed, as would a couple of vans for cover. Each agent would cost about twenty dollars per hour, with time-and-a-half for overtime. It would cost several thousand dollars a day for this surveillance.

With that in mind, Trent and Watson wanted to be sure it would be effective. If surveillance was started during daylight, there was a good chance the Simses would spot the agents. Watson knew that Robert already believed the DCI had been watching him for some time, even before Heather disappeared.

To be sure they stayed covert, they wouldn't set up before dusk—sometime between 6:00 and 8:00 P.M.

So, thirty years of combined experience in police work between the two lieutenants was applied in an intelligent, well-reasoned, logical, and crucial decision. Months later, Trent and Watson would mock themselves for trying to be too crafty, and for letting that cost them a chance at the big score.

Chapter 11

The public access area on the west end of the old Locks and Dam 26 is tucked away about a half-mile off U.S. Route 67 in St. Charles County, Missouri, near the small town of West Alton. The turnoff is only a few hundred yards from the decrepit old Lewis and Clark Bridge that soars high above the Mississippi River to connect Alton on the east to the commercial districts in the St. Louis area on the west. The rocky, bumpy road leads off the highway and through the trees, crosses a set of railroad tracks, and then smooths out into a wide, gravel parking lot. Just over the earthen levee is the river, and a popular spot for some pretty good fishing. The view of Alton across the water is unobstructed, and the white stone walls of the police station are unmistakable.

Charles Saunders of nearby Overland, Missouri, had fished there often for years. On Wednesday, May 3, he pulled in just before 7:00 P.M., walked over the levee, and fished for a half-hour or so. When he got back to his car, he took a few minutes to add a quart of STP Oil Treatment to the crankcase, walked over to the sidewalk near the rest rooms, and dropped the empty can into a trash barrel.

The black plastic trash bag sitting on the bottom of the barrel caught his eye. It was kept company only by a Taco Bell drink cup, an empty soda bottle, and the STP can. A knot had been tied in the top of the bag and there was a bulge in one end, about the size of a head of lettuce. Mr. Saunders hefted the bag. It obviously was too heavy to contain just a small amount of garbage. He took out his pocket knife, reached in and slit the plastic.

It could have been a doll lying there in the bottom of the bag. But Mr. Saunders knew immediately that the perfectly preserved, pink and naked body of the infant lying face up in that bag probably was the missing little girl from just across the river, Heather Lee Sims. It was a heartbreaking, gut-wrenching sight.

"Oh, my God," Charles Saunders murmured in a choked whisper.

Rick McCain had been able to get home at a decent hour Wednesday, about 7:00 P.M., much to the surprise of his wife, Janet. Her parents were visiting, and the discussion had turned to the Sims case about the time the telephone rang, just before eight o'clock. A police dispatcher told Rick that the St. Charles County Sheriff's Department thought Heather's body had been found in a trash can. Rick ordered Ventimiglia, Dooley, and Hayes called out.

McCain dashed to his car. For the first time in his career, he slapped the red, emergency "Kojak" light on the roof of his unmarked Ford T-Bird and drove like a lunatic across the narrow bridge to the access area. He thought immediately of the FBI's psychological tactics.

"Son of a bitch. It worked."

But remembering 1986, he wondered about the condition of the body, and he worried over losing control to another police agency.

He was the first Alton cop there and found that there were only a couple of detectives from St. Charles County at the scene. Rick was met by a young detective named Steve Roach, who asked him to stay in the parking lot, well back from the barrel, until the detectives had a chance to check out the scene and until St. Charles County Sheriff Edward Uebinger arrived to take charge. McCain agreed, even though he was anxious to confirm that it was Heather. He hoped that Roach's request was a positive sign that the St. Charles County guys would handle the scene carefully and professionally until Alton could take over.

Ventimiglia and Dooley arrived a few minutes later. Ventimiglia laughed as he told McCain that the two detectives mistakenly had gone to the construction site of the new locks and dam downstream. They had startled three construction workers drinking beer in the mobile-home office by walking in and asking where the body was. The unsuspecting workers had been more puzzled than the cops.

But McCain's account of what the St. Charles County detective had said soon changed Ventimiglia's mood. He didn't take McCain's patient, philosophical view of being kept away from the body.

"This is our case," he sputtered angrily. "We should be up there supervising the scene. At least they ought to let us up there to help. They're acting like we don't know what the hell we're doing."

Rick tried to calm him down.

"Come on, Tony. It's their case right now. They're just trying to preserve the scene until they figure out what's going on and can collect the evidence. That's fine. Let them do that. They'll let us up there pretty soon, and when we verify that it's Heather, then it'll be our case."

Dave Hayes was in a Lamaze class with his pregnant wife, Julie, when his beeper went off. His cop's intuition was on target. *This is the body,* he thought.

The DCI surveillance teams had swung into action right on time Wednesday evening. Cars set up at each location about 6:30, just as dusk fell. They had been in place about an hour when Agent Rich Kruse, who was watching the Sims house, decided to call home to let his seventeen-year-old daughter, Kelly, know that he would be out late, if not all night. Kruse called from a nearby pay phone, and Kelly's first comment floored him.

"Hey, you guys done good."

"What do you mean?"

"You found the body."

"Wait a minute. What do you know that I don't know?"

"I just heard it on TV. They said you found a body that you think is her in a rest area over in West Alton."

Kruse couldn't believe it. Could it be true? If it were true, that meant that they might have caught the killers redhanded if they had set up surveillance earlier that day. "Shit."

While Kruse was getting the word, the other agents

were picking up radio traffic on the Alton police fre-
quency that was suggesting the discovery of the body.

Trent was driving to Alton from home sometime after 8:00
P.M. to check on the surveillance when he heard Kruse radio
the other DCI agents about the news. Trent was stunned.
The pressure had worked, and someone dumped the body.
And DCI could have caught them if they had set up earlier.
Trent could only think of one word. *Shit*.

The cops had been wrong on two major assumptions.
The body had not been disposed of already, as everyone
assumed. And now, what they had been sure wouldn't
happen, had happened. It had been moved right under
their noses. They thought surveillance might catch someone checking on the hiding spot for the body, or going
to talk to someone about what had happened. But no one
had suspected that the body would be moved. Damn.

Shortly after Sheriff Ed Uebinger arrived at the access
area, he came over and introduced himself to McCain.
He was a tall, mustachioed young man who seemed
pleasant enough. He wanted everyone kept away from the
barrel until the evidence had been collected. McCain still
was trying to be open-minded, and he wanted to avoid
causing a problem with another agency. But he thought
the sheriff was overdoing it a little, and he didn't much
care for what seemed to be a slightly superior attitude by
the sheriff. Uebinger obviously wasn't interested in any
comments from the Alton police.

When another deputy came over a few minutes later
and asked the Alton cops to move their cars farther away
from the scene, McCain thought Ventimiglia would blow
a gasket.

"Who do they think they are? We wouldn't treat another agency like this. This *is* our case, after all. These
clowns don't know the first thing about this case and
they're not even asking us."

The reporters had begun arriving and were being kept
at the rear of the parking lot. Uebinger released some
sketchy information about how the body was found and
described it as "fairly well preserved." Part of his account, however, turned out to be inaccurate. He said that

the body had been found by a fisherman who had seen someone acting suspicious near the trash can. When the fisherman approached, the other person left, and the fisherman then found the body. Uebinger would not identify the suspicious person as a man or a woman.

The press would not learn for six months that Uebinger had blended statements from two different men. Charles Saunders had found the body, but it was another fisherman who had seen a young man standing idly near the trash barrel. The fisherman later helped the police put together a composite drawing of the other man, but it wasn't a good match for anyone close to the case. The man was later assumed to be uninvolved and probably just waiting for someone in the rest rooms.

But Uebinger's sessions with the press that night infuriated the Alton cops, who feared that too much information would be released before they could figure out what had happened and what was appropriate to say publicly.

Roach finally came over to McCain and said one officer from Alton would be allowed to view the body. McCain figured it was Ventimiglia's right as case agent. But Tony shook his head.

McCain urged him again.

Finally, Ventimiglia said, "Look Rick, I've got to be honest. I can't go up there and look at the body."

"What do you mean you can't go up there? This is your case."

"Hey, look. I've seen dead bodies before. I've seen a lot of dead bodies before. But I cannot do it on a kid. Not on a baby."

So McCain turned to Dooley. As Dooley approached the barrel, he braced himself for a view of a badly decomposed little corpse. But when he peered over the edge of the barrel, he was amazed to see the perfectly preserved body. Her head was turned slightly to the right, but it was clear that it was Heather.

Roach looked up. "It's yours, isn't it?"

Dooley nodded slowly. "Yeah. That's her."

The body was in such good condition that Dooley thought she must have been dead for a very short time. But then he noticed that the lividity—the red tone to the

skin caused by the settling of the blood after death—was
on the front. The body had been face down for some time
after death, and death had come long before the body
was placed in the barrel. Dooley also noticed a bright
red mark on the baby's left cheek.

He walked back to McCain and nodded. "It's Heather.
There's no doubt about it. It's ours, all right."

Then he offered his surprising conclusion.

"It looks like she just died within an hour. But the
lividity is wrong and she has a bright red mark on her
face that must be freezer burn. I think this kid has been
frozen or something. There's no other explanation for all
of that."

Over the next few minutes, Dooley felt the full impact
of what had happened, and the hair on the back of his
neck stood up. This was for real now. Heather was really
dead, and her little body was in that silver-colored barrel,
right over there. He surveyed the parking lot. There had
to be at least forty other trash barrels, and the body was
in the one where it was most likely to be seen—right by
the rest rooms and the sidewalk.

Dooley wondered about the person responsible for this,
and he felt rage, frustration, and disgust course through
him. *Who the hell are we dealing with? What kind of
person does any of this?*

Ventimiglia was angry, too, but his anger was directed
at St. Charles County. Despite that, he still was offering
some good advice to the other detectives. He suggested
calling in the crime scene technicians from DCI—Dee
Heil or Mark Johnsey—so they could use their "electro-
static lifter," a device that could life footprints from dust.
That would preserve the several footprints visible in the
soft, loose dust about twenty feet from the trash barrel.
Heil and Johnsey were experienced crime scene techs, and
probably could be at the scene within thirty minutes. But
the reaction from the Missouri cops made it clear they
didn't want assistance from any Illinois cops.

It wasn't long, however, until Uebinger announced that
he had called in the FBI.

Ventimiglia's minimal patience was evaporating rap-
idly.

"What do we need the FBI for? They're great at what

they do, but I don't think there's been a bank robbery here. They do bank robberies. This isn't even a federal case. They can't even file a murder charge.''

His anger was spreading contagiously to Dooley and Hayes, but Dooley was trying not to sway McCain into doing something he might not want to do.

The final straw for Ventimiglia came when Uebinger led a line of photographers from the media up to the scene, within ten feet of the body.

''We're over here sitting on our thumbs, and he's escorting the damned press up to the scene? We can't get within 100 yards, and the press is walking up there like they own the place. They're getting more information that we are, and it's our case.''

He stormed off and sat in his car. It wouldn't take much for him to throw a punch at the sheriff and, although that would do wonders for Ventimiglia's disposition, it wouldn't help the case.

The St. Charles County crew spent about three hours photographing the scene and collecting evidence. They scooped up bits of broken glass, soil samples, and bits of trash and debris from the barrel, the area around it, and the nearby rest rooms.

Finally, the word came that Hayes would be allowed to come up and take some pictures and videotape. They were preparing to take the body out of the barrel and put it in the crime-scene van for delivery to the medical examiner's office. An autopsy by the medical examiner, Dr. Mary Case, already was being scheduled for the first thing the next morning.

Hayes and McCain were thrilled that Dr. Case would do the autopsy. She had hosted the seminar they had attended the week before, and they were impressed with her expertise. Although Heather couldn't speak, the cops knew that her little body would tell everything it knew to Dr. Case the next day. McCain told Hayes and Dooley to attend the autopsy and get as much information as they could from the doctor.

But Hayes's first thought was that taking the body out of the barrel now was exactly the wrong thing to do. They should leave it as is and take it to Dr. Case so all of it could be processed at the morgue to avoid losing fingerprints or other evidence. There was no hurry to get the body out now. But St. Charles County obviously wasn't interested in advice. Hayes just took the pictures.

As the bag was lifted out and Heather's tiny, naked body was placed on a white sheet on the ground, the woman detective taking the photos for St. Charles County broke down into loud sobs and cried uncontrollably. Hayes couldn't help but think about his baby that would be delivered within a few weeks. Heather and Hayes's baby might have known each other. They might have gone to school together. But that would never happen now.

When the FBI arrived, McCain was introduced to Special Agent Carl Schultz from the St. Louis office. Schultz was an impressive man with the perfect FBI presence. Even without seeing the Marine Corps tie tack, it would have been easy to guess that kind of background. He carried himself like a career military officer and exuded an aura of command. His deep, resonant voice announced his confidence and competence.

McCain told Schultz that the Alton police had been dealing with Tom Salp of the FBI's National Center for the Analysis of Violent Crime. Schultz knew Salp by name, but had never met him. Schultz graciously offered to put McCain in contact with Salp immediately to see if he had any instructions on how to proceed after discovery of the body.

The next several minutes made Rick feel like a hero in an exciting cop movie. Schultz used his car telephone to call his office and get a call placed to Salp in Washington. Within a few minutes, the FBI had patched a sleepy Salp through to Schultz's phone at the scene, and the agent handed it to McCain.

McCain was dazzled. "Just like in the movies."

He sat in Schultz's car and told Salp what had happened. McCain tried not to sound too excited, trying to retain something of a professional cool.

"It worked, Tom. We found the body. I did exactly what you said to do, and it worked just like you said it would. They made the mistake and we caught them."

Salp was elated. He told McCain to continue to be upbeat in his comments to the press to keep on the pressure. The tactics apparently had worked so far, so it made sense to stay the course. Keep stressing that the police were confident of a successful conclusion to the case. And he said to push hard for new interviews with Robert and Paula as quickly as possible, hopefully within the next twenty-four hours. Salp told McCain to call him back regularly to keep him informed.

Shortly after the body was removed from the barrel, McCain was stunned to hear that the copy of Heather's footprint that Robert had given the police earlier had failed to match the body. The fingerprint analyst for St. Charles County had made the comparison. Had Robert given them a phony footprint in hopes of throwing them off? If he had, he had just opened himself up to some serious trouble—like a charge of obstructing justice.

McCain told the St. Charles County detectives that his officers would get a copy of Heather's footprint from the hospital the next morning to make another comparison. Although it was a surprising development, everyone was sure it would be straightened out the next day with a positive identification as Heather.

(It would be weeks before McCain would find out that the footprint supplied by Robert was genuine, and that the analyst for St. Charles County had been wrong. During those weeks, the police hoped that Robert was open, at least, to an obstructing justice charge that could be used as leverage against him or Paula.)

It was nearly 2:00 A.M. when Uebinger told McCain he was preparing to shut things down. The sheriff invited McCain to bring his men back the next morning to help decide how to proceed and to make a complete search of the access area.

By then, McCain was as angry as his detectives. And it had gone beyond just feeling insulted. McCain and his men had come to hate Uebinger's guts. A good cop wouldn't have played some kind of control game in this case, leaving the cops who knew the facts sitting on the sidelines. Uebinger had treated them with disrespect by keeping them away from the scene and he had insulted them by showing no interest in their suggestions.

When Uebinger suggested that McCain might want to assign one of his detectives to sit with Uebinger's deputy at the scene overnight, Rick's first thought was, *Drop dead. You've slapped us in the face, and now you want one of my detectives to baby-sit one of your patrol deputies. No way.*

McCain politely declined the sheriff's suggestion, but agreed to return the next morning to help search the area.

Driving home, McCain's thoughts were filled with the possibilities. Unlike 1986, they had a nearly perfect body that would yield a cause of death. They had a trash bag, and perhaps other physical evidence. And God only knew what the next day would bring. Following Salp's advice would require convincing Robert and Paula to come in for interviews. That wouldn't be easy, and getting anything out of them would be tougher.

But McCain already was beginning to anticipate facing off again with Robert. Things were different now. This was a murder.

Live news bulletins were being broadcast from the access area that evening, and the discovery of the body was the lead story on all the television stations at 10:00 P.M. It was another incredible event in an already incredible story, and the media ate it up.

Don Weber saw a bulletin when someone flipped on the television at his parents' house while he was there helping them pack up; he was driving them to their new home in Virginia the next day. When the news broke, Don was stunned. He had been convinced the body would never be found. He called Bill Haine, and got the details on the trash bag and the barrel. Don wondered immediately about how much evidence could be collected from the body and the trash bag, but the thought of trying to match the bag to others at the Simses' house never entered his mind.

He hoped some fibers might be found that could link the bag and body to the Simses, or their house or car. Some direct connection between them and their dead baby. Weber had been in Atlanta attending a seminar on violent crime on the day in 1982 when Wayne Williams was convicted of a series of brutal murders. The trial had focused attention on the emerging use of fibers as evidence. If that kind of evidence could be found in Heather's death, it would be a big boost to the prosecution.

Back in Alton, Robert and Paula Sims heard the news the same way as everyone else in the area that night. About 10:30 P.M., Orivlle Blew and Linda Condray arrived almost simultaneously at the Sims house, where a crowd was gathering in the street. Linda stayed with Robert; Orville collected Paula and Randy and took them back to the Blews' home. A photographer for the Alton *Telegraph* captured the scene through Orville's car window. The next day, Paula's stoic face, with little Randy's head tucked against her neck, appeared on the newspaper's front page.

In another eerie parallel to 1986, Paula would never return to her home after the discovery of her daughter's body. The Simses would put the house up for sale for $39,900 on May 16, and would sell it a week later for $35,000.

Thursday morning was overcast and cool. The police and FBI began arriving at the access area about eight o'clock, and the press corps started gathering soon after that. A deputy at the entrance told the reporters that Sheriff Uebinger had said they would not be admitted and there wouldn't be any statement until much later. A steady, cold rain began to fall, scattering the reporters to their cars and vans.

In the motor home brought to the access area as a mobile command center by Uebinger, a meeting of the top police officers in the case was under way. The sheriff conducted the meeting, and McCain realized quickly that it would be more of the same bull he had endured the night before. Uebinger and the FBI were discussing how "they" were going to go about investigating this case, and it wasn't long before McCain tuned them out. It was still Alton's case, and it was going to stay that way. But only a week into his tenure as chief of detectives, McCain decided he wasn't ready to alienate the FBI and the St. Charles County sheriff. McCain hoped to keep his job longer than that.

Larry Trent had met the still-smoldering Tony Ventimiglia at the Alton police station earlier and got a full account of the night's activities. Ventimiglia was angry over the poor treatment, and had serious concerns about the competence of Uebinger and his department. Ventimiglia worried that vital evidence would be lost because of Uebinger's conduct.

Dave Hayes described the condition of the body to Trent, and added that it appeared to have been refrigerated, maybe even frozen. That was a new twist, and Trent realized that it opened up a lot of possibilities about what had happened.

McCain took more than twenty volunteers from the department back to the access area for the search on their own time—from dispatchers to lieutenants. He was proud to show that kind of dedication to Uebinger.

The search was directed by an FBI agent, and Trent was amazed at how poorly it was organized. Sergeant Bill Fitzgerald from Alton had stood over a cigarette package for more than an hour waiting for a photographer to get a picture.

After nearly four hours of covering the area, nothing of value was found.

In the command center, McCain was watching Trent's reaction to the discourse by Uebinger and the FBI. Rick hoped the look on Trent's face meant he was as put off as the Alton cops had been. About twenty minutes into the meeting, Ventimiglia stormed out in disgust. Trent joined him for a cigarette and agreed that his assessment of Uebinger had been accurate.

Trent was amazed that Uebinger was talking about compiling information about the 1986 case and asking for information about the Simses' psychological make-ups. Trent had expected the discussion to concentrate on the search. How could Uebinger assume he would be so deeply involved in the rest of the investigation? It was Alton's case, and Trent didn't see how the discovery of the body in St. Charles County altered that appreciably.

Trent thought McCain was doing a good job of dealing diplomatically with Uebinger. Rick was going out of his way not to cause a problem among the agencies. But Trent could see the growing frustration and impatience in McCain's face.

* * *

McCain's chance to push things in the right direction came sometime after noon. The telephones at the command center failed when the cops tried to call Salp. McCain quickly suggested that his office, just two minutes away, was the most convenient spot to resume operations. That would get the case back into his jurisdiction.

It was obvious to McCain that Uebinger and the FBI were attracted by the lure of publicity, and that meant politics would be creeping into the investigation. McCain wasn't going to stand for it. Chief Downey and Mayor Voumard hadn't interfered or brought politics into it, and McCain wasn't going to let this room full of "strokes" foul this up now that something might be about to break.

So everyone headed for Alton, easing their way through the pack of reporters waiting at the entrance to the access area. No official word was released, but some of the cops mumbled that the operation was moving back to Alton.

While McCain was straining to get things under control, Hayes and Dooley were standing in the autopsy room with an FBI agent and Detective Marsha Hill from St. Charles County. Hayes and Dooley had attended other autopsies before, and sadly, this was the second for an Alton baby in a week. They had attended Terria Graves's the week before.

Dooley looked up as a woman walked in, dressed to the nines in obviously expensive clothes and jewelry. Dooley wondered who she was; she looked like she should have been shopping at the exclusive Frontenac Plaza in nearby Clayton. But Hayes knew her from the seminar. "That's Mary Case," he whispered.

When she came back into the room in her surgical garb and went to work on the autopsy, her expertise was obvious.

She soon called Hayes over. She had curled back the baby's upper lip, and she pointed to three small, vertical cuts on the inside of the lip.

"This is important. Take some pictures of this. These lacerations mean this baby was smothered; this was a homicide. The cuts result from something being held against the outside of the mouth and pushing the inside of the lip against the bony gums underneath.''

When Dr. Case opened up the chest cavity, she immediately said, ''This baby's been either refrigerated or frozen. There are early signs of internal decomposition that are inconsistent with the exterior of the body.''

Hayes and Dooley looked at each other. It make sense and it fit with the theory that there had been an effort made to make it look like Heather had just died shortly before the body was found.

Sometime during the autopsy, the FBI agent muttered, ''I can't take this.'' He left the room.

Dr. Case asked who has handling the case for the state's attorney. Dooley told her it was Don Weber.

''My favorite attorney,'' she said. ''We worked together on the bite mark case several years ago. We used Lowell Levine, the bite mark expert from New York. It was the uh, uh . . .''

''Karla Brown,'' Dooley and Hayes said in unison.

''That's right. The Karla Brown case. I remember that case very well. Don was an assistant state's attorney when it happened and couldn't get anything done on it. Then he became state's attorney, and went back and exhumed the body to get the bite mark evidence. I did the new autopsy on the body and Levine did the bite mark work.''

So Dooley and Hayes left with what they had hoped for, a cause of death and an expert medical opinion that Heather's body had been frozen, and the bonus of close cooperation from an expert who liked the prosecutor.

Three weeks later, when Hayes's daughter was born and weighed in at nine pounds, twelve ounces, Hayes's memory would drift back to Heather and the autopsy. Heather also had weighed nine pounds and twelve ounces that day.

Rick McCain felt back in charge as soon as he arrived at his office with Uebinger, Schults, and Trent. Rick was buoyed by the autopsy report from Dooley and Hayes. The doctor's conclusions were the kind of breaks the police needed to solve this case. And Rick had learned that Heather's footprint from the hospital matched the body, removing that nagging uncertainty.

The cops agreed that the Simses should be brought in for interviews that night. And they decided that the cause of death, the freezing, and the positive identification of Heather would be withheld from the press until Robert and Paula had been interviewed. That way, details that came out during the interrogations would have to be from the Simses' independent knowledge, not from the media reports. A confession with that kind of information couldn't be recanted later.

McCain called Salp to fill him in and get his advice on the interviews. Rick was expecting Salp to reaffirm him as the one to handle the interview with Robert. They already had talked about the rapport that Rick had cultivated with Robert. Robert seemed to like him. So Rick was sure that Salp would give him the go-ahead to take this crucial last shot at Robert.

Instead, Salp began to describe the characteristics of the person who should face Robert. He shouldn't be too young or too old. He should have an authoritative approach and a deep, radio-type voice. He should have a somewhat militaristic and strong manner, polite but firm. The kind of person who would stand out in a crowd as a recognized leader.

McCain looked across the desk at Schultz. Salp was describing his fellow FBI agent to a "T." The only thing missing was Schultz's Marine Corps tie tack. From Salp's description, the man to interview Robert Sims had to be Carl Schultz.

That was a blow to McCain and his ego. He considered himself one of the best police interviewers around, and he certainly wanted another shot at bringing Robert down and solving the case. But McCain couldn't go against Salp now, not after the body had been found. He couldn't reject his advice after he had been dead-solid-perfect on the psychological tactics. So Rick swallowed hard and decided that, if he was going to be wrong, he was going to be wrong on the side of following Salp's advice.

But that meant the FBI would be involved officially in the case now, and Rick didn't like that. He wasn't crazy about the FBI or some of the ways it worked with local police. But the real rub here was more technical. If this were a murder in Madison County, the FBI wouldn't even have jurisdiction.

McCain was bothered by a nagging suspicion that he had been set up. Was the FBI brotherhood at work here? Salp's description had been too close to Schultz to be anyone else. Had it been planned that way, to move the FBI into the inner workings of the investigation now that something might be ready to pop? Rick liked Salp, and he didn't really want to think that had happened. But he wasn't naive, either.

By the time he hung up the phone, he was a little confused and disappointed, and very irritated. It wouldn't take much for him to blow, and Uebinger managed to say exactly the thing that would do it. The sheriff immediately began to plan the "joint" interviews of Robert and Paula, discussing how they were to be done and when they were to be done and by whom they were to be done.

McCain felt his guts tighten. As he stood up, he turned angrily toward the man who had become an expert at infuriating Alton cops in a very short time. This could be Rick's last act as the chief of detectives, but he would go down in style.

"Sheriff Uebinger, you may do anything you want to do, but you and I are not doing anything together." Rick's voice was shaking as the volume rose. "And from now on, we're going to work our investigation and you work yours. If there's something that you need that we have, we will supply you with it. But this joint investigation thing is ceased, as of right now. This is our case, and we will take it from here."

McCain turned stiffly back toward his desk, and glanced over at Trent. There was a slight, almost fatherly nod of approval. Within a few minutes, Uebinger was gone. No one would know how or when he had left. But that was the last contact between the men, and the sheriff's last contact with the case.

McCain apologized to Trent and Schultz.

"I'm sorry, guys. Maybe I shouldn't have done that, and maybe you think I'm being arrogant. But I'm tired of the S.O.B. He doesn't know what he's talking about, and he treated us like crap last night. And I'm not taking it anymore. I've only been chief of detectives for a week, and I don't have all the answers. But I'm sick of him.''

Rick interpreted Schultz' shrug to mean he didn't necessarily disagree. And Trent was nodding again.

An unexpected look into the private side of the Simses, and especially Robert, came about 4:00 P.M. Thursday when Sergeant Bud Pyatt interviewed one of Robert's coworkers with the memorable name of Bill Bailey. A blunt and plainspoken man, Bailey said he had known Robert since he started at the plant in 1974. Robert had been more outgoing then. In some of their many conversations, Robert had revealed that Paula had proposed to him, and that he had accepted, with one condition.

"Robert said he told her that her retarded brother could never set foot on their property and, even if her parents died, the condition would still apply.''

Bailey said Robert had become strange and a loner after Loralei died. Some days, when Bailey spoke to Robert, he would respond. Other days, he would just stare, and then turn away. Robert had become quick to anger, and a chronic complainer at work. He filed repeated written complaints with the company that Bailey said almost always were unfounded.

And, reminiscent of the problems with the woman coworker at the credit union years ago, Bailey told of Robert harassing a black woman at work. Bailey said Robert had put dead cockroaches and a used condom in her sandwich.

Tony Ventimiglia and some of the other Alton officers disagreed with McCain about letting Schultz handle the interview. Ventimiglia was convinced Rick was the right guy for the job. In fact, Ventimiglia thought of himself as the best choice to talk to Paula while Rick was hammering Robert. But McCain said he had to go with Salp's program, since it had brought the case that far.

As plans were made for the rest of the evening, two more ideas emerged.

The first was using women officers to interview Paula again, since Sievers and Morgan had come so close to success in 1986. They obviously couldn't do it again;

Paula would never sit down with them now. Trent offered to bring in two women he knew from the DCI office in Marion, about seventy-five miles south. They were good agents and could be there in time to be briefed before going head to head with Paula while Robert was talking to Schultz.

The second point was the need for more searches at the homes of the Simses and Blews, and of the Simses' two vehicles parked in their driveway. The police hoped to find hairs or fibers that could link the Simses to the dead baby.

But one other major piece of evidence the police were counting on was an opened roll of black plastic trash bags that Sergeant Richard Wells remembered seeing on some shelves in the basement stairwell at the Sims house. The other bags seized by Hayes at the house had been white. Only Wells had remembered seeing the black bags, and he knew right where they were. Thanks to his memory, the police realized that there was a distinct possibility that those bags could be matched to the body bag.

The searches also would focus on the freezers and refrigerators in the family's home, since the police now knew that Heather's body had been kept cool for some time before it was so callously dumped in the trash.

A massive search-warrant raid was planned for that night so all of the targets could be hit while Robert and Paula were at the station being interviewed. The police called Bill Haine and filled him in. He agreed with all of the ideas, and sent Randy Massey to Alton to draw up the search warrant applications with Hayes.

The jury in the rape trial prosecuted by Don Weber had begun deliberations that morning. Weber asked Haine to take the verdict so Don could leave town with his parents as soon as possible. By all accounts, Weber had resumed his career in fine form and a conviction was imminent. But three hours later, the jury returned a surprising and disappointing acquittal, an inauspicious return for Weber. He knew his critics in the defense bar would be rejoicing. But he had other things on his mind.

Amid everything else that was happening, Weber bid an emotional good-bye to the home where his parents had lived for forty years, and where he had been raised. The

Weber family pulled out of town about 5:00 P.M. and headed east.

As Don drove along Interstate 64, cutting through the heart of southern Illinois, the Sims case monopolized his thoughts. With the cruise control engaged and the flat, straight highway in front of him, he had a lot of time to consider the various angles and twists in the case. Maybe the body had been kept in a cooler or ice chest in some isolated area. Could the Blews be helping Paula cover up the deaths of their own grandchildren?

What about the satanism angle? There were so many rumors. No, Don had rejected that as baloney. He had learned a long time ago that such far-out theories usually were just that—too far out and invariably wrong. No, it all came back to Paula Sims. And it was frustrating for Weber to be so far removed from the action in a major case. He liked to be in on the interviews, to trap the suspects by their own statements about alibis. Don knew how such stories unraveled in court if they hadn't been nailed down months before trial in detailed interviews.

He was so lost in his own thoughts that he missed his turnoff at Interstate 57. He had planned to take that route south, and then turn east across the top of Kentucky. He was at least thirty minutes past when he realized he had missed it. He had to adjust his route and head on toward Indiana. He spent the night at Evansville, and got a briefing by phone from Haine on the eventful evening that was just unfolding back in Alton.

Chapter 12

An assembly of reporters and television trucks unlike anything ever seen in downtown Alton, or anywhere else in the St. Louis area, had massed outside the police station Thursday afternoon. Every police officer or prosecutor who arrived or departed was mobbed by hungry reporters who hadn't been fed even a tidbit that day. After days of habit-forming news conferences, gorging themselves on the abundance of minor facts, the reporters were suffering withdrawal pains amid the news blackout.

Bill Haine later compared struggling through the reporters to fighting his way through a band of extra-persistent Hare Krishnas at the airport.

Despite the emergence of the sun by mid-afternoon, the day had turned unusually cool for May. Most of the reporters, equipped for such climatic changes during media stakeouts, had donned heavy coats to wait on the sloping sidewalks outside of City Hall.

On a smaller scale, another blitz was shaping up at the home of Paula's parents. Backup crews from the television stations had arrived in front of the small brick ranch house. The press knew Paula was there.

In the depths of the Alton police station, careful preparations for the all-out assault were under way. Schultz was getting a detailed briefing from Sievers and others on the deaths of Loralei and Heather, the quirky personalities of Robert and Paula Sims, and everything else the cops could remember.

Trent had gone back to his office in Collinsville, and had arranged for DCI Agents Pam Burke and Monica Joost to drive into Madison County to interview Paula that night.

Massey and Hayes were working on the affidavits Hayes would sign to convince a judge that search warrants were justified. The affidavits had to list what items were expected to be found in each of the residences and vehicles, and the basis for that belief.

Pam Burke was driving back to Marion after a training session at DCI headquarters in Springfield when she got the call to go to Alton and meet Monica Joost. They would interview Paula Sims. Pam Burke was vaguely aware of the Sims cases, and she knew she and Joost were being called in because the police hoped women would get farther with Paula.

In an unsettling coincidence, Pam Burke was pregnant with her second child. Her first thought about this assignment was about that maternal paradox.

"Here I am, going to have my second child, and I'm about to confront a woman the police believe has killed her second child."

No one else knew Burke was pregnant. She wondered if her supervisors would have given her the assignment if they had known. She had been pregnant for just over three months, and she hadn't announced it yet because she didn't want to lose good assignments or get special treatment. Her first child, a boy named Robbie, was just a few months older than Randy Sims. Six months later, Pam Burke would deliver a daughter, Karla, and would look back sadly on the night that she faced Paula Sims.

Burke arrived at Trent's office in the late afternoon, and he gave her some of the background. he told her what had happened with Sievers and Morgan in 1986, and what the police hoped she and Joost could accomplish that evening. Burke drove to Alton about 6:00 P.M. and got a detailed briefing from Sievers. Burke tried to hold onto everything Diana told her; she would need it all later in what probably would be the toughest interview of her career.

She also was put on the phone with an FBI psychological profiler from Quantico. He told Burke to do all the talking at first, not giving Paula a chance to speak. Burke was to be sympathetic and understanding, one mother to another. She knew how easy it was to get upset and lose control when the baby kept crying. After painting a sympathetic portrait of such a situation, Burke was to steer Paula toward a confession by saying, "Is this how it was? Is there anything else you want to tell us?"

But based on what she had learned from Sievers, Pam Burke doubted Paula would fall for such a simple approach. She would refuse to talk, or she would try to outmaneuver the cops again. The expert's other advice was to let Paula leave if she wanted.

Burke wondered if it was a crying baby that was behind the crime. Or could it have been the strange boy-girl thing some of the other officers were talking about? How else could you explain a boy that was fine, and two dead daughters? Although the sexual-preference angle was intriguing, Burke thought it would be easier for Paula to "come in" on the crying-baby story. Surely that would be more palatable for Paula.

Meanwhile, Monica Joost had driven in from Marion, meeting Trent on Interstate 55–70 near the DCI headquarters in Collinsville. He led her on a ninety-five-mile-per-hour drive to Alton so she would have time for a briefing from McCain.

Burke and Joost had similar and connected careers. They had been trooper cadets together five years earlier, and both had shifted over to DCI after two years on patrol. They had been in DCI training together, too. Now they would be together when they faced the strangest case of their lives.

When McCain returned to the station after getting something to eat late that afternoon, he was mobbed by reporters again. One asked if McCain was aware that the FBI in Springfield had confirmed that it was Heather's body. McCain mumbled that he had not heard that, and then pushed through the crowd.

Rick was furious. The FBI had violated the agreement by releasing the identification. Rick had hoped to dangle that in front of Robert and Paula to get them into the station for the interviews. But now the Simses would hear it on television. The FBI's blunder could sink the plans, and Rick was irate. It was more proof that some participants were trying to grab a little piece of the Sims case publicity while Alton did most of the work.

* * *

McCain had ducked calls from Robert Sims all day, waiting to speak to him when the trap was set.

As time to pull the Simses in drew closer, McCain still felt uneasy about acquiescing to Schultz. He seemed like a bright guy, apparently very experienced. He certainly seemed confident and in command. But Rick didn't like passing off an important role in his biggest case ever to someone he hardly knew. And his concern about Schultz's interviewing style grew as the agent began setting up the room. He planned to sit across a desk from Robert, contradicting what McCain had learned in several courses on interview technique. He had been taught to sit near the person, to observe body language and perhaps touch the subject on the arm to make him comfortable or gain his confidence. Schultz even admitted it had been some time since he done an interview like this.

But the die was cast. By 6:00 P.M., everything was ready. It was now up to McCain to lure Robert and Paula into the station. He called Robert, who was upset that he had been unable to reach McCain all day.

"Where have you been? You told me I could always call you and they'd get you for me. I've been calling you all day."

"Well, Robert, I've been really busy. Don't you want me working on the case? I'd certainly think you'd want me working on the case rather than taking phone calls. Now, I want to tell you about the baby."

"Well, they said on the television that it was Heather. Was it really Heather?"

McCain shook his head. Robert still wasn't excited. He still was speaking in the calm voice that was so hard to take.

"That's what I wanted to talk to you about. But I don't want to do it on the telephone. Can you and Paula come down to the station tonight?

For the first time, McCain actually could sense some apprehension, maybe even fear, in Robert's voice. He obviously was concerned about what the police might have now. He didn't mind being an informed witness, but he didn't want to be a suspect.

"Well, uh, I don't know if we can make it. We've got

to take care of Randy, and I just don't see how both of us can come down there, and—''

McCain bluffed, his voice impatient. "Well, fine, Robert. You tell me you want information about Heather and you can't even come down to the station to get it. I can't leave the station and come over to your house to tell you. You know the press will follow me if I do, and you'll have all those reporters at your front door. Is that what you really want me to do?''

"Well, no. But, uh . . .''

"I'll tell you what I'll do. If you come down here, I'll open the basement door for you and wait for you there. The press will see you, but you'll be able to drive right into the building and I'll close the garage door behind you.''

Robert hesitated briefly to weigh his options. "Well, I'll come, but Paula can't come. She needs to stay with Randy.''

"Hey, look. I need to talk to both of you about this. I can't talk to you on the phone about it. You know how the press is. They might be listening to us now.''

"Okay. We'll come down.''

McCain hung up, and then nodded his head in victory. Robert probably knew what McCain was doing, but he couldn't resist the challenge. His curiosity compelled him to find out what the police knew, and even fear couldn't stop him. That's what McCain had counted on; just like Salp had said. The combination of guilt and his belief that he was so intellectually superior to the cops wouldn't let him stay away. No matter what the cops had, Robert knew he could handle it.

The detectives formed two squads to execute the search warrants that night. Ventimiglia, Hayes, and Dooley would go to the Sims house, joined by McCain later. They also invited Detective Roach from St. Charles County to accompany them. Meanwhile, the search of the Blews' house would be conducted by Sullivan, Wells, Pyatt, and Patrolman Larry Parks, the evidence officer. The groups would leave the station and hide from the reporters until McCain radioed the signal to descend on the targets.

Dooley and Hayes left the station and made a couple of quick turns to ditch the television crews. The cops pulled into a parking lot on Broadway and laughed as the television minivans zipped up and down the street looking for them.

At 8:30 P.M., McCain opened the basement garage door to let Robert and Paula into the station. Rick was surprised to see them in a car he didn't recognize being driven by a man he didn't know. The chauffeur was Herb Condray, a new cast member for Rick.

Three minutes later, McCain gave the signal for the searches to proceed.

Trent thought Schultz seemed tense as he waited to talk to Robert. As the agent started to leave the room, one of the cops wished him luck. Schultz turned and said quietly, "You guys say a prayer for me." A couple of the cops chuckled, reacting as if Schultz were joking. Without a hint of a smile, Schultz said, "I'm serious, guys. I'm serious. Would you say a prayer?"

Trent realized that Schultz's comment was genuine. The FBI agent knew the importance of this interview, and he was seeking help from a greater power. So Trent said a prayer.

McCain had escorted his three guests upstairs. He thanked Condray for helping the Simses and asked him to wait in the lobby. Rick asked Paula to wait there for a minute, and he took Robert through the door into the hallway outside of McCain's office. Robert didn't know that there was a growing number of cops and prosecutors hiding just behind McCain's door. Rick dropped his voice.

"Look, Robert. It was Heather, the body that we found. I wanted you to know that.'

No reaction. Robert didn't blink. McCain, still thinking Robert had given the police the wrong footprint, noted that Robert didn't show any surprise at the identification.

Robert asked calmly, "Are they sure? Are they really sure?"

"Yes, Robert. They're sure."

McCain began walking Robert toward the detective room and the waiting Schultz.

"The FBI is here. They're involved because this could be a kidnapping case and the body was found in Missouri. They would like to talk to you. You don't have to talk to them if you don't want to. But the man would like to get the information from you like you gave it to me."

"What does he want to ask me?"

"He wants to ask you the same kind of questions I did. Robert, just go in there and, if you don't like the man and you see a problem, don't talk to him. At least give him a shot. He's a nice guy. I worked with him today."

Robert nodded. Another chance to square off with the feds.

McCain took Robert into the room and introduced him to Schultz. As the men shook hands, McCain walked out.

He stuck his head into his office and announced, "Well, I got one. Now, I'll go for the other one."

He called Paula into the hallway.

"Paula, the FBI is here and they're talking to Robert. He wanted to talk to them and he's back there talking to them now."

McCain was sure Robert had told Paula not to talk to the police. Rick was hoping Paula would think Robert had changed his plans and was back there cooperating with the FBI, maybe even incriminating her. McCain steered Paula into a nearby room and sat down with her.

"I wanted to let you know that, unfortunately, it was Heather that we found over there. Please accept my sympathy. I'm very sorry to have to tell you that."

McCain spoke softly, and in the same monotone that the Simses usually used.

"Robert's in there talking to the FBI. He's going to try to help us get this straightened out, and I hope you'll do the same. We're not here to cause you trouble. But you know there are some problems with this case. You know that. Now, you and I seem to get along okay, and I don't have any problems with Robert."

About that time, Pam Burke and Monica Joost walked down the hall past the open doorway. McCain feigned surprise, and then called them into the room. He introduced them, and then pretended that he had to take a phone call. It was a transparent story, but it was the best he could do.

Pam Burke sat down next to Paula and Monica Joost sat down closer to the door, a little behind and to the right of Paula. As she had been instructed, Burke started talking without allowing Paula to speak.

"Paula, you know, I'm a mother, too. I can understand these things. I can sympathize. I've had nights where the baby was colicky, and I understand what that's like, how it can get to you."

As she parroted the FBI's instructions, she watched for some reaction. Not much, perhaps a little anger or resentment about being there. But she was cold, no emotion. Burke had expected a few tears, perhaps, from a woman who had just been told her baby was found in the trash.

"I know what it's like to be tired and frazzled, and the baby keeps crying. I know . . ."

Without a word, Paula pushed her chair back and stood up. She had heard enough. She turned and walked out of the room.

Pam Burke was shocked. She felt the bottom fall out of her stomach. Her first thought was that she had been given this important duty and big opportunity, and she had failed.

The agents followed Paula into the hallway, where she obviously was looking for Robert. She began to call out for him.

"Where's Robert? I want to see Robert. Robert said I didn't have to talk to you. Where's Robert? We're leaving right now."

Trent came out of McCain's office as Paula started down the hall toward the room where Robert was being interviewed. She was getting louder, and Trent was afraid Robert would hear her.

But she turned and went back out to the lobby where Herb Condray was waiting. Within minutes, Trent heard Herb protesting loudly, calling for Robert to be sent out so they could leave.

Trent and FBI Agent Jim Quick hurried into the lobby and told Herb to quiet down. But he kept blathering that the police had no right to do this and that he was going to call a lawyer. Paula was chiming in, too, demanding that her husband be sent out so they could go home immediately.

"We don't care what you do," Trent finally told them. "If you don't like it, leave. But Robert is not coming out. If you want to call a lawyer, call a lawyer. We don't care what you do."

Herb Condray added a new threat. "Well, I'm going to go out and talk to the press."

Trent almost laughed. That group of reporters out there would eat him alive. "The press is right out there. Go ahead and talk to them."

Herb suggested to Paula that they leave without Robert; she agreed. Trent followed them to the basement garage and watched them drive away.

Pam Burke walked dejectedly over to Diana Sievers. "Diana, I blew it."

"No you didn't, hon. There wasn't anything else you could have done. She would have done the same thing to anyone tonight. It wasn't your fault, so don't blame yourself."

Burke and Joost stayed the rest of the evening, waiting with the other cops to hear what was happening with Robert. Burke was terribly frustrated; she knew McCain and Schultz had pinned their hopes on that interview with Paula. Burke couldn't help but wonder if there was something else she could have done. What if she had started with the boy-girl thing? Would Paula have stayed to hear her out, or tried to debunk the idea? Those questions would stay with Pam Burke forever.

And she wanted desperately to tell someone she was pregnant that night. She felt the need to share that secret with someone after facing Paula that way. But she bit her tongue. She would wait another two weeks before telling the others that her thoughts that night also had been on another baby. Two mothers, from different worlds.

By the time the detectives arrived at the two houses with the search warrants, large crowds were forming at both locations. And the reporters who had staked out the homes were waiting.

The doors at the Sims house were locked, and Dooley

gave some thought to kicking in one of them. But he realized that nothing would look sillier on the news at ten o'clock than a cop's unsuccessful attempt to kick open a door. And, if he kicked the door and it didn't open, chances are he would fall on his butt. That would make some great news footage he would never live down.

He went to the window on the front of the house and tried to force up the wooden sash to pop open the lock. Instead, the glass in the window shattered.

To the cops' surprise, a loud cheer went up from the several hundred people crowded along the Simses' property under the glare of the television lights; the ovation described the mood in Alton about the Sims family. The people lined the fence along the west side of the driveway and were pushed up against the five-foot chain-link fence around the front yard, straining to see every move the cops made on the front porch.

As the window splintered, Dooley stepped back and tried to look as if he had meant for that to happen. As he and Hayes glanced at each other and shrugged, shards of glass fell out of the frame at their feet. The smaller Hayes crawled through the window, trying to avoid the remaining pieces of glass in the frame, and hoping that he wouldn't tear the brand-new suit he was wearing. He unlocked the front door to let in Ventimiglia, Dooley, and Roach.

Hayes went right to the shelves in the basement stairwell and picked up two rolls of black "Curb Side" brand trash bags from K-mart. Each roll contained fifty bags; one was opened and one still was sealed. Hayes also picked up two black bags full of trash outside the house.

The importance of all of the bags was becoming clearer. Hayes realized that the difference in the white and black bags could be significant. If they got a break, maybe the perforations on the bag Heather was in would match those on the one sticking out of the roll.

The search of the Simses' refrigerator and its freezer drew a blank. A dusty freezer in the basement, hidden by some wallboard and other scrap, apparently was unused and yielded no evidence. A pair of tennis shoes was taken to check the pattern on the sole with the footprints

188 Don W. Weber and Charles Bosworth, Jr.

left near the trash barrel. The FBI might be able to compare them to the photos of the footprints.

One of the many books on the Simses' shelves also caught the detectives' attention. It was called "The Stash Book," and one chapter discussed how to hide a person in a house using methods such as false walls. The book appeared to be a primer on hiding drugs. But the chapter on hiding a person qualified it as possible evidence, so it was seized.

McCain drove up just as the detectives were finishing the search of the house. As he stepped out of his car and was recognized by the crowd, the people burst into cheers and applause. For the second time in as many evenings, Rick had the feeling that he was living a role from some movie. It was strange, but he had to admit it felt good. Cops don't always get cheers like that from the public.

But the crowd seemed to be in such a jovial mood that some of the reporters wandering through the people were troubled. How close was that to a vigilante mentality, or to a lynch mob? The people didn't seem violent or threatening. But it was obvious that they believed the Simses were responsible for their daughters' deaths, and the crowd seemed to sense that justice might be near. It was a partisan crowd, and the cops were the heroes.

A newspaper photographer suggested, "Someone ought to set up a refreshment stand." It wasn't long before a neighbor of the Simses, who had been interviewed by nearly every reporter on the story, sent her children through the crowd to tell the journalists that free coffee and doughnuts had been set up for them at the woman's house.

Downtown, the huge press corps at the police station had been joined by a growing crowd of curious citizens as the word spread about the night's dramatic events. The group wasn't as boisterous as the crowd outside the Sims home. But word of the events on Washington Avenue was spreading outside City Hall.

After the detectives finished in the Simses' house, they moved to the garage. A pair of boots in the bed of a pickup truck had a design on the soles that looked similar to some of the footprints at the access area. Hayes also vacuumed the carpeting in the brown Chevy station wagon and the silver Jeep CJ-5 to try to collect fibers.

In Cottage Hills, the four detectives were admitted into the home by a polite but reserved Orville Blew. Interesting discoveries were being made there, too. What appeared to be a blonde hair had been found in the bottom of the Blews' freezer in the basement. And an infant's sleeper-pajama, with a bunny pattern like the one Heather had been wearing, was found in a spare bedroom. The police also took a roll of black trash bags from the basement and a single bag that was lying on top of a refrigerator next to the freezer. A hairbrush and some hair in the bristles were seized in the spare bedroom where Paula had been sleeping.

The detectives also took a pair of bib overalls from a hallway closet, two pairs of boots, and two pairs of gloves.

Robert had taken the FBI bait just as the police had expected. It would be an interesting matchup: two calm, cool men staring into each other's eyes and waiting for the opponent to blink first.

Schultz took command immediately.

"Mr. Sims, I want you to understand that you are not under arrest. You are not in custody. You may leave at any time you wish and no one will try to stop you."

"All right."

Schultz made sure his voice was commanding, but not intimidating. He spoke softly, but with the edge of authority that would establish him as the one in charge.

"Now, I don't want you to say anything right now, or to try to answer any questions. I just want you to sit there and listen to me for a minute. Mr. Sims, you should know that all indications point to you and your wife as the prime suspects in the disappearances and deaths of both of your daughters. The stories your wife has told in both of these incidents are totally preposterous, and no jury in its right mind would believe them in a trial. It is completely absurd to claim that one person—one kidnapper and killer—has singled out a family over a period of three years and has come into that family's house twice and taken the family's children—both girls—and then

killed them. I have never heard of anything like that, and
neither has any other policeman on this case. How can
you expect anyone to believe that? How can you expect
anyone to believe anything other than that your wife is
responsible for your daughters' deaths, and that these ridiculous stories were concocted to cover up for her acts?''

Robert had been staring calmly at Schultz. As the agent
finished, Robert began to shake his head. It was his move,
and he slipped right into his pat story.

''All I can say is that we have told you the truth. We
have told you what happened and everything that we
know about what happened. I don't have any firsthand
knowledge of what happened to my daughters. I haven't
been involved in this directly. All I can tell you is what
my wife has told me and what I know about it. I have no
reason to doubt what Paula has said happened in either
case. I believe her, and I am being totally honest and
truthful about all of this.''

The two men bantered back and forth for a half-hour.
Finally, Schultz excused himself and told Robert he
would be back in a few minutes. He walked out, leaving
Robert alone.

Trent had been pacing the hallway outside the interview room, listening carefully and nervously to some of
the dialogue that filtered out through the ventilating duct.
He was surprised when Schultz walked out of the room
and closed the door behind him.

Schultz stepped back into McCain's office and poured
himself a cup of coffee, surprising the rest of the cops.
Another FBI agent wrote down the time Schultz walked
in, and later recorded the time he went back into the
interview room. Schultz told everyone that he was encouraged because Robert was talking freely, but added
that he was sticking firmly to the story. It appeared Robert was enjoying the game.

By then, reports had come in that the police at the
Blews' had found what was thought to be a hair in the
freezer and had recovered a baby's sleeper like the one
Heather was supposed to have been wearing. Schultz was
glad to get some hard facts to use against Robert.

When the agent returned to the room, he informed
Robert that search warrants had been executed at his

house and the Blews' home. Robert was surprised, but he held his reaction to a minimum.

Watching for more reaction, Schultz told Robert about the hair in the freezer and the baby's sleeper.

This time, Robert's reaction was more obvious. He looked down at the desk, and slowly began to shake his head. He was silent for a time, and Schultz let him sit there. That rattled him, the agent thought.

When Robert looked up, he said, "I've never wanted to believe that Paula was involved in our babies' deaths. But now, I think I have to."

That deliberative voice was even softer now.

"Paula has been a good mother and a good wife, and I don't think she would have hurt the children on purpose, or that she would have meant to do it. If she did, then she needs help. She couldn't really have known what she was doing at the time."

Schultz sensed that the tough veneer around Robert was starting to crack. It was time to apply the pressure and to give him a chance to take himself out of it, and to implicate Paula.

"Mr. Sims, if your wife did it, as you say you believe now, how could she have done these things without you knowing about it?"

"Paula had keys to her parents' house and she has access to the house any time. Her mom and dad were out of town. She could have put Heather's body in the freezer sometime while I was asleep. And she could have taken the body over and put it at the dam area while I was asleep. I wouldn't have known about it."

Robert was moving in the right direction. He asked if any tire marks from Paula's station wagon had been found at the access area. Schultz bluffed, saying he couldn't divulge all the evidence.

When McCain and the other detectives returned to the station after eleven o'clock, Schultz was on another coffee break.

McCain was floored. Schultz had left Robert alone in the room in the middle of an interview? That violated everything McCain had ever learned in classes and in experience. Leaving Robert alone with his thoughts could only strengthen him, giving him time to work on his answers.

But McCain was encouraged by Schultz's report that Robert had said Paula might have had something to do with the girls' deaths.

When Schultz returned to the fray, he asked Robert if he was worried about his son.

"Randy is the number-one interest in my life. I would do anything for that boy. I've been thinking that, if Paula was invoved in the babies' deaths, and I have to believe she was now, then Randy could be in real danger from her. Is there some way the authorities could take Randy from Paula right now? Some way to put him in protective custody with my brother in Texas, or maybe Paula's relatives near Kansas City?"

"I don't know about the local laws, Mr. Sims. That would be something for the local authorities." Schultz wondered if Robert was using Randy to steer the interview away from the killings.

Robert was shaking his head again. "I'm very concerned for Randy's safety."

He held his fists together out in front of him, and twisted them.

"Paula could wring his neck in just a few seconds. I think he could be in danger from her at any time."

Schultz took another break.

Just after 10:00 P.M., while Robert and Schultz were in the middle of their standoff, another startling development began shaping up in the small vestibule at the entrance to the police department. Donald Groshong, the lawyer from Alton who had handled Robert's divorce eleven years ago, walked into the station and asked to be admitted into the interview with Robert.

Charlie Bosworth, the lead reporter on both of the Sims cases for the *Post-Dispatch*, was talking to an editor on the pay telephone in the vestibule when Groshong walked in. The two men knew each other well after years of trials and hundreds of cups of coffee. Bosworth hadn't heard what Groshong had said to the dispatcher, but it wasn't hard to guess.

As Groshong passed, he nodded and smiled faintly, a

look that the reporter immediately understood. Bosworth was well acquainted with Groshong as a crafty and resourceful criminal-defense attorney, and a friend of Weber's. What a battle it would be if those two squared off on this case!

While Bosworth was getting off the phone, Groshong was buzzed through the security door and went over to the desk. The dispatcher asked him to wait until someone in charge could be reached in the detective section.

Bosworth signaled for Groshong to come back out into the vestibule. As Groshong came through the door, he grinned again, and the game was on. Bosworth returned the grin, and the men leaned against the wall.

"Don, what are you doing here?"

"Well, I'm here."

"I can see that. Why are you here?"

"I'm here."

"Right. Might you be here representing a client who might be here being interviewed by the police?"

"Let's just say I'm here."

Bosworth grinned again. "Why do I suddenly feel like Robert Redford?"

Groshong laughed out loud. He knew immediately that Bosworth was referring to the scene in the movie *All the President's Men,* where Redford, playing *Washington Post* reporter Bob Woodward, was trying in vain to get some information out of an attorney at a court appearance for the Watergate burglars. The exchange had been almost identical to the one between Groshong and Bosworth. The reporter knew that Groshong, a movie buff, would catch the reference easily.

McCain had just arrived at the station after completing the searches when he was told that Groshong was demanding to be allowed in to talk to Robert. McCain immediately denied the request, and confirmed his decision with Randy Massey, the assistant prosecutor who was in Rick's office that night. Robert wasn't under arrest and he hadn't asked for an attorney. To McCain, Groshong had no right to be involved.

Groshong still was refusing to acknowledge why he was there when Lieutenant James Gabriel called Groshong to the window at the desk.

"Sergeant McCain said you are not to be admitted. Mr. Sims has not asked for an attorney. He is not under arrest and he is not in custody. Sergeant McCain said you have no right to see him now."

Groshong appeared to be stunned.

"You can't be serious. You have to let me talk to him. I've been asked to represent him and I am here to see him. You can't deny me the right to confer with my client."

Gabriel was unmoved. "I'm just telling you what I've been told."

"Well, we'll have to see about that, won't we?" Groshong replied defiantly.

He borrowed what would be the first of several quarters from Bosworth and began a series of telephone calls. He started with his partner, Edward Moorman, who suggested calling a judge to get an order admitting the defense into the interview. Groshong called Circuit Judge Paula E. Riley, whom Groshong had worked for when Riley was the county public defender. Riley said Groshong should call a criminal judge for a ruling.

As the pay-phone drama unfolded, Bosworth was joined by his colleague from the *Post*, Pat Gauen, who also had to dig into his pocket to supply quarters to Groshong. Soon, the other reporters began drifting in. As the intensity of the calls increased, some of the television stations carried live bulletins to cover Groshong's desperate, long-distance legal challenge. His policy of not discussing his cases with the press evaporated as mini-cameras picked up every word he said on the phone.

After failing to find a criminal judge at home, Groshong called Chief Circuit Judge P. J. O'Neill and explained that Robert Sims was "in the slammer" while the police kept his attorney outside. O'Neill called the detective section, but was satisfied with assurances from McCain and Massey that Robert was free to leave at any time and had not requested an attorney. O'Neill called Groshong back and denied his request for intervention.

By 11:50 P.M., Groshong had abandoned his efforts and left the station.

For the second or third time, a tired Carl Schultz had just told Robert Sims that the interview seemed to be going nowhere. But, for some reason, Robert appeared to want to stay and talk. The conversation turned to what things were like in the Sims house after Heather was born, and Robert explained the separate sleeping arrangements. He and Randy needed their sleep, uninterrupted by a crying baby.

Not particularly enlightening, Schultz thought. But then Robert offered a comment that not only stunned Schultz, but would mystify everyone connected with the case from that day on and inflict irreparable damage to the Simses' image as distraught parents.

"After Heather was kidnapped, Paula and I started sleeping together again. On Monday or Tuesday night, Paula and I had the best and longest-lasting sex we've had in a long time."

Schultz was speechless. Had this man before him really just said that while his infant daughter was missing, he and his wife were having the best sex of their lives?

Schultz took another break and told the other cops what Robert had said.

"Can you believe a guy would say something about sex like that in the middle of this case?"

Schultz said he thought he had gotten as much out of Robert as he could; the agent looked tired. But the others encouraged him to go back and try one more time.

Schultz began to hammer Robert with the logical conclusion tht Paula had killed the babies. Robert wouldn't go that far, but he did admit that he had to believe she had something to do with their deaths.

Then he surprised Schultz again by offering to go home and "work on" Paula to try to get her to admit some involvement in the deaths.

"I might be able to get her to admit it. You guys never will. She'll never talk to the police again. If any local police try to talk to her, she'll zip her mouth shut and demand to see her attorney."

At 12:38 A.M., Schultz ended the interview. He went back to McCain's office and said, "He's all yours."

McCain turned to Ventimiglia. "You want to go in with me and work on Robert?"

"No, thanks. You go ahead."

McCain looked back across the room full of seasoned

cops, and his gaze settled on Dooley. "Mick, you want a shot at him?"

Dooley was surprised that Rick would pass over all the talent in that room and pick him. But it felt good, and, hell yes, he wanted a shot at Robert.

McCain and Dooley decided they would try to call Robert's bluff on getting an admission from Paula, and that they would stay in that room as long as Robert was willing to talk. Rick decided the best thing to do was try to rock Robert with a tougher approach to force him to offer solid proof of his innocence.

"Robert, do you really expect anyone to believe that you're not involved in your daughter's death? You're right in the middle of this."

Robert stonewalled him. "Sergeant McCain, I've told you the absolute truth. I didn't have anything to do with any of this."

"Yeah? Well, let me tell you what has happened tonight, Robert. We have executed search warrants at your house and at the Blews'. A roll of black plastic trash bags has been taken from your house and will be sent to the FBI laboratory in Washington to be compared to the one Heather's body was found in. We found a blonde hair in the freezer at the Blews, and a sleeper like the one Heather was supposed to be wearing was found there, too.

"I also want to tell you that when Paula was examined at the hospital Saturday night, there was no evidence that she had been injured. It's highly questionable whether she could have been struck on the head and knocked unconscious for forty-five minutes."

Mick chimed in. "And you have to admit, Robert, that it is awfully improbable that your family could have been the victim of two such similar kidnappings by some masked men. It just isn't very probable, Robert."

Robert nodded. "I know. And I have to admit that, after this happened to Heather, I am suspicious of Paula. I know I didn't kill Heather. And if Paula did it, I have to believe it was an accident."

McCain again. "Let me ask you this, Robert. Is there any reason that tire tracks at the scene where the body was discovered might match the tires on either of your vehicles?"

"I don't think so. Not that I know of."

McCain had just used one of his favorite techniques, and Robert had given the guilty, wishy-washy answer. When a hypothetical question suggesting evidence of guilt is proposed, an innocent person will answer definitely, comfortable with the knowledge that there could be no such evidence. But a guilty person will hedge, because he doesn't know what evidence he might have left behind.

McCain jabbed again with the same technique.

"Is there any reason that the hair found in the freezer at your in-laws' house would be Heather's hair?"

"I don't think so." Wrong answer again.

"The body was found in a black trash bag. Is there any reason . . ."

Robert almost jumped. "Now wait. My fingerprint might be on that bag if it came from the roll at our house." He was talking faster now. "I'm the one who takes out the trash. And, when you're pulling off a trash bag to use, you have to grab the bag behind it to tear it off at the perforations. So my fingerprint might be on the bag, but that wouldn't prove that I had anything to do with it. That's just how my fingerprint could be on it."

McCain and Dooley were getting excited, and they started pulling out all the stops. After another round of denials, Dooley decided to throw in the "good cop, bad cop" bit. Sure, it was old. But sometimes it worked.

His voice boomed through the small room. "Robert, I've had enough of this. You can't expect us to believe this. You're not being straight with us, and I'm not going to listen to any more of your self-serving crap until you are."

Dooley spun around, stormed out of the room, and slammed the door.

McCain just shook his head. "Robert, Mick's got a hot temper sometimes. He can't stand for someone to jerk him around like this. He'll cool down. But you've got to be straight with us."

"I want to cooperate Sergeant McCain. I'm trying to cooperate."

"No, you're not, Robert. And if you're going to lie, we might as well just stop it right here."

Dooley came back in and sat down. "Robert, how do

you expect anyone in the world to believe this story Paula
has told?''

"I have to believe my wife."

McCain seemed to be getting angry. His turn to be the
bad cop.

"Robert, look. Everyone knows there wasn't any masked
man. Everyone knows that. It's a fact. So someone else in
that house had to do it. It had to be you or Paula or Randy.
You tell us you didn't do it, and I assume we can eliminate
Randy as a suspect. Do you agree with that?''

Robert nodded slowly. "Yes."

"Well, Robert?''

"Then she must have done it. But I don't want to believe that and, even the way you say it, I still don't know
it for sure. And if she did it, it must have been an accident. I know she couldn't have meant to kill the girls.''

It was McCain's turn to stomp out of the room.

When he returned a few minutes later, he asked Robert
about his concern for Randy's safety. Robert offered to
sign a statement saying he believed the girls' deaths might
have been accidental and Paula may have caused them,
if that would get Randy placed with another relative to
protect him. Robert started to write on a legal pad.

McCain stopped him. "I'm not interested in a statement that says what you believe might have happened,
Robert. We want to know what you know. We want to
know what happened."

Robert looked up. "Is there some way you can get the
state to put Randy in custody of my brother in Texas?
Can you talk to the state and get them to do that?''

McCain injected a sarcastic tone into his voice. "You're
his father, Robert. You do it. You call the Department of
Children and Family Services and tell them why Randy is in
danger and why he should be in someone else's custody.
We'll go with you to DCFS and to get him.''

Robert was wearing down. He looked at both of the
detectives.

"I know you guys don't believe me. You still think I
had something to do with Loralei's and Heather's deaths.
But I know that Paula won't let me go to jail for something I didn't do. I'll go home and talk to Paula about
what happened. If you promise you won't say anything

to the press before then, I'll bring her back to the police station before noon to confess. She'll tell you I had nothing to do with this.''

McCain remembered that Robert's first wife had confessed to making harassing calls to his coworker. So there was a precedent there.

Robert continued. ''I think Paula needs psychological help. If she did this, there's something wrong with her.''

Okay, Robert. I'll agree to that. I won't say anything to the press. But I'll tell you right now, I know you won't be back. I know you won't keep the bargain.''

''Yes, I will. But I don't want to say anything more now.''

It was 3:15 A.M., Friday, May 5. Before McCain and Dooley drove Robert home, they got him to agree to be fingerprinted and photographed. The fingerprinting went well, and the camera flashed when the picture was taken. But when the film was developed later, the shot of Robert was nowhere to be found. The negative didn't even indicate that the picture had been taken. McCain and Dooley never figured out what had happened. Spooky.

While they were driving Robert back to the Blews' house, Dooley could feel a deep depression coming on. They had hit Robert with their best shot, but they hadn't brought him down. Dooley tried to console himself with tomorrow's promised session with Paula, and with the thought that it would have been worse if Robert had walked away before McCain and Dooley had their shot at him.

But it was a small consolation indeed.

Rick's mind was running along the same lines. He had been in on a hundred confessions, he guessed. And he had never tried harder.

When McCain pulled up in the driveway at the Blews' house, Robert opened the back door of the car and started to get out. He turned to McCain and said, ''I know you don't believe it, but I will bring her in by noon.''

An exhausted Rick McCain looked back over the car seat and shook his head. ''I don't believe it, Robert.''

Chapter 13

Friday morning was spent packaging the evidence the cops hoped would bind Robert and Paula inescapably to the body of their murdered baby. The right results from the FBI analysis of the trash bag and hair—those fragments of this horrible act—would give the police powerful new weapons to destroy the kidnapper story. The cops might even learn whose hand had smothered the life out of that baby.

McCain was busy, but he couldn't help watching the clock. He had little hope that Robert and Paula would walk through that door by noon. But there was that slim chance.

In front of the station, the battalion of reporters was growing by the hour. There were crews from the three network affiliates and an independent television station in St. Louis, and several radio stations. The print media was represented by the Associated Press and about a dozen reporters from local newspapers: The *Post-Dispatch*, Alton *Telegraph*, Edwardsville *Intelligencer*, Belleville *News-Democrat* and some smaller weekly newspapers. The Chicago *Tribune* and Kansas City *Star* had sent in reporters, and *People* magazine had dispatched a reporter and a photographer. McCain was getting a lot of calls from across the country, and a production company already had inquired about turning the Sims case into a movie.

For the first time, State's Attorney Bill Haine was becoming a major player in the case because of what Robert had said about Randy's safety. The chief prosecutor had begun to worry that something might happen to the only surviving Sims child. If there were a real danger, Haine believed he had a responsibility to protect the child. That

probably meant taking Randy into state custody and
foster care until a judge could review the evidence and
decide if such action was warranted.

Haine called Schultz and asked about the tone of Robert's comments. Schultz said he had taken Robert seriously.

"Based on your reading of Robert and what he said,
should we be concerned for Randy's safety?"

"Yes, I would be concerned," was Schultz's blunt reply.

Haine also got the agent's promise that he would testify in court about the twisting motion Robert had made
with his hands when he said Paula could wring Randy's
neck. That was sinister.

Haine asked assistant prosecutor Kit Morrissey to call
the regional office of the Illinois Department of Children
and Family Services and report the allegations against
Randy's safety. Kit informed the supervisor of the child-
abuse team that it was likely that state custody would be
sought, and asked that a caseworker stand by.

Haine checked with Rick McCain, and he agreed with
Schultz about the threat to Randy's welfare. Haine was
even more convinced he would have to act, and soon.
State law allowed the prosecutor, on his own volition, to
order a child taken into protective custody. But the decision had to be supported by a juvenile custody petition
and reviewed by a judge later. Haine asked Kit, who had
been handling juvenile cases, to prepare the petition and
set a hearing before a judge for the next week.

Haine had given Weber a status report when he called
in that morning from his motel in Indiana, and asked him
to check in regularly while he was on the road that day.
When Haine told Weber that Don Groshong would be the
defense attorney, Weber had to smile. He always had
wanted to face his old friend on a major criminal case,
and it looked like he finally would get his wish.

Weber knew Groshong approached his cases with the
same intense strategy that he applied to his championship
chess game; the defense attorney even kept a chess clock
on his desk. He plotted each move carefully, anticipating
his opponent's reaction, always a step ahead. Weber knew

he would have to stay several jumps ahead of Groshong in this game.

Weber called Haine again about one o'clock from a pay phone near Lexington, Kentucky. Haine was close to deciding to take Randy into state custody. But Weber, painfully aware of the legal ramifications of that decision, urged caution.

"Bill, once you take this into juvenile court, you're really crossing the Rubicon. Once that's done, we have to open this whole case up to Groshong. He'll have access to all the police reports, everything in the case file. He'll have subpoena power and he'll be able to take depositions from all of the witnesses. It's awfully early in this investigation to have that happening. We shouldn't have to provide the defense with that information until charges are filed. But if we go ahead with the juvenile petition now, we'll have to let Groshong inside."

"I know, Don. But I just can't take the chance that something could happen to that child after we've been warned. What if someone in that house goes bonkers and harms the kid? We have to weigh the danger to Randy against the tactical problem of letting Groshong into the case. And I think I have to come down on the side of protecting Randy."

"Okay. You're the state's attorney, and it has to be your decision. I know from experience that there are some things the state's attorney alone has to decide, and I think this is one of them. But take a couple more hours and think about it before you make the final decision. I'll call you again in two hours, and we'll see what's happening."

"Okay."

This was a tough call in a very tough situation, and Bill Haine was handling it alone. As a state's attorney with only four months on the job, Haine would need good solid adivce, Weber knew. But Bill certainly seemed to be guided by the right motivations.

In Alton, the police work was continuing. Tony Ventimiglia had received an important bit of news from a man who called about the discovery of the body. Ernest Springer, a sixty-seven-year-old Alton resident, had been checking for aluminum cans in the trash barrels at the access area the day before, and saw the black trash bag in the barrel by the rest rooms. He hadn't disturbed it. But, after seeing the news on television, he realized that the bag was the one that contained Heather's body. Springer's story could be crucial; it put the bag there at a specific time—1:00 P.M. Wednesday.

Ventimiglia and Sullivan drove over to the Alton Memorial Hospital later that day and spent four hours interviewing twenty-six nurses and other staff members about their memories of the Simses. Most of the comments were similar to what the police had heard in 1986. Paula was a quiet, cooperative patient and Robert was a quiet, rather unusual man.

But there were more telling comments, too. One nurse in the maternity ward remembered that Robert had "cried and cried" when Randy was born, and had prohibited photographs of the baby or a birth notice in the newspapers. Paula had been pleasant, but she chain-smoked and seemed nervous. Another nurse remembered that when Paula's second and third children were born, she had not shown the kind of emotion expected from a mother who had lost her first child. The Simses also had asked if the door to the nursery was kept locked, and had ordered that their babies not be shown to anyone without one of the parents present.

Another nurse described the Simses as unenthusiastic about the births of all three children, and yet another described Robert as especially uninterested in Heather's birth. One nurse said it seemed that feeding Heather was a chore to Paula, and that she usually sent the baby back to the nursery as soon as she was fed.

A nurse who remembered Loralei's birth related to Ventimiglia a conversation with the parents. The nurse asked Paula, "What child is this for you?" Paula responded, "The first," and Robert added blankly, "And the last." It hadn't seemed like a joke, the nurse said ominously.

Many of the nurses shared some memories of Robert after Heather's birth. He never came to the hospital without Randy, and seemed extraordinarily attentive to the boy. Robert obviously was much less interested in the new baby girl. The nurses also remembered that Randy had scored a coup—he was the first child ever who had attended the "Stork Club" dinner that was given for the parents the night before they took Heather home.

When they left the hospital, Ventimiglia turned to Sullivan and summed up the comments. "Robert and Paula are some very weird people."

McCain's prediction was on the money. Noon came and went, and no Simses. That canceled all bets, and he began filling in the reporters on the events of the last thirty-six hours. He hoped that would increase the pressure on the entire Sims family. McCain announced that Robert and Paula now were suspects, and that other family members could be suspects, too. McCain went so far as to predict that the police planned to seek murder charges eventually against Robert and Paula, based in part on the evidence collected during the searches. He explained that the trash bags, hair fibers, and baby's sleeper were being flown to Washington for analysis.

He also said the parallels between the deaths of Loralei and Heather could lead to charges in the first case. But he was quick to point out that such charges would be up to the authorities in Jersey County.

McCain's reference to the Simses and some of their relatives as suspects added fuel to the media's burning interest in the case. The television stations dispatched extra crews to the Blews' house for stakeouts that continued around the clock for several days. Live updates were aired each evening, often with no more to report than someone setting out the trash. Other Virginia Avenue residents were interviewed repeatedly, attesting to what fine neighbors the Blews had been. Some of the residents were taped while they were eating dinner. Crowds gathered at all hours and cars cruised by as the passengers craned their necks to look at the house illuminated by the TV lights. A woman with a sign reading, "We love our daughters" showed up; that played well on the news.

The congregation of media trucks, cars, reporters, cameramen, and curious onlookers grew to such a size that the Groshong called the sheriff's department to complain that the street in front of his clients' home was almost impassable. Sheriff Bob Churchich posted a deputy and some barricades on the street to restrict traffic.

Shortly after live bulletins were broadcast Friday afternoon reporting McCain's description of the Simses as suspects, Robert and Paula left her parents' house and drove to Groshong's office, only three blocks from the police station. Television cameras recorded their every move.

A soft rain had started to fall as Don Weber was crossing the pleasant green countryside in Tennessee. By the time he pulled into a service station near Oak Ridge, a driving rainstorm had moved in. He ran to a telephone booth, which stood alone on a hillside near the station.

"What's the situation now, Bill?"

"It hasn't really changed, Don. I just don't see how I can do anything but take Randy into custody. I couldn't live with myself if something happened to him, and I hadn't moved because I was worried about Groshong. I can't make this kind of decision on that basis. It's the wrong foundation. Do you see any way around it?"

The wind was sweeping the rain under the sides of the phone booth and Weber could feel his feet, wet and cold.

"Well, I'll tell you. Two hours ago, I didn't think I would agree with you. But I've had a lot of time to think about it, and you're right. For better or for worse, we have to cross the Rubicon. I think we have to grab the kid."

"Good. I'll give the order. We'll grab him today."

It was a tough decision for Haine. But as the father of seven children, he had great empathy for what the toddler must be suffering. His little sister had disappeared not long after she had arrived, and now he would be torn from the rest of his family to be placed in a home full of strangers. But the alternative was to leave him with parents who were under suspicion in the deaths of his baby sisters. If the obvious were true and even one of the Simses were guilty, there was some deadly pathology in the family that might be triggered again by all the stress. If Robert were to be believed, Randy was in danger from his mother, a woman whose husband believed she was, at best, suffering from some psychological impairment. Haine just didn't see any other choice.

Weber hung up and looked through the glass of the phone booth. What an incongruous situation. He was standing in a driving rainstorm, making a decision that would up-end the life of a little boy hundreds of miles away. The kid was about to be taken from his parents, a man and woman who were claiming that their infant daughters had been kidnapped and murdered by masked gunmen in two attacks three years apart, in two different cities. How could any set of circumstances be more unbelievable?

Once Haine had made the decision about 3:15 P.M., things moved quickly. He met caseworker Susan Redman from the Department of Children and Family Services at the Alton police station. He explained that she would be accompanied by Detective Tim Botterbush from Alton and Sergeant Ewin Knezevich from the sheriff's department to the Blews', where Randy was to be taken into custody on Haine's orders.

Robert and Paula were at Groshong's office when Knezevich knocked on the Blews' door and was greeted by Nylene.

"Mrs. Blew, we have a court order for the Department of Children and Family Services to take custody of your grandson. It's only temporary custody and there will be a hearing on it later for a judge to review it. Miss Redman is from the Department of Children and Family Services. I'm sorry, but we have to take him now."

It wasn't surprise that Knezevich saw in the grandmother's eyes. It probably was the pain of giving up her only remaining grandchild—pain tinged by a hint of hostility toward the legal authority that would come to her house and take that boy. Knezevich could understand that; he didn't really blame her.

The group moved through the living room and into the kitchen. Nylene was holding Randy by then. He was a cute little boy with bright red hair and a scrubby-clean look. Nylene started sobbing. But Orville took it calmly, with an air of resignation.

Nylene pleaded, "Do you really have to do this? Do you have to take him now? Where are you taking him?"

Susan Redman nodded, "Yes ma'am, we have to take him now. We'll be putting him in a foster home under department supervision. There will be a hearing next week for a judge to review Mr. Haine's order and to decide whether there is enough evidence to keep Randy in state custody."

Nylene passed Randy to his grandfather. The boy was getting scared and confused. Nylene disappeared down the hallway to gather up some clothes, bottles, and toys.

While they waited, Knezevich surveyed the home of a family firmly in middle America. Nothing fancy, but comfortable, and definitely lived in. He had been involved in seizures of children by the state before, and sometimes the situation was so bad that he was glad to be taking the child out, to be rescuing the kid from an environment of danger or neglect. But he didn't feel that way this time. This child obviously was loved by these people, these very caring grandparents.

Nylene reappeared in the kitchen with a paper bag filled with supplies. She hugged the boy again, and whispered, "I love you, Randy."

Orville was crying now. "I love you, Randy. I love you." As he handed his grandson to Susan, the boy began to cry. It was a heartbreaking cry that Knezevich could almost feel inside.

By the time Susan got to her car in front of the house, Randy was wailing and the fear was painfully obvious in his face. As she leaned into the front door of the car and strapped him into the safety seat, the television cameras zoomed in. The tape of the pitiful event was the lead story on the news at five o'clock. The emotional scene was played repeatedly over the next few days, and would be resurrected innumerable times for months to come.

Later that night in a motel room in Marion, Virginia, Don Weber flipped the television to the Cable News Network and settled down with a slice of pizza. He felt a million miles from the events unfolding back in Madison County. But within minutes, Sergeant Rick McCain's serious face appeared on the screen, announcing that he expected murder charges against the Simses. Weber couldn't believe his eyes. The case had followed him all the way across the country.

As he listened to McCain's voice—which reporter Pat Gauen would describe that weekend as "the sparse, Dragnet-style monotone of Sergeant Joe Friday"—Weber realized that he was in for a real roller-coaster ride. This case was bigger than he had thought.

Late Friday, Groshong made his first, and one of his very few, comments to reporters. He insisted that the Simses denied any wrongdoing, and he said the police had told the couple "that there was so much pressure from the media that someone would have to be charged with something." It was bluff, but it played well in the press and provided some public defense of his clients.

At the news conference on Saturday, McCain disclosed that Randy had been taken into custody because of Robert's statements during the interview. But it was at a joint press conference with Yocom on Sunday that the full story emerged. McCain quoted Robert's statement that he believed Paula may have killed both of their daughters accidentally. McCain described Robert as saying he was "somewhat suspicious" about Paula's kidnapping stories.

"Mr. Sims was unsure of his wife's story . . . and his belief was that his wife may have been involved in the deaths of Heather and Loralei." Rick added later, "I don't think he believes it was intentional. He believes it was accidental."

Yocom said he was not surprised that Robert would point the finger at his wife. "He appears to be the stronger of the two people. I think he could have been looking for a way out of his own problems in this situation."

And for the first time, McCain offered the official suggestion that the motive in the deaths could have been the bizarre gender preference. His surprising explanation that the Simses had been upset at having daughters instead of sons was backed up by Yocom's disclosure of the statement by Paula's hospital roommate from 1986, Julie Fry, saying that Paula had made a tearful call from the hospital to Robert to apologize for having a daughter instead of a son. The roommate said Paula had told her, "I wish we could have had a boy. We wanted one so bad."

The sheriff rubbed his chin. "The only motive I can come up with—and it's pure speculation on my part—is the fact that there's been several comments made by them on the male–female issue."

McCain also went into his observations about the lack of decorations and toys for a little girl in the Sims house, while Randy's room was nicely decorated and the house contained "dozens and dozens of things attributed to a boy."

McCain, trying to keep the pressure on the Simses, issued a plea for Robert and Paula to call him to discuss the situation again.

The long-awaited interview with Stephanie Werner came off on Monday. It was worth the wait. The twenty-year-old woman—a slim, attractive brunette—had come to the station with her mother to tell the story about being Paula Sims's roommate in March. While Ventimiglia sat there in near astonishment, Stephanie Werner described how Paula had confused the details of the kidnappings in 1986 and 1989, some six weeks before the second kidnapping.

Werner related that she and Paula had been discussing the deliveries of their children—a son for Werner and a daughter for Paula. Paula had delivered her son and her new daughter by caesarian section, but said she understood Werner's description of natural labor as "hell." When asked how she would know, Paula responded that she had delivered a baby girl naturally three years ago. She had named her Loralei. And then, in a very unemotional manner, Paula described how the baby had been kidnapped.

"Paula said she had been taking out the trash or burning the trash—I'm not sure which way she said it—and a masked gunman came up to her and ordered her into the house. He hit her in the head and knocked her unconscious, and when she came to, all that was missing was the baby and the diaper bag."

Werner told the story in a rather matter-of-fact tone. But the words sent a chill up Ventimiglia's spine as he considered the implications of this new twist. Paula was lying in that hospital room just hours after she delivered Heather, planning how to pull off the next one. That made it premeditated murder, and ruled out the accidental death theory.

Stephanie Werner had thought the story was odd, and asked if the police had found Loralei's kidnapper. Paula said the police had given up on it and, instead, had blamed her and her husband. They still were paying off the legal bills from the case. Paula then told her roommate that the body had been sent to a laboratory in Atlanta and never returned for burial. Paula was not convinced it was Loralei's body, anyway, and believed the kidnapper was someone who had lost a baby recently. She said she had a pretty good idea who it was, but had not pursued it because the chances were so slim of finding a baby who might have been sold on the black market.

Paula went on that, because of what had happened to Loralei, the Simses never allowed anyone to baby-sit for Randy, not even his grandparents. In fact, Paula seemed withdrawn when her parents visited her in the hospital and did not seem to want her mother to hold Heather.

While Paula was talking about Loralei, Robert had walked into the room with Randy. When Paula told what she was discussing, Robert looked down and shook his head. Stephanie Werner thought he looked disgusted. Nothing more was said about it after that.

The women's first meeting had not been pleasant. Werner had delivered little Jacob the day before—on St. Patrick's day—and was in the room already when Paula was brought in after delivering Heather. Paula was upset about having a roommate, and said she had requested a private room when she filled out the hospital pre-admission form some time ago. Paula even suggested that Werner move, and Stephanie had refused. That had seemed to settle the issue.

In fact, the roommates got along well enough after that for Werner to remark later that it would be "neat" if Jacob and Heather met years later and became boyfriend and girlfriend, only to learn that their mothers had been roommates. Paula's cool response was, "That would be neat, but I doubt it.'' Another conversation Paula seemed anxious to end.

Paula was more responsive when asked about postpartum depression. "The baby blues," Paula said and shrugged nonchalantly. "No problem. You feel a little down for a couple of days, but there's really nothing to it."

Ventimiglia had to make sure of this story, since the back of his mind was sending him messages that said, "This could be a big break." Stephanie's account was so bizarre that it would be easy for a defense attorney to attack later. He suggested she had read the details of the two events and confused them. But Stephanie was adamant. She didn't read newspapers and she didn't watch the television news. She admitted that she wasn't very well informed, because she just wasn't interested.

Ventimiglia wanted to make sure this young woman understood the stakes.

"Okay, but we have to be sure you're right, and that you're telling us the truth. This is very important, and we can't have it come out later that it didn't happen this way."

Werner's defensiveness gave way to anger and she snapped, "Why would I be lying to you? I don't have anything to gain by coming in here and lying to you. I didn't say anything sooner because I was worried about my son. I thought he might be in danger from the kidnapper or even the Simses."

Werner backed up her story by adding that she had told her mother what Paula had said a day or two after the conversation. Her mother, Barbara Werner, nodded. Her daughter had recounted the details while she still was in the hospital. Barbara Werner remembered the trash bag and the knock-out blow, and they were what caught her attention when she heard the story of Heather's kidnapping later.

Ventimiglia wanted McCain to hear this story firsthand. He pulled Rick from a meeting in the chief's office, telling him, "Mac, you gotta' hear this."

McCain tried to shake her just as hard as Ventimiglia had. She stuck fast to the story, never contradicted herself and, to McCain's delight, she didn't sound like a goofball. She even offered to take a polygraph test to prove her veracity.

As Ventimiglia reflected on this new story later, he realized that everything the Simses ever said seemed rehearsed. Everything had been well planned, except for the dumping of the body. Even when Paula had told her roommate the wrong story about Loralei, the details had come out so smoothly and so calmly. Was it possible that the story the police got on April 29, 1989, had been a version drafted, and then rejected, for June 17, 1986? Was Heather's death being explained with a second-hand lie made up for her sister? Another chill ran up the sergeant's spine.

The first court hearing in the Sims case began the next day, Tuesday morning, in the Madison County Courthouse in Edwardsville. The seventy-year-old, white stone building is a massive, three-and-a-half–story rectangle, built around a huge central atrium. Standing at the railing on any floor, observers can see virtually the entire building across the open center.

Associate Judge Ellar Duffwilliams (she would later change her name to just Duff) would decide whether there was probable cause to support Haine's petition to make Randy a ward of the court, which would keep him in state foster care until a full hearing was held later. Haine had asked Kit Morrissey to handle the first hearing. She had filed the petition and she knew the judge well. Don Weber had just arrived by plane late the night before, but would be with Kit for moral support and to assist her if anything unexpected happened.

The petition charged that Randy Sims was a neglected minor because living with the Simses constituted an injurious environment that could endanger his welfare and physical safety. As required by law, the judge had appointed a "guardian ad litem" to represent Randy at the hearing. The guardian was Tom Jackstadt, an assistant public defender.

McCain would be the only witness. To prepare, he had to bone up on all the reports his men had filed over the last ten days. He also had to compile a set of the written reports to comply with a subpoena served on him the day before by Groshong. The powers bestowed on the defense, as Weber had feared, already were being exercised.

Before the hearing, Haine and Weber met with McCain to explain that the prosecutors had decided to put a lid on the publicity about the case. There would be no more public statements. Weber said there was little chance Robert and Paula would be making any more mistakes under Groshong's guidance. And Weber was worried about the proclivity of some judges to let defense attorneys go way too far in their complaints about pretrial publicity. Such complaints could result in almost endless hearings before trial.

McCain was glad to hear about the end to the news blitz. He had grown weary of the media circus around the station and the constant, harassing calls from reporters.

So, the first of many Sims hearings opened. As would be the rule, the hallway outside the courtroom was jammed with reporters, camera crews, and newspaper photographers. Courthouse workers who drifted by to get a look at the Simses were disappointed to learn that Robert and Paula would not be attending and the public would not be admitted. Under Illinois law, juvenile hearings can be attended only by the press.

Kit Morrissey was in charge, but Weber and Haine sat with her. Morrissey was a trim, attractive brunette who had gone to work for Haine five months earlier, and already was earning a reputation as an up-and-coming young prosecutor. Haine knew she was nervous about the hearing, but he was confident she could handle it.

After Judge Duffwilliams denied a motion by Groshong to dismiss the petition outright, Rick McCain testified for two hours, sitting on the hot seat he would ride nearly twenty times before this case was completed. He gave the judge basic accounts of the Simses' story and the investigation, and described the similarities between the Loralei and Heather cases. He said nothing had been found to support the Simses' versions, and all the evidence pointed toward the parents as the suspects.

But it was Rick's account of Stephanie Werner's statement—although he didn't identify her by name—that galvanized the press with the news that Paula apparently had blundered and had given her roommate the details of Heather's kidnapping six weeks before it happened.

Groshong objected to protecting Stephanie's identity. It gave him his first chance to criticize the police and prosecutors for "manipulating the media" and creating hysteria, and then trying to suppress certain facts, such as the name of a major witness.

Judge Duffwilliams disagreed and ordered the name to be withheld. But she agreed with Groshong on one issue. "The media has gone hog-wild with this," she said.

On cross-examination, Groshong hammered at Mc-Cain on several points and argued that there was no evidence that the Simses were involved in their daughters' deaths. McCain responded that expert analysis of evidence such as the trash bags and the hair from the freezer was under way, and the real lack of evidence was in support of the Simses' kidnapping stories.

"In our estimation, we've ruled out the masked-man theory," McCain said.

An inconsequential exchange led to a laugh that relieved some of the tension. Groshong was questioning McCain about *The Stash Book,* and asked if McCain had noticed that there also was a copy of the Bible in the Sims home.

"Yes, sir, I think I did see a copy of the Bible in the home. But it didn't have a section on hiding bodies in it."

At the end of the hearing, Judge Duffwilliams ruled quickly and succinctly. She said the evidence showed that Randy Sims "may be subject to harm and injury from his environment" if left in his parents' custody. He would remain in state custody, and she ordered a hearing on permanent custody set within 120 days.

Outside the courtroom, Haine dropped the bomb on the press. Surrounded by reporters in a media assault unlike anything he had seen yet, Haine announced the news blackout by his office and the police. There were several reasons, including his desire to avoid charges later of prosecutorial misconduct. The investigation was now under the jurisdiction of the prosecutor's office because of the juvenile hearing and plans for a grand jury investigation.

Pushed by the reporters for a better explanation of the decision, he offered one of the most quoted lines from the case.

"I would like to try this case somewhere in the Western Hemisphere, and even that's becoming a bit difficult in this matter."

While McCain was at the hearing, the detectives were delivering subpoenas for appearances before the grand jury on Thursday by Paula, her parents, and Herb and Linda Condray. The detectives relished that duty.

Paula was handed her subpoena later in the day as she left Groshong's office. Dave Hayes and Tim Botterbush, hidden by several television crews, had been lurking around the corner from the office doorway. Robert and Paula were standing at the elevator when Hayes reached over her shoulder and handed her the paper. She took the paper, but never looked at it or Hayes. Groshong reappeared at his door and motioned for the Simses to return.

Robert was omitted from the first round of subpoenas, partly to cause more friction between him and Paula.

Hayes and Botterbush then joined Patrolman Larry Parks to execute search warrants on Robert's four lockers at Jefferson Smurfit. For a moment, Hayes thought the most remarkable aspect of the lockers would be the pictures of Randy hanging in each one, and the absence of photographs of either of the dead Sims girls. But in Robert's tool locker, Hayes found a library of fifteen paperback books with titles that sent some eyebrows into space.

The Abnormal Wife, *The Abnormal Ones*, *One More Time*, *The Secrets*, *Traded Wives*, *The Watcher*, *The Sex Shuffle*, *Love Too Soon*, *The Shame of Jenny*, *The Education of Lydia*, *The Girls in the Office*, *Mistress of Moorwood Manor*, *Girl High*, and *Nina*.

And one other book: *The House of the Seven Gables*.

The detectives also found a handkerchief-sized piece of cloth that bore a drawing of a naked woman sitting on a large skull. Hayes just shook his head; really strange.

From the other lockers, the detectives got a pair of bib overalls, a pair of work boots, a hairbrush and a gym bag. None of the items ever would be used in court.

That night, Chris Sullivan got another peek into the Simses' personal life when he interviewed Dave and Linda

Heistand. The couples had met in 1985 when the Simses bought a waterbed from the Heistands' store. Robert and Paula were quiet and reserved and a little strange, and therefore hard to get to know. But eventually the four became good friends.

But after Loralei's body was found, the Heistands had stopped seeing the Simses. Robert called and invited the Heistands to come and see newborn Randy; they declined. The news of Heather's disappearance had given Dave Heistand "goose bumps." The Heistands thought Loralei's death might have been an accident that Paula was unable to admit to Robert. But they had no explanation for the second death. They reluctantly had come to the conclusion that Paula had a real problem with little girls and, in fact, must have real mental problems.

On Wednesday morning, May 10, the public got its first glimpse into the Simses' backgrounds in lengthy profiles of Robert and Paula published by the *Post-Dispatch* under the headline, "Bits and Pieces of Two Troubled Lives." The reporters, Bosworth and Gauen, had spent the better part of three days gathering information on the couple, and Gauen had been the first reporter to visit La Plata, Missouri, for a look back at young Paula Marie Blew.

His story disclosed that Paula had been emotionally devastated by the death of an older brother in a car wreck in 1976, and had been known as a caring and compassionate sister to her other brother, Dennis, who was stricken with a seizure disorder. The story portrayed Paula as quiet and occasionally sour, a tomboy and an outstanding basketball player. But the newspaper had not turned up much information on her darker side—the reputation for running with the rougher crowd and the reports of petty theft, drinking, and drug use.

The profile of Robert focused on some problems dealing with women, including the harassment charges by a female coworker that resulted in a criminal charge against his first wife. It recounted the failure of that marriage, the navy's decision to classify him ineligible for reenlistment, and his arrest for shoplifting in 1979. And the story hinted at the reaction of the police when they were faced with the incredible orderliness of Robert's extensive workshop.

While the public was gobbling up the little morsels about Robert and Paula, Heather's body was being buried next to the unmarked grave of the sister she never knew. Robert, Paula, and about fifteen relatives and friends attended the funeral at the First Baptist Church in Bethalto, and then drove to Woodland Hill Cemetery for the burial of the tiny white casket. Unknown to the family, the police were following along, recording the license plates and makes of all the vehicles and taking pictures of everyone there.

The graveside service was brief. Paula wore a dress for the first time any observer could remember, and Robert wore a three-piece suit. They were flanked by the Blews and the Condrays. Paula appeared to be crying at the grave.

But a television reporter swore later that Paula Sims had walked over Loralei's unmarked grave without even a glance.

After the family left, camera crews and photographers rushed to the grave and morbidly captured the lowering of the casket. It was a ghoulish site that bothered even veteran reporters. And it initiated the first serious examination by the press of its own behavior in the case. In the first of many stories that would run in newspapers and on television, the *Post-Dispatch* published a piece the next day about the increasing debate among journalists over coverage of the Sims case. Most of the editors and TV news directors said they had serious concerns about the publicity and whether the authorities had manipulated the press to assist the investigation. They didn't want to try the Simses in the media, but admitted it had been difficult to restrain coverage amid the news frenzy that surrounded the couple. Some editors and defense attorneys complained that the police had released too much information about the case.

McCain had expected that. He had been warned that the press would turn on the cops after the news blackout was imposed. His friendly relationship with some of the reporters already had begun to sour. Now that the feast was over, the host was being devoured.

Chapter 14

The leaders of both Sims investigations convened at six o'clock Wednesday evening in the shabby, dusty law library in the Madison County state's attorney's office. Weber and Haine had called them in to discuss the direction, or maybe the lack of direction, in the case, and to decide what to do about it.

There were good points, to be sure. Weber was encouraged by the trash bag and the blonde hair, even though it would be a while before the FBI lab returned its findings on them. The case was strengthened dramatically by the results of the autopsy on Heather's body, and by the medical examination that showed no injury to Paula.

There was Robert's statement to the police. That did some damage to the Simses' credibility, casting doubt on Paula from the person who would have wanted most to believe her. But it really didn't nail anything down, and Robert's opinions would be inadmissable in court.

Stephanie Werner's statement was a dramatic and chilling testament to the murderous plot that had simmered in Paula's mind since the hour of Heather's birth. To Weber, that seemed conclusive that Paula had committed the killings herself.

But Don was worried by a jumble of unanswered and potentially dangerous questions. Questions about times and opportunities, and about what the people closest to the Simses knew. No one had collected their accounts of the crucial hours and facts in the case; there were no signed statements from the Blews or the Condrays.

Even Paula's whereabouts were undocumented for most of the time between Saturday and Wednesday. What about the hours between Tuesday night and Wednesday morning? Weber deduced that the body had been placed in the barrel sometime Tuesday night. Not earlier, because decomposition would have been more advanced. Not later, because it was unlikely the body was dumped in broad daylight. But even those assumptions were in doubt because the FBI had learned that the gates to the access area had been locked Tuesday night.

In the background, public pressure was mounting. Each day the press repeated McCain's statement anticipating murder charges, and the reporters always asked, "When?"

Weber had concluded that the authorities were going to have to force one of the Simses or their relatives to make an incriminating statement against themselves, or someone else.

That was how he laid out the situation to the other investigators and prosecutors that night. They sat around the long conference table, drinking Cokes or munching on chips while Weber offered his appraisal, and a modest proposal.

"We've got to put pressure everywhere we can, on everyone we can. We've got to force a mistake by someone. This case is not going to be solved from the outside. It doesn't look like someone who saw something is going to come forward. We've got to act and make our own breaks."

He suggested arresting Paula on some charge other than murder, and leaving Robert untouched. That would separate the seemingly inseparable Simses physically for a while, and maybe even drive a wedge between them emotionally. There already had to be a considerable amount of friction from Robert's statements to Schultz and the subsequent seizing of Randy by the authorities. The Simses had sold their house and had been cloistered at the Blews' since Heather's body was found. Except for trips to Groshong's office, they never left the house. The constant togetherness had to be creating some serious tension, and jailing Paula while leaving Robert alone might be the last straw for her.

Maybe Paula would talk while she was in the slammer. She would be getting a preview of a long stretch in prison while Robert was free. Maybe the Blews would talk just to keep their daughter from bearing the full blame alone.

One hitch in Weber's plan was Orville Blew's substantial bank account and the certainty that he would post Paula's bond. But Don's scheme addressed that, too.

He wanted Jersey County to charge Paula with obstructing justice in Loralei's death. Paula would be arrested and forced to post a high bond. Then Madison County would hit her with similar charges in Heather's death, forcing her to post another bond. By the time Madison County followed up with murder charges and an even higher bond, Orville might have exhausted his bank account, and she would stay in jail.

It was a rather audacious effort, but it was the best plan anyone could offer. And Weber was desperate for some hard evidence.

While he was talking, Rick Ringhausen paced nervously around the conference table. The new prosecutor from Jersey County was a slim man whose pointed features were accented by his black hair and beard. He had been elected only six months earlier, and he had no experience with major crimes. He knew charges on anything but murder in the 1986 case had to be filed within the next month, or the three-year statute of limitations would expire. Murder has no statute of limitations in Illinois, so Paula could be hit with that at any time down the road.

Weber reassured Ringhausen, promising that Madison County would issue its charges right after Jersey County, and that Madison County would try Paula first. Ringhausen finally accepted Weber's promise of support and agreed to charge Paula with obstructing justice.

Weber asked Sievers to go through her reports from 1986 and come up with three statements Paula had made that would be the easiest to disprove. All that had to be alleged in the charges was that Paula furnished false information to the police in an effort to obstruct the prosecution of "the person responsible" for Heather's disappearance and death. Her statements that Loralei was kidnapped by a masked gunman were grounds enough for the charges.

Sievers suggested that Paula's interviews with Yocom

on June 17 and June 18, and with Sievers on June 24 contained statements that could be disproved.

Yocom turned to Weber. "Don, can't we charge her with concealment of a homicidal death, too? I'd really like to get something against her that refers to homicide in Loralei's death. I think Paula ought to face a charge that says Loralei's death was a homicide, just like Heather's was. We know it was, and I really want homicide in there somewhere."

Weber thought for a few seconds.

"Yeah, we can charge her with concealment of a homicide for furnishing false information to the police when she knew Loralei had died by homicidal means."

Yocom beamed. "That's great. That's great."

He had waited a long time for this. And he told the others that this could be perfect timing because a known snitch already was in jail. If Paula talked to her at all while they were cellmates, Yocom would know in a flash what had been said.

Weber dictated the charges so they could be typed up and Ringhausen could take them back to Jersey County that night.

The plan was to file the charges late Friday afternoon. Paula would be arrested too late in the day to post bond before the banks and court offices closed for the weekend. That would give authorities some time to try to squeeze her while she was in jail in Jerseyville over the weekend.

Everyone swore themselves to secrecy so the plan would not leak to Groshong before the trap was sprung.

About 10:00 P.M., as Haine was reading in bed, the telephone on the nightstand rang. Ande Yakstis, a reporter for the Alton *Telegraph*, was calling to ask Haine some very specific questions about the charges to be filed Friday against Paula. Haine was stunned. How the hell had Yakstis learned about the plan so quickly after everyone had sworn themselves to secrecy in a blood oath?

Yakstis said nothing would be published before the arrest. That helped soothe Haine's anxiety, but he still couldn't believe that the plan had leaked out so quickly.

He called Weber and told him what had happened. Weber shook his head. The best-laid plans seem to go astray awfully easily in Madison County.

On Thursday morning, Randy Massey opened the grand jury investigation into Heather's death. Weber had not been sure it was the right time, but he had not tried to dissuade Massey. Paula, the Blews, and the Condrays, accompanied by Groshong, assembled early that morning in a small room near the courtroom where the grand jury would start at 9:30. As they were called, one by one, into the grand jury room, the television cameras rolled. As the press closed in on Linda Condray, the blonde who was built like a linebacker threw a shoulder into one television reporter who got too close. The reporter was staggered, but unhurt, and one of the cameramen for another TV station captured the bump on tape. It was played often for weeks.

Paula and her parents were in the room so briefly that it was obvious they had refused to testify, citing the Fifth Amendment. Herb and Linda were in the room just long enough to answer some general questions from Massey. Paula, Groshong, and the others refused to speak to reporters as they left the building. All the while, Paula kept the deadpan look on her face that the public had seen for nearly two weeks.

Weber's review of the transcripts later found nothing of any real value from the testimony of Herb and Linda. They had not been pinned down on any details that would keep them from giving alibis for Robert or Paula later. That would have to be done later. Weber decided that he would begin presenting evidence to the grand jury the next week. He might even call Robert.

Friday morning, Dooley and Hayes drove to a home in Cottage Hills, not far from the Blews', to interview June Gibson, Paula's friend since high school. The interview was another view of a strange life behind the doors of the Sims house, with Gibson describing Robert as "the strangest person I know." Gibson visited Paula only when Robert was gone, and said Paula had become increasingly frustrated with her husband's excessive rules. He insisted that everyone take off their shoes before entering the house and wash their hands as soon as they came inside. Robert ordered anyone with a cold or sniffle to stay away from the baby, and no visitor could hold her baby.

The rules had forced Paula to cancel a visit to her house by some of her relatives from Missouri who wanted to see Heather. Robert was so inflexible that Paula finally called her mother and said the visit would be too much trouble for everyone. Paula also had quoted Robert as saying that he did not want Randy visiting the Blews because their house was too dirty, and that he would not let Randy out of the stroller at the hospital when Heather was born because the floors were too dirty.

Gibson had visited Paula a couple of weeks after she came home with Heather. When Gibson arrived, Paula was smoking marijuana; Gibson finished the joint after Paula offered it to her. It wasn't long before Paula blurted out that she and Robert probably would be getting a divorce. Paula didn't know how much longer they would stay married if the separate sleeping arrangements continued.

Gibson remembered bumping into Nylene Blew at a garage sale shortly after Heather's birth. Nylene also had said Paula and Robert were not getting along and probably would be divorced. And Nylene claimed to have been suspicious of Robert's involvement in Loralei's death.

Gibson ended the interview by admitting that the death of Paula's second infant daughter was bizarre. But she said she never would believe that Paula had anything to do with it.

About two and a half hours later, June Gibson called Dooley at the station and gave him another tidbit. Paula had said Robert was having nightmares about his experiences in Vietnam and was having a hard time dealing with the things that had happened there. Gibson said she had been surprised to read in the *Post-Dispatch* that Robert had never been in Vietnam, and that he had an ex-wife that Paula had never mentioned. More strange little things.

Weber was pleased with the Gibson interview. Her statements could lend support to the idea that Robert had pressured Paula to get rid of the little girls. He had even

withheld himself physically in the separate bedrooms upstairs and downstairs—the males superior to the females.
Paula had admitted that she didn't know how much longer she could take it if things didn't change. So she had
changed them. Weber thought a jury would find that believable.

June Gibson may not have realized the importance of
her statements, but the cat was out of the bag.

Weber had been anticipating eagerly the events of Friday afternoon, May 12. For the first time, Paula would
be faced with the official accusation that she had lied,
and the implication that she had murdered, too. She
would endure the humiliation of arrest and handcuffs and
jail. It would be a surprise, and big news, for Paula to
be arrested in the death of Loralei amid the investigation
into Heather's death, and only two days after her funeral.

Don hoped it would be a good move strategically
against Groshong, an offensive he wouldn't have expected and wouldn't be prepared to handle. Just like a
cunning move to check in a chess game. It wasn't check-
mate, and it wouldn't win the game. But it might throw
off the opponent's plan and force him to begin reacting
defensively instead of attacking; it could force a mistake.

Don expected the maneuver to come off about four
o'clock, leaving Paula in jail over the weekend. Instead,
Don got a call about one o'clock saying that Paula would
surrender at the jail, and bail already had been arranged
by Groshong. Weber learned that his crafty plan had been
shot down in flames by what seemed to be a horrible and
unlikely coincidence. Yocom had gone before the only
judge in Jersey County to get the arrest warrant signed;
Groshong had appeared mysteriously, and announced that
he would bring her in voluntarily that afternoon. Bail
would be posted immediately, and she wouldn't spend a
minute in the clink. Yocom had been floored to see Groshong, and understood that Groshong had been in the
judge's chambers discussing a divorce case when he overheard the sheriff apply for the warrant on Paula.

It would be a year before Weber learned that Groshong
had been tipped off by someone who knew about the

plan. But that day, Weber was furious over the apparent coincidence.

By mid-afternoon, word had leaked out to the press and they jammed the hallway outside Groshong's office, waiting to follow Paula to Jerseyville. Her hasty exit down a stairway sent the reporters and cameramen scattering through the halls and dashing around the outside of the building to catch her.

Even that moment was tempered by the undeniable style of Groshong and his law partner, James Williamson. Williamson had driven his classic white 1961 Rolls-Royce to the office that day, and volunteered to chauffeur Groshong and Paula on the fifteen-mile drive to Jerseyville. As Williamson turned onto the square outside the old courthouse, even the reporters seemed stunned by the mode of transportation. That kind of unexpected and flamboyant touch delighted the partners. Weber thought it was slightly overdone under the circumstances.

By the time they arrived, dozens of people had gathered outside the courthouse and newer sheriff's department next door. When Paula, escorted by Groshong and Yocom, walked the fifty feet to the rear entrance of the courthouse after being booked at the jail, she was greeted by hoots and cheers. One woman yelled, "Let's see some justice now."

Groshong heard what sounded like a threat on Paula's life. He later filed a motion asking for better security because he had heard someone in the crowd yell, "Shoot her! Shoot her!" It would be some time before he learned that the voice had belonged to a cameraman for KSDK-TV. The battery in his camera had failed as he was taping Paula. He was yelling to the other cameraman, who was taping the crowd, to turn his camera toward Paula. "Shoot her! Shoot her!" he had yelled.

A time or two, Paula glanced nervously at the reporters as she made the short walk. Her face was grim and her eyes betrayed some anxiety. But she generally looked straight ahead, ignoring the microphones thrust toward her and the shouted questions.

In the same courtroom where a coroner's jury had returned a verdict of "undetermined" on the cause and manner of Loralei's death, Paula made her initial appearance before Circuit Judge Claude J. Davis. He read the four charges and asked if she understood them. In her only comment that day, Paula said softly, "Yes."

Judge Davis set Paula's bail at $100,000. Orville Blew submitted a cashier's check for $10,000, listing himself as the remitter. That satisfied the 10 percent cash requirement, and Paula was free to go.

Before Groshong left, he filed a written plea of "not guilty" and an unusual motion asking that Paula be kept in segregation if placed in jail. It was signed by Paula and said she intended to remain silent. She wanted to be kept away from other prisoners to avoid the possibility that they might try to gain favorable treatment for themselves by claiming she had made incriminating statements. Groshong knew Weber's style, too. The defense had seen the cellmate interviews before.

After Paula and Groshong left, Yocom and Ringhausen told reporters that evidence developed during the investigation into Heather's death had assisted their case. It could lead to charges against Robert, too, and murder charges against Paula might be filed later.

Yocom said he had waited for this day for three years, and had never given up hope that charges would be filed. The sheriff shook his head as he said, "It certainly has been on my mind for a long time. But I hate to think there had to be another death involved to get this thing resolved."

Back in Edwardsville, Weber was depressed. The whole point of this plan was to get Paula in jail for a few days. It had been derailed by what seemed to be a stupid mishap. There would be no progress in the investigation, and a tactical move had been wasted. The only saving grace was that the plan to arrest Paula in Madison County could continue. Maybe then something would break loose.

A few more useful tidbits would come in from interviews with witnesses over the next week or so. Ventimiglia talked to Dr. Duk Kim, who had examined Paula in the emergency room. The doctor said a blow to the back of the head or neck that would render a person unconscious would have caused damage to the bones and tissue there, and the damage would have been more obvious than the slight red mark he saw on the skin. He said Paula had shown a full range of motion that night and had been oriented to time, place, and person. She had shown none of the confusion that usually accompanies a head injury.

Weber was encouraged when Ventimiglia called and said the doctor's opinion would be that it was medically impossible for Paula to have suffered a head injury.

On May 16, Hayes interviewed the Heistands again. They said the Simses had wanted a boy because they had enjoyed the Heistands' sons so much. After Loralei was born, however, the Simses seemed happy with her. But the Heistands remembered that, sometime around Loralei's birth, Paula had said she was worried about her baby being kidnapped. After Loralei disappeared, the Heistands stayed close to the Simses because they could not believe their friends were involved.

That belief had withered after they talked to Robert about the failed lie detector tests. Robert had claimed that they had passed a second test arranged by their attorney. But the attorney had told Heistand that no second test had been given. Robert later called and told Heistand, "I wish you wouldn't have said anything to my attorney about the second polygraph." That was pretty curious conduct for an innocent man.

Heather's death was beyond belief for the Heistands. They told Hayes that they probably knew the Simses better than anyone, and they believed Paula was capable of being involved directly in both deaths. They felt the deaths could have resulted from the Simses' desire to have boys, not girls. It was possible that Paula had killed both babies accidentally, and that Robert was involved only in the coverup. The Heistands even offered to go to court to assist the police in finding the truth.

It was all opinion again, useless in court. But it helped to paint a picture of the Simses.

The next day, Hayes was interviewing Paula's former coworkers at the National Food Store when he called Jeff Reed from nearby Florissant, Missouri. Reed remembered talking to Paula just a couple of days before she was fired. He was going to be married soon, and she

asked if he and his fiancée wanted children. He said he
wanted to have a couple, and was surprised by her response.

"I hope I never have any kids. And if I do, I hope it's
a boy, because I don't like little girls."

Reed thought that was a strange comment from a
woman. But he always had thought Paula was strange.
She seemed needlessly rude to customers sometimes, and
once went off the deep end and railed at a janitor who
had failed to stock the Pepsi soda machine.

Another coworker had similar memories of Paula, and
recounted how another employee had suspected that
Paula had slashed her tires after an argument at work.

An interesting interview about Herb Condray popped
up a week later. Alton police officer Bonnie Parker got a
call from a woman who said she was a friend of Herb's.
Herb had been visiting her and her roommate, a black
woman, two or three times a week for the past year at
their apartment in Alton. He gave the roommate about
$100 a week to play bingo, and he occasionally would
accompany the woman and play bingo with her. Sometimes Herb and the woman would just spend some time
together. He seemed to know a lot about the Sims case.
He had told both of the women that the Alton police were
dumb and that, even with the FBI's help, they would
never convict the Simses because they had no evidence.

The woman also quoted Herb as saying he was a math-
ematics teacher and had been on a sabbatical leave for a
year. Th police later confirmed that Herb was on a medical leave from Sumner High School in St. Louis, where
he had taught algebra and geometry.

The next several weeks failed to bring anything that
cleared the muddy waters much for Weber. The FBI's
analysis of the evidence was slow, and Weber decided to
ignore the mounting public pressure for some action in
Madison County. He delayed indefinitely the grand jury
session that had been set for May 18.

There was some maneuvering on the charges in Jersey
County, where Groshong filed a series of motions seek-
ing dismissal of the charges and a reduction in the bond.
On May 30, Ringhausen obtained a grand jury indict-

ment of Paula on the same charges from May 12. The prosecutor wanted to avoid a preliminary hearing on probable cause, which was not required under an indictment. It had no real effect on the case.

That incredibly tumultuous May faded into a calmer June. There was much less publicity about the case, but the public still seemed fascinated and it remained a major topic of conversation everywhere.

It was about that time that perhaps the most sardonic example of the black humor brought out by the case surfaced. In a line repeated often throughout the court system, it was said that the name "SIMS" stood for "Sudden Infant Murder Syndrome." The cynical joke became so widespread that it even was written under a photograph of Paula that hung in the detective section at the Alton police station.

In Jersey County, Groshong lost efforts to get the charges against Paula dismissed and to move the trial out of the county because of the publicity. Ringhausen's response was that Paula had created the publicity with her own ridiculous statements that her babies had been kidnapped by masked gunmen.

Meanwhile, there was plenty of activity behind the scenes.

Weber's suspicion that Heather's body had been in the Blews' freezer until it was dumped in the trash barrel suffered a fatal blow. The FBI had interviewed Orville Blew's brother-in-law, Thomas Ewigman, from Peculiar, Missouri. He and his wife, Orville's sister, had returned with the Blews the day after Heather disappeared and had arrived in Cottage Hills about 3:00 P.M. Ewigman told the FBI that Paula and Randy had spent the evening at the Blews' house, and that Donna Ewigman had made stew for dinner with meat she had taken from the Blews' freezer in the basement. Ewigman said there was not much else in the freezer, and his wife certainly would have noticed if there had been a dead baby among the edibles.

That was a pretty solid body punch to Weber's theory. Ewigman's testimony would be unimpeachable, and Weber would have to find a different freezer for the body between Saturday and Wednesday.

The analysis of the rest of the evidence had begun to dribble in, and it wasn't coming out the way Weber had hoped. The FBI had found nothing useful from the debris collected at the access area, and the photos of the footprints at the scene could not be matched to any of the shoes or boots the police had confiscated. The state police crime lab had found nothing in the Simses' mop, the diapers, or the garbage in the trash bags. And the state lab had determined that the footprint Robert had given to the police was, indeed, Heather's. The chance to charge Robert with providing false evidence disappeared.

And another major piece of evidence evaporated when the FBI finally reported that the hair from the freezer actually was just a carpet fiber.

Weber didn't get any good news until the report on the trash bags. After the FBI's experts visited the plant in Minneapolis, where the bags were manufactured, they conducted their analysis and concluded that the bag that Heather's body was in matched the bags from the Simses' house. Don didn't know the exact details yet, but he knew it finally was the kind of answer he had been waiting for. It was that direct link between the murdered baby and her parents.

On June 9, Weber appointed McCain a special investigator for the state's attorney's office so he could interview Dr. Mary Case with Don. That would insulate McCain from a deposition by Groshong and, since McCain took no notes during the interview, no police report would be generated.

Weber needed to know everything about the condition of Heather's body and what it meant to Dr. Case. From his experience with her in the Karla Brown case, he had great respect for her ability to interpret every medical clue from a body and translate each into a meaningful lead in a criminal investigation. The doctor's conclusions would have a great impact on Don's theory, how he would investigate the case, and how he would present it to a jury.

Her first three points were beneficial to Weber. Heather

had been smothered. The cuts inside her upper lip were evidence of that. That made it murder, pure and simple.

Dr. Case also concluded that Heather had died shortly before she had been reported missing. At the latest, she had died right about the time the police were called Saturday night. With that opinion, Weber could defeat any claim that the baby had been killed sometime after she was out of the Simses' control. Dr. Case had just locked the killing into the time when Heather still was in her parents' custody.

And any kind of natural death, such as sudden infant death syndrome, could be ruled out.

"How?" Weber asked.

"Because SIDS deaths don't present themselves in a trash bag in a trash can in a remote access area along the Mississippi River."

But her third point made Weber wince. Dr. Case was adamant that Heather's body had been frozen, not just cooled. He argued with her.

"Are you sure it couldn't have been packed in ice or even dry ice?"

"No. The level of decomposition of the body proves that it was not just refrigerated, like a body would be in a morgue. It had to have been frozen, and I mean at thirty-two degrees Fahrenheit or below. Probably at twenty-three or twenty-four degrees."

Weber tried for forty-five minutes to shake her conclusion. But she stood firm, and that shot down his theory that the body had been stored in an ice chest, maybe even packed in dry ice. Dr. Case was his expert, and he had to go with her opinion. But it meant that he not only had to put someone in contact with the body on Tuesday or Wednesday, but he had to put them near a freezer connected to electricity.

That became particularly knotty for Don because he couldn't suggest the body had been in the Blews' freezer the whole time. Ewigman's statement to the FBI had squelched that. It was a major point in the scenario, and Don was stumped.

In a conversation later with his wife, Virginia suggested that the body could have been stored in the kind of refrigerated locker where fishermen kept their catch.

Her father had been a fisherman, and he rented storage lockers for that. It was a reach, but Don was out of ideas. He sent the Alton police on a search for all the frozen food, meat, and fish lockers they could find in the Alton, Jersey County, and Brighton areas. But only a few were found, and none of them could be linked to the Simses.

One other conclusion by Dr. Case had been helpful. Don wanted to know when the body had been left at the access area. She said the freezing of the body complicated efforts to determine that. The body would have been frozen from the outside in, and then thawed the same direction. Decomposition is affected by body enzymes, and the chemical process would change after freezing because everything was decomposing at different times.

But she concluded that the body was placed at the access area as early as Tuesday night or as late as 1:30 P.M. Wednesday. That allowed Weber a very wide time frame to put someone together with the body and the freezer and the opportunity. The less precise he had to be on the time, the harder it would be for the defense to provide an alibi.

For Don, the whole case was coming down to giving Paula the means and the time to freeze the body, to retrieve it later, and to dump it. Even if he could get a jury to believe a mother would do any of that to her baby, he still had to prove that the mother had the opportunity to do it without getting caught.

In early June, Weber decided that Herb and Linda Condray had to be interviewed at length to nail down everything they knew about the case. Weber had to know if they could alibi for the Simses during the pivotal times.

Don assumed the Condrays, by then, had to hate the Alton police. It would be better to send someone else, so he called in two of the best cops he knew—Captain Robert Hertz of the sheriff's department and DCI agent Dennis Kuba. He had worked with them on several major cases, and knew both of them to be intelligent cops who could handle themselves well in a difficult interview. They also were good-looking guys, and Don hoped that Linda might not mind talking to them. Don thought the blond Kuba even looked a little like Robert Redford.

A chance for that interview while Groshong was otherwise occupied soon presented itself. Groshong had scheduled a deposition of Stephanie Werner for June 13. Weber would send Hertz and Kuba to the Condrays while Groshong was in the deposition. That way, the Condrays would have a hard time reaching their attorney if they were hesitant to talk to the cops.

Linda Condray agreed to be interviewed, and was more than willing to offer her opinion that Robert and Paula had nothing to do with their daughters' deaths. She had seen the way the Simses behaved toward those babies, and it reflected nothing but genuine love and affection. Their deaths had left the couple grieving deeply. They had loved and wanted both of those children.

And then Linda dropped her own theory of the two cases on the unsuspecting officers, leaving them almost speechless.

Linda believed Loralei's disappearance was a genuine kidnapping, but Heather's death had been the work of Sheriff Frank Yocom. Linda had learned that Yocom had been so frustrated at his inability to nail Robert and Paula in Loralei's death that he decided to have another of their children killed so he could frame them. Linda's novel solution to the case came from information provided by an anonymous woman who had called Linda and said Yocom had been overheard in a hardware store saying that he knew the Simses were guilty. He was quoted as saying, "By God, I'm going to get them any way I can." The woman said she knew Yocom was capable of such things, because she had been forced to flee Jersey County in fear of her life after having some unspecified dealings with the sheriff. The woman had refused to identify herself, and Linda never heard from her again.

After they recovered from the shock of that story, Hertz and Kuba began to narrow the scope of the interview to dates, times, and places. What about Sunday? Linda said Robert and Paula had stayed at the Condrays' home most of that day, until Paula's parents came and picked up her and Randy sometime that afternoon.

Linda had to break off the interview because of a photography appointment, but she agreed to talk again the next day. Kuba had other commitments, so Hertz was joined by Chris Sullivan. Linda was joined by Herb. Neither of the Condrays could remember their whereabouts on Tuesday, May 2, or Wednesday, May 3, the day Heather's body was found. They checked their calendar, and found only a note about a photography appointment at 10:00 A.M. on Wednesday.

Asked where Robert and Paula had been between April 29 and May 3, the Condrays said they believed the Simses had been at their home on Washington Avenue. They had not stayed with the Condrays, so Herb and Linda weren't absolutely sure.

They rejected the authorities' claim that Robert had said Paula might have killed the girls accidentally and needed psychological help. The Condrays said Paula's mental stability probably was more sound than Robert's, and that she had been a fantastic mother who was overly concerned with her children's safety.

They also had definite opinions on the suggestion that the Simses disliked little girls—"foolish and stupid." They never had seen any indication that it was true and thought that suggesting it as a motive for two murders was ridiculous.

They related that the whole family recently had contributed toward the $2,000 cost of a headstone for the girls' graves. Robert had been upset by newspaper stories suggesting that some members of the public were thinking about buying a headstone. That was the family's responsibility, Robert had said, some three years after Loralei's death.

As Hertz and Sullivan left, they saw Robert sitting in a chair outside the Condrays' front door. No one spoke.

Weber thought he had most of what he wanted from the interview. The Condrays had eliminated themselves as possible alibis for Paula or Robert at the crucial times, without being able to recall anything specifically. That would prevent them from coming in later with sudden memories and new alibis.

Weber also liked the crazy allegations against Yocom as some kind of avenging devil who had haunted the Simses, returning to kill a child and frame the parents. How absurd could things get? Don filed that away as some great material for impeaching Linda's credibility later if needed. *Only a space cadet could come up with something like that*, he thought.

During the first day of Linda Condray's interview, Weber was sitting through the deposition with Stephanie Werner in Groshong's office. Groshong wasn't feeling well that day, his forty-second birthday; Jim Williamson handled the questioning. Weber liked Williamson and considered him something of a Renaissance man. He was a millionaire several times over from his substantial law practice in personal injury and railroad cases. Like Groshong, Jim was incredibly well read and a devotee of opera. Despite his claim of being a heathen, he was an expert on the Bible. He and the fundamentalist Christian Weber argued often about biblical points.

Williamson was an imposing physical presence as well; a large, barrel-chested man who was never seen in anything but dapper three-piece suits. He walked with a slight limp from an old football injury and carried a cane, adding an air of sophistication that suggested a retired British general who had not let his noble title prevent his service in the wars in India.

Despite his gentlemanly ways, Williamson had hammered Stephanie Werner on a couple of points, and had insisted that she could have confused the details of the two kidnappings after reading the both versions in the newspapers. And he was adamant that she say whether she had ever used drugs or marijuana. Weber objected to the question as irrelevant unless it was narrowed to the time in question. But Williamson insisted that she answer as to any use, ever. Weber told her she didn't have to answer, and she refused to do so.

Williamson was angered by that and said the question would be certified to a judge, the process by which a judge determines if a deposition question has to be answered. Weber responded that Williamson was trying to intimidate and bully Stephanie Werner.

In some of the many off-the-record and friendly conversations being held during that period among Weber, Groshong, and Williamson, the prosecutor insisted that the marijuana question had been "indecent" and an intrusion into a citizen's privacy. Williamson would laugh and brush Weber off, saying the defense had a right to know about a prosecution witness. During the months preceding the trial, the three men would get together often in Groshong's office to tell war stories, argue literary points, listen to opera and, invariably, discuss the case. It was a sophisticated effort to draw out each side's strategies without giving away too much, and the three men enjoyed the sessions. Williamson took endless pleasure in accusing Weber of lying about the evidence, such as the freezer hair. "You're a Nazi," Jim loved to tell Weber.

The day of the deposition, Weber made a startling discovery about Stephanie Werner. He was driving her from Groshong's office to the police station four blocks away, where she had left her car, when she turned to him and asked a surprising question.

"What is the big deal with what Paula said to me?"

It dawned on Weber that Stephanie really didn't understand the contradiction involved.

"Don't you understand that what she told you isn't the way it happened? She told you she got knocked out in 1986 by a bandito. But she didn't get knocked out in 1986. That was what she told the police when Heather was kidnapped six weeks *after* she told you that."

Stephanie looked surprised as it sunk in.

"Oh, I didn't understand that."

Don knew her surprise was genuine. Actually, that was better for him. It proved that she had not made up this story and come forward for some other reason, like hope of getting a reward. She was telling the truth. Paula had made a baffling blunder, and had made Stephanie a key witness.

As the end of June approached, it was time to move on to Phase Two of Weber's master plan. He had delayed partly because he had promised Groshong that nothing would happen while he was on his sailboat with his family in the Bahamas for two weeks in June.

But Groshong was back. At a meeting in Haine's office, the prosecutors and investigators decided that Paula would be charged again with obstructing justice and concealing a homicidal death, this time in Madison County and this time in Heather's death. Don appreciated the plan as another parallel between the cases that was ironically appropriate.

The charges would be filed over the long July Fourth weekend. The Fourth was a Tuesday, and if they busted Paula the Saturday before, they might be able to keep her in jail for several days before her father could get to a bank for the cash for bond again. That had failed in Jersey County, but it was worth trying again in Madison County, where Weber felt he could control the situation.

The charges would be four counts of obstructing justice and two counts of concealment of a homicidal death. Two obstructing charges referred to Paula's statements to Patrolman Eichen that Heather had been kidnapped, and the other two were for her statements to McCain that she had been knocked unconscious.

The honor of bringing Paula in on Saturday, July 2, went to Dooley and Hayes, and they would be assisted by a deputy sheriff because the Blews lived in the county venue. Since it was a Saturday, they went to the home of Judge O'Neill in Alton for him to sign the warrant. But he couldn't because it had not been file-stamped by the circuit clerk's office. The supervisor of the clerk's criminal division, Paula Wardle, lived in Alton, and she agreed to go to the office with the cops to get the warrant stamped. The judge signed it on the second visit to his home, and set the bond at $250,000. It would take $25,000 cash to secure Paula's release this time.

Hayes's knock on Blews' door was answered by Orville, and Robert was standing behind him. When Hayes said he had a warrant for Paula's arrest, he saw Paula dart around the corner into the hallway, headed toward the back of the house. Hayes yelled for Dooley to cover the back door. As Dooley turned the corner, he saw Robert part the curtains on the door window and peer out. But by then, Paula had reappeared in the front room, and sat down on the couch to pull on her shoes.

As she stood up, Robert embraced her and Hayes thought he heard Paula whimper softly. She hugged her father, and walked over to Hayes to be handcuffed. Without a word, she handed Hayes a folded piece of paper. It was the same motion Groshong had filed in Jersey County saying she would remain silent and wanted to be held in segregation.

Paula was placed in a sheriff's car and driven to the county jail in Edwardsville. As she was booked by a jail matron, Paula refused to give her name, address, age, and other personal history. Hayes told her that her right to remain silent did not include refusing to provide the jail with personal data. When she still refused to answer the question, Hayes threatened to leave her in the holding cell until she cooperated.

Finally, in a sarcastic and clipped tone, she answered the questions.

This time, the plan had worked. With the banks closed, Orville was unable to get to his reserves for the $25,000 needed to satisfy the bond; Paula would sit in jail until Monday. But it turned out to be for naught; she had been well prepared by Groshong, and she refused to speak to anyone.

The arrest had caught almost everyone by surprise, especially Groshong. Haine explained to reporters that Paula had been arrested on a Saturday because "things just jelled" on Friday. But he also said that the timing of the arrest also was an effort to reduce the amount of publicity accompanying the action.

Groshong was sailing on Lake Carlyle, fifty miles east of Alton, when he got the word. He was incensed that Weber had pulled that kind of stunt over a holiday weekend.

Just before Paula was to make her initial appearance in court Monday morning, a well-tanned Groshong pulled Weber into the judge's empty chambers and angrily ripped into him. Haine walked in, and Groshong directed some of the invective in his direction, too.

Pointing his finger at Weber, Groshong said, "You're on my shit list. What you did was terrible and I'm pissed off. I didn't think you would pull something that sneaky and underhanded. I thought you would be more honorable than that with me. I assumed you would play your cards close to the vest, but I thought you would be straight with me. I'm on my sailboat and I have to hear from someone else that you've had Paula arrested. I had to cut my weekend short and come back early to handle this."

Weber was surprised by Groshong's angry attack, but he rejected the allegation that he had done something improper.

"Come on, Don. We're both big boys here and this is a grownup fight. Neither of us is going to pull our punches. I'm taking my best shot and I always said I would. That's the way it's going to be. We've got two dead babies and we're going to get to the bottom of this. I promised you last month I wouldn't do anything while you were in the Bahamas. But I never promised anything this month."

After Haine left the room, Weber looked at Groshong and asked, "You're really mad, aren't you?"

Groshong shrugged. "Not that mad."

But Weber knew Groshong well enough to know that he was genuinely angry. It wasn't an act.

The battle shifted into the courtroom before Chief Criminal Judge Edward C. Ferguson. Groshong asked for Paula's release on a recognizance bond without posting cash, or at least a reduction in the bond to $100,000. She had appeared at all hearings in Jersey and Madison counties, and she was not about to flee while she was contesting state custody of her sole surviving child. The high bond, he said, was punitive and an attempt to keep her in jail in case she would talk to other prisoners. "If her name was anything other than Paula Sims, you would never, ever see a bond this high," Groshong said.

Weber responded that a high bond was proper because she may have tried to flee when she was arrested. And then, as added incentive for the judge to keep the bond high, Don dropped a sledgehammer on her.

"A murder charge against Paula Sims is imminent in this case."

Weber was struck by the irreconcilable philosophies at work in the courtroom. Groshong was arguing that every defendant had constitutional rights to be protected and honored, even by the prosecutors—purely abstract points. For Weber, the issue was flesh and blood—justice for Loralei and Heather by prosecuting their killer. Constitutional rights were important; so was justice.

Judge Ferguson refused to reduce the bond. But again Orville Blew's checkbook came to the rescue. He immediately submitted a check for $25,000, and Paula was free again. Weber was surprised; he had no idea that he hadn't come close to breaking Orville's bank.

The day still held more controversy, however. That afternoon, the Alton *Telegraph* ran a story quoting Herb Condray accusing Weber of trying to extort a statement out of Robert that would incriminate Paula. The leverage used by Weber was an offer to return Randy to his father in a letter Weber had sent to Groshong.

Actually, Weber's letter had been an offer to consider returning Randy if Robert could provide evidence that Paula was guilty and would testify against her. But it wasn't the heavy-handed extortion attempt portrayed by Herb Condray. It was a simple suggestion that Robert and Paula knew more than they were telling, and the prosecutors would be glad to let one of them testify against the other.

But Weber couldn't defend himself publicly against Herb's attack. The letter had been private correspondence between the attorneys about a juvenile case in the middle of a news blackout. So Weber had to keep his mouth shut and take the galling abuse from Herb.

By the time Don got home that night, he was exhausted. And he was worried over Groshong's wrathful outburst. Weber told his wife that he was afraid Groshong was too angry to let what had happened pass. It was possible, Don thought, that their friendship might not survive. That certainly was one result of this damned case that Don hadn't anticipated and would sincerely regret.

But Groshong called that evening from his office, where he and Williamson had been talking for some time over drinks. Groshong was in a much better mood. He and Don chatted and laughed, and Don knew the cloud had passed.

Chapter 15

July Fourth wasn't a holiday for Weber and the Alton police. They were preparing to fire up the grand jury that the prosecutor would ask to indict Paula Marie Sims for murder. Not only did the evidence point toward Paula as the person who actually committed the killings, but charging her with murder might be enough to make her ''roll over'' on Robert if she had not acted alone.

Weber also wanted to keep the pressure on in Loralei's death. He appointed Ringhausen a special prosecutor in Madison County so he could sit in with the grand jury to hear any testimony that could be useful in Jersey County.

Hayes and Sullivan had the holiday duty, delivering subpoenas to the whole Sims clan for appearances before the grand jury for the next Monday, July 10. Robert and his in-laws were served at their home, and the cops then drove the few blocks to the Condrays' house on Rose Street to hand them their subpoenas. But the detectives weren't finished. Weber couldn't find an answer in the file to another question that had crossed his mind. Did the Condrays have a freezer? One way to find out, and maybe pick up a little intelligence on the Condrays at the same time, would be to canvass their neighborhood.

After Sullivan and Hayes served the subpoenas, they spent a couple of hours knocking on doors along Rose Street. Nine of the neighbors said they knew nothing about the Condrays. The only tidbit the police picked up was one man's suggestion that Linda was angered easily when kids got into her yard. The only other neighbor who answered his door said he knew Herb and Linda, but he refused to discuss them and closed the door in the cops' faces.

That kept the record intact. Several neighborhood canvasses over three years in two infants' deaths had yet to produce a single piece of valuable information.

Don had subpoenaed Robert as a precaution. He probably wouldn't be called to testify, since he was certain to take the Fifth. But it might be necessary to have him there in case something, or someone, broke in front of the grand jury and the defense case started to crumble. Don might have a window of opportunity of about two hours to act before the defense could start making repairs, and Robert's presence could be essential. If Don let that opportunity slip away, he might lose the only chance at finding the truth.

But the testimony from the other witnesses could be very important. Weber wanted to close the door on any possible alibis for Paula. He wanted, finally, to get some answers to the questions about where everyone had been during those crucial time periods. Just how much did the Blews know about this whole thing, and what could be learned about their freezer?

Weber also saw the grand jury session as an opportunity to weaken Groshong's control over the extended Sims family. As long as he was the attorney for all of the relatives, he could keep them all going the same direction. If Weber could split them up, he would have a better chance of getting information from them and keeping information from Groshong. Weber was sure Orville Blew had been paying Groshong's fees, so the defender would stay with Paula if he had to choose between representing her or Robert. Everyone knows a lawyer will follow the money.

But the start of the grand jury investigation also presented Weber with a new challenge. In Illinois, a lawyer is permitted to stay in the grand jury room while his client testifies. If Groshong were allowed to sit through Weber's questioning of the Blews and the Condrays, the defense soon would figure out Weber's theories. That would put Weber at a distinct, if not fatal, strategic disadvantage. Groshong could start closing up holes before Weber got to them.

When Monday arrived, Weber had a plan ready. Nylene Blew was the first witness brought before the grand jurors in a courtroom on the third floor. Groshong sat there as she nervously cited her right under the Fifth

Amendment to refuse to answer questions that might tend to incriminate her. Without any hesitation, Weber ordered Nylene taken before Judge Ferguson on the second floor.

Weber, Haine, Groshong, and Nylene filed out of the room and walked down the stairs to Ferguson's courtroom, with a line of reporters tagging along behind them.

Nylene stood anxiously in front of the bench as Weber announced that she had taken the Fifth Amendment, and that he was seeking a grant of immunity from prosecution for her testimony. She could not be prosecuted for anything she said to the grand jury, unless she committed perjury. As an immunized witness, she could be held in contempt of the grand jury and jailed unless she testified. Ferguson issued the immunity order and explained to Nylene that she had to answer the questions.

The line marched back up to the grand jury room. But it was time for a special maneuver from Weber; he stepped into the doorway in front of Groshong and shook his head.

"You're not going in there, Don."

Groshong arched his eyebrows. "Yes, I am. I represent her and I'm going in there."

"No, you're not. It's a conflict for the attorney for the target of the investigation to sit in on the grand jury testimony of other witnesses, and you're not going in there."

"Well, let's see what the judge says about that," Groshong responded emphatically.

So they trooped back down to Ferguson's courtroom with the press in tow. Weber stated his objection and asked Ferguson to bar Groshong from the room. Groshong protested, saying Nylene had a right to her choice of attorneys and the prosecution had no right to exclude him. Nylene wouldn't be making any incriminating statements against anyone, and there was no harm in letting him in with her. But Ferguson agreed with Weber that "multiple representation" created a conflict for an attorney defending the target of the investigation. It would threaten the integrity of the grand jury and destroy its confidentiality if the target's attorney heard the testimony of another witness.

Weber added that he would be taking the same action with Orville. Ferguson gave the Blews until the next morning to obtain new counsel.

Weber's ploy to push Groshong farther away from the

center of the investigation had worked. Groshong would get all the reports on the investigation through the discovery process, in which both sides must disclose their evidence to the other before trial. But by the time the reports made it to Groshong, Weber hoped to have everything vital to his case nailed down.

That evening, Don got a call at home from one of his best friends, Tom Long, who said the Blews had asked him to represent them before the grand jury. Long was the chairman of the Republican Party in Madison County, and an expert civil and tax attorney who had been one of Don's assistant prosecutors when he was state's attorney.

Weber loved the irony in Groshong's decision to steer the Blews to Long. Don thought of the night of his wedding, on December 30, 1983. He was preparing to leave for the church when he was stunned to see a huge white limousine wheel into his driveway. Out of one door popped his tuxedoed best man, Long, and out of the other door jumped the tuxedoed Groshong, who was to videotape the wedding. The three friends enjoyed their chauffeured drive to St. Louis for the wedding, lounging in the back of the limousine and having a few refreshments. It had been a complete surprise, and the kind of moment that makes great memories.

Long told Weber that the immunity orders for the Blews would be challenged on the grounds that immunity in Illinois did not protect them from prosecution in Missouri, where the body had been found. The Blews would refuse to testify without immunity in Missouri. But Weber explained that the U.S. Supreme Court had ruled long ago in a case called *Murphy V. The Waterfront Commission* that a grant of immunity by one prosecuting authority extended to all prosecuting authorities.

Before court started the next morning, Weber approached Groshong with a smile.

"Nice touch with Tom, Don. The first thing I thought of was you guys picking me up in the limo the night of my wedding. Now all three of us are in this huge case together."

Groshong returned the kind of smile that can pass only between close friends. "I thought you'd like that."

But it was time for business. At last, Weber would have the people closest to the Simses before the grand jury, and he would have Groshong on the outside. Nylene testified for about two hours. After lunch, Orville was called in. He took the Fifth Amendment and the scene from the day before was repeated in Ferguson's courtroom. As Orville's attorney, Long objected on the immunity–jurisdiction issue; Weber cited *Murphy* v. *Waterfront*. Ferguson ordered Orville to testify.

His testimony lasted ninety minutes. Weber was satisfied with the information from the Blews. He had established several points. Paula had keys to her parents' home and could use them whenever she wanted, giving her access to their freezer when they were out of town. Orville could alibi for Paula on Tuesday night and Wednesday night, but not Wednesday morning, when Heather's body could have been dumped.

And the grand jury had a pretty good picture of some of the oddities about Robert and Paula Sims, such as Robert's restrictive rules around the house and his distant relationship with his in-laws.

The Blews' testimony and the interview with the Condrays the month before combined to make Weber hope he had what he needed—some time periods, including Wednesday morning, when no one knew Paula's whereabouts. If that held up, the only person left who could alibi for Paula during those crucial times was Robert. Would a jury believe him?

After the Blews testified, Weber put on the cops who knew the Sims cases so well—Yocom, Sievers, McCain, Ventimiglia, and Hayes. With all of that information before them, Weber was confident the grand jurors would do what any normal, reasonable person would when confronted with Paula's preposterous stories and the facts—point the finger and cry, "Murder."

So the moment that so many people had awaited for so long arrived. Paula Sims finally would face a murder charge for the cold-blooded murder of her own six-week-old daughter. Weber presented the charges he wanted the grand jurors to return in an indictment, and he took the unusual step of asking them to return a special report he had prepared. Then he left the jurors to their deliberations.

At 5:50 P.M., the grand jury returned an indictment charging Paula with two counts of first-degree murder. Under state law, multiple counts of the same charge can be filed to allege different legal theories of guilt. One count charged that Paula had smothered Heather with the intent to kill. The second charged that Paula had smothered Heather with the knowledge that it could cause death or bodily harm.

The charges also were phrased to give Weber the most flexibility in presenting the evidence. The charges said that the killing had been committed by Paula Sims "or one for whose conduct she is legally accountable." Under that language, Weber could invoke the state's accountability law that says a person is just as guilty of murder if he participates in the planning or commission of acts that kill someone. Weber could argue that Paula's obvious involvement in the killing and coverup would be enough to constitute guilt of murder, even if someone else actually snuffed the life out of Heather.

That was backed up by the grand jury report. It pledged that the grand jury would continue its investigation into the possibility that Robert Sims had been involved in his daughter's death. The implication of the two documents was clear, and not particularly subtle. It fell just short of an accusation against Robert.

As requested by Weber and Haine, Judge Ferguson ordered Paula held without bail. This time, Orville's bank account couldn't come to Paula's rescue. Even if the bond was reduced later, Paula would spend some time in jail.

The indictment was returned amid the kind of media attention the case had attracted all along. Just outside the door to the grand jury room, Haine and Weber were encircled by reporters and cameras. Weber deferred to Haine, who explained that there was "very important" physical evidence to support the charges, and that the Alton case was relevant to the case from 1986.

Haine also confirmed that prosecutors might seek the death penalty for Paula under two provisions in state law—a victim under twelve and a killing committed with "exceptionally brutal and heinous behavior indicative of wanton cruelty."

Again, Weber had backed up the indictment with the grand jury report. It also said, "The proof is evident that the death resulted from exceptionally brutal and heinous behavior." Another hammer blow from the grand jury.

The report served several purposes for Weber. It kept the pressure on Robert, and served notice that death was a possible sentence in the case, putting even more pressure on Paula.

Haine refused to offer a motive for the seemingly senseless killing. "Only the accused knows the motive; anything else is speculative."

And then he offered a personal comment. "This is a sad, terrible case. We just have to deal with it."

Even the most experienced reporters in the crowd had to admit there was a heightened sense of energy surrounding that piece of paper. It was identical to the ones they had seen with dozens of other names on it. But this time, it was Paula Sims's name.

Ten miles northwest of the courthouse, a small group of cops was poised. For the first time, Sergeant Tony Ventimiglia had decided to step into the spotlight. He had worked hard at staying in the background. But this time, with the big pop coming on his case, he wanted to be out front. He wanted to arrest Paula and he wanted the television "tape at ten" to show him escorting the handcuffed defendant to the car. He would be accompanied by Sievers, another cop who had earned the right to be in on this arrest, and by a new city detective, Jody O'Guinn.

When word of the indictment reached the waiting police at 6:30 P.M., they converged quickly on the Blews' house; the press already was there in force. Ventimiglia told Orville that they had come to arrest Paula on murder charges. Orville and his daughter were not surprised. With no small amount of satisfaction, Ventimiglia told the steely-eyed Paula she was under arrest and handcuffed her. As they started out of the door, Orville caught Ventimiglia by the arm and asked if he knew what the bond would be. While Ventimiglia was explaining that the judge had denied bail, Sievers and O'Guinn walked Paula outside and put her in the car as the cameras rolled.

Tony Ventimiglia missed the one television shot he had been waiting for since April 29.

Weber went home right after work that night, grabbed a can of beer, and collapsed into a chair. He closed his eyes and leaned his head back, and let the events of the

day sink in. Oddly, he felt none of the elation or relief
that often comes at such a turning point in a major case.
After some murder indictments, Weber would go drinking with the cops to celebrate a job well done. But this
night was different. He was thinking only that the die
was cast, and there was a lot of work ahead. Time had
shifted to Groshong's side. He would have access to all
the police reports and other information now. Weber
could waste no time finding answers to the questions in
his mind before Groshong realized their importance.

There was one bit of satisfaction, however. Don knew
there was a good chance Paula Sims had spent her last
day of freedom.

The orange jumpsuit, standard issue for prisoners at
the Madison County Jail, was much too big and baggy
for Paula as she shuffled clumsily into the courthouse in
ankle shackles and handcuffs early Wednesday morning.
She was dwarfed by Jim Neumann, the six-foot-four deputy who had escorted Paula as she was driven through
the jail's motorized rear gate, down the narrow alley, and
around the corner to the side entrance at the courthouse.
As she got out of the car and was led down the ramp into
the basement, the photographers closed in. She was ush-
ered through the dingy hallway past the snack bar and
loaded into the elevator for the ride to the criminal division on the second floor. The photographers dashed up
the stairs, racing the elevator to be waiting again when
its doors opened and Paula was led into the courtroom.

It was a scene that would be repeated dozens of times
without variation, and would lead the courthouse regulars to assume that videotape must be very cheap.

But this first time was vintage Paula. No emotion, eyes
front. She was whisked into Judge Ferguson's courtroom.
As the press filled the two rows of wooden benches in
the back, Ferguson read the charges and told Paula she
could face a prison sentence between twenty and sixty
years, or sixty to one hundred years if the case fell under
the more severe provisions of an extended term. She also
could get life in prison without parole, and perhaps even
the death penalty. Groshong entered a plea of not guilty
and filed motions asking that bond be set and that Paula

be held in segregation. The judge set all motions for Friday, the same day as the preliminary hearing on the earlier charges of obstructing justice and concealment of a homicidal death.

With that, barely ten minutes in court, Paula's first appearance as an accused murderer was over and she hobbled back into the elevator with Neumann.

The scene was repeated two days later, on Friday, July 14. Paula was brought back into Ferguson's courtroom, this time to appear before Judge Duffwilliams in the preliminary hearing. Weber knew the reporters and spectators jammed into the room would get to hear a lot more than they expected. And to increase the dramatic tension, Robert was sitting in the front row just behind Paula's right shoulder.

Weber knew the press would jump all over the story that day because so much information would come out. They would play it so big that it probably would eliminate any chance of trying the case in Madison County.

Weber figured Groshong would use the hearing as a free peek at Weber's theories on the case. That was okay, because a good prosecutor could do the same thing to the defense. By listening carefully to the questions the defense asked, Weber usually could figure out what the other side's game plan was. He even could tell how the defense was planning to handle certain pieces of evidence or testimony, especially when he knew an opponent this well.

Groshong opened the hearing with a typical gambit, a motion asking Judge Duffwilliams to recuse herself because she also was hearing the juvenile matter involving little Randy's custody. Weber responded with the gracious suggestion that the judge was capable of discerning what evidence applied to which case. The judge refused to step aside.

Weber's first witness was Frank Yocom, and with him came the first test of Don's "modus operandi" theory in the Sims cases. As soon as Weber asked Yocom the first question about the report from Paula about a missing child in 1986, Groshong objected. It was totally beyond the subject of the indictment and the hearing.

Weber was ready, and he explained quickly that the 1986 case bore striking similarities to the 1989 case.

"Under the well-known, established law of 'modus operandi,' a prior incident is admissible in court if it tends to prove an element of the crime charged."

He held his breath as the judge started to rule.

"The objection is overruled. You may proceed, counsel."

Fantastic, Don thought. The cornerstone to his case had survived the first storm, even though Judge Duffwilliams was hardly an experienced criminal judge and the rules of evidence were less stringent at a preliminary hearing.

Yocom went methodically through the Loralei case. The parallels to Heather's death were shaping up nicely, and Weber was pleased with the way it was sounding from the witness stand.

But Yocom startled Don by suggesting that Paula's story had been reenacted by the police in 1986. Don didn't remember seeing anything in the reports about that. Yocom explained that it only consisted of having several officers lie on the floor and then run up the stairs when they heard the door close. The exercise suggested to Yocom that Paula probably wouldn't have been able to see the kidnapper on the driveway at night if she had waited until the door closed to chase him.

On cross-examination, Groshong asked if Yocom had checked to see if the date of Loralei's disappearance had any significance on the satanic calendar. That sent a ripple of satisfaction through Weber.

"It was insignificant," the sheriff said.

But to Weber, the question meant Groshong still was looking into the satanism angle, eliminated long ago by the authorities. The defense was running several weeks behind, just as Weber wanted.

Weber's second witness was Rick McCain, and he provided the most dramatic testimony of the day by disclosing the FBI conclusion that the bag with Heather's body had been made on the same machine within twelve hours of the ones in the opened roll found at the Simses' house. Weber didn't have the full report yet, and he still wasn't aware just how impressive that evidence would be later.

Weber surprised the press by offering his first suggestion of a motive. While McCain was recounting June Gibson's statement about Robert's rules around the house,

Weber asked if Paula had told her friend that the rules were causing marital problems. Groshong objected to the question as irrelevant.

But Weber responded, "The information she gave to a police officer is that a masked man kidnapped her child. The evidence that she, in fact, murdered her child tends to prove that her story to the police is not true. The evidence that the children caused a problem and were about to cause a divorce in the family gives the defendant a strong motive to murder her child and to obstruct justice by lying about what really happened."

The judge overruled Groshong's objection without comment.

Groshong cross-examined McCain closely on most issues, but hit especially hard on the trash bags and focused on the FBI's inability to match the perforations on the edges of the bags. That meant Groshong had not received much expert assistance on that evidence yet because he didn't know that the stretching of the bags before they tear made matching those points nearly impossible.

Groshong also was careful to suggest to McCain that Stephanie Werner could have confused the newspaper accounts of the details of the two kidnappings. That attack on Stephanie's credibility would allow Weber to call her mother as support. To Weber, Barbara Werner's supportive testimony could be more important than her daughter's.

McCain was starting to enjoy the give-and-take with Groshong. In fact, McCain knew Groshong's reputation and had expected him to be much tougher in the courtroom. Their exchanges even provided a few chuckles that day. Groshong was drilling McCain about the good care the Simses had given Heather, including the trip to the doctor for treatment of diarrhea. As the defense attorney listed the good points of the baby's condition—no bruises, no broken bones—McCain added one more factor: "And the death of the baby."

Groshong looked up and smiled. "That's a nice shot."

When Weber returned for redirect examination, he gave McCain the opening they both had been awaiting.

"After Heather disappeared, what happened to the sleeping arrangements in the Sims home?"

"According to Robert Sims, during the interview with

Special Agent Schultz of the FBI, Robert and Paula slept together and, on either Monday or Tuesday of that week, had better and longer-lasting sex than they had had for a long, long time.''

In a dramatic movement, Paula spun her head around and looked back over her shoulder at Robert. She shot him an icy, withering stare across the silent courtroom. But he didn't react, even under his wife's glower and after a very private detail of this very private man's life had been disclosed.

"No further questions," Weber gloated.

Groshong shrugged it off. "I don't have any questions about that."

Judge Duffwilliams ruled quickly that probable cause had been established and ordered Paula bound over for trial.

Groshong entered not guilty pleas on all counts and filed several motions. He asked for a gag order to end "the conscious effort on the part of the police and prosecutors to try this case in the press and other news media." He requested that the trial be moved out of Madison County because of the "extensive, adverse pretrial publicity." He filed copies of dozens of newspaper stories to support the argument that Paula could not get a fair trial in the county. He also filed a motion asking that the indictment be dismissed because it did not properly state an offense.

Weber was pleased with the hearing. He had learned some useful things about Groshong's case without giving away too much from the prosecution. Groshong had not delved into the time of death or the time when the body was dumped. That left him searching for an alibi from Saturday night until Wednesday, a long time that would be difficult to cover. Groshong didn't know that Weber had narrowed the period when the body was dropped into the barrel from midnight Tuesday to 1:00 P.M. Wednesday.

Paula was starting to settle in at the jail. But a curious problem arose. Paula protested indignantly when she learned that a male trusty was doing the women's laundry. Paula told Lieutenant James Newsome, the jail superintendent, that she didn't want a man touching her underwear. Newsome shrugged and responded, "Then

you do the laundry." He was surprised when she agreed.
So Paula took over the laundry service for the women's
cellblocks. Her undies were safe.

When grand jury day drew near, Weber decided that
Herb Condray needed a little lesson in cooperating with
the authorities. Don was still smarting from Herb's blast
in the press over the letter to Groshong. Don and the
Alton police decided Herb's mood might improve if he
knew his bingo partner, the black woman, was waiting
in the wings during the grand jury session. So they subpoenaed her and arranged for her to be standing nearby
when Herb and Linda arrived that morning.

Weber got there early, and found Dooley escorting the
woman, who was wearing a rather low-cut, and very
bright red, dress. *The lady in the red dress. How appropriate,* Weber thought. Dooley stationed his guest against
the railing by the courthouse atrium, directly across from
the stairs and the elevator Herb was most likely to use.

It was worth the wait. As Herb rounded the corner a
step or two behind Linda, he glanced over and saw Dooley and the woman. Weber was standing nearby, and read
Herb's widened eyes and fallen expression as "suppressed anxiety."

It didn't take a Pulitzer prize-winning reporter to notice the lady in red. There was a lot of speculation among
the reporters, and they spent most of the morning trying
to pry her identity out of friendly sources.

The report that fell widest from the mark came from
a reporter from KTVI-TV, Channel 2, who told his viewers that sources had identified the woman as the fisherman who discovered Heather's body. That brought a
robust guffaw from the cops. One reporter who learned
the real story had it confirmed simply by approaching
some of the official sources and saying, "Bingo." The
huge smiles were more confirmation than Deep Throat
ever offered Woodward and Bernstein.

With the preliminaries over, Weber turned to the business
of the day and called Linda Condray before the grand jury.
He didn't expect her to help his case, but he wanted to make
sure she couldn't hurt him with some unexpected alibi at the
trial. He would take her methodically through that week,

hour by hour, testing her memory of times and places. And he wanted Linda to tell the grand jury a little more about the Simses' emotional makeup and their marriage.

Linda testified for about fifty minutes, and Weber was getting essentially the kind of information he had expected. But as he asked her about arriving at Robert's Sunday morning, he got a response that whacked him right between the eyes. He knew he had just heard something very important, but he couldn't decipher it as he stood before the grand jury, looking at the husky woman with the bleached-blonde hair.

"Now, when you got there, who was there?"

"Lots of police; my brother, Bob. I believe Paula was there, but she was preparing to leave with Randy to go to her parents' house because Bob wanted her to."

Weber was stunned. This distraught mother, who supposedly had been knocked unconscious by a man who kidnapped her infant daughter some ten hours before, was going to her parents', where she would be alone? Everybody knew the Blews were out of town. Paula going there then was completely inconsistent with the rest of the story, and it caught Don off-guard.

"That's on Sunday?" he asked almost clumsily.

"Yes, to my best recollection, that's correct."

"Did she leave then?"

"If I recollect correctly, she did. She took Randy, put him in the station wagon; she was packing a few things. Bob wanted to buffer her from all that was taking place. 'Go to your parents' house. You can't be of any use here.' And to my best recollection, she did leave and go to her parents' house in the station wagon, which we now own."

Weber wasn't sure what this meant. Had Robert sent Paula to her parents, knowing that no one else was there to comfort her? Don stowed it away mentally and would try to plug it into the case late some night when it was just him and the file.

He waited until the end of Linda's testimony to get into her theory that Yocom was responsible for Heather's death. Weber let her tell the jury essentially the same weird story she had told Hertz and Kuba. When that was over, Weber politely invited Linda to leave.

Herb testified for seventeen minutes, offering nothing of substance.

Troy Sims, Robert's father, was on the stand for twelve minutes, and Weber thought, *He doesn't know anything.* But as the slender old man with the slicked-back hair and neatly trimmed little moustache took the stand, Weber couldn't help but think of the reports that Troy often had accompanied Herb to play bingo. *A family just full of intrigue*, Don thought.

One adjective for Dr. Mary Case that just about every man involved in the Sims investigation—cops, prosecutors, defense attorneys, and reporters—could agree on, was "intimidating." Her commanding presence was the sum of several factors. Foremost was her obvious expertise as a forensic pathologist, coupled with her ability to present her conclusions in a way that nearly precluded any disagreement. She didn't come off as cold, but just a little aloof. Her professional bearing was reinforced by a stunning appearance. She was fashionably slender and her short blonde hair was cut in the latest style. Her clothes were perfectly tailored and obviously expensive, and were set off by stunning, sometimes massive, jewelry. She carried herself in a way that suggested she could have been a model, but actually bespoke the confidence of a recognized leader in her field.

At only forty-six years old, Dr. Case already had amassed a curriculum vitae that was overwhelming; it was eight single-spaced pages of accomplishment. In addition to her residencies, fellowships, and assistant professorships, she had served as assistant or chief deputy medical examiner in St. Louis city and county, and currently was the chief medical examiner for St. Louis County and, fortunately, St. Charles County. She had published fourteen papers and eight abstracts with titles such as, "Patterns of Injury and Recognition of Homicide"; "Accidental or Inflicted Injury in Children: A Study of 160 Child Deaths"; and "Delayed Death Produced by Manual Strangulation." She had presented 31 talks on subjects such as child abuse, brain death, and head injuries.

On August 3, Dr. Case sat for a deposition in her office

at the St. Louis University Medical Center and answered questions about the autopsy of Heather's body. Jim Williamson handled the questioning for the defense. Weber and Kit Morrissey were there and Tom Jackstadt appeared as the court's guardian of Randy.

Williamson repeatedly drilled in on Dr. Case's two primary conclusions—that Heather was smothered and died about the time she was reported missing, and that her body was frozen soon after she was killed. Dr. Case explained several times that she had concluded the baby was smothered because of the three tiny lacerations on the inside of her upper lip and the absence of any other disease. Those tears occurred when someone put pressure on the outside of the baby's mouth, forcing the soft skin under the lip against the bony maxillary ridge where her upper teeth would have appeared later. A hand or even a pillow could have been used. The doctor said she had seen a case where an infant was smothered by a stack of blankets.

Williamson suggested that those cuts would be unusual with an infant who had no teeth. But Dr. Case was unbending and said that teeth would not have been required to cut the soft tissue there.

"Would you agree that it's difficult, hard, virtually impossible to make a diagnosis of suffocation of a child without teeth?" Williamson asked.

"No. I do not agree," was the blunt response.

She also defended her conclusion about the freezing of the body. The body appeared to be very well preserved, but there were "cherry red" marks on the left forehead, cheek, and neck that indicated exposure to cold. Her suspicions were confirmed when she examined the internal organs. The state of decomposition there was more advanced than it should have been in comparison to the outside of the body. She said the body had been frozen, probably in temperatures in the 20s, soon after death. If it had been very long after death, the cherry marks would not have appeared.

The body had lain face down for some time after death because the blood had settled in the front of the body— the livor mortis condition. The body was found face up, but the blood meant it was not that way right after death.

Don wondered if the killer had been unable to look Heather in the face after the deed was done.

Dr. Case explained that freezing also would account for the stage of rigor mortis in the body, another issue raised repeatedly by Willamson. She had found the rigor mortis fading away, a stage usually reached thirty-six to forty-eight hours after death. But she said she believed the baby had been dead for about 72 or more hours, or since about the time she was reported missing. Freezing would have slowed the rigor mortis process, making the discovery of the body seem closer to the time of death.

Weber had been hoping that Williamson could shake Dr. Case's conclusion about freezing. The freezing made Weber's job a lot harder.

Williamson fared no better when he asked Dr. Case if Heather could have died from sudden infant death syndrome. Based on all the facts and the body's condition, the doctor said, SIDS could not be considered.

"Why not?"

"A SIDS case occurs in the home. When children are found dead, they are brought in to be examined. Why would a SIDS case be found in a plastic bag abandoned in a trash can?"

"Well, it's possible, isn't it?"

Dr. Case stiffened. "No. Never in this jurisdiction or any jurisdiction in which there is a proper forensic pathologist, would this be adjudged a sudden infant death, meaning, 'I don't know why this child is dead, but it's natural causes.' This is a very suspicious death, obviously. It's a child abandoned in a trash can in a plastic bag and later identified as a child who was removed some days earlier. Obviously, very suspicious circumstances. Children like that are never considered SIDS, properly. If you don't know why they die, you simply say, 'I don't know why they die and I don't know what the manner of death is.' But it's totally improper to consider that as sudden infant death."

Despite the battling back and forth between Williamson and Dr. Case, it would turn out later that the most important answer she gave was not even noticed by any of the lawyers that day. At the beginning of the deposition, she said she was board certified in three specialties—anatomical, neuropathology, and forensic pathology. No one even paid any attention to the one in the middle.

Chapter 16

Don Groshong had stood behind the defense table on hundreds of criminal cases over the last seventeen years, including two dozen murder cases. He was best known for his defense of Susan Davidson and her lover, Bill Gill, who were charged with the brutal killing of Davidson's husband. Groshong had beaten the odds in Gill's trial, coming away with a verdict of voluntary manslaughter in a bloody beating with a piece of firewood, supplemented with a couple of gunshots to the head. The remorseful Gill pleaded self-defense and got seven years in prison.

But by the time Susie got to trial, Groshong had run out of miracles. A cache of love letters exchanged between Susie and Bill before the killing had fallen into the hands of the prosecutors after a prolonged court battle that helped build Groshong's reputation as a resourceful pretrial tactician. The jury, faced with Susie's writings about her fears that she and Bill would be caught and punished, convicted her of murder. She was sent to the Dwight Correctional Center for women for thirty years.

Groshong knew his way around murder cases. And he had never seen one with less evidence against the accused than the case of Paula Sims. He had never seen a file that thick with less in it.

That was his attack on August 7 when he asked Judge Matoesian to set a reasonable bond on the murder charges. Groshong's only witness was Sergeant Rick McCain and, with Robert in the audience again, Groshong went right to work on the cop.

"Do you have a confession?"

"No, sir."

"Do you have any prior testimony of Mrs. Sims under oath that would implicate her in this matter in any way?"

"No, sir."

"Do you have any eyewitnesses who saw Mrs. Sims do anything in this case?"

"At this point, no, sir."

"You don't have a videotape confession or audiotape confession, do you?"

"No, sir, I do not."

Groshong went down the list, eliminating one type of evidence after another. No fingerprints or tire tracks or lineup identifications. Nothing in the autopsy report linked to Paula. The perforations on the trash bags hadn't matched. It only took a few minutes, and Groshong was pleased by the time he said, "No further questions of this witness."

Not bad, Weber thought as he stood for his turn. But Groshong had used the old defense trick of focusing on what the prosecution didn't have. Don would present what they did have.

McCain explained that Paula Sims had "absolute, last control" of Heather, and the evidence overwhelmingly contradicted her story about the kidnapping. The list he offered for Don was different than the one Groshong had drawn from him. This was a recitation of the peculiarities in these two cases and the holes in Paula's story.

McCain also mentioned that Dr. Case had concluded that Loralei's death was a homicide. That obviously took Groshong by surprise. It hadn't come out at the doctor's deposition four days earlier. Groshong asked if there was a report on such a conclusion. McCain said Dr. Case had made the statement in an interview with Weber about two months earlier, but McCain had not written a report on it because Loralei was not Alton's case.

Groshong clearly was concerned that he now could be facing allegations about two murders, not one murder and one unexplained death.

To keep the defense off balance, Weber pointed into the audience and told Matoesian he would like to call Robert Sims to the stand. Groshong objected; Robert would refuse to testify under the Fifth Amendment. Weber complained that it was improper for the attorney for the accused to prevent the prosecution from calling some other witness. But Matoesian shook it off and told Weber that Groshong's statement would stand as citing the Fifth on Robert's behalf. He could not be called to the stand.

Groshong turned to his argument for a reasonable bond, reminding the judge that Paula already had posted $35,000 in cash, through her father, and still was trying to regain custody of her son. The defender offered his evaluation of the state's case against Paula Sims with a typical comment.

"If you find one shred of evidence that Paula Sims moved the body of her baby, I will personally eat the pen sitting in front of me."

Weber asked that bond be denied again with a response in kind. "Anybody who can move a dead baby around to thwart the police investigation is certainly capable of taking it on the lam," he said sarcastically.

And then he surprised everyone by saying the investigation indicated that Orville Blew had the financial resources to meet any bond up to $7 million—which would require $700,000 in cash. Weber had heard scuttlebutt that the Blews had more than $300,000 in investments to add to his pension plan benefits from Amoco.

Matoesian took three days to read the transcript from the preliminary hearing, and then denied bond without comment. That same day, Groshong filed the kind of motion that had built his reputation as a crafty defender. He asked the judge to dismiss the murder charge because there was no evidence that the crime had occurred in Illinois. The judge added that to the list of motions that were to be argued on August 22.

Before the hearing began in the courtroom that day, Weber and Groshong met informally with Matoesian in his chambers. Groshong started to justify his motion for a change of venue with the results of a professional poll he had commissioned showing that 75 percent of the potential jurors in Madison and Jersey counties knew about the Sims case, and half of that group had an opinion about Paula's guilt or innocence.

But Weber stopped him, explaining that the judge already was planning to move the trial. Weber wouldn't oppose the idea, since television coverage had been far in excess of anything he had ever seen.

Judge Matoesian said he favored Bloomington, a small college town in central Illinois, or Peoria, a larger town farther north that had been the location of the famous Richard Speck trial in 1967 when it was moved out of Chicago. Speck was convicted of butchering eight student nurses in their dormitory in Chicago; he is still serving a life sentence. Matoesian said he would decide on the location after he made some calls. He decided later to go to Peoria.

Inside the courtroom, Judge Matoesian announced the change of venue and a trial date in January or February. But the venue change was the only motion Groshong would win, and the news that Paula Sims would be tried outside of Madison County got bumped down a couple of notches in the media reports that day because of unexpected announcements and comments by Weber.

Don decided to take advantage of something he had learned about a conversation between Frank Yocom and a confidential informant who knew Paula. Yocom had given his word that the informant would not be identified and the information would not be divulged. Although that bargain would be tested later, it didn't mean Weber couldn't use the insight to his advantage then.

The informant had revealed that Paula was terrified of the death sentence. Weber would take advantage of that by announcing then that he would seek execution for Paula if she were convicted. She might bargain off the truth, or maybe even turn against Robert to get herself off that gurney where the lethal injection would be pumped into her arm.

Weber always had supported the death penalty in appropriate cases, and to him, the conclusion that this one was entirely appropriate was inescapable. What could be more brutal and heinous, in the words of the law, than smothering your own six-week-old baby? In fact, execution was deserved in both cases.

When Matoesian called the motion asking for the prosecutor to declare on the death sentence, Weber responded in his most dramatic style. Standing about ten feet from

Paula, Don turned and leveled his gaze directly at her. He spoke slowly, so the words would sink in.

"We are seeking . . . the death penalty . . . for Paula Sims. If she is convicted of murder, the state will seek to put her . . . to death."

Paula had no immediate reaction. But as Don stared at her, she turned her eyes away, and then lowered her head. It was more reaction that he ever had seen from her before. For once, he felt that something had broken through that barrier of stone. But it took a direct threat on her life to make a crack.

Don dropped another bomb when Groshong was challenging the indictment because it did not identify the person referred to when it said the killing had been committed by Paula "or one for whose conduct she is legally responsible."

Weber responded, "There is circumstantial evidence that Robert Sims, in fact, participated in the killing and the coverup."

Groshong shook his head. "That's not worth responding to."

Weber had been holding back when it came to Robert, hoping that something more solid would develop. With the existing evidence, Don was afraid a charge against Robert wouldn't make it past a defense motion for a directed verdict of acquittal. A judge could rule, after the prosecution rested, that there was not enough evidence for a jury to convict. That acquitted the defendant without letting the case go to the jury. Directed verdicts of acquittal were rare, but they certainly weren't unheard of and they barred any further proceedings later.

Don knew Robert really wasn't "in the loop" of the evidence that had led to Paula's indictment. On the surface, at least, Robert only had repeated what Paula had told him. Circumstantial evidence justified suspicions about Robert. But evidence in a trial had to prove more than reason for suspicion.

Weber was hoping that Robert or Paula would crack under the mounting pressure. Orville and Nylene had thrown Robert out of their house after Paula was arrested, and Robert had been staying with his sister. Weber hoped that Orville might pry the truth out of his only daughter someday. But Weber had just about given up hope that Paula ever would plead guilty. Groshong had said Paula was insistent that she hadn't done anything wrong, and would never consider anything more than a plea to a misdemeanor in return for probation. Weber had offered a sentence of twenty-five or thirty years, but only for a plea to murder. It was a stalemate there.

Groshong lost two other important motions that day. The judge refused to order Paula held separately from other jail inmates, despite Groshong's claim that she feared for her life and that prosecutors were known for hauling cellmates into court to testify that a defendant had made a jailhouse confession. The cellmate then bargained for a good break on his or her own case.

The judge also rejected Groshong's challenge to Illinois's jurisdiction in the murder. Groshong argued that, absent any evidence to the contrary, the jurisdiction should fall to the venue where the body was found. He said Illinois law required the courts to presume the murder happened in St. Charles County, and the authorities there should prosecute the murder. Groshong even worried that Paula could be exposed to double jeopardy if she were acquitted in Illinois and then charged in Missouri.

Weber rejected the whole argument and called McCain and Ventimiglia to testify that all the evidence in the case was found in Madison County, and it all pointed to the Simses' house as the murder scene.

Matoesian agreed with Weber again, and that set the die. Madison County would prosecute Paula for murder and seek her death, but the trial would take place in some other county's courthouse.

Two days later, Weber sent Dave Hayes into the county jail for the first interview with one of Paula's cellmates. A twenty-five-year-old woman quoted Paula as complaining that the police were basing the charges on the confused account from Stephanie Werner. Paula had cried several times, and was heartbroken over losing custody of her son. The cellmate thought Paula was innocent.

Officials at the jail posted a notice saying that Sergeant Ventimiglia in Alton should be notified before any female prisoner was released so an interview could be arranged. They may as well have sent Groshong an engraved invitation to complain again.

The Sims case was not the only one on Weber's desk that summer and fall. Although it was difficult to focus on other cases, there were some that were just as disturbing, in their own ways, as Paula's. The last week of August, Don went before a jury in Judge Matoesian's courtroom to try a man from Granite City in a particularly nasty sex abuse case in which the victims, ironically, were two little girls. *I can't get away from cases involving two little girls,* Don thought.

Charles Nash, a thirty-six-year-old, bearded behemoth, had sexually and physically abused his girlfriend's daughters. They were six and eight years old, and Nash had showed them pornographic movies before making them perform sexual acts with him. He had slapped and beaten them, and he once placed a plastic bag over the younger girl's head until she nearly passed out. He had threatened to kill them and their mother if they told anyone what he had done.

The girls were excellent witnesses against Nash. It was the kind of crime that fueled the fires of righteousness in Weber. It wasn't difficult to ask the jurors to punish this man. They deliberated about ninety minutes before convicting Nash. He seemed shocked and was crying like a baby when he was lead from the courtroom by deputies.

Weber felt like he was back in the saddle again. He had lost his first trial as a reborn prosecutor in May, and he needed this victory, especially in such a revolting case. A slumping prosecutor is like a slumping hitter in the big leagues. He loses his self-confidence and begins to doubt that he'll ever hit again. He focuses on the wrong things and makes the wrong moves, and the problem intensifies. But after knocking this one out of the park, Weber knew he had his stuff back.

In September, Matoesian sentenced Nash to twenty-five years, and he cried again.

Weber immediately tried another child molester in Matoesian's court. Robert A. Votava, a former city councilman from the small town of St. Jacob, was charged with repeatedly assaulting a girl from the time she was six until she was fifteen. It was an unimaginable story of nighttime rides into the woods, where Votava would tie up the girl before sexually abusing her. He once tied her to a tree before raping her, and he often would hit her if she resisted. A psychologist testified the girl was suffering from "rape trauma syndrome" and was having severe emotional problems. Weber called Votava "a sociopath and a predator," and the jury agreed. He was convicted and Matoesian gave him thirty years.

Weber also handled a murder case investigated by DCI agent Dennis Kuba. Keith Gaultney, a laborer from St. Jacob, was shot twice in the head while he slept in his own waterbed. The normally quiet town was being rocked by murder and child molestation. Gaultney's wife, a plump blonde named Kathy, said she had returned from shopping with their four-year-old son and found her husband dead. But Kuba knew that Keith Gaultney had informed on his wife, who was one of the principals in a huge marijuana ring that had been under investigation by the DCI and the U.S. Drug Enforcement Administration for about a year.

As happens so often in cases that involve Weber, even Kathy Gaultney's arrest had a goofy twist. The day that Weber was filing the murder charge against her, he was standing at a traffic light in Edwardsville after having lunch with Kuba and Agent Chuck Brueggemann. Weber had just asked the agents what Kathy Gaultney looked like when a woman's voice said, "Are you guys busy today?" It was her; she had spoken to them from the passenger's side of a van that was stopped at the light. Brueggemann pointed at her and said, "She looks just like that." They arrested her a few minutes later at her attorney's nearby office.

Kathy and Paula got to know each other in the county jail, and Kathy later would have something to say about that. But one report said the women once parted with the comment, "See you in Dwight." It was an assumption that they soon would be moving to the women's prison in northern Illinois, where they could meet up with Susie Davidson.

Weber won a conviction against Kathy Gaultney the

next February, after the jury deliberated for about thirty minutes. Judge Ferguson sentenced her to forty-five years in prison—in Dwight.

The Gaultney case also drew a comment that Weber took as testimony, and a compliment, about his reputation on the other side of the law. It came from a man who was arrested on charges that he helped Kathy Gaultney set up a phony motive for her husband's killing. He asked the police who was prosecuting the case, and was told it was Don Weber.

Drawing out the words, his response was, "Ooohh, shiiit."

Judge Matoesian's decision that Madison County had jurisdiction in Paula's case didn't settle the question for Groshong, of course. On August 24, two days after the hearing, the defense filed a petition for a writ of habeas corpus in U.S. District Court at East St. Louis against Matoesian and Sheriff Bob Churchich. It asked for a federal judge to rule that Illinois had no jurisdiction, and to order the charges dismissed.

Three weeks later, District Judge William D. Stiehl denied Groshong's petition, ruling that he had not exhausted all state court remedies before turning to the federal courts.

In September, Groshong and Williamson made a trip to New York to satisfy one of their passions. They went to the Metropolitan Opera to hear *Aida*. Aside from enjoying the performance immensely, Williamson had the added experience of standing next to actor Paul Newman in the rest room. Williamson decided that the appropriate thing for one to do under that circumstance was to smile politely and nod graciously. It was no time to ask for an autograph.

Weber knew about the trip to the opera, but he didn't know the defense team also would be paying a visit to the chief assistant medical examiner for New York City, Dr. Jay Dix, in hopes of using him as their expert witness. He reviewed the case files and reached conclusions that contradicted Dr. Case. Dr. Dix believed that the marks on Heather's upper lip came from something placed inside her mouth. He couldn't offer a suggestion on what, however. And he was not at all convinced that the body had been refrigerated or frozen.

For Groshong, that wasn't very useful. In fact, Dr. Cases's opinion on freezing was beneficial to the defense. It forced the prosecution to explain how the body was hidden, frozen, moved, and dumped, all under the watchful eyes of the cops and the media. Groshong was convinced the Simses had been under police surveillance all along.

When the attorneys got home, they told Weber about the opera and the restaurants, but not about the doctor.

The month of October was filled with pretrial activities initiated by Groshong. He renewed his request for Paula to be held in segregation at the jail after learning of the interviews with the cellmates. He also filed a petition with the Illinois Supreme Court asking for a quick ruling on the jurisdictional question—an effort to exhaust state court remedies as suggested by the federal judge. In two weeks, the Supreme Court denied the motions without comment.

On October 25, Groshong filed a baker's dozen motions with Matoesian, leading with several challenging the constitutionality of the state's death penalty statute. One motion said Paula had run out of money and wanted the county to pay the expense of hiring experts for the defense.

October slipped into November, and the first day of the month brought another series of losses on the recent defense motions, including the challenges to the death penalty. But Groshong was undaunted, and he greeted the month with another blitz of motions. He wanted Matoesian to bar Weber from using thirty-eight pieces of evidence, including any mention of Loralei's death. He wanted to keep out the testimony of Stephanie Werner and her mother, the Heistands, and Jeff Reed. The defense wanted to suppress all the statements Robert had made to FBI agent Schultz, and to McCain and Dooley in the long interviews on May 4 and 5. Any testimony about Paula's life in La Plata was included in the motion, as was any information about her "personal relationship" with her late brother.

November 9 was an incredibly busy day for Weber. At a morning hearing, he had to argue against Groshong's request to question jurors individually instead of in groups. To Weber, picking a jury in a death penalty case was an exact science. The jurors' answers to two special questions determined whether they were considered. The first was the question he asked in every case, and he looked the juror right in the eye when he asked. "If I produce enough evidence to satisfy you beyond a reasonable doubt that the defendant is guilty, will you convict him?" The only acceptable answer was an unequivocal yes.

The second was tougher, and Don would point directly at the defendant as he asked. "If, after hearing all the evidence, you are satisfied that the defendant is guilty, that he qualifies for the death penalty, and that there is no mitigating factor sufficient to preclude imposing the death penalty, will you come back in this room and impose the death penalty on this person?" The answer to this one had to be yes, too.

Don had picked five of the six of the death penalty juries that had been selected in Madison County since the state's law took effect. Don knew Groshong had never picked a death penalty jury, and probably would spend his challenges culling out jurors who had read about the case.

Before the hearing that morning, Weber, Groshong, and Matoesian were standing in the doorway to judge's chambers when he told the lawyers, "I'll give you guys two days to pick this jury. If you don't get it picked in two days, I'll take over the questioning."

Weber was bothered by that, even though he knew that state law gave the judge every right to do it. Don thought it would take about two and a half days, and he certainly wanted to do it himself.

"Judge, we're going to need a little longer than that," Don said coyly.

Groshong set his jaw. "No, there's no way we can do

it in two days. It will take me two weeks to pick this jury, and that's all there is to it.''

Matoesian's friendly countenance hardened. ''Well, you can't have two weeks.''

Groshong shot back, ''Well, I have to have two weeks, and I'll take as long as I want to pick this jury. My client's life is at stake.''

The judge's response escalated the hostilities. ''You know, I don't have to let you ask any questions.''

Warning bells were going off in Weber's head. The judge and the defense attorney were about to argue each other into corners, and the judge was going to be the winner by picking the jury himself. Groshong didn't realize how serious the judge was. Andy Matoesian was an affable man, but he didn't like to be challenged. Groshong's next comment was exactly what Weber didn't want to hear.

''Well, you just go ahead and ask the questions and I'll get you reversed by the appellate court in a minute. I absolutely demand that there be no time limits on jury selection.''

Weber could see his tactical advantage sliding away. All his plans for how this jury selection and trial would proceed were about to be shot down by a dispute between the other parties.

Matoesian spun around and stalked back to his chambers. He bellowed angrily back over his shoulder, ''Well, that's it. Nobody's going to ask any questions. I'll pick this jury.''

Groshong stalked away, leaving Weber standing there alone. ''Oh, great. Boy, am I glad this happened.''

He followed Matoesian into his office and tried to soothe him. ''Look, Judge. Don't worry about it. We'll be able to pick this jury in two and a half days. We'll all be reasonable about this.'' It took some talking, but Don finally got the judge to agree to that much time. But Matoesian still was threatening to take over if it wasn't done on time.

Groshong was standing in the hallway smoking a cigarette by the time Weber found him and told him what the judge had said. Groshong didn't disagree, and Weber took that as tacit assent.

The hearing began in the courtroom, and the day got better for Weber. Matoesian denied Groshong's motion to question the jurors individually and for the county to pay for experts for Paula. But more importantly, the judge denied Groshong's motion asking for dismissal of the charges because of prosecutorial misconduct. Groshong had complained about efforts by the police and prosecutors to manipulate the media to put pressure on the suspects. He noted there had been no press release announcing that the "hair" from the freezer had turned out to be carpet fiber.

Weber defended the authorities' tactics with a simple statement.

"Well, it worked. These actions were absolutely legitimate in the pursuit of the dreadful perpetrators of this crime, and they worked. The perpetrators were rattled into dumping the body."

The rest of the day proved to be more enjoyable for Don. That afternoon, a secret meeting was held in a very unexpected place. At the small house outside of Brighton where the police had assembled more than three years earlier to look for Loralei Sims, Weber met with some of those same investigators again: Frank Yocom, Diane Sievers, Debra Morgan, and Wayne Watson. The cast was joined by Haine, Ringhausen, and Sergeant Robert Biby, the DCI's electronics expert.

Weber had decided to act out Paula's account of Loralei's kidnapping and videotape the results. He was sure it would prove that it was physically impossible for things to have happened as Paula had described them. And Don was sure the tape would be admissible at trial to impeach Paula's credibility.

Watson lived in Brighton and knew the current owners of the house. They had agreed graciously to allow the almost ghoulish imposition. They understood the fascination with the house and the case. When the cops arrived, the family cleared out.

Biby set up two video cameras. One was by the pole holding the dusk-to-dawn light in the driveway. It was aimed at the front porch to capture the escaping kidnapper and the pursuing Paula, to be played by Watson and

Morgan. The second camera was set up over by the pond, to get a better view of the entire scene.

Weber felt like Cecil B. deMille. The crew arranged some timbers on the front porch where the Simses had furniture. A truck was parked in the driveway, exactly where Robert's truck had been. The furniture in the basement family room was rearranged the way the Simses had it, and a picnic basket was placed by the stairs to serve as Loralei's bassinet.

Weber and the others used walkie-talkies to tell the actors in the house when to go into "action," and their movements were timed. Morgan lay on the basement floor, just as Paula had said the gunman had told her. When Watson made his getaway and Morgan heard the door close upstairs, she jumped up and ran up the stairs, out of the door and down the driveway.

On the first run-through, Morgan burst through the screen door about eight seconds behind Watson, close enough to see him well, even at night. Watson was not very far down the driveway. That was what Weber had hoped. Paula's story that the kidnapper had disappeared down the driveway, vanishing even before she got to the road, just didn't hold up.

In the second take, Watson carried a pistol and a doll to simulate more closely the conditions under which the kidnapper would have been escaping. Morgan picked up a second on him.

On the third and fourth attempts, Watson ran to the rear of the house, darted into the woods, and made his way down the slope to the spot where Loralei's remains had been found. He scrambled back up the hill, through the thicket, back around the house, and down the driveway. That was the effort needed for the kidnapper to dump the body where it had been found.

On the first try of that scenario, Watson was empty handed. Debby Morgan had been standing in the driveway, looking for the kidnapper, for twenty-nine seconds when Watson reappeared from behind the house. On the next run-through, he carried the pistol and the doll, leaving the doll at the marked location in the woods. The times were the same, proving to Weber again that it was ridiculous to argue that some bandito killed the baby while running around the house, removed and kept her clothing, dumped her body in the woods, and then escaped down the driveway without being seen by Paula.

The fifth and sixth attempts were the same, only Watson assumed that the baby had been thrown into the woods. Without the props, Watson reappeared in the driveway eight seconds after Morgan stopped under the light. It took two seconds longer to stop at the woods and heave the doll down the slope. He wasn't even able to throw the doll all the way to the spot where the body had been found, almost 100 feet into the dense woods.

Someone in the group dubbed the event the "First Annual Paula Sims Baby Toss." As a break in the afternoon's grisly activities, even that dark-humored remark seemed shamefully funny.

Weber was thrilled with the results of the reenactment. The term was inappropriate, because there had been no real event to reenact. But Weber hoped the tape would prove to any jury that Paula had lied. There had been no kidnapper. The killer had to be the person who had made up the incredible lie.

Weber ended the tape with a scene that he wasn't sure anyone would understand. He had Biby walk through the family room, out the sliding-glass doors at the rear of the house, across the small yard and to the edge of the woods. From that spot, the camera panned down toward the bare spot in the underbrush.

Don was showing the route he believed actually had been taken by the killer to dispose of Loralei's body.

Chapter 17

The light in Don Weber's tiny office was the only one burning that night in the former convent occupied as temporary quarters for the county prosecutor and his staff. Everyone else had already gone home on a chilly November day that had dissolved into a rainy evening. Converting the old convent into offices for prosecutors had seemed an absurd juxtaposition of people and places, except for the boss, the devoutly Roman Catholic Bill Haine. He had taken some merciless ribbing as the father of five daughters moving into a convent. To avoid any further abuse—and perhaps to stave off divine disapproval—Bill had resisted the temptation to put his office in the small chapel with the stained-glass windows.

The convent had been the only available building near the courthouse when the old bank used as the offices for the prosecutor, public defender, and others had to be evacuated. The county was razing it to make room for a $17-million administration building where they all would have new offices.

Weber's office on the second floor had been one of the nun's sleeping rooms, and Don certainly felt cloistered there. It was a claustrophobically small room with concrete walls. Don had barely enough space to hang his treasured possessions. On one wall were his medals and awards, such as those from the DCI for his work on the Karla Brown case. He also had hung his other plaque remembering the bite mark evidence against Karla's killer, John Prante—"You can lie through your teeth, but your teeth don't lie." On the opposite wall, he displayed his gallery of favorite photographs of him with Ronald Reagan, Robert Bork, and Edwin Meese—Weber and three staunch conservatives he admired.

But the room was dominated by the pictures of two military geniuses who seemed appropriate for a prosecutor's wall. Don had learned a great deal studying the tactics and characters of General Robert E. Lee of the Confederate States of America, and Major General George Armstrong Custer, late of the Seventh Cavalry.

Lee was the consummate tactician, the man who fought against all odds and had held off the Army of the Potomac for four years. And, in the end, he had been elegant in defeat. A stately portrait of the general hung behind Don's desk.

On the opposite wall was Custer—brash, courageous, aggressive, fearless. But Custer's heroism, which made him the youngest general in the Union Army during the Civil War, was tempered by his final act, one of the biggest blunders in tactical military history. Don had penciled in above the portrait, "Never Underestimate Your Opponent."

In that philosophical environment, Don was delving deeply that night into the bizarre case of Paula Sims. The time for guesswork and maybe was past. It was time for Weber, with sincere prayer to the God who had guided him so often in similar times over the years, to assemble the hard facts into some reasonable, logical explanation for these most unreasonable, illogical acts.

Don was facing the most serious courtroom test of this case so far and he had to be ready soon. Judge Duffwilliams would review Randy Sims's custody as a ward of the state in a full-blown, adjudicatory hearing set to begin Monday, November 27. It was barely ten days away, and part of that precious time would be taken up by Thanksgiving. If Don didn't manage this hearing right, it could be a disaster. He would have to justify seizing Randy by proving three propositions—that there was sufficient evidence to believe that Paula Sims killed her other two children, that Robert was involved to some degree, and that the Sims home was a dangerous place for a child.

Don's first concern about the hearing was the legal doctrine of collateral estoppel. It held, essentially, that a prosecutor who could not prove his case at a hearing such as this, where the burden of proof was 51 percent, could be barred from proceeding to criminal court, where the

burden was "beyond a reasonable doubt." If Weber lost
at the juvenile hearing, Groshong's pretrial expertise
probably would get the charges against Paula thrown out
before they reached the trial level.

To be sure he would win at the upcoming hearing, Don
would have to present most of his evidence. But he was
determined not to reveal everything. He felt sure his wily
opponent still had not grasped the significance of the
timing between Tuesday night and Wednesday. Weber
wanted to avoid tipping his hand, and sending Groshong
off to find an alibi for Paula before the trial.

The hearing was a high-stakes game of "The Price is
Right." Don had to find the point at which he had presented enough evidence to win, without giving away everything that he was planning to use in the big show in
January in Peoria.

Don also felt like he would be dealing with two adver-
saries at the hearing. He considered Tom Jackstadt, the
court-appointed guardian for Randy, an ultra-liberal defense attorney who would be difficult to convince that
Randy was in danger from his own parents.

So the process of pulling the case together began in
Don's tiny cubicle that night. He had gone through all of
the police reports once, setting aside about half of them
as irrelevant. He ran through the remaining half again,
and eliminated more than 50 percent of those, until only
the important pieces of evidence were left. He filed those
reports in a logical order and used them to draw up a list
of witnesses. The reports were stacked into little piles
that made up the raw material for Don's case. Now it was
time to put those parts together into a finished product.

The easiest way to present the case was chronologically. Don organized the reports and witnesses that would
tell the story of Loralei's disappearance and death first.
Then he would bring in Stephanie Werner—the bridge
between the Loralei and Heather cases—to emphasize her
striking testimony and to make sure the import of it was
obvious, even to a judge.

But now it came down to Heather's death. And the
perplexing factor in that case was the freezing of the
body. Where had the body been? It was a major point in
this hearing.

But it would be even more critical at the trial. Weber had to put Paula, the body, a freezer, and electricity together somehow, somewhere. He had to give Paula the time to get the body and dump it. He had to have a consistent, plausible explanation for the jury on how all of that could have happened. He knew the judge and jury would demand it.

The Blews' freezer was out. Someone had reached into it Sunday night, and there had been no baby there. It wasn't the Simses' refrigerator, because the cops checked it Saturday night. And, even though Don didn't like Herb and Linda Condray, he was convinced they weren't involved; it wasn't their freezer. The search for meat lockers, fish lockers, or any other kind of rental freezer had shown nothing either. So where had the baby been?

Don was ruminating on Sherlock Holmes's favorite advice for deductive thinking in crime solving: "Eliminate the impossible, and whatever is left, however improbable, is the answer."

The second that entered his mind, Don remembered Linda Condray's testimony to the grand jury: Robert had told Paula Sunday morning, "Go to your parents' house. You can't be of any use here." What had Robert meant by that? If Don could crack the code, he could crack the crime.

Think. If there wasn't anything more Paula could do at home, what could she do at the Blews'? The Blews were out of town. Robert had called them in Peculiar, Missouri, to tell them about Heather, and Orville volunteered to come home later that day. Paula had been surprised by that, Robert had said.

Then the fireworks went off, and the light exploded in Don's mind. He pressed his fingertips against his forehead.

"Now I get it," he thought. "She had taken the body to her parents' and put it in the freezer there, so the cops wouldn't find it at her house. She knew her parents would be out of town. That was more than just a coincidence. It was part of the plan. Robert's statement Sunday morning meant Paula had to go to her parents' to move the body before they got home. That explains why she didn't show up at the Condrays until later that afternoon."

So, where did she put the body after she retrieved it from her parents'? It wasn't any of the places he had already eliminated, so, as Holmes would have asked, what was left?

It was the freezer in the Simses' own refrigerator. It was improbable, but it had to be the answer.

Don frantically rifled his police reports to look for the time when the cops had left the Simses' house Sunday morning—about eleven o'clock. Then he searched for any mention that they had gone back into the house. Only once, when Mick Dooley picked up a copy of Heather's footprint and Robert's divorce decree on Monday afternoon. No search then, however.

Incredible! It worked, and it had to be the answer.

Don rocked back in his chair and locked his fingers behind his head. His gaze drifted up and riveted onto the audacious General Custer, who was so successful because he always did things his opponents never expected.

"Paula, you're just like General Custer. You brought that baby's body back to your house on Sunday after the cops left, and put her in your freezer. That's why you were so nervous, and that's why the psychological tactics that the FBI recommended worked on you. That's why you made that big mistake on Wednesday when you dumped the body. It wasn't just because they were playing on your guilt. It was fear, because you had that dead baby in your house and, if the police came back, the ballgame was over." Don shook his head. "Paula, that was the most audacious thing I've ever heard of."

It all crystallized. Don had it now. He went back through all the police reports, and there was nothing inconsistent with that theory. That had to be what had happened, and it would be Don's theory of the crime from that point on. A woman capable of murdering her baby was capable of doing this. If she could let Loralei's body rot and be desecrated by animals right behind her house, she could plop Heather's body into the freezer behind the turkey and the corn.

Don realized that Heather's life span had depended on the Blews' departure for the weekend. If they had left a week or two earlier, Heather would have died then. Her death had been ruthlessly premeditated.

Don pushed his chair back from his desk. Champagne was appropriate, but a beer would have to do. He walked out of the office, crossed Vandalia Street, and bought a six-pack at the National Food Store on the corner. He went back to his office and shared one with the generals before heading home.

He was excited and anxious to share his theory with Virginia. She was watching the ten o'clock news when Don walked in, dropped into a chair, and popped open another beer.

"Let me tell you a little story."

As he explained his idea, Virginia nodded. When he was done, she asked what seemed like a thousand questions. But Don welcomed them, because he needed to have this revelation tested. And it passed. He could answer all the questions without damaging his theory. And Virginia, his closest confidante, accepted the idea as valid.

"You've got it. You've unraveled the mystery of Heather's whereabouts."

The next day, Don told Haine, and he liked the explanation. Kit Morrissey agreed with Weber's revelation, and seemed stunned that he had figured it out. Weber passed it on to McCain and Ventimiglia and, to his surprise, they didn't buy it. They just couldn't see it as possible. But Don was reassured by the old pro, Bob Trone. Don valued Bob's opinion as a master prosecutor as he valued few others. And he was relieved when Bob nodded. "You know, you're probably right," Bob growled slowly.

The new theory became something else Don would keep secret at the adjudicatory hearing. He didn't want the defense attorneys to spend two months looking for a way to punch holes in it.

His theory would leave him way out on a limb with no safety net. If he failed with it, Paula probably would be acquitted and it would be his fault, personally. He decided he wouldn't even call Linda Condray as a witness at the adjudicatory hearing to avoid telegraphing anything to the defense. Her statement was locked in by her grand jury testimony, and she could never recant.

The hearing began that Monday with all of the expected media fanfare. The reporters knew it would be a preview of the trial in January, and they jammed into the tiny courtroom where Judge Duffwilliams presided. The room was so small that it accommodated only one table, and all the attorneys and the Simses crowded around it. Don Weber sat almost directly across from Paula, and Robert sat just to her right. It was the closest Weber had been to the Simses; maybe he would be able to read something up close that he had missed before.

The opening statements were brief and to the point. Weber said he had to prove a very narrow issue—that Randy Sims was in danger from his environment and from his mother when the state seized him in May. The evidence to support that was the preposterous stories the woman had told about how her infant daughters had died, and the logical conclusions that she had killed them.

Groshong's response was just as succinct. There was not a single fact in the state's custody petition to support the allegations that Randy was in danger.

Weber kicked off his case with a few witnesses who recounted the Loralei case. While Sheriff Yocom described the discovery of Loralei's scattered remains and how the tiny bones apparently had been chewed on by an animal, Don glanced over at Robert and Paula. She was staring at the judge's bench and didn't flinch. Robert shifted briefly in his chair, but his blank expression didn't change.

Wayne Watson testified about his role in the reenactment of Paula's story. Judge Duffwilliams agreed with Groshong that the videotape of it should not be played because there were too many discrepancies between the conditions at the house in 1986 and when the tape was made.

Despite the loss of that evidence, Weber enjoyed State Trooper Mike Donovan's description of the extensive canine searches. His articulate testimony elevated the status of tracking dogs almost to high art, establishing that the dog would have found the scent if any interloper had run down that driveway that night. Don made a mental note to use more canine officers at the trial.

He was looking forward to putting Stephanie Werner on the stand to see if her story would be considered as dramatic as he had found it. When she stated her name as Stephanie Werner-Cook, Don realized she had been married since the spring. In a straightforward manner, she recalled Paula's mismatched account of Loralei's kidnapping.

Groshong's cross-examination had a sarcastic edge to it, indicating that his plan was to portray her story as malarkey from someone unworthy of belief. But Stephanie wouldn't be bullied and responded rather caustically to Groshong's tone. Weber thought she had come off a little too nasty; he made a note to work with her on that. But her story had emerged pretty much intact—the still-chilling testimony of a devastating slip of the tongue by Paula.

And, since the defense suggested that Stephanie had made up the story, Don could call Stephanie's mother to establish that her daughter had told her about Paula's statements while they were still in the hospital and before Heather disappeared.

After court ended for the day, Kit Morrissey broke some bad news to Don. The FBI had refused to send its experts to the hearing. They testified only in criminal trials, and they weren't going to bend the rules for this case. Don was stunned. The loss of the expert testimony on the trash bag would be damaging, perhaps fatal. It would cost him the one direct link between the body and the parents. If the lack of the evidence caused Weber to lose the juvenile case, it could prevent the prosecution of Paula completely.

The danger was too serious to let pass. It called for some inventive action under the old saw about skinning cats. Before court the next morning, Weber told Ventimiglia to find Charlie Bosworth from the *Post-Dispatch* and tip him that the case might be thrown out before trial because of this FBI rule. That would be a great story, and Weber knew Bosworth would call the FBI immediately to check it out. That kind of media scrutiny would be unwelcome, and the chances for better cooperation would increase with the public perception of "The Bureau" at stake.

At a recess after Barbara Werner testified, McCain and Ventimiglia told Don that Bosworth had called the FBI office in Springfield. The agent in charge responded that he knew nothing about the problem, but would check into it immediately. Weber was sure that would do the trick.

He began calling Alton police officers to the stand as he turned the hearing toward Heather's death. But the drama began when Lieutenant Peggy Neer from St. Charles narrated the videotape taken at the access area when Heather's body was found. Robert, the attorneys, and the reporters shifted to the far side of the courtroom so they could see the television on a stand in front of the jury box, just behind Paula's left shoulder. Paula sat dead still in her chair, staring away from the screen.

As the camera tilted over the edge of the barrel and zoomed down to the bag, the horrible, heartbreaking view of Heather's body came into focus. She was naked, lying on her back with her face turned up and slightly to her right. The upper part of her face was obscured by the bag. But her tiny right hand was pulled up and clenched in what Weber thought was almost a gesture of defiance. The "cherry red" marks on her neck and face were plainly visible.

Robert Sims was watching intently as his daughter's body came into view. He closed his eyes and turned his head, and tears trickled down his face. He pulled a handkerchief from his pants pocket and dabbed at his eyes. Paula kept her gaze locked on the table in front of her, but she had to know that everyone in the courtroom was looking at her—including her husband.

As the tape reached the point where the body was about to be removed and placed on a white sheet, Judge Duffwilliams called a recess and asked the attorneys to step into her chambers. Through a grimace, she asked if she really needed to see the rest of the tape. Weber agreed that she had seen enough. When they returned to the courtroom, the tape was turned off without explanation to the observers.

Weber called FBI Agent Carl Schultz as his next witness. Over repeated objections by Groshong, Schultz related the details of the long interview with Robert. The agent twisted his fists together as he mimicked Robert's fear that Paula could wring his son's neck. That little movement was so ominous when made in the Sims case.

Weber shifted gears quickly. "Did Sims indicate what the sleeping arrangements were before Heather was murdered?"

The question drew an immediate objection from Groshong as irrelevant and hearsay. But Weber responded that Paula's old friend, June Gibson, would testify the next day "that the sleeping arrangements were one of the driving forces in the murder of both of these children. They slept in different parts of the house because of the baby. Paula was very upset because of that."

Duffwilliams allowed Schultz to answer.

Then Weber moved in for that unbelievable line about the great sex. Not only did it portray some weird pathology in the family, but it provided a basic part of the motive. It was all tied together grotesquely: Robert wanted the baby girl gone, and he removed himself from the marital bed until it was accomplished. When the deed was done, the sex was great.

Weber asked the sex question three times before the judge overruled relevancy objections by Groshong. Finally, Schultz was allowed to say, "On that occasion, it was better, it lasted longer, and that it was better than normal."

On cross-examination, Groshong tried to minimize the sex line and the worry about wringing Randy's neck with a rapid-fire series of questions.

"And it wasn't until two or three days later that this incident that the prosecutor thinks is the motivating force of this case took place, right? Where they had sexual intercourse together?"

"Yes. On the Monday or Tuesday after the disappearance."

"Bob Sims didn't tell you that they immediately ran out to a motel room or anything, did he?"

"No, sir, he did not."

"He didn't tell you that they immediately ran up to the bedroom and jumped in the sack together, did he?"

"No, sir, he did not."

"It was several days later, wasn't it?"

"Yes, sir."

"Do you know whether Robert and Paula Sims were married?"

"No, sir, I do not."

"All right. You said that Bob Sims told you that, or you speculated that, Paula could wring the child's neck in seconds, right?"

"Yes, sir. That's what he told me."

"So could anybody, couldn't they, if they were near the child?"

"Yes, sir."

The defense could cross-examine all day, but Robert's statements still were devastating.

Groshong also suggested that Schultz had exaggerated the evidence, such as the hair and the pajamas, to mislead Robert into thinking there was a strong case against his wife. Schultz denied that. He had only told Robert what had been found, and had not tried to mislead him.

After court recessed for the day, Don learned that the FBI had called Haine's office and said there must have been some communication problem. "The Bureau" would be more than happy to send its experts.

Weber immediately called one of them, Agent Allen Robillard, to discuss the testimony. It was this kind of evidence that made Don thankful for his engineering background. As Robillard talked, Don realized that what the experts could say would be convincing indeed. Robillard also agreed to Don's request that a chemist be added as an expert, and that he use a mass spectrograph to analyze the plastic for chemical composition.

Robillard said the experts wouldn't be prepared or available for about two weeks. Weber would get a delay in the hearing to accommodate them.

When Don had been able to steal a few seconds away from the business at hand, he had watched Paula for some flicker of humanity, some suggestion, however slight, that there was a real, flesh-and-blood person behind that steely countenance and those cold eyes. But he had not seen that. He had seen, instead, a puzzling series of little things, idiosyncracies that reinforced his view of her as a frustrating enigma. While witnesses were testifying about her and, in some cases, accusing her of murder, Paula was quietly arranging several pencils so that they were exactly perpendicular to the edge of the table. When she poured a glass of water, she was careful to avoid spilling even one drop. When she set the pitcher or glass down, she put them precisely back on the spots where they had sat before. Robert's workbench and Paula's water pitcher—what a couple.

The Simses seldom spoke to each other, and when they did, it was brief and whispered. It appeared to be no more than idle conversation. There was no suggestion of any serious disagreement between them, despite the incredible pressure they had lived under for six months.

The next morning, Wednesday, November 29, seemed normal enough. Don planned to put June Gibson on the stand, finally getting this strange business of the sleeping arrangements and Paula's thoughts about divorcing Robert on the record from someone in whom Paula had confided her most personal thoughts. Don also would present Dr. Kim for his medical opinion conclusively eliminating the possibility that Paula had suffered a knockout blow.

But within minutes, Don's case seemed to be collapsing around his ears. Weber told Ventimiglia to take June Gibson into an interview room and go over her testimony. Weber pulled Dr. Kim aside to ask him about Paula's supposed head injury. The doctor was a Korean immigrant who had a heavy accent and was rather difficult to understand. But that was the least of Don's problems.

Instead of a medical conclusion of "impossible," as Ventimiglia had promised, all Kim would say was, "I don't think so" or "It was highly unlikely." And he ended by adding that he wasn't an expert on head wounds. *Great,* Don thought. *That's hardly "impossible" or the accepted legal standard of "to a reasonable degree of medical certainty."*

Then Ventimiglia came out of the interview room wearing that crooked, one-sided grimace that meant trouble. He walked up to Don and said, "Guess what? She says it's all bull."

"What is?"

"Practically everything in her statement to Dooley. The line about Paula thinking about divorcing Robert, all of it. She's not even sure about saying Paula had a problem with the sleeping arrangements."

Don's heart sank. His medical testimony had just turned to dishwater, and now the basis for the motive was going down the drain. He decided to tackle June Gibson first, using his best cajoling, affable manner. But he was confronted by a resolute woman who was adamant that the police had completely misquoted her. The Simses were happily married and loved their children. Despite Robert's rather odd rules around the house, Paula never had suggested divorce. Within minutes, Don's friendly demeanor dissolved. He exploded out of the room and slammed the door.

He called Dooley over and asked him about Gibson's denials. Dooley stood firmly by his report. He specifically remembered her saying everything he had written. Weber told Dooley and Hayes to go back to Gibson and get the problem straightened out immediately.

Don had barely turned around when he was told that Jeff Reed, Paula's former coworker, was grumbling about losing a day's pay to testify. Don promised to try to work something out for him. In the end, the prosecutor's office administrator, Don Greer, would prevail on Reed's employer to pay him for the day.

It was ninety minutes past time for court to start. The judge was leaning on Don to get under way. The reporters wanted to know what was happening. And his two major witnesses were scuttling his ship. It was eleven o'clock, and Don already felt like he needed something a little stronger than the three Cokes he had guzzled. This was the kind of day that drove trial lawyers nuts.

Dooley finally emerged and told Don that an agreement of sorts had been reached. "Here's the bottom line. She'll agree that Robert had these strange rules and she will say that Paula complained about the sleeping arrangements. She will quote Paula as saying, 'I don't know how much longer I can take this.' But she won't say that Paula used the word *divorce*."

Weber sighed in relief. That much still was useful because it established Paula's discontent with the sleeping arrangements. Weber told the cops to be sure and get a signed statement from Gibson before trial.

Don called the reluctant witness to the stand. She described the sleeping arrangements and quoted Paula as saying, "Things had to change because she couldn't go on like this anymore." She added that Paula had said the "rules and regulations were starting to get to her."

Groshong questioned Gibson about the calendar on the wall in the Simses' kitchen. She had noticed some writing on it about how much Robert and Paula loved their children. Paula certainly seemed to love her children and appeared to be a normal mother, Gibson added. And Groshong got her to agree that the rules and regulations might have been more of a problem than the sleeping arrangements.

It wasn't the testimony Weber had anticipated. But it suggested that something was amiss between Robert and Paula, and it centered on the children.

Dr. Kim's testimony was cautious, but he said he had seen nothing to indicate that Paula had suffered any trauma to her neck or head sufficient to render her unconscious for forty-five minutes. He had not even felt obligated to take X-rays; the police had requested them.

Under cross-examination by Jackstadt, Kim said he had never examined anyone who had been struck by a karate chop and had no way of determining medically whether anyone really had been knocked out.

Groshong tried to draw a comparison to injuries from whiplash, and got a response that had Dr. Kim comically rocking his head back and forth to simulate that action. The doctor said whiplash usually was accompanied by a neck injury; Paula had none. Groshong pointed out that the doctor had written "head injury" as the diagnosis on the hospital records.

But Dr. Kim responded, "We just have to go by the history because, you know, in medicine we just have no way we can say, 'Oh no. You're lying. No, that's not true.' There's no way we can really do something to counteract those kinds of claims."

But Groshong got the doctor to admit he was unable to say that Paula had not been knocked out. "I cannot tell you that," he said.

Kim was the second major witness to give Don watered-down testimony within an hour. Don wondered if anyone else knew what a miserable morning he had just survived. As soon as he walked out of the courtroom for lunch, he took Ventimiglia aside and gave him a new assignment.

"Tony, I want you to get on the phone and find me an expert in the field of blunt trauma to the head."

"Where should I start?"

"I don't know. Start with karate experts and go from there. They should be able to tell us how much force would be required to knock someone out for forty-five minutes. And we need a medical expert to testify that what Paula is claiming is impossible. Dr. Kim's 'I don't think so' doesn't cut it. We've got five weeks to find someone who'll give me 'impossible.' "

That afternoon, Don wrapped up his case with testimony from Mary Lynn, supervisor of the child abuse team from the Illinois Department of Children and Family Services. She testified that her review of the case had led to her recommendation that Randy be put in temporary custody and that the state obtain a court order for guardianship.

Don's case ended with a whimper.

Groshong opened his case with Robert Gaston, the fisherman who had seen the suspicious fellow by the barrel. Gaston identified the composite drawing he helped the police create. Groshong obviously believed that was evidence of the real perpetrator. The person in that drawing wasn't Paula or Robert.

Linda Condray took the stand to identify several sets of photographs she had taken of Robert, Paula, and their children. She also testified about the calendar and metallic memo board that hung in the Simses' kitchen, and said she had seen Robert and Paula write notes on them.

Weber's cross-examination was brief, and he steered clear of Sunday morning and Linda Condray's suspicions about Sheriff Yocom.

As Weber had hoped, Groshong's witnesses exposed the defense strategy. He hoped to muddy the waters with confusing testimony about minor points to suggest some doubt about what had happened. Weber called that the "octopus defense." You squirt out enough ink to cloud the waters so no one can see anything clearly, and then you try to escape in the confusion.

The first witness Groshong called for that was Joy

Hokenson, a young woman who had been in downtown
Alton about noon on Wednesday, May 3, and saw a mustachioed man in a business suit get out of a parked car.
He passed a bundle wrapped in a baby blanket to a man
who had stopped a car in the traffic lane. The car turned
in the direction of the Lewis and Clark Bridge, which led
right past the access area.

Weber asked no questions, suggesting that there was
nothing significant to inquire about.

Curt Brown, a young man from East Alton, testified
that he and his girlfriend had been at the access area
Wednesday evening about dusk to take photographs of
the sunset. They had seen two black men in a black Ford
Thunderbird speeding out of the area.

Weber asked no questions. But he wondered how the
black judge would like the defense's obvious implication
that two blacks leaving the scene must have been up to
no good.

McCain was next, called to offer more testimony about
the calendars. Weber was tired of hearing about them,
and he wondered if Groshong really thought they would
impress anyone. If Paula Sims could murder her babies
and hide the bodies, she certainly could scribble some
misleading phrases on the calendars.

Weber challenged the calendars as irrelevant and inadmissable as hearsay. If Groshong wanted that evidence
in, let him put Robert or Paula on the stand to testify
that the writing was genuine. Weber would love that.

His tactic had some effect. Groshong and Robert had
a heated discussion indicating Robert wanted to testify.
Groshong won, and Robert didn't take the stand. The
judge refused to admit the calendars as evidence.

Ventimiglia was Groshong's last witness, and he confirmed that the pictures of the shoeprints taken at the
access area did not match any of the shoes or boots seized
by the police.

During Ventimiglia's testimony, Weber got his first
glimpse inside the mind of Robert Sims. Weber had been
glancing back toward the media gallery occasionally to
see how they were reacting. It was interesting to see what
sent them scribbling furiously, or what had them fighting
to stay awake. Weber had looked toward the reporters

while Ventimiglia was describing the cloth picture of a naked woman sitting on a skull that was seized from Robert's locker. But instead of seeing the press, Weber caught the eye of Robert Sims. Robert was looking at the prosecutor with those cold, dark eyes. He smiled slightly and arched his eyebrows in a look that Weber interpreted as asking, "Don't you wish you had a picture of a naked woman sitting on a skull in your locker?"

It was an eerie look, and Weber decided that June Gibson and the others were right: Robert Sims was the strangest person he had ever met, too.

The hearing was recessed until December 14, when Weber would return with his FBI experts.

But after the first part of the hearing, Weber thought Groshong was left with little more than the "Some Dude" defense, the lame claim by so many suspects that "someone else did it." If that was Paula's story, it was fine with Weber.

The first two weeks of December rolled by quickly and uneventfully. It soon was the fourteenth, and Don was putting on the testimony from three FBI experts and Rex Warner, vice president of Poly-Tech Inc., the company in Minneapolis that manufactured the trash bags.

Warner was a pleasant, engaging man who explained the manufacturing process in relatively simple terms and drew a sketch of the mechanisms on a large pad of paper on an easel. Pellets of polyethylene resin are heated at 400 degrees and pushed into a circular die that forms the tube of plastic sheeting that becomes the trash bags. The bottoms of the bag are welded shut by a hot blade called a heat seal. As the seal is working, another blade makes the perforations so the bags can be ripped off the roll by the consumer.

Warner explained that throughout the process there are little markings left in the plastic tubing. The thickness of the sheet may vary slightly, and imperfections in dye color can be found. Dust or bits of plastic build up on the rollers or the heat seal, and leave identifiable marks in all the bags that run through. To minimize that, the heat seals are changed at least every twenty-four hours, and can be changed as often as every two hours. Warner said he had shown the FBI experts through his plant in May to acquaint them with the process, and they had seen the same machine that manufactured Heather's shroud.

Finally, it was time for Weber to roll out the long-awaited experts. Agent David Nichols, a chemist and biologist from the FBI lab's material-analysis section, concluded that the bags were made of the same type of plastic.

Agent David Attenberger was a document examiner whose expertise was typewriter and tool-mark identification. He had studied the manufacturing machinery and had compared the heat-seal marks on the bag that held Heather's body, the bags in the opened roll of bags at the Simses' house, and the two bags the Simses had filled with trash. His conclusions were about to rock the quiet courtroom.

"The same heat seal was used to make those bags in a relatively short period of time—close proximity to each other."

Weber asked, "Will you tell the court what 'close proximity to each other' means to you?"

"Within ten seconds."

Everyone in the courtroom was stunned, as Weber had been when he had heard the conclusion the night before.

Groshong looked up in shock. "What was the answer?"

Attenberger's slight southern drawl echoed softly, "Within ten seconds."

Weber sat down. "No further questions."

Groshong launched into a series of questions about the heat seal, and Attenberger insisted that the same heat seal had been used on all of the bags, including the unopened roll found at the Sims house. Those bags had the same characteristics as the others, but some additional marks indicated they had been made some time after the others.

Allen Robillard, the most professorial of the experts, was the clincher. He had an impeccable moustache and carried himself with an air of distinction. His voice was soft but authoritative, and he spoke with precision. He was the chief of the unit that examined hairs and fibers. He had examined hundreds of trash bags to find matches,

and he ran through a list of characteristics that started
with the obvious—color—and included size and construction. He was careful to distinguish, by spelling the words,
between *dye* marks that were affected by the coloring
agent in the bags, and *die* marks that were left by the
tool through which the bags passed during the manufacturing process.

Robillard's conclusion was that none of the bags had
been connected directly to any of the others. But the
markings in the plastic indicated that the bag with the
body had been the first one off the roll at the Sims house,
or the first bag wound onto the next roll.

Jackstadt asked about matching perforations, and Robillard explained that such a match seldom could be made
because plastic stretches and distorts as it tears.

Groshong, seeming to concede that the bags matched,
asked about their order off the roll. The agent had concluded the body bag was first off. The two that had been
used for trash came after that, but Robillard believed that
there had been other bags between each of the three.
Those other bags had not been found, he said.

Robillard's testimony closed the hearing in what Weber
thought was grand style. The FBI testimony had been
more decisive than he had expected. How could anyone
believe the bandito who took Heather just happened to
have a trash bag manufactured within ten seconds of the
roll owned by her parents?

Don even allowed himself to hope that the strength of
the state's case would force Paula to consider a guilty
plea to pare a few years off her sentence and leave her
with hope for freedom after a long stretch in the pen.

Weber's closing argument was brief. To return Randy
Sims to his home, the judge would have to believe that
his sisters had been kidnapped and killed in the way
claimed by their mother.

Jackstadt surprised Weber by agreeing with him. He
had been swayed by the testimony of Stephanie and Barbara Werner.

Groshong argued that there was no evidence linking
Paula Sims to her daughters' deaths. He shrugged. ''All
the state says is, 'We believe Paula Sims lied. Therefore,
she has to be guilty of murder.' ''

Judge Duffwilliams called the attorneys into her chambers and announced her ruling. Weber sighed in relief as the judge said she believed there was "more than a preponderance of the evidence that the stories Paula Sims told in relation to the disappearance of her two daughters are not believable."

But then Duffwilliams stunned Weber. "But I don't believe the evidence is sufficient with respect to Robert."

For the first time in the case, Don was genuinely caught by surprise. He responded quickly that the hearing had been focused on proving that the environment had been dangerous. The next step, a hearing to decide ultimate custody, would be the place to discuss Robert.

The judge disagreed, saying it had been Weber's choice to focus only on Paula. Once Paula was removed from the environment, the danger ceased. Considering the proximity to Christmas, the judge ordered Randy returned to Robert that day.

She moved back into the courtroom and announced her ruling. Robert and Paula stood and embraced each other, and both began to cry. It was the most emotional exhibition by the Simses in four years. Robert hugged Groshong, and Paula comforted her husband by patting him on the shoulder. Paula was flirting with the death penalty, but Robert got the comfort.

Weber viewed the decision as a significant judicial mistake, and he resented the judge's suggestion that he should have proven the case against Robert then. He worried that the decision could damage the criminal case if Paula was buoyed by this partial victory. She might reject any plea negotiations before trial, hoping she could beat the rap in Peoria just as she and Robert had pulled off this small victory.

Robert waited in the corner of the courtroom while Groshong arranged Randy's return. Robert's comment to reporters was, "I praise the Lord. That's all I have to say." But several reporters pressed, even after he added, "I just wish you guys would leave me alone now." He finally responded that he believed his wife and had faith in her. She had been a good mother. It had been painful living under the harassment from the media and the police. He said his religious faith had helped. "God. God gets you through."

Weber watched as the reporters encircled Groshong. It was one of the few times the defense had been able to relish even a partial victory. When a reporter mentioned that the burden of proof would be even greater at a criminal trial, and Groshong grinned and said, "You bet 'cha." Was he optimistic about Peoria? His eyes twinkled as he smiled, "We will have to see."

Weber knew that look, and it meant the chances for a plea bargain were dimmer now, not brighter as he had expected an hour earlier.

As the crowd dispersed, Weber walked over to Ventimiglia and asked about an expert on head injuries. Ventimiglia gave Don a knowing smile.

"I've already called all over the country and everyone keeps referring me to the same expert."

"Who is it?"

"Dr. Mary Case."

Neither man could imagine how important those three little words would be.

Chapter 18

Once the court system had Paula Sims in its grasp, she found herself on the fast track toward a sensational trial. She had spent more than five months in jail as her attorney had little luck in his pretrial battles. Even the judge who returned her son to his father added an affront by acknowledging substantial evidence that Paula had murdered both of her daughters. But the heaviest blow in all of those proceedings fell on December 18, when Judge Matoesian decided that Weber would be allowed to present evidence about Loralei's death to the jury trying Paula for Heather's murder.

Everything Don had learned about jurors—about people—told him that his best chance at a conviction was giving twelve normal people the choice between convicting Paula or accepting her claim that the Sims house had been visited by such incredible evil twice, without any explanation for why the baby girls in that family had been targeted for annihilation.

To win the use of evidence on Loralei, Don wrapped the issue in a solid legal argument he had been refining since the poison-doughnut case ten years earlier. It was the ''doctrine of other crimes and modus operandi'' argument, and it cut to the very heart of this case.

In a hearing before Judge Matoesian, Groshong argued against the use of evidence about Loralei by claiming there was no proof that her death had anything to do with Heather's. But Matoesian disagreed, and ruled there were enough similarities to bind the cases together in an ''M.O.'' argument.

Weber also won the judge's approval to do something he really didn't want to do—play for the jury the videotape of the autopsy on Heather's body to prove that Heather was smothered. Groshong argued that photographs would be sufficient, and that the ghastly nature of the tape would do nothing but inflame the jurors' passions and prejudices.

The next day, Don and Virginia were leaving town for a two-week Christmas break. Don had prepared a list of things to be done in the final days before the trial on January 8. First, he wanted all of his witnesses to get copies of their statements to the police so they could review them and refresh their recollections, and he asked Virginia to work with Stephanie Werner-Cook on her testimony. Virginia had been Don's office administrator when he was state's attorney, and had worked with his victim-witness program. Don respected her expertise in drawing out the extra details that made a good witness a great witness.

But one of the most important items on his list was the filing of a motion "in limine" to try to defuse Groshong's strategy for the trial. Don's would ask the judge to prohibit Groshong from using unsupported testimony on unrelated events to try to muddy up the waters. Weber wanted to derail the stories about the bundle-swap on the Alton street and the black men speeding away from the access area. He wanted to avoid the red herrings like the unidentified shoe prints in the dust on a public sidewalk twenty feet from the trash barrel. The motion said that testimony or evidence suggesting a "third-party suspect" had to identify the suspect and specify a connection linking him closely to the commission of the crime. If it failed to do that, it was barred.

The motion was filed the day after Christmas, while the state's attorney's office was still smarting from a damaging loss in a double-murder trial on December 12. Weber wanted to avoid the fate that had befallen another experienced prosecutor, Rich Rybak, when a jury acquitted Thomas Reidelberger in the shootings of his sixteen-year-old son and a man who was visiting Reidelberger's estranged wife, Kathleen. The case had seemed airtight, topped off by an audio recording made of an emergency call to the sheriff's department by Reidelberger's son just as the killings began. A voice admitted to be Reidelberger's could be heard screaming hysterically at his wife, "Look what you made me do. Are you happy

now?'' Kathleen could be heard begging frantically for
him to let her get help for their dying son.

Reidelberger's attorney had overcome that powerful
evidence by attacking the wife's character and suggesting
that there had been another, unidentified, person in the
house at the time of the shootings. Reidelberger always
proclaimed his innocence and, after the verdict, sought
unsuccessfully to have the police re-open the investigation. Reidelberger was still seeking a new look at the
case a year later.

The acquittal had been a serious blow to Haine's administration and Weber wasn't about to be the next victim of the ''octopus defense.'' There wouldn't be any ink
fogging up the waters in the Paula Sims case.

Don was hoping that this time off would allow him to
get away from the pressure building up as the date in Peoria drew closer. They would visit relatives in North Car-
olina for Christmas, and then go to Chicago over New
Year's on a special mission. Don was to serve as godfather
for the infant daughter of one of his best friends from
college, Phil Troyk. Phil held a doctoral degree in electri-
cal engineering and was a professor at the Illinois Institute
of Technology, as well as a consultant to the Ford Motor
Company. But to Don, Phil's most impressive faculty was
his ability to repair Don's worn-out televisions. Don usually packed one along when he visited his old friend.

Don was especially thrilled to be godfather for little
Melissa. Few German Protestants served in that role for
Roman Catholic children, and he readily accepted the
honor. The christening was set for December 30, and
Don attended a party with his friends the night before.
He could hardly believe it when the conversation turned
to the Sims case. When he offered to explain that the facts
were not quite as the group was discussing, someone
asked how he would know. He told them.

At the ceremony the next day, Don couldn't help but
ponder the irony as he stood and looked at the joy of a
new mother and her baby daughter, and remembered the
twisted, ugly side of that relationship that faced him.

That evening, Don and his friends attended a dinner
theater where the audience joined in the play to figure

out the culprit in the murder mystery. Don's expertise led him to a guess that turned out to be so far off it was laughable. He hoped his theories would fare better in Peoria.

Tuesday, January 2, arrived faster than Don could believe, and he found himself back at work to put the finishing touches on the Sims case. He met Tony Ventimiglia at the office of the medical examiner in St. Louis County to interview Dr. Mary Case again. This time, however, she wouldn't be the forensic pathologist who had performed the autopsy on Heather's body. This time, she would be the neuropathologist who was an expert on head wounds, brain injuries, and the nervous system. And she would be talking about Paula.

Don explained to the doctor that he hadn't been able to get the medical conclusion from Dr. Kim that was needed to disprove Paula's claim of a blow to the head that had knocked her out for forty-five minutes.

"I need 'impossible.' He's giving me, 'I doubt it.' "

He recounted some of Paula's story, and waited for a reaction from the expert. Dr. Case didn't give Don what he wanted. She offered, "Based on what I know, it's very unlikely, but it could be."

So Don started over. If he had to stay there all day, he was going to get "impossible" from her. He could tell that he was going to have to ring the right bell to get it.

"Okay. What about this? No bruises, no soreness, no lacerations, no bumps or lumps. The only redness is from her fingers pressed against her neck. What about that?"

"Well, I don't see how that could happen."

"Is it possible?"

"Well, it's possible."

Nuts. Try again.

"Okay. Here's the medical report. Full range of motion. Oriented as to time, place, and person. Is that enough?"

"Well, that's completely inconsistent with being knocked out. I'd have to say that that's extremely unlikely."

"Okay. Can you testify, to a reasonable degree of medical certainty, that Paula Sims was not knocked out?"

"Based on what you have told me, I can't testify to

that. I don't think it happened. But I can't say it was impossible.''

Another miss. So Don spent another half-hour going over it again and again. She was being friendly and helpful, but he couldn't get her to take that last, crucial step. Once more from the top.

"Okay, Dr. Case. Here's how Paula says this happened. She said she went outside to empty the trash, and this bandito confronted her outside.''

Dr. Case leaned forward a little and her eyes narrowed. Don continued.

"She said he told her to go back in the house. Then he knocked her out.''

The doctor was listening intently.

"She told Detective Dooley that she got struck on the back of the head. She pointed to the back of her head and she told Dooley she remembered feeling the blow.''

Dr. Case leaned back in her chair and crossed her arms in front of her.

She said softly, but very emphatically, "Now, *that,* is impossible.''

Don looked at Ventimiglia; the cop looked back with that crooked smile and arched eyebrow that said, "Bingo." Both of the men knew they finally had what they had come for, and what they had been searching for all this time.

Weber turned back to the doctor.

"Okay. Let's make sure we understand each other. Do you mean that, to a reasonable degree of medical certainty, you can testify that this didn't happen—that it's impossible?''

She nodded slowly. "That is impossible.''

In very technical detail, the doctor explained how memory was formed in the brain. It takes some time for each bit of memory to created by an electronic impulse sent into the brain; the impulse has to create a track that becomes a memory as time allows it to deepen and define the information. If that process is interrupted somehow, such as by a blow to the head and unconsciousness, the memory does not have time to form. When the person regains consciousness, there is no memory to recall. The loss of memory may go back several minutes before the loss of consciousness.

Dr. Case called that "retroactive amnesia." Paula could not have remembered feeling the blow, or walking back into the house. She might not even have remembered taking out the trash or being confronted by a kidnapper. And because the brain is so traumatized, she would have been disoriented and groggy after she came to. She couldn't have remembered where Heather should have been and she would have been physically unable to run up and down the stairs, searching the house.

Dr. Case explained that she had been knocked out in a car crash and later had no memory of her car entering the intersection where the crash occurred. When she came to, she was very concerned because she knew, as a neuropathologist, how serious being unconscious was, medically. It almost always required hospitalization.

As the men walked out of the doctor's office, Don wondered if he was required legally to disclose this new medical opinion to Groshong. No, he decided, he didn't have to ask the questions for the defense. He had no duty to disclose this conversation to Groshong. After all, Groshong had seen her qualifications. He and Williamson had interviewed her; they even had taken her deposition. It was up to them to ask the same questions Weber had asked.

So Don had another surprise for his old friend at the trial. Not only would he spring the theory about Paula's Sunday morning trip to her parents' freezer, but now he had Dr. Case's conclusion. In a sense, the doctor's opinion might be the only real knockout blow delivered by anyone in the Sims case. Now, if he could just keep it quiet until the right moment.

The next day had been scheduled for the activity that every good prosecutor does—the visit to all the scenes important to the case. Just after noon, Don was joined by Kit Morrissey, Bill Haine, and DeeDee Duburow, a law clerk who worked part time for the prosecutors. They were met in Alton by Ventimiglia and took a quick look through the photographs that could be used as evidence. Don looked at the bassinet, but he didn't expect to use it at trial. They piled into Ventimiglia's Ford and drove to the house on Washington Avenue, where Don figured Heather had died.

Don looked around the yard where Paula said she had been confronted by the bandito. That was the word that was beginning to pop into Don's mind more and more; it seemed to convey the right sense of the ludicrous. As he walked into the house, which was being remodeled by the new owner before renters moved in, it felt cold; no warmth from the events that had transpired there. As he checked every room, the place struck him as nothing more than an average little house.

When they pulled away, Don told Ventimiglia to note the time and distance to the next destination—the access area. They headed west on Washington and made a right turn north onto Broadway. They drove right past Groshong's office. A couple of blocks farther, Tony made the left turn onto the Lewis and Clark Bridge and they crossed the Mississippi. They had just landed in Missouri when Tony made a right turn into the access area—it was the first turn after the bridge. The prosecutors looked at each other in amazement. They hadn't realized just how close the body had been to the Sims house—barely five minutes and only 2.7 miles. What a convenient spot for Paula to conduct her business.

The group wandered around the parking lot and looked into the trash barrels. Don felt some sparks there. And the scene reinforced his belief that the baby had been dropped into that barrel for convenience, not so it would be found. It ended up there for the simple reason that the barrel could be reached from a car window.

Paula could have leaned out and lowered the bag into the barrel without getting out of the car.

Haine had begun to feel ill while he was there, so they drove back across the bridge to the police station, where he could get a ride home.

The next stop was the St. Charles County Sheriff's Department, about forty-five minutes farther west in Missouri. Don was surprised to learn that the only evidence there was the trash barrel. It was symbolic of the department's role in the case. While he was there, he picked up a copy of an FBI wanted poster on one of the criminals he found most intriguing—Ted Bundy, the serial killer executed in Florida.

The troop crossed back into Illinois and drove north to Frank Yocom's office in Jersey County, arriving at the last stop of the trip about dusk. Don was moved when Yocom handed him a small box that contained some of

Loralei's bones and the vials of blood that had been used by the laboratory to identify the remains.

So this is what Loralei has come to, Don thought. *Some tiny bones, a couple tubes of blood, and a report from a lab in Atlanta.*

Kit raised the issue of the confidential source who had given the sheriff some compelling details about Paula. The man had been the origin of the information about her fear of the death penalty. But he also had passed along even more damaging information that Yocom had sworn not to divulge. Kit and DeeDee Duburow suggested listing him as a witness, in case he became a last resort.

But Yocom reminded the lawyers that he had given his word the man's identity would not be divulged and the information never would be used.

Kit wanted to consider the options. "Don, this is a real close case. We could lose it. The source is a witness. He talked and he has to bear the responsibility."

DeeDee Duburow agreed. "This guy knew what he was doing. You at least have to list him as a witness, in case you have to use him in an emergency."

Ventimiglia was unsure. He wanted to use the information to convict Paula, but he understood the sheriff's reluctance to break his word.

Frank Yocom was listening. Nobody wanted Paula more than he did, but he had given his word.

Don was listening, too, and he was remembering some advice Judge Matoesian had given him at particularly difficult time years before—"When you're in command, command."

The group was walking back to the car when Don spun on his heel and went back into the small brick building. He stuck his head through the doorway into the sheriff's office.

"Frank, a man's word is his bond. I understand that. We're not going to use this witness. For better or for worse, he's not a part of this case."

Frank nodded and smiled. "I appreciate you doing that, Don."

The last hearing before the trial came up on Thursday. But before the hearing, Don had one more item of business to clear up. Groshong had disclosed that his medical expert would be Dr. Jay Dix, and Weber had to talk to him. Dr. Case knew Dix, and told Don she was interested in what her well-qualified colleague would say. To Don's surprise, Dix rejected Case's conclusion that Heather had been smothered by a hand held over her mouth. The cuts under her lip should have been accompanied by bruising, he said. But he admitted that the color on the videotape of the autopsy that he had viewed might not be good enough to show such bruises.

As Don performed a brief "cross-examination" over the telephone, the doctor agreed that the history of how a body was found and presented was the most important part of any diagnosis. He called this "a negative autopsy," since the body was in good condition except for the tiny marks under the lip. Those marks alone would lead to an "undetermined" cause of death. But the marks and the location of the body—in a trash bag in a trash barrel—led him to conclude that the cause of death was homicide and "probably asphyxiation."

That was a relief to Don. Dix would not contradict Dr. Case's conclusion of a homicide. And there was no legal difference between death by "suffocation" or asphyxiation."

Dix also expressed some doubt that the body had been frozen. Freezing should have been accompanied by microscopic changes in tissue and a "doughy" texture to the flesh. If it had been frozen, why weren't the "cherry red" marks found on other parts of the body? He added, however, "The spots of red do make me wonder."

Weber asked for an explanation for the cuts under the lip. "I don't know," was Dr. Dix's frank reply.

Don also wanted to know the doctor's conclusion on a cause of death for Loralei. "Homicide," Dix said.

He also gave Weber the same basic, and chilling, description of death to an infant from smothering that Dr. Case had offered. Dix said, "Death would come within minutes, but the baby would struggle some."

Don decided to see if the defense expert would be able to counter the prosecution's surprise evidence about Paula's head injury. Dix answered frankly again, "I'm not an expert on that. All the people I see are dead." He agreed when Don asked if the best source for an opinion on head injuries was a neuropathologist.

* * *

At the hearing, the judge was to decide on Don's motion to strike a number of Groshong's witnesses and bar some of the evidence that he insisted proved that the Alton police had ignored a number of other leads because they had made up their minds that Paula, and perhaps even Robert, were guilty. But the judge agreed with Weber that the evidence did not establish a link to another suspect.

But Matoesian handed Weber a setback, too. The judge refused to allow the jury to see the videotape of the reenactment of Paula's story about Loralei's death. But Weber knew the reenactment might be mentioned by witnesses during the trial, giving him another shot at getting it before the jury.

When the attorneys and Matoesian sat down in the judge's chambers after the hearing, Groshong was upset. He frowned at the judge.

"I guess you realize that you just suppressed practically my entire case and ruled that I don't even have a defense. There really isn't any point for me to even go to the trial."

Matoesian shook his head. "It isn't that bad, Don."

The three men took their conversation into the judge's outer office, where they were joined by Charlie Bosworth. Groshong made another comment about having his case gutted by the judge.

Bosworth jokingly asked Groshong, "Don, are you even going to go to Peoria now?"

Groshong's voice brimmed with sarcasm as he answered, "Well, I was going to drive up, but maybe I'll just take the train, since it seems the *railroad* is running."

Matoesian was walking out of the room when the defense attorney fired his verbal shot at the judge's ruling. Andy glanced back over his shoulder, but just smiled.

Weber thought that was a pretty funny line from Groshong, a guy who had just been hammered by damaging rulings in the courtroom.

Weber asked Groshong to meet him later to talk seriously about the case. Weber wouldn't divulge Dr. Case's opinion, the single biggest piece of news he ever had developed in his professional life. But he felt compelled to offer his old friend and adversary one more chance to enter a guilty plea and avoid a trial—and perhaps the death penalty.

Groshong walked into Weber's office later and sat

across the desk from Don. The usual jokes and sarcastic give-and-take were gone, and Weber took on a very serious tone of voice as he suggested a plea to the murder charge. He looked down at his hands folded on the desk, and then looked back into his friend's face.

"At this point in the case, I am very dangerous to your client's life."

Groshong wasn't sure, at first, how to take his friend this time. He looked at Don for about fifteen seconds as he weighed the comment.

He finally shrugged and responded, "Well, I'm sure I'm going to win, too. But I will convey to Paula what you have said. I'll go over to the jail and talk to her, and I'll let you know. But I've already talked to her about this several times."

"Okay. But I have to tell you—I think one of us is misreading this file and one of us is really wrong about it."

Groshong smiled. "Well, I'm sure you're wrong. And you're going to lose this case."

Weber had discharged his conscience, as he always did in a death sentence case. He had given the defendant a chance to plea bargain for her life. That done, he could seek the death penalty knowing he had offered mercy first. It would be Paula's choice.

Don knew Groshong was sincere in his reading of the case. But the defender was starting with Paula's story and trying to figure out what had happened from that. Weber felt this case had to begin by assuming that Paula was lying at her convenience. Believing his client had caused Groshong to ignore the question of timing that was so important to Weber.

The attorneys held their final conference Friday afternoon in what probably is the most public location in county government. They met in front of the bronze statue of James Madison in the courthouse lobby. Both men were dressed casually in jeans, leather bomber jackets, and ball caps. Groshong hadn't shaved.

Weber knew the answer before he asked, "Did you talk to Paula?"

"Yeah. We had a big fight. I even threw a pencil at her. But in the end, Paula said, 'I didn't do it and God knows I'm innocent, and I'm not going to plead.' "

Weber shrugged. "Well, I'll see you in Peoria."

"See ya.' "

As the men parted, Don was thinking, *Well, Paula's got guts. She's a gambling woman. She's telling me, "Prove it. I'll bet my life you can't."*

He went back to the office to talk to Haine. Instead, he was staggered by an unexpected jolt. Kit Morrissey came in and said she was on the telephone with Ernest Springer, the man who had seen the trash bag in the barrel at one o'clock. But now he was adding that he had checked the barrel about 10:30 that morning, and the bag wasn't there. Don snapped straight up in his chair. If the time when the body was dumped could be narrowed to 10:30 A.M. to 1:00 P.M., it would be much easier for Paula to find an alibi. And it raised other questions. Where was everybody during that short time span? Where were the Simses? The cops? The press?

The glories of the last week seemed to fade.

Weber grabbed Haine's telephone and called Springer. The man confirmed Kit's account, and then asked bluntly, "Do you understand what I'm telling you? What I'm telling you is that the baby was dumped in broad daylight between 10:30 and 1:00."

"Have you told this to Groshong?"

"No, I've never talked to him."

Weber hung up and called Tony Ventimiglia. Don had to restrain his anger that the police had not drawn that information from the witness earlier. Ventimiglia said he didn't think there was anything in the file that would give the Simses alibis for that time period. But Don told him to talk to the television stations in St. Louis to determine if they had had the Simses under surveillance at that time. If they did, and the Simses had an alibi, Don's whole theory about Paula dumping the body could be destroyed, and the case could be lost.

The police worked quickly. Ventimiglia called Weber at home Saturday afternoon to tell him nothing in the file was a problem and the television stations had no way of knowing if they had the Simses under surveillance. Dave Hayes even had checked the aerial photographs taken by the police to be sure that no television vehicles showed up near the Sims house.

Weber felt better after that. He allowed himself to reason the situation backward. Paula was guilty and she dumped the

body. Therefore, she couldn't have an alibi. But the new timing meant that Paula had indeed dumped the body in broad
daylight. *What audacity,* Weber found himself thinking again.
The effect of the FBI's advice for a media blitz must have
blown Paula's mind to make her do such a risky thing.

The shorter time period would affect Robert Sims, too.
He could put himself deeply into "the loop" of guilty
knowledge if he gave Paula an alibi for such a short time.
And if he didn't, Paula might be willing to roll over on
him. Weber knew he had to be prepared to present a
somewhat harsher picture of Robert to the jurors to make
sure they would not accept an alibi from him.

Weber played his regular Saturday tennis match with
his team that day. Most of the other players were agents
from DCI, and Weber was shocked when one of them,
Terry Klutts, offered his opinion that the jury would acquit Paula. Klutts saw the shock in Don's face, and
quickly added that he thought Paula was guilty. He just
didn't think Weber had enough evidence.

Weber worried, "If you can't convince a cop, what
about regular jurors?"

Peoria is 160 miles north of Madison County, a long
trip across the monotonous prairie of central Illinois on
a cold night. The drive gave Don three hours to think,
and he used this first Sunday trip to concentrate on looking at the case from Paula's point of view. He was convinced that Paula hadn't hated Heather; she had sung to
her in the hospital and had showed some other signs of
being a normal mother. Despite that, Don believed Paula
had been planning Heather's murder all along. Robert disliked little girls, and Paula had been through it all before,
three years ago. Even the sleeping arrangements were the
same this time, the same pressure on Paula again.

It seemed to Don that Heather's bout with diarrhea
may have been the last straw—the final irritant that put
the plans in action. Trying to break Paula's code, Don
wondered if she had confessed allegorically when she
said she had been taking out the trash because of the dirty
diapers; Robert didn't like the smell of the dirty diapers.
Paula had treated Heather like another bit of trash, stick-

ing her in the bag and dumping her in the barrel because she didn't like having her around.

Don reached the Continental Regency Hotel in Peoria later than he had expected, and late for a meeting with Haine. Bill and his private law partner, Randy Bono, had brought in two jury selection consultants from Des Moines, Iowa, who Randy had used in his civil trials. Haine was paying their fees from his interest in the law firm. Theresa Zagnoli, a psychologist, was vice president of the consulting firm; Phyllis Henry, a research analyst with a doctoral degree, had been a cop for ten years.

Weber wasn't sure about using consultants. He knew how to pick a jury and he wasn't sure he wanted them involved in his case. He met the group in the hotel restaurant and was introduced to the women. They seemed to go out of their way to make Don comfortable and to defer to his expertise. He assumed they had been warned that he was a prima donna with a temper. But he soon found their questions provocative and beneficial. He realized that they were helping him focus on some pitfalls he had known instinctively that he wanted to avoid, but hadn't given a lot of thought to. They suggested avoiding any portrayal of Paula as a docile, pathetic woman, a victim controlled by a domineering man. She should be shown as an independent, strong woman, capable of murder to meet her own ends. And they warned him to steer clear of any juror who seemed to be a militant feminist who would tend to blame the man for the problem, despite the evidence.

Don realized that he would have to be more conscious of those concerns during the jury selection and trial. But he was confident that Paula's conduct throughout the years would show her to be a willful woman who had acted on her own to solve her own problems, even when the solutions were the murders of her own babies.

Don got to his room about 11:00 P.M. and went to bed. As he settled in, he assessed the way he felt with one of his favorite phrases from Mark Twain—the calm confidence of a Christian holding four aces. He slept well.

Chapter 19

Monday, January 8, 1990. It was the day that everyone, it seemed to Don Weber, had been awaiting. All the planning and thinking and discussing were over. It was time for the prosecutors and the cops to put an end to the abominations of Paula Sims. And it all would happen in the courthouse where the infamous Richard Speck had been convicted twenty three years earlier, and in the town immortalized by Richard Nixon's question about whether it would "play in Peoria."

And Don felt way too tight. He had been under pressure before, but not like this. Not under the microscopic examination this case was receiving. And not when another man's career could depend on it, as Haine's could on this case.

And there was the man on the other side of the aisle. Weber wasn't about to underestimate Groshong. He was capable of presenting a masterful case and destroying his opponent. Weber's case could come apart about fifteen different ways, and it was up to him to keep it from disintegretating under Groshong's attack.

Weber and Haine were escorted through the rear door of the Peoria County Courthouse by a deputy assigned to them by the sheriff. They took their files to a small room provided for them in the offices of State's Attorney Kevin Lyons. Don heard he was missing quite a scene outside the courtroom.

The Paula Sims trial was opening with all the fanfare and media attention everyone had predicted, even 160 miles from her home. The three major television stations from St. Louis had rented parking spaces in front of the courthouse for their microwave vans what would beam their live reports back to St. Louis and Madison County.

Even the television stations in Peoria had been running advance stories about the trial, and their reporters and camera crews were on the scene. Reporters from a dozen newspapers, the Associated Press, and several radio stations swelled the media ranks to almost thirty. The artists who would sketch the courtroom scene started staking out their front-row seats.

The reporters were admitted around the long line of spectators that had queued up outside the glass doors to the hallway on the second floor of the courthouse. The line ran along the railing around the open balcony and past the courtroom where Speck had been tried. Two courtrooms away, through the doors and down the hall, was Courtroom C. It was a long, narrow room set off by dark paneling from floor to ceiling and huge marble slabs that rose gracefully on the wall behind the bench. There was surprisingly limited seating for spectators in the four rows of wooden benches and the row of chairs behind them. An aisle divided the seating, and the benches on each side would hold six comfortably, seven relatively easily, and eight, if they jammed in. Maximum seating in the room was about eighty.

The front bench on the right side was reserved for Haine's staff and other officials. The press quickly filled up most of the other seating and watched Weber's first act in the courtroom; he rearranged the prosecution and defense tables, swinging them around to face the jury box. The judge's bench was to Weber's left, and the defense was to the right.

As Weber was rearranging the room, the focus of all the effort was arriving outside. Paula was escorted into the courthouse under the probing lenses of television cameramen and newspaper photographers. She looked pale and gaunt, even thinner than before. Her dark brown hair hung limply along the sides of her face. She wore a long-sleeved, V-neck knit blouse of light blue and maroon stripes, and light blue polyester slacks that seemed sadly out of style.

She walked about twenty feet from the transport van to the unfinished sally port that was part of a new addition to the courthouse. The covered entrance would be ready the next day, however, and Paula would be the first prisoner to use it. During the rest of the trial, she would be driven into the structure as the overhead door closed quickly behind her, shutting out the cameras.

At 8:53 A.M., Judge Matoesian called court into session as his court reporter, Dorothy Warren, began filling the first of seventy steno books with her shorthand notes. Matoesian quickly denied Groshong's motions to sequester the jury and to gag the attorneys to stop comments to reporters during the trial. Groshong cited the front-page story in that morning's Peoria *Journal-Star* as evidence of the need to reduce the publicity.

Groshong also lost a motion to keep Weber from discussing the death penalty with potential jurors. Weber argued that the jurors should know they might be asked to order Paula's execution because the evidence would show that "murder had been percolating in her malignant little heart."

The reporters who weren't familiar with Weber's style seemed almost shocked, but it was a great line.

At 9:45, Matoesian had the first group of jurors brought into the courtroom and the tedious jury selection began. The judge told Paula to stand as he introduced her and the attorneys to the jurors. The judge read and explained the charges, and told the panel that the death penalty was a possible punishment. He ran through a long list of ninety names of potential witnesses, including Paula Sims, to see if the jurors knew any of the witnesses.

Although Groshong was refusing to confirm that Paula would testify, a reporter from KTVI in St. Louis immediately aired a live report saying Paula had been confirmed as a witness on the list. That was not true then, but it turned out later to be accurate. It was another incident of "premature speculation," an affliction suffered by some media members who get excited too quickly.

Paula sat grimly through the proceedings. She usually stared straight ahead, and only occasionally allowed herself a glance at the jurors. Sometimes she sipped nervously from a cup of water.

Despite the deadly serious tone, Matoesian's comments led to a few chuckles. He remembered aloud the time he had asked a divorced woman what her ex-husband had done. She replied, "Nothin'. That's why we're divorced."

The procession of jurors brought in seemed to be a legitimate cross-section of life in Peoria—secretaries, homemakers, a stockbroker and a number of workers at Caterpillar, the heavy-equipment manufacturer and major employer in town.

The judge excused three of the first twelve on the panel—one who was opposed to capital punishment and two who said their opinions would be impossible to overcome.

When the remaining nine were turned over to Weber, he began his quest for a panel of normal people. As he questioned one young man about capital punishment, Don pointed directly at Paula and asked, "Would you have any hesitation about imposing the death penalty on that woman right there?"

It was a startling and effective ploy. Don knew he had to confront the jurors with the reality of the case. The death penalty was a real possibility for a real person— "that woman right there." If the jurors couldn't answer that question without blinking, they probably couldn't do the deed later.

Groshong's questions surprised Weber a bit. The defender asked the jurors if they knew anything about sudden infant death syndrome. How could Groshong use that in his defense when his own medical expert had ruled it out? Groshong also asked if any of them were members of right-to-life groups or neighborhood crime-watch groups. He concentrated on questions of whether everyone convicted of murder should get death, the confusion over the jurisdiction between Illinois and Missouri, and the evidence about Loralei's death.

At the lunch break, Weber met with Haine, Kit, Dee-Dee, Bono, and the consultants. The consultants suggested that Weber was not friendly enough, coming across as too harsh and tense. He might alienate the jurors. Weber reacted emotionally to what seemed to him to be criticism from people unqualified to offer it. He blew up.

"If you guys are so smart, you try the case yourself. I've picked five death-penalty juries. I know what I'm doing and I don't need help from you. I don't want the jurors to like me. I just want them to listen to my arguments. I'm trying to convict a woman and sentence her to death. I can't come in here like some clown and entertain them. If you can do this better, then you do it."

Weber stormed out of the room and stalked down the hall. He was standing by the balcony railing when Haine caught up with him.

"Look Don, I know you're nervous and upset. These guys are just trying to help. But I've got ultimate confidence in you. You're the only guy who can handle this case. So you do it the way you want to."

His words cooled Weber down, and he realized that his reaction was the irrational result of the mounting pressure. It probably was better that he had exploded and released the steam that was building up. Don met again with Theresa Zagnoli, and realized that her suggestions made sense. When court resumed, Don applied her ideas and felt much better about his performance.

By the end of the day, twenty people had been questioned and four jurors had been selected. Weber and the others who had seen this process a few times already figured Juror Four would be the panel's foreman. Harold Ryan, Jr. was an engineer at Caterpillar; he always wore a suit, unusual for most jurors, and generally peered out at the courtroom over the top of half-lens reading glasses.

That evening, the first bull session was held among the attorneys at Sully's, a great sports bar around the corner from the courthouse; it quickly became the favorite eating and drinking spot for the lawyers and reporters. Weber, Haine, Kit, and DeeDee traded thoughts over a couple of drinks with Groshong and Williamson.

The discussion turned to a videotape the defense planned to use as evidence. Recorded at Randy's first birthday party, the tape showed a seemingly normal mother, obviously pregnant again, playing with her son. In one scene, Randy was crawling down the hallway while his mother trailed behind, teasing, "Mommy's gonna' get you" in a twangy drawl. Randy was peering back over his shoulder with some apprehension.

Groshong taunted Weber that the jury would love that tape, seeing Paula as a loving and playful mother.

But Don snapped back, "Right. And I'm going to have a

lot of fun with the line 'Mommy's going to get you.' That line has a very different meaning when Paula Sims says it."

The tape was never played.

Tuesday morning started with a surprise. Weber gave Groshong a copy of a written statement taken by the Alton police from murder suspect Kathy Gaultney at the Madison County Jail the day before, when the police followed Weber's orders to interview all of Paula's cellmates.

Gaultney had quoted Paula as saying that Heather's kidnapper had appeared suddenly in the house and walked into the room where the baby was sleeping. He struck Paula in the back of the neck, knocking her out. She awoke later, found Heather missing and Robert and Randy still asleep upstairs.

Don thought the change in some of the details of the story was interesting, and might be used to show that Paula was having trouble keeping her lies straight.

As the questioning of potential jurors resumed, Groshong became irritated by Don's habit of pointing at Paula. From Groshong's seat between Don and Paula, he was seeing the full impact of the prosecutor's ploy. Groshong even attempted to defuse it once by leaning forward and making a funny face directly into the outstretched finger of his opponent. But the defender finally had enough of it and objected. He told the judge that Weber was trying to intimidate the defendant.

Matoesian shrugged it off. "Some people talk with their hands. Overruled."

The selection process dragged on through the day with a considerable number of people dismissed by the judge or removed with one of the fourteen challenges allowed for each attorney. Weber removed jurors who were too hesitant about the death penalty or struck him wrong some other way. Don, Kit, and the consultants seemed to be agreeing on all the choices. The consultants gave the "disqualify" signal by putting a pencil in their mouths. But Don and Kit usually had decided that already.

By the end of the day, twenty-five jurors had been dismissed, and no more had been chosen. But progress had been made. With few challenges left, a jury would be seated the next day.

* * *

But Wednesday got off to a frustrating start as the judge, Weber, and Groshong bounced the first twelve jurors off the panel. It seemed that an outbreak of contagious opinion was sweeping the panel as the jurors realized that claiming to have a firm opinion about guilt or innocence, or opposing the death penalty, would get them excused. Matoesian decided to treat the epidemic by bringing the jurors into the room one at a time. That speeded things up, and before long, the panel of twelve was seated.

Kit Morrissey handled the selection of three alternate jurors after the lunch break. Even that turned out to be somewhat difficult. Nine in a row were excused by the judge for opinions or opposition to capital punishment. But within an hour, three more men were seated.

So the jury was set. They had gone through eighty-eight candidates to find the eight men and four women who would serve. But Weber liked the panel. He had a hunter who had worked with dogs; he would enjoy the testimony about the canine searches, and would vouch for the dogs' abilities with the other jurors. There were two black women. The older one was married to a park ranger, and she had commented that many people went to the parks to take drugs. She wouldn't like the idea of Heather's body being left in a trash barrel at a park. The younger one struck Don as someone who had come up the hard way, using her own strength and character to build a good life. She would be tough on someone like Paula.

The rest seemed like good, solid citizens. Weber couldn't ask for more in a case like this.

Groshong finished the day by winning some motions. Matoesian barred Weber from mentioning the grants of immunity to the Blews at the grand jury, and he threw out the results of blood tests that showed that Paula had smoked marijuana the night Heather disappeared.

Don had watched Paula as often as possible during those three days. She had been almost stoic. How could she display so little emotion and seem so disinterested while everything that went on around her involved the death of her babies and the possibility that she might be executed? She had sat so still, her hands folded in her lap and her gaze fixed on some far-off point. Even when she looked directly at Don, he saw nothing in her eyes. He would expect a look that said, "I hate you," or "I'm innocent." But he got nothing. How could he convince the jury that a cold-blooded killer lived behind those blank eyes? Was that expressionless face really just another mask? That was how he would play it. The many faces of Paula Sims. A different mask to meet the need of the moment. The loving mother. The faithful wife. The caring daughter. The old friend. The merciless killer. The lying suspect. The innocent defendant.

That evening, Don worked to refine the opening statement he would deliver to the jury the next day. He worked from an outline to keep it spontaneous; never a prepared text.

But he needed a special way to describe this nonexistent kidnapper, a word that would cut with just the right edge of sarcasm. In a meeting in his hotel room that night, Don asked everyone what they thought of the term "bogey man." It seemed perfect. It was something from everyone's childhood. It described an imaginary, evil figure who would come in the night and take a child away. No one had ever seen the "bogey man," and there was no evidence he really existed.

But Don was concerned about a possible racial overtone. Was there a popular assumption that the "bogey man" was black? Everyone agreed that might alienate the black jurors. Kit called Duane Bailey, a black prosecutor Weber had hired while he was in office. Bailey warned that the term invoked a threatening black man and could insult the black jurors.

Weber decided he was going to have to come up with something else. He didn't like the current, popular horror figures, like Freddy Krueger from the *Nightmare on Elm Street* movies, or even Darth Vader from *Star Wars*. They were too real to fit this situation. He needed a term to convey the idea that this guy never really existed, except in Paula's malignant imagination.

He laid awake for about an hour that night. It wasn't just the search for right phrase. He knew that the next day was the biggest of his career.

Chapter 20

Judge Matoesian leaned back in his chair.

"The court recognizes Mr. Weber for opening statements."

The prosecutor stepped before the jury box and began a relentless assault on Paula Sims in a courtroom packed with spectators and reporters. He was ready to pull together the results of years of investigation for the twelve people who would decide if Paula Sims was the victim of two horrible crimes, or the killer of two innocent babies. Don would present the cases chronologically, and he wasted no time in letting the jurors know what they would hear about Loralei's disappearance and death.

"What Paula Sims told the police was as close to a fairy tale as you can get in a murder case. She told a fairy tale about a roving Rumpelstiltskin who showed up on her doorstep one night and snatched her infant baby for ridiculous motives, under preposterous circumstances, and in an unbelievable manner.

"And, again in 1989, this roving Rumpelstiltskin showed up on her doorstep in a ridiculous manner, in an impossible way, she says. Her second fairy tale is a little bit different from the first because it was refined, because she had experience. But it is equally preposterous."

Don was making eye contact with each juror, slowly and deliberately; their eyes showed they were staying right with him as he went through a detailed account of Paula's story from 1986 and destroyed it, ticking off each bit by impossible bit.

Then it was time to make it personal.

"During this trial, I expect that you are going to see a number of faces of Paula Sims. One face is going to be Paula Sims, the actress, and she was really pretty good.

She can act upset. She can act emotional. She can act distraught. She can act like they act on TV. The problem is that she doesn't know how to act medically, in real life. And, during the second abduction—alleged abduction—I think you are going to be able to tell that her story of that event also is untrue.

"There is another face of Paula Sims you are going to see, and that's the one with her guard down a little bit. That's the one she showed to Stephanie Werner, when she was in the hospital in March of 1989 having Heather."

Don described how little Randy was "doted on by his father; adored by his father; treated like he would break." And then he gave the jury the motive, that attempt to explain these irrational acts in some rational way.

"And something else that's quite curious. Apparently this roving, fairy-tale figure doesn't care about Randy. He just takes Heather. There have been three children born to the Simses. The boy survives; the girls are dead. Now, is it a coincidence, something that we can discount, that this person just happens to take baby girls, who Paula does not want, and leaves the baby boy, who Robert does want?"

After touching the important evidence, without divulging too much, it was time to close.

"The faces of Paula Sims that you will see are going to be varied, because she is quite a personality."

As he prepared to fire the first of many dramatic lines toward the jury, he glanced at Paula. She wore the vacant, stony look he had seen so often, and that he hoped she would be wearing for him again at this moment. He pointed at her again, as he had for the last three days.

"But the important face of Paula Sims is that cold-blooded, merciless face that you see now. And that was the last face that Baby Loralei and Baby Heather saw."

Don turned slowly away from the jury and walked back to his seat. It had worked, and Paula had posed perfectly for him. He felt sure the jury now understood what this case was all about. And he had used the words "cold-blooded and merciless" because they were part of the death penalty criteria. He already had begun to condition the jurors for that decision.

As Groshong stood, Weber was glad he had worn his almost-white linen suit. It contrasted perfectly to the black suits worn by the defense attorneys. The Lone Ranger pitted against Darth Vader and the Emperor of the Evil Empire.

Groshong calmly approached the jury and spoke softly.

"Mr. Weber, Miss Morrissey. If it pleases the court. Ladies and gentlemen. My name is Don Groshong and this is my client, Paula Sims."

He suddenly stabbed his right index finger into the top of the lectern and his voice rose.

"I want to get one thing straight right now. Paula did not kill those children. She didn't kill her children. She's innocent. Right now, she's innocent. We have a terrible tragedy. We've got two children who are dead. That's a terrible tragedy. But she didn't kill those children. She's the victim, and the evidence will show you that she's the victim, not the perpetrator of anything."

Groshong put his own spin on the most damning part of the case—the incredible repeat performance.

"Is that unusual? You bet it is. But that is not the question. The question is, 'Did Paula kill her daughters?' The answer to that question is, 'No, she did not.' And the perpetrator of that is still at large."

He claimed a lack of evidence, and charges built only on theory.

"The state's case is outlined this way: Paula's account of what happened in 1986 and 1989 is unusual. I think Mr. Weber described it in the words 'preposterous, unbelievable, ridiculous, impossible, and imaginary.' The police did not believe Paula. The prosecutor did not believe Paula. Therefore, they say, since they don't believe Paula, she killed her daughters.

"The fact that the state doesn't believe Paula is beside the point. Really, whether you believe what Paula said is beside the point. Even if you disbelieve her, that doesn't prove murder. But the point is, what she says is true. And, when she testifies in this courtroom—and she will— you judge her credibility when you hear her."

Weber had his answer. Groshong had just locked Paula into testifying, no matter what the state's case revealed.

Groshong warned the jurors that they would find Weber's theory of the crime more incredible than anything Paula Sims ever said. Groshong said Paula and Robert were "fairly humble people, fairly simple people." He added, "We are not talking about Albert Einstein here."

He glanced back at Paula. "No offense."

But her unremarkable intelligence made it ridiculous to believe that this simple woman had pulled off two shocking baby murders without leaving any evidence that a staggering investigation could discover.

And his voice nearly dripped with incredulity when he described Weber's acceptance of Stephanie Werner's statement.

"What you have to believe is Paula had to have made up her mind to kill that child in the hospital room on the day of the delivery, and told a perfect stranger about that. And six weeks later, she did exactly what she told the girl. That's incredible."

He discounted the trash bag as evidence with a startling and, Weber thought, pretty intriguing theory of his own. Groshong compared the trash bag to the pillow slip that a burglar would use to carry off his loot. And then he turned that around to make the state's use of the bag seem like another half-baked accusation.

"When a burglar comes in and steals your stuff and puts it in a pillow case and takes it out, and they recover the loot, and it's in your pillow case, they don't indict you for the burglary. They look for the guy that did it. That is not what happened here. Because it's her pillowcase, they indict her."

Groshong closed, "So now, I think after you have heard all the evidence, you have viewed all the exhibits, we are right back to square one. We don't know who killed and who kidnapped these children, but you will know that Paula Sims didn't do it, and that whoever did it is still out there. And I think that will establish for you a reasonable doubt of her guilt, and that she is innocent."

Weber was pleased that Robert and Paula would take the stand. He had been hoping for a chance to stand face to face with them and force them to justify their absurd stories. He remembered a law-school adage that cross-examination was the most effective means of fact finding known to man.

He plunged into the evidence with his first witness, Jeff Reed, who repeated Paula's comment about not wanting to have children, especially girls. Julie Fry followed him with her story about Paula's weeping telephone call to Robert, apologizing for having a daughter when Loralei was born. Don liked her; she was an articulate witness with a good memory and no reason to fabricate a story.

Sheriff Frank Yocom was next, and he gave the jury its first glimpse at the pathetic remains of Loralei. As he described the condition of the tiny skeleton and identified the photos of what was found, Weber passed the pictures among the jurors. It was a sobering experience for the twelve in the jury box, and Weber knew it would be a big step toward hardening their hearts against Paula. Weber was surprised when Groshong's cross-examination drew out more disturbing details about the condition of the body, including the grisly likelihood that it had been chewed on by animals.

Don and Minnie Gray took the stand to paint a vivid picture of their young neighbor appearing hysterically at their front door. Weber was careful to draw from both of them that they had not seen or heard anything from some mysterious kidnapper in the still of that summer evening. In his cross-examination, Groshong got Don Gray to agree that a path had been cleared through the woods behind the Sims house by a crew installing lines for cable television, the implication being that a kidnapper might have escaped along that path.

But while Groshong was questioning Minnie Gray, he walked into the first blind-side punch in the bout. Groshong innocently asked about Paula's dog, Shadow, hoping to show that the dog was too meek to have attacked a kidnapper.

"It was a family pet," Minnie agreed, and then added, "but Paula told me she was never afraid back there because she said Shadow heard everything, so, you know, she said she wasn't afraid."

Bingo, thought Don. His opponent had fallen into the

classic trap of asking one question too many, and had taken a hard right to the nose for his trouble.

Weber strode quickly to the lectern for re-direct examination, asking only two questions to show that the dog had not barked that night, obviously because there was nothing to bark at. Weber was barely able to squelch the smile that he felt tugging at the corners of his mouth. Through the prosecutor's mind was running the same phrase that was being whispered sarcastically among the reporters—"The Shadow knows."

Yocom returned to the stand to describe the long investigation. Weber wanted to establish that the police had done everything possible—from searches by dogs to airplanes to divers—to check out Paula's story, and never could find a single piece of evidence to back it up.

Groshong focused his questions on sixteen tidbits from Paula's story that the police had confirmed as true, using a line-by-line dissection of Paula's written statement to Yocom and Bivens.

On re-direct examination, Weber began to lay the trap that could lead to getting the videotape of the reenactment admitted as evidence. Since Groshong had asked about efforts to verify Paula's story, Weber asked Yocom to recount the reenactment and the conclusion that Paula easily would have seen the kidnapper in the driveway.

When Groshong came back on re-cross, Weber watched as his opponent fell into the trap, asking many more questions about how the reenactment was performed.

In the audience, Bob Trone watched as his colleague drew in the defense attorney. When the trap was sprung, Trone leaned over to his wife and whispered, "Now Don will shove that tape right down Groshong's throat."

It was well into the afternoon when Weber called his eleventh witness, the first of four canine officers who would describe their futile search for scents on the Sims property. Groshong agreed to let Trooper Michael Donovan testify as an expert, and Don used the affable trooper to educate the jurors about how the dogs performed their jobs. Donovan explained that dogs are able to identify and file in their memories 150 odors within a minute of arriving at a location. The dogs are trained to ignore those scents and search only for the one that their handler has told them to follow. When tracking humans, the dogs sniff out the odor of the body cells that flake off the skin every time a human being moves. If someone were running, the scent would be enhanced because of the sweat.

Weber asked for Donovan's opinion on whether an unknown man had run down the driveway that night. After Matoesian overruled an objection from Groshong, Donovan responded, "It didn't appear, to the way the dog was working, that anybody had gone out to the road and gone in any direction that we could find."

Great, Don thought. With a dog handler on the jury, surely that opinion would carry some weight.

Donovan described Judd's discovery of Loralei's body the next week and then told the jury how he had gone to the Simses' house in Alton three years later to conduct an unsuccessful search for Loralei's missing sister.

Groshong's cross-examination was lengthy, indicating he was trying to learn about police dogs as the trial progressed. But as he pushed with insistent questions on the dog's success rate, Groshong gave the trooper the chance to boast that dogs have a 95 to 100 percent success rate finding human scents, although they locate the person in question in only fifteen to twenty percent of the cases. The longer Groshong drilled, the more infallible the dogs seemed.

State police sergeant James Buysse was next, and he offered a clear opinion about the phantom kidnapper. "I believe that there was no one running from the house," he said.

When Groshong cross-examined him about his dog, Bear, Buysse vouched for him in no uncertain terms.

"If the guy is there, he will find him."

Groshong started a snappy exchange when he said Paula had run down the driveway, creating the kind of "hot scent" Buysse said Bear could find.

"You didn't pick that one up, did you?" Groshong asked.

"No."

"There you go. No further questions," Groshong retorted in triumph.

But Weber wouldn't let that stand on his re-direct.

"Let's assume that, rather than being an excited, emotional mother who had just had her baby kidnapped, she just sauntered down that lane. Would she leave a hot scent?"

"Not as hot a scent as someone running nervous, excited."

Sergeant Charles Yoways of the state police said he and his dog, Sergeant, found no scents at the scene, either. Yoways's hometown was given away by his thick accent and his use of "a block" to describe how far into the woods he had searched. Weber smiled as he asked his last question.

"You're not from Chicago, are you?"

The audience laughed as Yoways responded, "Yes, I am."

When the first day of Paula Sims' trial ended, Weber felt great. He had run through fourteen witnesses without a hitch, and the dog handlers had capped it off well. The juror who knew about dogs had paid close attention, as Weber had hoped. And Groshong seemed to have locked himself into a pattern of cross-examinations that were bringing out details that made Don's case stronger. It was a good, solid start.

The testimony would be more dramatic, Weber knew, on the second day, Friday, January 12. The first witness would transport the jurors back into those woods behind the Sims house and let them see just how little was left of Loralei by the time Judd found her.

Mark Johnsey, the DCI crime-scene technician and forensic anthropologist, took the stand with the bearing of an expert. With scientific detachment, he described the painstaking effort of collecting the little bones found in the woods on June 24, 1986.

"As you go down the hill, less and less bones were found. The only conclusion I could draw was that some type of animal was eating on the skeleton or the remains, and it was being dragged down the hill."

A woman in the audience gasped at the gruesome suggestion. Loralei's mother showed no reaction.

Groshong's cross-examination was brief, but the ques-

tions allowed Johnsey to put out the disturbing news that
Heather's left arm and left leg were missing, as well as
a number of other bones. Weber knew the jury would
find it disgusting that this woman had sat in her house
while her baby's body was being savaged and dismem-
bered by hungry animals barely a hundred feet away.

Weber then steered the case toward a direct attack on
Paula's kidnapper story by calling DCI Agent Debra
Morgan to recall how Paula had claimed to have seen a
"shadowy figure" running down the driveway. That
would be important to Don's attempt to discredit Paula
with the taped reenactment.

Groshong went after Debby hard from the start. He
insisted that she had focused on Paula as a suspect from
the beginning and had interviewed her only to get incriminating information; he hammered her about not
writing her own report of the interview and for not using
a tape recorder or video camera to record it.

Don had to admit Groshong was being pretty effective,
and the interview technique by the agents, while common and appropriate, wasn't looking too good in front
of the jury.

Groshong suggested that the reenactment was done
solely to manufacture evidence to use against Paula at
the trial. Morgan said that was not her purpose; she was
doing what she had been asked by Agent Watson.

Weber thought Agent Morgan had held up well under
tough questioning. But others, maybe even some jurors,
would think Groshong had scored his first points with his
questions about the agents' interview techniques. Don
decided then that her partner, Diana Sievers, had to be
brought in from a training session in Washington, D.C.
to testify on Monday, regardless of the problems involved.

Don was glad that Dr. Michael Graham, the chief
medical examiner for St. Louis, was his next witness.
His testimony would be a surprise, and it would help
shift the focus off Groshong's cross-examination of Morgan. Graham wouldn't be a major surprise; just a nice
little land mine for the defense. He had examined Loralei's remains shortly after they were found.

"After having done your examination, were you able

to determine within a reasonable degree of medical certainty the cause of death of Loralei Sims?''

"In a general sense, yes.''

"What is that opinion?''

"It is my opinion that she died of homicidal violence.''

There it was. For the first time in public. Weber now had an expert opinion that Loralei Sims was murdered. Most of the jurors and spectators looked at Paula. She never moved a muscle.

Groshong had to dilute the impact of that announcement. He got Dr. Graham to agree that he could not say how the baby had been killed. But Groshong's efforts to get Graham to admit it could have been accidental failed. Graham said the body's condition and its location ruled that out, and he refused to let Groshong isolate the factors from the medical conclusion.

In re-direct questioning, Weber asked Dr. Graham about the verdict by the coroner's jury in Jersey County classifying the cause of Loralei's death as unknown. He disagreed, and would have listed it as "homicidal violence of an undetermined nature.''

As the last dog handler, State Trooper William Rogers, was about to complete his testimony, Groshong noted that Rogers's dog was named "Rocky.'' To laughs from the spectators and jurors, Groshong asked, "Who names all these dogs?'' Rogers answered that the dogs usually had been named before the police acquired them. But Groshong's question started a running gag that he would continue throughout the trial. Anytime a dog was mentioned in any context, Groshong asked about its name. He always got a laugh.

Six nurses took the stand in quick succession to describe their observations of the Sims family during three births. Generally, they testified that the Simses were a quiet couple who had been very happy and excited at Randy's birth, and less so when their daughters were born. After Heather was delivered, Robert always brought Randy to the hospital and seemed more attentive to him than to the new baby. A couple of the nurses never saw

Robert hold Heather; he had always held the newborn Randy.

The oddest exchange came when Don called Jane McElroy, the team leader on the OB floor when Heather was born. It was one of those moments trial lawyers dread, but are powerless to avoid.

When Weber asked if she had observed Robert's conduct toward Heather, the nurse said, "No, sir."

Don looked down at the police report, in which Ventimiglia had quoted her as saying Robert seemed "disinterested during the birth of the victim, Heather Sims." Don asked again, and still she had nothing to offer.

He decided the best thing to do was grin and bear it. A little comic relief. He smiled and shrugged.

"No further questions."

There was a low ripple of chuckles through the courtroom.

The next nurse, Bernice Stupperich, helped Don redeem himself. She said Paula had looked at Heather with a blank face—no emotion when she was handed her newborn daughter. After thirty-eight years as a nurse, that was not the kind of reaction she was used to seeing from a mother.

The first real fireworks of the trial were about to start, and Don was eager. He called Stephanie Werner-Cook to the stand. He had just learned that she was pregnant with her second child, and that certainly couldn't hurt her credibility in this case about baby killings.

Virginia Weber's work with Stephanie was apparent. She wore a demure dress and seemed more calm and reflective as she told her story.

Groshong approached Stephanie with obvious disbelief. He zeroed in on the disagreement about the room and Paula's supposed comment about signing for a private room on a preadmission form. Groshong seemed victorious when he produced a copy of the form to show that Paula had marked the box for a semiprivate room, and then offered a copy of the nurse's notes that had no mention of any disagreement.

It was obvious from his voice that Groshong believed he had just destroyed Stephanie's credibility. But Weber didn't believe the incident over the room was of any import, and he would present it to the jury that way later.

Groshong seemed incredulous at Stephanie's insistence that she had not been so curious about the case of her roommate's baby that she had devoured the newspapers. But she said she was too busy with a job, a baby, and college classes to do that.

Weber was pleased that Groshong had used the newspapers again, because Stephanie's mother could be called for corroboration. She would be the last witness for the week, a strategic move he hoped would send the jury home on the right note. Barbara Werner took the stand to recall how Paula's account had come to mind amid the first news on television of Heather's disappearance.

"I said, 'Oh, my God. That's Stephanie's roommate, and she was taking out the trash again.' That's what stuck in my mind."

It reverberated through the courtroom. *She was taking out the trash again.* The comment came out better than Don had hoped, and he knew it would stick with the jury. *She was taking out the trash again.*

It was a great way to end the first week. Weber never had run through twenty-six witnesses in less than two days; in fact, he never had that many witness in a whole trial before. And he was impressed that the system set up by Don Greer, the administrator in the prosecutor's office, had delivered each day's witnesses to Peoria in a rented van, on time—no easy task.

Don headed home for the long weekend, with Monday off in honor of Martin Luther King, Jr. Don felt great on the drive south. He had watched the jurors taking some notes during the testimony, and he had felt the piercing stare from the jury foreman. But the juror had sent that same look toward Groshong, too, apparently scrutinizing things closely.

On the other side of the table, the defense was just as pleased. Groshong felt he had destroyed Stephanie Werner's credibility, showing positively that she had lied about the dispute over the hospital room. He would nail that down later with more hospital witnesses of his own. If she had lied about something so inconsequential, how could she be believed about something more important?

How could anyone accept the basic premise of her story? Who could believe that, just hours after Heather was born, Paula sat in her hospital room and schemed to murder the infant? And then she revealed those thoughts to a total stranger? That theory had to be at the top of any list of unbelievable stories.

Weber was glad to get home to talk to Virginia. She had hours of videotapes from the television news, and Don enjoyed sitting there watching them. He was overwhelmed with the kind of coverage the trial was getting in St. Louis, but he wasn't thrilled with the artists' sketches that seemed to add sixty pounds to his frame. Virginia told him she had heard that the trial was the major topic of conversation everywhere, from the taverns to the beauty shops to the backyard fences.

Don spent the weekend in his normal pursuits, trying to stay away from trial matters to relax. He played tennis Saturday and Sunday, and, as usual, his team lost.

Chapter 21

Even the risk of her very life had failed to draw Paula Sims out of the silent monolith that had encased her since 1986. As soon as the assault on her began then, her humanity had given way to this emotionless countenance, an icy stare. It remained intact even when she sat in a courtroom and was bombarded by hideous details of her daughters' deaths that made others recoil. She never flinched, even when she had to know that everyone would expect an innocent woman to weep in horror. Instead, Paula stared off in the distance, past the judge and jury.

Don wondered if she had locked herself in another world somewhere to insulate herself from reality. But he watched Paula in the courtroom and what he sensed was a woman determined to remain in control, a woman who was not about to be brought to tears for the amusement of the mob. Her obsessive personality held her in check, and made her put the water bottle back in exactly the spot it had been, with the stopper turned just the proper way. She walked into the courtroom stiffly each day and sat erect at the table for hours without moving.

But Don, and everyone else there, knew the toll was being taken. She appeared thinner by the day and her haggard face showed the strain. At night, the jail guards could see her sitting doubled over on her bunk, rocking back and forth. Weber thought Groshong was right when he said Paula already was dead inside.

Groshong was making an effort to communicate with Paula. He and Williamson spoke to her as often as possible, often touching her arm or putting their hands on her shoulder. Groshong occasionally would wink at her as he returned to the table. But all of that lessened as the activity of the trial grew more intense and the attorneys' attention was pulled in other directions.

At 9:00 A.M. on Tuesday, January 16, Don Weber renewed his request that Judge Matoesian allow the videotape of the reenactment because Groshong had raised the specter of the police "trumping up" evidence against Paula. Groshong argued that he had been compelled to ask the police about it when Weber brought it up. But the judge agreed that Groshong's extensive cross-examination had made the tape admissible.

But first, Weber brought in Diana Sievers to rehabilitate her report on the interview with Paula. Diana could be a bulldog, and Groshong wouldn't be able to shake her insistence on the report's accuracy. She remembered that Paula had been positive about seeing the figure running down the driveway and hearing his footsteps crunching in the gravel. "It wasn't a probably or a maybe," Diana said flatly.

She and Groshong sparred a bit, but neither drew blood and the agent held up well.

Lieutenant Wayne Watson took the stand to describe the reenactment as an attempt to determine if it was "physically possible" to reconcile the location of Loralei's body to Paula's description of her actions and the alleged abductor's movements. On cross, Groshong asked repeatedly why Wayne had neither kept running north through the woods behind the house, nor hidden in the bushes or behind the trees along the driveway in the front. Wayne said Paula had reported seeing and hearing the man run toward the road, so that's what Wayne had done.

The television sat up high on a metal rack, tilted downward slightly so the jurors could see it. They watched intently as the six recreations were played, showing Watson dashing to the front door and Morgan following seven or eight seconds later.

On the fourth take, as the jury waited forty-five seconds for Watson to reappear after dumping the doll in the woods, Weber looked at Juror Four—Harold Ryan—the likely foreman. He sat back, took off his reading glasses, and shook his head slowly as he stared at the television. The look meant, "No way." It didn't telegraph a conviction. But Don knew the foreman was rejecting the idea of a kidnapper dumping the baby behind the house and escaping down the driveway in the front of the house. The tape showed it was physically impossible—clearly, convincingly, and without a doubt.

The last scene on the tape was the walk across the family room, out the back door and over to the edge of the woods. Weber scanned the jurors to look for any sign that they were comprehending his message, "This is the route used to take the body to the woods." The jurors didn't respond as he had hoped. Oh, well, he was still glad he had done it, even if for his own amusement.

Weber had Watson relate Paula's startling comment after he suggested she leave while the divers searched the pond: "No, no. I want to be here when they bring her body up." Don had feared the comment was too ambiguous to use. But he had to admit, it played well in the courtroom.

Groshong asked if Watson thought Paula had meant the body would be brought up from the water, specifically.

"No. She meant 'bring the body up' from somewhere. I can't say what was in her mind."

Groshong shot back, "Well said."

Weber took a deep breath. That concluded the evidence on Loralei, and it had gone well. Now it was time to transport the jury three years forward in time, to the subject of these murder charges.

June Gibson was Don's first witness as he moved into his case on Heather. All he wanted from her was confirmation that Paula was disturbed about the sleeping arrangements. June nodded, "She said she didn't know home much longer she could handle it."

Groshong's cross-examination brought out more about Robert's rule of conduct around the house, and how upset Paula had been when the rules had kept her family from coming to see Heather. But June gave Paula some support by describing her as very happy about Heather's birth and a normal mother in every way.

Weber was glad to begin the first of an avalanche of damning testimony from the Alton police. Robert Eichen, the first cop on the scene, was now a firefighter. He gave the jury a calm, factual account of his initial contact with the Simses as they told their story for the first time. Weber asked sarcastically if Eichen had decided to "just round up the usual suspects," using the wonderful line from *Casablanca*. Eichen shrugged and said all he could do was call in the vague description of the kidnapper that had been offered by Paula.

Groshong asked if Paula had been hysterical, and Eichen stung him with the response, "Not as hysterical as I would have been."

A neighbor, Ruth Ann Miller, told the jury she had taken her dogs into the front yard about 10:45 that night, and had noticed nothing unusual at the Sims house across the street.

When Groshong made more jokes about the dogs' names, Don decided it was time to stop laughing. He didn't want this case laughed out of court, and he didn't want the jury laughing along with Groshong. Weber sat silently and without a smile in response to Groshong's line. It would be the last laugh that counted.

Janet Harkey-Dawson, the emergency room nurse, told the jury there had been no evidence of a substantial injury to Paula, nor did she show the head-injury characteristics of being confused and disoriented.

Don hoped Groshong would assume that the prosecution had nothing more dramatic to offer about the head wound. Don was beginning to get nervous about keeping Dr. Case's testimony a secret. He had guarded it closely, and very few people knew about it. But even some reporters were beginning to smell something in the air, and Don worried that a leak could lead to a courtroom battle that could dilute the element of surprise and the impact of Dr. Case's testimony.

Ernest Springer testified about seeing the trash bag in the barrel at 1:00 that Wednesday afternoon. Then he dropped the bombshell, and said it had not been there when he looked at 10:30 that morning. The import of that revelation was not lost on the defense. Immediately after court, Groshong subpoenaed the logs or time records from the television stations in St Louis, hoping he could prove the Simses were under surveillance during that period. He sighed in serious disappointment when Weber told him over drinks that night that the ground already had been covered a couple of weeks ago, without any luck.

Weber's last witness provided another dramatic closing at the end of a day. Charles Saunders testified about cutting open that trash bag that he thought might contain a head of lettuce. Weber showed the gray-haired man a picture of Heather's body lying in the bag at the bottom of the barrel, kept company by some assorted trash.

"Is that what you saw?"

Saunders's voice cracked and he choked on the emotion as he said softly, "Yes, yes."

The courtroom was left in a strange hush. Don hadn't expected that from the witness, and he felt the impact in his belly. It had to affect the jurors, too. For once, there was some genuine emotion, a most human reaction to the horror that was this case.

After adjournment, Weber spoke briefly with some of the reporters about testimony they hadn't expected: Dr. Graham's conclusion about Loralei's death, Watson's story about Paula's comment, Springer's time element, and Saunders's emotional reaction. Weber had managed to bring in some surprises, even though most of the media thought they had seen his full case in November.

Don tried to be coy about it, but that never had been his long suit. He couldn't restrain his exuberance and, before he realized it, he blurted out, "There are going to be some other surprises in the next day or so."

Several reporters used his comment in their stories, and it was played prominently in the Peori *Journal-Star* the next morning.

Wednesday started on a light note when Judge Matoesian presented the jurors with intricately formed wooden pens he had turned on his lathe at home. The judge's hobby was woodworking, and many lawyers, reporters, and others in Madison County were the proud owners of an original "Andreas," the Armenian judge's middle name.

Weber had been anxious for this day. He would get deeply into the investigation of Heather's death, and set up the knockout punches he expected the next day from the FBI and Dr. Case. They would complete his case and, hopefully, seal Paula's fate.

Mick Dooley took the stand to describe the trip to the emergency room with Paula. It was clear that he never believed Paula's story. But Don also was using Dooley subtly to prepare the jury for Dr. Case's testimony. Don repeatedly asked if Paula was remembering the things she was describing for Dooley, stressing the word "remembered" each time. Few people knew why he was doing that. But it would become very clear for everyone the next day. The facts in the hypothetical question he would pose to the doctor were being introduced into evidence right then.

Before Don called Dr. Kim, Kit Morrissey discussed his testimony with him again. Now the doctor suddenly was willing to say "impossible." Kit knew that would create a credibility problem when Groshong demanded that the doctor explain the harsher opinion. Kit calmly urged the doctor to stick with his earlier conclusion. Discretion was needed here, Kit decided. Weber was thankful he had someone as bright as Kit backing him up.

Even so, Dr. Kim's testimony was a little more emphatic. He would have expected to see more than some slight redness on her neck if she had been rendered unconscious for forty-five minutes.

"In medicine, anything is possible. I thought, at that time, that it was highly unlikely to impossible to correlate what she told me to the findings I had gotten." Kit smiled. That was easier to handle.

Groshong pointed out that the doctor had examined Paula for five or ten minutes, some three hours after she would have been struck, and noted that Dr. Kim had written "head injury" as a diagnosis on the chart.

Groshong said emphatically, "Based on your examination of Paula, you can't tell us she wasn't knocked out; you can't tell us that."

Dr. Kim shook his head. "I cannot tell she was not knocked out."

That's okay, Weber was thinking. *The real knockout comes tomorrow.*

After Sergeant Rick McCain had described for Weber the "karate chop" motion Paula had made, Groshong started a sharp and pointed cross-examination. He wasted no time sticking it to McCain over the failed tape recorder that prevented the jury from hearing what Paula really said during the interview. And he charged, with great indignation, that the police never seriously investigated anyone but the Simses.

McCain got a laugh from the crowd when Groshong asked why he had not written any reports on his activities.

"I guess you could say that's the advantage of being the chief of detectives."

Weber had Dave Hayes describe the blanket folded neatly over the edge of the bassinet, and how nothing else in the house had been disturbed. And Don used Hayes to set up part of his theory on the hide-and-seek game with Heather's body by explaining that the police had left the Sims house early Sunday, and never went back until after the body had been found.

Chris Sullivan told the jury about the hours he spent canvassing the neighborhood with no results. Groshong got slapped again when he asked Sullivan for more details, and the detective mentioned that one woman had walked her dog right past the Sims house between 10:30 and 11:00 without seeing a thing. Groshong tried to recoup by asking, "Did you get her dog's name?" The crowd laughed again; Weber didn't.

Detective Marsha Hill from St. Charles County was called to identify an autopsy photograph of Heather as the body from the barrel. And Weber then had her identify the silver-colored barrel as it was wheeled into the courtroom on a dolly. It was an unexpected and striking tactic, and the story in the *Post-Dispatch* the next morning described the barrel as a silent but powerful witness.

Weber finished the day with Rex Warner, the vice president of the company that made the "Curb Side" trash bags. Don was relieved to be getting to the trash bag evidence as Warner drew a chart to explain the process and the machinery that would play such an important part in matching up the bags. Groshong drew some impressive numbers from Warner. The company made almost five million pounds of bags for K-mart—22,222 rolls of bags each day.

* * *

The phone rang in Weber's hotel room about nine o'clock that night. Groshong growled, "My sister tells me the word is out that you've got a big surprise coming up for us tomorrow."

Weber laughed self-consciously. He hoped Groshong wouldn't read anything into it. "Oh yeah? I don't know where that came from. You know I never talk to the press." His old friend knew better.

"Well, she says everyone is talking about it."

"I wouldn't worry about it. It's not that big a deal. I'll see you tomorrow."

"Okay."

Don hung up, and grinned. Boy, the press could make a big deal out of so little.

Chapter 22

The facade of the building was not particularly impressive. Concrete-gray. A high, stark wall marked only by large letters proclaiming it to be the Peoria County Courthouse.

As Weber walked past that wall the morning of Thursday, January 18, he paused and looked up. He thought again about the Speck trial, and wondered if what would happen to Paula Sims in that building today would go down in history alongside the other trial. Don could feel the anticipation welling up inside. Several times over the last couple of days, he had to force himself to stop thinking about it.

The number of reporters had stayed relatively steady so far, usually about twenty. The "civilian" crowd, the private citizens, had leveled off at about twenty because of the limited seating and the lines. But on Thursday, the crowd had grown again and the line that jammed up outside the courtroom had rivaled the first day.

Before court started, Weber delivered to Groshong a statement from another cellmate of Paula's in Madison County. The woman was in jail on a minor charge and had told police that she once had seen Paula sitting on her bunk in a trancelike state, her eyes rolled back in her head. She was almost chanting what sounded like a prayer, and the woman thought Paula had said, "God sacrificed his son, so we had to sacrifice our daughters."

The report had been so weird, almost creepy, that it made the hair stand up on the back of Weber's neck. But he decided it was too bizarre to use, even in this case. He didn't want to suggest satanism or some other occult angle that could only muddy up the waters.

Weber finally called the case agent, Sergeant Ventimiglia, who had been invaluable as background support during the trial. Not only did he know the case inside and out, but he had helped prepare witnesses and make sure Don had what he needed when he needed it. Ventimiglia had been allowed to sit in the courtroom when he wasn't on some other assignment.

He didn't like testifying, and wasn't thrilled about facing cross-examination by a defense lawyer who seemed to be getting increasingly testy with Alton cops. He used a large aerial photo to explain how close the access area was to the Sims house—2.7 miles by his odometer, five minutes and forty-eight seconds on the road. He reaffirmed the time the police had left the Sims house that Sunday morning; he knew because he had been the last man out.

Kit Morrissey came into the room with the white bassinet where Heather had slept. After so much had been said about it, it seemed oddly unremarkable, except for the coating of fingerprint dust. Ventimiglia identified it for the jury.

Don's pulse jumped when he called his first FBI expert; the end was nearing.

Special Agent David W. Nichols took the stand with the air of confidence one would expect from an expert with the world-renowned FBI crime lab. In an unemotional, flat voice, he described testing the five trash bags to see if they were comparable. Conclusion—there was no difference in the polyethylene plastic used in the bags.

As he testified at some length, an artist capturing the scene leaned over to the reporter next to him and whispered, "In hell, there will be only FBI testimony."

Groshong had Nichols explain that there was nothing useful found among the boots and shoes confiscated, or the broken glass and other debris scooped up near the barrel.

On to the second expert. Special Agent David W. Attenberger strengthened the link between the bags. He directed the jurors to strips of enlarged photographs of the marks left by the heat seal, slipping a telescoping pointer from his shirt pocket. Doesn't everybody carry one? The bags all had the marks; they all were made with the same heat seal.

By now, several of the jurors were standing to see better as they took notes. This was a new story to them.

Attenberger offered his scientific opinion that the bag Heather's body was in and the first bag he pulled off the opened roll from the Sims house were made within ten seconds.

"It's my opinion that the bag was made within ten seconds of the outermost bag on the K-4 roll."

Groshong went through a dizzying series of questions that Weber thought had lost the jurors. The result was Attenberger's conclusion that only thirteen bags would be made in ten seconds. Weber looked at the jurors. Had they realized the implication? Paula's bandito had to have one of only thirteen bags in the whole world similar to those at the Sims house, and he used it for Heather's body.

After lunch, Weber's final FBI expert created a scene in the courtroom unlike anything Don had ever experienced. Special Agent Allen Robillard obtained Matoesian's permission to stand in front of the jury box and lay long strips of photographs on the railing to explain his conclusions. After he had answered a few questions from Weber, the agent seemed to take over the courtroom with his professorial style. Weber stepped back and let Robillard assume command, explaining his efforts at will. Weber was surprised Groshong didn't object. Within minutes, the jurors in the back row were standing and the alternates had left their chairs in front of the jury box to squeeze in around the end. Judge Matoesian was standing at the far end of the jury, too, and Weber just stepped back to stare in awe. Robillard was the best expert witness Weber ever had seen, and the jury was eating it up.

At one point, Robillard looked up and asked the jurors, "Is that clear?" They all nodded.

He described the different types of marks that could be left in the bags as they were manufactured, including "fish eyes," the swirled dots left in the plastic by dust or other particles.

Robillard said his analysis convinced him the bag with Heather's body could have come from the roll at the Simses. If it did, it probably was the fiftieth bag—the

outermost bag. If not, it was one of the very next bags
manufactured, which would have made it among the in-
nermost bags on the next roll as they were wound around
the spool.

Robillard also explained that during manufacturing the
column of plastic that will become the bags is twisted as
it moves over a pair of rollers. If there is something causing a continuous mark in the plastic, it will show up in
a spiral track along the column of bags. By comparing
the locations of the marks in individual bags, Robillard
said, he could determine how close they were to each
other.

His conclusion was that the three bags he studied represented every other bag on the end of the roll from the
shelf; a bag was missing between each of them.

Groshong put it simply in his cross-examination.

"The bottom line is, we're missing every other bag.
Aren't we?"

"Exactly. That's clear," the expert responded.

Weber leaned back in his chair. It had been incredible,
and the jury loved it. But after this recess, he hoped to
deliver the *coup de grace*.

Dr. Mary Case had arrived while Robillard was holding sway over the courtroom. As Ventimiglia escorted
her into the witness room, she turned to him and asked,
"Does the defense lawyer know what I'm going to testify
to?"

"No."

The doctor grinned and shook her head. "He's gonna'
shit."

She had brought a couple of books on suffocation
deaths, and Weber delivered them to the defense lawyers
at the recess. They asked for a chance to talk to Dr. Case
before she testified, and that unnerved Weber. He could
feel the trap about to spring, and any pressure from the
wrong direction now could trip it too soon, missing the
prey by inches.

He paced the hallway for what seemed hours, and was
pleasantly surprised when Groshong and Williamson finished their meeting with the doctor in no more than ten
minutes. Don felt sure the doctor was smart enough not

to volunteer information on her testimony. She would answer direct questions, but surely she wouldn't give up the surprise unless asked directly.

As the defenders walked past Don in the hallway behind the courtroom, Williamson pointed toward the judge's chambers.

"Let's go see the judge. We have a motion to make."

As Don turned to follow them, he could feel his heart pounding. He sat down at the table across from Williamson. Groshong stood in the back, smoking a cigarette.

Williamson turned to Matoesian. "Judge, we want to make a motion that Dr. Case not be allowed to testify that, in her expert opinion . . ."

Don felt his heart jump into his throat. His mouth went dry. Had they figured it out?

". . . that, in her expert opinion, Paula Sims did it."

Weber took his first breath in several minutes.

He grinned at Williamson. "Jim, that's not it."

Then he turned back to Matoesian. "Judge, I don't have any objection to that."

Weber turned and floated out of the room.

The time had come to spring the trap. Don was thrilled when he called Dr. Mary Case as his next—and last—witness.

The doctor wore a tailored white suit over a glimmering, silver blouse with a high, ruffled collar, and silver shoes. A multistrand pearl necklace hugged the collar of her jacket and large earrings dangled beside her face. When she walked into the courtroom, several male jurors perked up immediately.

In contrast to the doctor's elegant entrance, but simultaneously, Paula Sims slipped out of the courtroom, almost unnoticed. The two women passed each other at the doorway without exchanging glances. Williamson quietly informed the judge that the defendant wished to waive her right to be present. Paula's sudden exit sent a ripple of whispers through the courtroom as the press and spectators traded guesses. Had she wanted to leave to avoid hearing the grisly details of Heather's death and autopsy? Or had her attorneys suggested she leave to avoid further alienating the jurors with her lack of response to this evidence? Later, Don would learn that the latter theory was correct.

As the doctor took the stand, Weber glanced around the courtroom. Those who knew what was coming were squirming in their seats. Don was trying to remain calm, but he was squirming inside.

He asked Dr. Case to list her specialties. She was board certified in three areas: anatomical pathology, autopsy and surgical pathology, and neuropathology. Don asked her to explain neuropathology, and the jaws of the trap clanged shut.

Two reporters who knew most of the details about what was coming leaned close together. Charlie Bosworth whispered to Jeff Fowler from KSDK-TV, "Here it comes." Bosworth nudged a colleague in front of him with his pen, a prearranged signal that the boom was about to be lowered.

Dr. Case answered, "It is the study of the nervous system, brain, spinal cord, and muscles."

The light went on in Groshong's head. He was leaning forward onto the table on his elbows. As her words sunk in, Groshong's shoulders slumped and his head bobbed down for a moment. He looked stricken. Then he sat bolt upright in his chair.

Bosworth whispered again, "Look, Groshong knows."

He did. "Your Honor, may I have leave to approach the bench?"

The attorneys assembled in front of the judge and Groshong strenuously protested.

"Judge, I object to any testimony by Dr. Case as a neuropathologist. The prosecution provided the defense with no discovery material about this and the state cannot bring this in as a surprise at this hour."

Weber was shaking his head adamantly; the crucial decision was seconds away.

"Judge, Dr. Case's qualifications as a neuropathologist are listed right on her curriculum vitae. I'm reading right off of it, and we provided that to the defense months ago. Don Groshong has had the opportunity to talk to her on several occasions. They've exchanged letters. The defense even took her deposition. Here it is; it's ninety-six pages. The state is not required to tell the defense what questions to ask.''

Matoesian shook his head. "The objection is overruled.''

Groshong bounced back. "I want a recess.''

The judge shook his head again. "You can't have a recess. Proceed.''

"Then I want to make a record on it.''

"You can make a record on it after she testifies. Proceed.''

Now there was a judge who knew how to be a judge, thought Weber. Don was not a fan of the bench in Madison County. But that was a judge.

While Weber was resuming his questioning of the doctor, Groshong and Williamson were conferring furiously and frantically in whispers at the defense table. Don tried to tune them out, but he knew he couldn't give them much time. They were dangerously resourceful, and given the time, they would figure out some way to brake the train that was bearing down on them. And it probably would be with one of those typical Groshong motions that would seem ridiculous, but would require a long time to hash out.

Weber spent the next thirty minutes having Dr. Case list her degrees, professorships, experience as a forensic pathologist and medical examiner, papers she had published and seminars where she had lectured. Groshong objected unsuccessfully several times to her testimony about seminars, especially when she told about delivering a paper in which she discussed "delayed death and manual strangulation." It focused on marks around the victim's mouth.

Groshong angrily objected when she commented that defense lawyers had not attended a seminar she had sponsored on head injuries. "That's wholly irrelevant," Groshong snapped. Matoesian agreed and sustained the objection.

Past her qualifications, Weber turned his questions to the autopsy of Heather's body. Dr. Case explained her conclusions that Heather had been suffocated and the body had been frozen.

Then Weber drew a series of answers from the doctor that shocked nearly everyone and had a dramatic impact

on the case—then and later. He asked how long it took
an infant to die while being smothered. The doctor explained that Heather would have experienced "air hun-
ger" and a burning in her chest very quickly, forcing her
to begin kicking her arms and legs frantically. Even at
the tender age of six weeks, Heather would have tried to
push away whatever was blocking her mouth and nose.
The death struggle would have continued for about two
minutes, until she passed out. As the blockage of her
mouth and nose continued after unconsciousness, Heather
would have died in another one to two minutes.

Four minutes! Who could smother a baby for four minutes?

Weber turned Dr. Case over to Groshong for questions
about her qualifications as a neuropathologist. He asked
if it were true that she never treated living patients. She
said she saw living patients, but did not treat them.

Groshong asked to speak to the judge outside the jury's
presence, but the judge refused and ruled that the doctor
was an expert.

Weber shifted his aim toward Paula, directly and personally in a way no one had ever expected.

He began drawing detailed explanations from the doctor about how the brain would react to a blow to the
head—such as a karate chop—that resulted in unconsciousness for forty-five minutes. Dr. Case called that "a
very serious loss of consciousness" and said it would
affect the brain stem. Coming to after something like that
would not be like waking up from sleep. It would be
more like coming out of a general anesthetic. The person
would be groggy and there would be a period of stupor.

"You don't just suddenly come out of unconsciousness," she explained. The victim would not be alert and
functioning well, even ten minutes later.

In very technical terms, the doctor explained how any
interruption in the process of memory formation would
result in "retroactive or retrograde amnesia." In this
case, she said, the loss would include the memory of the
blow, certainly, and as much as five or ten minutes of
what had happened before that.

"Is Paula Sims's story medically possible?"

"I would say no."

"Is it possible for her to remember the blow?"

"No, she would not remember the blow. Memory can't be made at the time the concussive force is applied."

"How far back would the retrograde amnesia go?"

"She may not remember any of that episode. Certainly, she wouldn't remember the blow."

Don had intended to ask several other questions, but decided to stop then to intensify the impact of Dr. Case's testimony. The trap had sprung shut, and Don hoped the quarry was snared. He could feel the tension in the courtroom as he turned and walked back to his chair. He knew it was the crowning moment in fifteen years of prosecutions. It was unquestionably the most dramatic.

Matoesian called a recess. It was four o'clock, and Dr. Case had been on the stand for an hour and twenty minutes. Again, a key witness called at the end of a long day for Don Groshong.

Weber was mobbed by well-wishers, from Haine to Kit to Ventimiglia. Weber had pulled it off, and they had never seen anything like it. The look on the judge's face also illustrated the impact of what had just happened in his courtroom.

Don met briefly with several of the reporters to explain that Dr. Case was one of the four of five people in the country certified by the American College of Pathology in forensic pathology and neuropathology. There were only a few people with such expertise, and one of them, who happened to be the medical examiner for St. Charles County, had just put that expertise to shattering use against Paula Sims.

For twenty-two minutes, Weber basked in the glow of this coup that had been planned for so long. He knew that the defense was huddled in a back room, searching desperately for some strategy to counter this devastating blow.

At 4:22 P.M., court resumed for what everyone expected to be a blistering cross-examination of Dr. Case. Weber assumed Groshong would be even more meticulous and probing than he already had been on some of the lengthy questioning he already had conducted. Don had omitted some details on direct-examination, assuming Groshong would draw them out.

Groshong asked if there had been any frozen tissue found in the body. The doctor said no. She couldn't tell how long the body had been thawed, and she could not determine the time of death.

Then Groshong stunned the courtroom by announcing, "Nothing further." His cross-examination had lasted three minutes.

Weber and Groshong traded a few more inconsequential questions for the doctor. She was excused at 4:30, after just eight minutes for cross, re-direct and re-cross, and the crowd was buzzing.

Matoesian dismissed the jury until one o'clock Friday; the morning would be for lengthy motions and other legal matters.

As Dr. Case left the courtroom with Ventimiglia, she asked why Groshong's cross-examination had been so short.

Ventimiglia responded in typical Ventimiglia style.

"Doc, you may not know it, but after your testimony, Groshong's case just went down the toilet."

As Dr. Case left the stand unscathed, Weber's case was complete after fifty-one witnesses. But he decided to wait until the next morning to rest his case formally, a quirk he had acquired from Bob Trone years ago.

Don wished there was some way to eavesdrop on the conversation as Groshong recounted Dr. Case's testimony for the absent Paula. It would have to be devastating news to the woman who had worked so hard to build a doubt-proof story the second time. Her own deceit had come back on her in a crushing contradiction.

For the first time in almost two weeks, Don celebrated that night. Gathered with the prosecution team and some cops, he allowed himself more than a couple of beers, and he let the pressure that had been building for eight months wash away. He felt sorry for his friend and opponent. It had been a hard blow to absorb without any warning, and he knew the weary Groshong had been staggered. But Weber assumed he would be facing some heavy counterpunches when Groshong started swinging the next day. You never beat Groshong until you beat him.

Chapter 23

To reserve their coveted seats in the gallery, the reporters had taped their business cards or scraps of paper bearing their names to the benches. The seats were guarded jealously and there was little claim jumping. Matoesian's trusty bailiff, Bill Portell, made sure of that. After weeks of trial, Weber knew exactly what he would see when he glanced back toward the press section. It was like looking out at a first-grade class; all the little faces were in their appointed places.

The crowd on the right side, however, changed almost daily, but the faces were familiar. Phil Kocis and Larry Trent sat in a often as possible; they still had a proprietary interest in this monster of a case. And Jimmie Bivens came, several days.

A few people attended almost daily, and the reporters quickly adopted one older man. He usually wore a hunting cap with earmuff flaps, made even more notable by billowing tufts of hair protruding from his ears. But his most noticeable characteristic was his habit—often maddening—of constantly jingling the change in his pants pocket. The reporters immediately named him "Mr. Change." He occasionally had to be shushed by one reporter or another as they strained to hear the testimony. But one of the first orders of the morning was to see if the dedicated Mr. Change had been able to get a seat that day. It was reassuring to see him seated in the back.

The crowds generally were well behaved, although some sharp words were exchanged between people scrambling for seats. Nearly everyone, at one time or another, would crane their necks to see if Paula was offering any reaction to some bit of testimony or a photographic exhibit. "She must be a wreck," one woman whispered to her companion. The number of spectators seemed to peak the last two days of Weber's case. No one could have predicted the crowd that would arrive to hear Paula later in the week.

Weber's strategy for offsetting the defense case was simple. He would use Groshong's witnesses to flesh out the prosecution's theories. After all, if the jurors were listening—and Don was positive they were—they had to be wondering where Heather's body had been before it was dumped. And when had Paula found time to stash the body in a freezer and then dump it? To prevent the jurors from getting wrapped up in the defense, Weber would drop hints regularly to keep them thinking about his answers to those questions. He would start telegraphing his surprising theory with intriguing clues from Paula's own witnesses.

Before the jury came in Friday morning, Groshong asked the judge for permission to use a letter to the Simses suggesting they had been targeted because of their last name. Weber humorously noted that the letter had been signed by AAHTTTU—which he pronounced as if it were a sneeze—an acronym for the Alliance Against Harassment, Torment, Torture and Terrorism Unlimited. Weber said it was too kooky to consider seriously. But Groshong argued that the police had made no attempt to check it out, so no one knew whether it was kooky or not. Matoesian rejected it.

As Groshong began his case, Weber put his engines on automatic pilot. DeeDee Duburow had arranged files on the witnesses alphabetically and Kit handed them to Don as each witness took the stand. He had decided to ask very few questions on cross, partly to de-emphasize the importance of the defense witnesses. He would save his energy for the grueling day when he would cross-examine Robert and Paula, one right after the other.

For the defense, Rhonda Scott, Paula's friend from high school and her maid of honor, was first as she recounted Paula's happy phone calls after each of the Sims babies was born. When Heather arrived, Paula said she was happy to have another daughter.

"She said the Lord had blessed them. She was so happy; I think we cried. She said she had counted all of her fingers and counted all of her toes, and she was perfect. She was beautiful."

Don felt sickened. He got the mental picture of Heather's hands and feet flailing hopelessly in the air as Paula smothered her. *I wonder if Paula counted every little finger and every little toe then,* Don thought.

But Don was troubled by the image Rhonda had drawn of Paula as a happy new mother. The contradiction between that Paula and the murderous mother bothered him, and surely it had struck the jurors. He would explain it the only way he could. It was more evidence of "the many faces of Paula Sims."

Groshong called Sheriff Yocom again to explain that he had called in the State Police and FBI because Loralei's disappearance was such a big case. The defense was contrasting that to the way the Alton police had handled their case.

Weber used his cross-examination to pull the jury back to his theory about Loralei's death.

"Was the body just laying there on the ground, like someone had just taken some trash out and thrown it in the back?"

"Yes."

Dave and Linda Heistand seemed to make good witnesses for the defense. They presented a sympathetic, more human portrait of Robert and Paula by friends who knew them. But Weber produced the police reports and reminded Dave Heistand of his comment that the Simses had said they preferred to have sons. When pushed by Weber, Heistand admitted, "I've had to question now, with both of these incidents, if she didn't have a problem with little girls."

Linda Heistand was more lively and glowing in her defense of their friends. "My husband and I thought they were going to make excellent parents." She agreed with Groshong that Robert had been a "proud papa" when the Heistands visited shortly after Loralei's birth.

Don wasn't sure how to figure the Heistands in light of their earlier statements so critical of the Simses and their knowledge of Robert's phony claim about a second polygraph test. The Heistands had mellowed, and Don wasn't sure why.

Groshong was making some points with the jury as he tried to portray the Simses as normal people caught in an abnormal situation that wasn't their fault. But Weber expected Groshong to make up some ground during the defense case. It wasn't a major concern yet.

Groshong had called ten witnesses, and Matoesian adjourned court to end the second week.

On the way home, Weber felt deep satisfaction with the week's events. He had pulled off the Dr. Case caper. The FBI witnesses had come off well; Robillard had been fabulous. All of the state's witnesses had been in Peoria when Don needed them, and that was a minor, logistical miracle.

He faced a major challenge next week when he would confront Paula and Robert in court. Paula was trapped on the issue of remembering what had happened before the blow, and Don guessed she would change her story to claim that she hadn't told the police she remembered those things. Even though another change in her story would be damaging, it would be better than sticking with the supposed memories and being destroyed by the opinion from Dr. Case.

As Don drove through Springfield, about seventy-five miles from home, he heard a radio-news account of a shootout in St. Louis in which a bank-robbery suspect had died, but only after he had killed one FBI agent and wounded another. Weber shivered. He hoped that wasn't Carl Schultz.

After Don got home, he and Virginia relaxed as they sat in bed until 2:00 A.M. and watched the tapes of the television news reports from the week. Don reveled in it; it was great fun. He was gratified that the reporters had played the surprise testimony from Dr. Case with the bombast it deserved. After everything he had gone through, he thought his case had played as well in Madison County as it had in Peoria.

Saturday afternoon, Don learned that Schultz had, indeed, been one of the agents in the shootout, suffering a serious leg wound. Schultz' longtime partner had been killed, adding a severe emotional shock to the bullet wound. Don was thankful that Schultz was not killed; but the prosecutor couldn't help but worry about how this would affect the case.

Don's standing tennis match rolled around Sunday and his team lost, as usual.

When the prosecution team assembled in the hotel lounge Sunday night, Don could sense the anticipation in the air. This would be the week. He was predicting jury deliberations and a verdict on Friday, with someone having a fabulous party over the weekend. He hoped it would be him.

Before another packed courtroom on Monday morning, January 22, Groshong resumed his attack. He would call eighteen witnesses that day. Some of them would cause Weber some genuine concern, and his mood would shift to a more serious tone. The first few concentrated on Groshong's effort to destroy Stephanie Werner-Cook's credibility over the hospital accommodations issue, and the defender was showing a sense of excitement for the first time. Weber was inclined to dismiss all of that without too much concern. He couldn't see why Groshong thought that was such a big deal. The essential part of Stephanie's story was solid.

A hospital administrator produced a copy of Paula's preadmission form—marked for a semiprivate room. Sandy Fink, the nurse who wheeled Paula into the room, was positive there had been no argument. Groshong was having fun now, and it was clear he felt he had the upper hand. Don thought the defense had rolled out a cannon to kill a gnat.

Sandy Fink had been the first witness Groshong had found before Weber. Don had called her Sunday night, and she was unshakable in her opinion that there had been no flap over the room. Don then asked about Robert Sims. The nurse had paused a long time before answering.

"I don't know if I should say this. But Robert is the strangest person I ever met in my life."

So Don tried to get that from her on cross-examination. She looked at him knowingly, aware of what he wanted her to say. But she wouldn't say it; her response this time was softer.

"He's just real quiet and reserved."

Don smiled at her slightly, and returned to his seat.

The next nurse called to the stand was Darlene Broadway, who testified that Paula had reacted to Heather as any normal mother would. She bonded well with her baby and kissed her often. Another image for the jury that bothered Don.

The next witness would be more fun for Don. Groshong called Linda Condray. Don had been waiting two months for this. Kit had reviewed Linda's testimony to the grand jury, and had marked the pertinent passages for Don.

As Linda answered questions for Groshong, Weber had to admit that she seemed very nice, perhaps excessively nice. He wondered if the jury would find her genuine.

But Linda produced the most powerful and inexplicable evidence of Groshong's case—a series of photographs she had taken of Robert and Paula and their children, mostly in the hospital soon after the births. The color pictures portrayed a normal couple, smiling happily and warmly embracing the newborn children. The photos of Heather included the cute and grinning, redheaded little Randy, completing the picture of an all-American family celebrating life's miracle of love.[1] Don was at a loss to explain those troubling photos, and even he couldn't question the genuine emotion reflected in Paula's face and smile. It was something he had never seen in Paula any other time. If it was having some effect on him, it certainly would have some effect on the jurors.

Groshong was firmly in charge now, and he slowly passed each photo among the jurors. As they studied the images on the paper, Weber thought they seemed visibly moved. Groshong continued his questions.

"On the occasion of the birth of Loralei Sims, when you were in the hospital, did you observe Paula with her daughter?"

"Yes, I did. And she was . . . Paula was very happy.

1. As reproduced on the cover of this book.

She was holding her daughter, singing, cooing. She seemed very happy with her daughter."

Linda was speaking softly and affectionately.

"Did you go when Randy was born?"

"Yes, I did."

"Did you see how she related to her son?"

"Yes. It was exactly the same. She sang with him and held him and talked about the beautiful little baby. That kind of thing."

"When you were in the hospital when she gave birth to Heather, did you observe . . . ?"

"Yes, I did. I was there with the entire family, and together they were talking to the baby and singing to the baby and, oh, goo-goo kinds of happy things."

Yuk, Don thought. *Hold the syrup.*

Linda identified the calendar that hung on the Simses' refrigerator, and said she had seen Robert and Paula write notes on it. Weber was sure he could negate that later, too.

Groshong asked if the police had searched her home after Heather disappeared.

"Well, yes. But it's a tad absurd."

Weber filed that for future reference.

As he began his cross-examination, he decided to rattle Linda by firing a shot across her bow. He would bring up Herb's "bingo" games with Troy Sims, her own father. Only a few people would understand the reference to Herb's "bingo" nights. Linda certainly would, and she was the important one. He wanted to take her to a flashpoint with an irritating personal question, and then pull her back. If she was thinking about personal matters, she might not be ready to duel over the important questions.

"You're sort of a close-knit family, all of you, aren't you? I mean, Robert and you and the Blews and Paula and Troy, Robert's dad?"

"Not particularly."

"Well, your husband, Herbert, and Troy, go out . . ." She didn't let him finish.

"Not any more," she said sternly.

"They used to, though?"

"They used to go to bingo." She emphasized the words

"used to" with such exaggeration that Don almost felt like chuckling.

She added, "He started taking Daddy to bingo after Mom died."

"They told you they go play bingo on those nights?"

"Yes." She clearly was agitated.

Now was the time to move quickly into the most important part of Linda's testimony, and the key to his theory on Paula's maneuvering with Heather's body. With a series of questions about Sunday morning, Don got Linda to agree that she had gone to Robert's house about 8:00. But she began to hedge after that. Had she figured it out? He pushed on.

"Paula was there, but she was getting ready to leave. Right?"

"I don't remember any more. It has been too long. I didn't take notes."

"Paula was there, getting ready to leave to go over to the Blews' house, wasn't she?"

"I said I don't remember. I didn't take notes. You probably know."

Don read from her testimony to the grand jury. She had said Robert told Paula to go to her parents' house.

"Now, does that refresh your memory as to who was there?"

"Yes."

"And Paula was going to the Blews' house?"

"Yes."

"Was Paula upset?"

"I didn't see Paula. She was preparing to leave."

Don's next question was designed to tip the jury.

"Did you think it was strange that her daughter had supposedly been kidnapped seven hours before, and she's going by herself over to the Blews' house?"

"No, not at all."

The answer really didn't matter. Don had made the suggestion, and anyone with any sense would see the contradiction.

Linda next saw Paula that afternoon at Linda's house, and she agreed that Robert and Paula had arrived separately.

Don had just established that Paula was at her parents'

home by herself Sunday morning; he would explain the importance of that to the jury later.

Weber decided to approach the report that Robert had banned his brother-in-law, Dennis Blew, from the Sims house. Weber asked if Robert and Paula were private people.

"Yes, they are."

"As a matter of fact, they've got a window shade over the window so you can see out, but no one can see in, right?"

"Yes."

"They have special windows for that, don't they?"

Linda snapped impatiently, "I don't know what kind of windows they have in their house. I haven't had a child kidnapped."

Don couldn't pass up that kind of straight line.

He shot back, "Well, they haven't, either."

He paused for just a second, letting the implication sink in.

"Now, how does Robert feel about people with birth defects?"

"Birth defects?" Linda was so shocked that she blurted out the words. The force of her exclamation startled the audience. Her reaction was so exaggerated, and so comical in retrospect, that it became one of the buzz words among the reporters. For days, no assembly of reporters could go more than a few minutes without someone blurting out, *"Birth defects!!!!"*

Linda's response was that she had no idea how her brother felt about the topic, although she agreed that she had never seen Dennis at Robert's house.

It was time for Don to close, and leave the jury with Linda's own absurdity as a remembrance.

"Now, you said you thought the search of your house was a 'tad absurd,' didn't you?"

"Absolutely."

"Is that because you think the real kidnapper is Sheriff Frank Yocom?"

Judge Matoesian rocked forward in his chair in surprise.

"I don't have the slightest idea. I have suspicions."

"You told the grand jury you thought Sheriff Yocom kidnapped Heather, didn't you?"

"No, I told the grand jury that I thought Sheriff Yocom had some knowledge of it. Obviously, he didn't do it."

She had been ready for that one; Groshong had prepped her well. But it was hard for Don not to gloat as he walked back to his chair. He had gotten everything he wanted from her, and he had enjoyed doing it. He could feel that grin coming on.

Groshong's next two witnesses were unassailable. Donna Ewigman, who was Orville Blew's sister, and her husband, Thomas, were fine people and Weber liked them. They had been at the Blews' house for supper that Sunday night, after driving in from Peculiar. Donna Ewigman had opened the Blews' freezer twice to get meat and bread.

Groshong showed Donna Ewigman a photograph of the inside of the Blews' freezer, and pointed out a ham in the picture. Then he asked the obvious question, coyly.

"Did you ever see an item in the freezer that was larger than this ham?"

"No."

"Did you see anything in a black plastic bag?"

"No."

The defense was pleased to be eliminating the Blews' freezer as a hiding place on Sunday night. Groshong still had no clue to Weber's answer.

On cross-examination, Weber had the Ewigmans explain how long the drive took that day, making it obvious that Paula had spent a long time at the Blews' house alone.

Weber dropped another hint in a question to Donna Ewigman.

"You have no idea what was in that freezer for the hours between Saturday night and Sunday, before you got there?"

"No.'

Groshong recalled Tony Ventimiglia, drawing out his denial that the Simses' house had been bugged or that they had been under surveillance until after Heather's body was found. Groshong also began to hammer Ventimiglia about the detectives' suspicions of the Simses. Weber had talked to the police about that point, urging them to admit readily that they suspected Paula and Robert from the start. "You guys are cops and you suspected them. We're proud of it, so say it."

So, when Groshong asked about the cops' suspicions, Ventimiglia said, "Based on the information from 1986, I was highly suspicious of them."

Groshong asked if it was the FBI's idea to "generate publicity" about the case.

"We didn't have to generate publicity. The press was sitting outside our door."

"Did the FBI say to manipulate the media?"

Ventimiglia frowned impatiently. "We didn't manipulate anybody."

On cross, Weber decided it was time to put the FBI tactics into perspective.

"It worked, didn't it?"

"We believe it did, yes."

The defense called Stephen McCassen, a document examiner for the state police, to testify that all of the notes written on the Simses' kitchen calendar were in Paula's handwriting. But Weber had been waiting for this chance, and had McCassen agree that there was no way to know whether Paula had written those notes after 10:00 P.M., April 29. After all, a woman who was capable of the things Paula had done surely could write some phony notes on a calendar.

When McCain took the stand again, Groshong went after him with a club. He deluged the cop with a flurry of questions about the press conferences. Had he used FBI psychological tactics before? Was he trying to pressure someone until they snapped? What about phone taps and homing devices? Groshong asked about surveillance at least three times before the cop's temper flared. McCain knew surveillance might have cracked the case in May, but holding off had been the right decision at the time.

He answered sternly, "It was discussed. But if Robert and Paula Sims were the perpetrators, they had plenty of time to do whatever they wanted to do with that baby before they called us. If it was not Robert and Paula Sims, we would be wasting a lot of manpower.''

Groshong asked why McCain hadn't taken the defense attorney's offer for use of the key to the Sims house. McCain was ready.

''I'd have your consent. It wasn't your house.''

The audience laughed, and the cop smiled victoriously.

For Weber, it was a decent way to end a long day. McCain had held up well, answering the questions—even the repetitive and insulting ones—openly and honestly.

That evening, Weber played tennis with Ron Warren, the husband of Matoesian's court reporter, Dorothy Warren. One of Don's forehand smashes had broken Ron's racquet, and the prosecutor hoped that was an omen for his cross-examination of Robert the next day.

Back at the hotel that evening, Don met with Kit Morrissey and Ventimiglia to discuss how to handle Robert. One of Don's weapons for impeaching this strange man's credibility was his prejudice against his brother-in-law. Don would use the report from Robert's coworker, Bill Bailey, about Robert's references to Dennis Blew's ''birth defect.''

Don called the police in Alton and told them to arrange to have Bailey brought up as a rebuttal witness. McCain called back later—Bailey was on a hunting trip and couldn't be located.

''Look,'' Don said., ''I don't care where he is. I don't care what you have to do to get him. Call out the National Guard. Call the president. Just get him here.''

By midnight, the police had told Don that Bailey was in Arkansas, but the cops were trying to reach him.

The idea of the night had come from Kit Morrissey. She suggested using Robert's ''best sex'' line as a closer for cross-exam. Don agreed it would be a great kicker.

Don thought again what a perfect cocounsel Kit had been. She had done the routine work professionally and without complaint. And when she offered some insight, she always was right.

When Don awoke the next morning, the words of the old song popped into his mind. He started humming, ''Won't you come home, Bill Bailey.''

Chapter 24

Orville Blew's journey across that courtroom Tuesday morning seemed to take a lifetime, each slow step weighed down by the wreckage of his dreams for his three children. A stricken older son. A mourned younger son. And a daughter branded as the murderer of her own children—his grandchildren. And now it all was being laid bare for this room full of strangers to gawk at. The limp in the man's walk seemed to be the least of his afflictions as he crossed the room and climbed achingly onto the witness stand.

"She's my daughter," he told the jury.

Even then, there was no reaction from his daughter.

When he said he had turned sixty-one the week before, Weber was surprised. Orville seemed at least ten years older than that; it had been a long sixty-one years, and the last three must have been excruciating. He seemed so tired.

Groshong guided Orville gently through a retelling of most of those years and the tragedies. Orville spoke in simple words. He loved his daughter and he had been devastated by his granddaughters' deaths. Paula had loved her babies, and she had treated them well. She had wept for them. His account of the days surrounding both deaths seemed to support what Paula and Robert had said. But there were no alibis. There was little for Weber to fear from Orville. If the jurors felt sorry for his loss, they would hold it against Paula, not the prosecution.

Even Weber's cross-examination was muted, subdued. But there were some facts that Don had to establish.

"When Robert called you at the Ewigmans', he didn't say for you to hurry back, did he?"

"No, sir."

Don focused on Paula's account to her father of the attack and Heather's disappearance. Paula had not offered many details, other than she was struck on the head. Most of what he knew about the attack had come from the newspapers. And then he volunteered a shattering line.

"We was [sic] standing up in the doorway and I had my arms around her. And I said, 'I thought you told me this would never happen again.' And she said, 'Dad, I was headed for the gun.'"

Don hesitated. Did Orville understand the impact of what he had said? It seemed crystal clear that he admitted that, despite his apparent acceptance of her stories, he really knew in his heart what had happened in 1986.

Don asked, "You loved both of those little girls like they were your own babies?"

"Yes."

Orville began to sob, and put one hand over his eyes.

"I don't break down very often," he said quietly. He regained his composure quickly; life had taught him how to do that.

Don drew from Orville that Paula had cried when her parents arrived home that Sunday, and that Paula wasn't in any condition to be alone. Don steered back on course.

"Did you know she had been over at your house earlier that day by herself?"

"No."

Don knew the jury had not begun to put all of the clues together yet. He would have to wait until the closing arguments to tie it all up.

The morning had begun dramatically, with many spectators who assumed Paula would testify that day lining up outside the courtroom about 7:00 A.M. It was unheard of in Peoria. By 8:00 about forty people were waiting. By 8:30, the crowd had grown so large that Bill Portell arranged to have the reporters slipped into the courtroom through a back door. Judge Matoesian ordered the coatracks behind the benches removed and replaced by another row of chairs on each side.

When the doors were opened at 8:50, the rush was barely civilized. The seats were full in less than two minutes, and many of the hopefuls waited outside for the first vacancy.

Even Groshong's routine changed that day. His son, Ryan, who would celebrate his eighth birthday the next day, had begun to have problems over his father's extended absence. So Groshong and his wife, Barbara, decided to bring Ryan and their ten-year-old daughter, Ashley, to court for the morning session. That visit with his father seemed to do the job, and Ryan was much assured about his dad's eventual return home.

The rest of the regulars were abuzz over something else. In that morning's St. Louis *Sun,* columnist John Racine had published a vicious personal attack on Weber that criticized his appearance and clothes and speculated about the effect of his "genetic shortcomings" on the trial. Haine and his staff were outraged, and the other members of the press seemed embarrassed.

Don kept the column in perspective; it wasn't worth getting too worked up over then, especially if that was the best Racine had to offer in the middle of a dramatic trial. Weber knew a conviction would be the best response.

As it turned out, the Sims case outlasted the *Sun;* it ceased publication three months later.

Orville's testimony took fifty-six minutes, finishing at 10:18 A.M.

And then it was time for Robert Eugene Sims.

He and Weber had passed each other in the hallway behind the courtroom that morning. Robert had squinted directly into Don's eyes, and Don had interpreted the look as a challenge. Kind of a "see if you can go ten rounds with me" look. Don had his game face on, too, and the nose-to-nose meeting was silent, but intense.

As Robert walked into the courtroom, the jury got its first look at the man they had heard so much about. Nothing very notable. A white sport shirt with faint blue stripes, his T-shirt visible at the unbuttoned collar. Blue slacks and a tan belt. There was a bit more gray in Robert's hair and beard, noticeable only to those who had seen him so often over the last few years and, especially, in the recent months. The odd gait in his walk was barely apparent as he mounted the witness stand. His eyebrows, as always, seemed arched in a question, and his dark eyes were noticeable even from the back of the room. The apprehension was apparent on his face. But it wasn't a look of fear.

Don thought Robert was making a real attempt to look like an average guy. That must account for the sport shirt when just about anyone else would have worn a suit.

Groshong moved directly into a rebuttal of Weber's suggestion of a motive, having Robert deny the couple had any preference for male children.

Robert's peculiar speech habits were striking from the witness stand. His voice was so soft, almost effeminate. And he spoke so slowly and deliberately that Don was having trouble paying attention while Robert finished a sentence.

And Don decided quickly that he was in complete agreement with the people who had assessed Robert as "the strangest person I ever met." While that thought was running through Don's mind, Kit leaned over and whispered, "This guy is a spook." Don nodded. He figured everyone in the room had to be reaching the same conclusion at the same time.

In the gallery, one reporter scribbled on his pad for a colleague to see. "What a spook." It appeared to be unanimous.

Even Groshong was worried about the droning tone of his witness's testimony. Robert probably was the only witness who ever heeded his attorney's advice about testifying— "Listen carefully to the questions and think about your answers." His effort to do that risked making him look too calculating and methodical. But Groshong hoped the jury would remember the testimony from many of the previous witnesses about how quiet and soft-spoken Robert was.

Groshong led Robert on a lengthy review of his married life with Paula. From home to home, hobby to hobby. When he mentioned that the Simses were "quite interested in all-terrain vehicles," Ventimiglia had to squelch a smile at the memory of pregnant Paula's posing on the three-wheeler.

Robert's testimony quickly took on the tone of, "This is Your Life, Robert Sims." Weber thought that was the wrong way to use Robert. He was boring the jury to tears, and the longer he talked, the more convinced everyone became that he was very strange. A few questions to show that he and Paula were just regular folks, and then a strong denial of guilt, would have been more effective.

Before Robert finished, Weber's boredom had led him to sort through his wallet and count the ceiling tiles overhead—ninety-six. Weber realized that Robert's testimony was very revealing of his intriguing and guarded character, but was presented in such a tedious way that few people would be able to stay interested.

As Robert described the couple's decision to start a family, he said, "And the first month we tried to have our first child, Paula got pregnant." There was a not-too-subtle hint of macho pride in the comment, and Kit slipped a sarcastic note to Don. "What a stud."

Robert said they had been thrilled and very proud when Loralei was born and he denied that Paula had been crying when she called from the hospital to make "a little apology" for not delivering a son.

"I wanted the child to carry on the Sims name," Robert said.

Don shook his head. What a burden for little Randy.

Robert's account of his actions the day of the kidnapping was incredibly detailed; he remembered each stop he had made on the way to work, and still had the rain check from a store that didn't have the item he was looking for. "Isn't that convenient?" Don mused.

Robert had arrived at work as usual, but the frantic call from Paula had come soon after that. His account of the first part of his trip home astounded Don. Like the trip to work, it was recalled in perfect detail as Robert ran stop signs and red lights in his haste to get home. Don noted the second-by-second description; if Robert had that kind of recall for those automobile trips, he should be able to remember just about everything else.

Robert's disdain for the police was obvious as he described the activities the night Loralei disappeared.

"They were just standing around in all the glory of all their big, fancy police cruisers, and nothing was happening, you know. Somebody just stole my child, and seconds and minutes could make a difference in catching them or not. I got the impression they didn't know what to do next."

Robert's voice fell even lower and more hushed than it

had been when he described how Sheriff Yocom had broken the news about finding Loralei's body. For the first time, Weber thought, Robert Sims's account of something was similar to the official version.

Groshong asked how Robert took the news that his daughter was dead.

"It hurt." Robert's voice cracked for the first time. "It hurt a lot."

As Groshong continued the questioning, Robert reached into his back pants pocket and pulled out a handkerchief. He gently wiped his eyes, and his voice still quivered slightly.

After they moved to Alton, Robert told the jurors, they made a lot of changes at the new place, mostly for security reasons. He frowned and shook his head slightly. "Too many nosy people watching you all the time, and we had to have a safe place for children, whenever we did decide to have another child."

When Paula became pregnant again, a sonogram showed that it would be a boy. He would be named Randall Troy.

Judge Matoesian broke for lunch after an hour and forty-two minutes of Robert's testimony. Weber felt as if he had aged a year. Listening to Robert Sims was the most tiring exercise Don had done in a long time, and he wondered if his reaction was just a manifestation of his prejudice. At lunch, he learned that everyone seemed to have the same reaction—Robert was a horrible witness.

He returned to the stand at 1:20 and resumed the detailed biography. Paula had become pregnant again in July of 1988. A sonogram failed to predict the sex of this baby, but both parents hoped for a girl to ease the pain of Loralei's death.

When Paula was in the hospital room, she and her roommate never discussed Loralei in his presence. When he took his wife and daughter home, everything seemed normal. Until April 29.

Robert delivered the same story of Heather's disappearance. As he recounted his awakening of the unconscious Paula, Weber dragged himself to attention. Each time Robert detailed Paula's responses and comments, Don knew the hole under the defense was deepening.

Paula still was coming out of unconsciousness with a memory of orientation to time, place, and person. She knew where she was and where Heather had been, and about the trash and the kidnapper. Robert had stuck to the story, and he had walked right into the brick wall Dr. Case had erected five days ago.

The first hours of the investigation by the police were hard for the Simses, Robert said. His voice became softer again as he said, "It was like we were reliving a nightmare again."

He reached Sunday morning and the departure from the house.

"I told Paula she needs to . . . she ought to go over to my sister's house and take Randy, and get Randy away from the press, and go over there and relax as much as she could. And I would stay there with the police until they got done, and I would be over to meet her."

Don drew the first big red star on his notes. Robert's critical mistake number one.

Robert said he next saw Paula about noon at the Condrays' house. The Blews arrived about mid-afternoon, and the Simses went home with them.

Robert described the reporters as camped outside the house constantly after the first day or so. "TV, newspaper, the whole nine yards. Looked like a circus."

Weber was relieved when Groshong began asking Robert about the activities of Wednesday, May 3, the day the body was found.

"Go anywhere that day at all?"

"I never left the house that day. Paula never left the house until shortly after the ten o'clock news."

Don drew another big, red star on his notes. Robert was "in the loop" now. He had just alibied for Paula during the time when she had to have dumped the body— 10:30 that morning to 1:00 that afternoon.

Robert told the jury that Paula never left until the announcement on television that a body believed to be Heather's had been found near West Alton. Robert called Orville, and he had driven over and picked up Paula and Randy "because the press was really starting to pile up after that."

The afternoon recess hit at 2:50 P.M. When it ended,

Groshong shifted to the interview with the FBI agent Schultz on the evening of May 4.

"They told me they had evidence against Paula and, under the circumstances, I must be covering up for her."

Robert was working up an air of indignation. His voice wasn't much louder, but it seemed firmer, to have more of an edge. He was almost angry as he said he had told Schultz "it was time to quit playing around and find this guy. And I wanted the murderer caught."

What did the FBI tell him about the evidence?

"They told me they had copies, impressions, something to that effect, of tire tracks from our 1979 Chevy station wagon that were found at the site where our daughter's body was found. They also told me they had hair samples out of Paula's parents' freezer that matched our daughter, Heather. And I asked them again, you know, 'Are you sure those are Heather's hair? I didn't want any mistake about any of this. And he said, 'Yes.' I asked him at least three times, 'Are you positive?' He said, 'Yes, it is her hair.' "

"That make you doubt your wife, did it?"

"A little bit, yes, it did. Because I knew I hadn't driven the car over there."

Robert told of agreeing to go home about three in the morning to try to convince Paula to go to the police and tell them everything. He described an angry confrontation with her at the kitchen table, with her father watching.

"I started drilling Paula, and said, 'Paula, you're not being truthful with me.' I said, 'I have been down to the police station, and they told me some things that I know, you are not being truthful.' And I explained to her, and she says, 'I don't believe it. You're going to believe them over me.' And she says, 'You let them get to you and make you believe I had something to do with our children's deaths.' And I said, 'I didn't want to, but after a couple of things they told me, I can see no other way that you didn't have at least something to do with this.' "

"Was this a nice quiet conversation between you?"

"No, no, no. I talked to Paula like I have never talked to her in eight years of marriage. And I didn't like doing it, but I had two dead children. And if she had anything to do with it, now was the time to come clean."

But she denied it all, he said.

Groshong asked, "Did you watch her face when she talked to you?"

"Yes, I did. I hurt Paula like I never hurt her in my life. I never wanted to hurt her like that, and after going through that conversation, I was the fool. I was the one that believed the lies that FBI agent had told me."

That was it for Weber. He would call Carl Schultz, despite his wound, as a rebuttal witness to refute the real lies, the ones that had just rolled off the witness stand in such rounded tones. Weber couldn't challenge the testimony about what had passed between Robert and Paula. But he could shoot down Robert's tale of a lying, conniving FBI agent. Fate had intervened in that, too, and Schultz would arrive for his appearance with even more credibility than Weber could expect.

It was time for Groshong to bring the long day of testimony to an end with a flurry of proclamations of innocence.

"Where were you between 10:30 in the morning and one o'clock in the afternoon on May 3, 1989?"

"I was in our home, 1053 Washington."

"Where was your wife?"

"My wife was in our home with me."

"Where was your son, Randy?"

"Our son was there with me."

"Where was the press? Where was the news media that day?"

"There was some of them out around the house."

"During that period of time?"

"Yes, sir."

"Did you participate in any way in the death of either one your daughters?"

"No, sir."

"Are you covering up for her because she did that?"

"No, sir. I would not do that. I love my children. I wouldn't cover up for anyone that would harm a hair on any of my children, no matter how much I loved them. I would never cover up for anyone."

"Did your wife kill your daughters, and you're covering up for her?"

"No, sir. No."

"Are you sure?"

"I'm positive. No doubt in my mind. Paula is a good mother, excellent mother. She's a wonderful wife."

"Your witness."

Robert's voice had been its most resolute at the end. But it was still so quiet. Robert had talked for three hours and thirty minutes.

And Don Weber had five big red stars on his one page of notes. Robert's testimony had been unimaginably tedious, and he hadn't said much of importance. But some of the things he had said could be dynamite. His version of Paula's destination Sunday morning contradicted his own sister's. He had alibied for Paula on Wednesday. The evidence was irrefutable that one of them had left their home on Wednesday morning with that black trash bag and its pitiful contents; one of them had made a quick trip across the Lewis and Clark Bridge, callously dropping the bag in a convenient trash barrel at the access area.

And Robert brazenly had called Carl Schultz a liar. So Don struck at that first, challenging Robert and promising to deliver Schultz the next day. Robert was not intimidated.

So the confrontational tone was set, and each man knew what to expect from his opponent.

Weber expected Bill Bailey to arrive in Peoria the next day, so the information from him could be used against Robert. Don asked about Bailey's statements, and Robert replied that he could not remember discussing any of that with Bailey. Robert denied that they had delayed having children for fear their offspring would carry Dennis Blews' health problems.

Had Paula had asked Robert to marry her? Yes, and Robert agreed that he had put a condition on the marriage when Paula proposed. Dennis would never be allowed to live with Robert and Paula full-time, because Robert did not want to tie them down to the twenty-four-hour-a-day job of caring for Dennis.

Weber, applying the language used by Bailey, asked, "Did you ever make the statement that the marriage was only on the condition that her retarded brother, Dennis, would never set foot on your property?"

For the first time in the trial, Paula reacted. She sat up an slid forward to the edge of her chair, her face pursed

in anger. It was real emotion, and Kit Morrissey watched
intently. It was the first time she had seen anything but
that stone face. The passion hadn't surged that way for
her two lost daughters, but it had at the insult to her
brother.

An indignant Robert jumped to Dennis' defense.
"First of all, her brother is not retarded."

Weber agreed.

"I know. You never made that statement to Bill Bailey?"

"No."

"Do you know where Bill Bailey is right now?"

"I don't care where he is. I know where he lives. He
could be standing out in the hall. Bring him in if you
want."

Don smiled. "Tomorrow." Bill Bailey was, indeed,
coming home.

"Fine."

It was an exchange right out of one of Don's favorite
movies, *The Caine Mutiny*. Weber had phrased his question about the surprise witness just as Jose Ferer had
asked Humphrey Bogart's Captain Queeg character as he
crumbled on the stand. But unlike Queeg, Robert had
remained defiant.

Weber kept up the attack. He noted that Robert had a
perfect alibi for the times when his daughters disappeared while in their mother's care. And, to keep Robert
off-balance, Don skipped to the issue of Father's Day
1986 and the disputed visit to the card shop in Jerseyville. Robert was adamant that Loralei never had been
out of the house, and never visited Gisella Rasp's Hallmark Shop. Don still hadn't figured out where this piece
fit in the puzzle, but it was curious that the Simses were
so adamant that it had not happened. It must be important enough to lie about. And besides, it was another
person that the Simses had to contradict.

On to Robert's discovery of his unconscious wife. As
Robert answered Weber's questions, he confirmed that
the awakened Paula had been alert and aware of her sur-
roundings and the events. Robert and Weber parried a
bit over the time Paula had said she was attacked. Robert
said he wasn't sure what she had said.

Don felt like he was in complete control now. It was time for Don to turn the heat way up while bringing Robert down a notch or two.

"Well, Robert," Don drawled, emphasizing the use of his target's first name. "You remember every stop sign you ran through on the way home with Loralei. You remember the intersections and the red lights. How is it you don't remember this?"

"I remember running every stoplight on the way home. And I know how many there are on the way home."

"Well, why don't you remember this detail?"

"I'm not sure." He wasn't so cocky now.

While he was on the topic of memories, Don asked about Paula's. Each time Don used the word, "remembered," he paused for effect. Robert confirmed that Paula had remembered her confrontation with the kidnapper, and being struck on the head.

"And she 'remembered' that, right?" Weber asked.

Robert nodded. And Don nodded. Even though the jury had been told by an expert that Paula couldn't remember these things, Robert just admitted that she was remembering little details from the seconds before she says she was struck.

Robert tried to hedge a bit, suggesting that she was pretty groggy and was staggering a bit. But it was too little, too late.

Robert offered, "She was not acting completely normal."

Don couldn't resist another straight line. "Well, what's normal for Paula Sims may be another matter."

To remind the jury about the motive, Don referred to Robert's direct examination when he gave the wrong dates for his daughters' birth dates, but had been right on the money about Randy's. Robert shrugged off the question, noting that his son was born on the first of the month—easier to remember.

Don turned Robert's attention to the crucial point of Sunday morning, preparing to pull things together for the jury. Robert denied telling Paula to go to her parents' house. He insisted that she had gone directly to the Condrays' about eight o'clock, as Linda arrived at the Sims house to stay with Robert. Had Robert realized that Don had figured out the Sunday-morning activities?

"Robert, Linda Condray says Paula didn't get there until three. How do you explain that?"

"I don't think she's remembering correctly. This is what I remember."

"What would Paula be doing over at the Blews' on Sunday by herself?"

"I don't know that she was there by herself."

It was time to let everyone in on Don's theory.

"So, if Paula had anything over at the Blews' house that she didn't want found, she would have to go over there and move it, wouldn't she?"

As if on cue, Robert asked the perfect question. "What would she have over there?"

Don paused, and then pounced. "A dead baby in their freezer," he said with cold precision. Some of the spectators exchanged shocked looks.

Robert was unfazed. "No, I don't think so." He answered with all the vigor of someone declining a second cup of coffee.

"If the baby was over there, she would have to move it, wouldn't she, because the Blews were coming back?"

"She got there right after she left, I'm sure."

Don moved to Wednesday, the next crucial day in the plot. Robert insisted that he and Paula had stayed home all day. Don had given Robert a chance to come off the alibi for his wife, but he had stuck with it.

"Now, when you talked to the FBI, you told them that your wife had keys to the Blews' home and she could have put Heather in the freezer while you were asleep, right?"

"I remember something like that, yes."

"And you told them you were real worried about Randy's safety?"

"After what they had told me, yes, I was concerned about Randy."

It was the perfect time to begin the crescendo to the finale. This was something Don had anticipated for weeks.

"And you were really wrung out at least until after Heather was found, right?"

"I have been wrung out for three years."

"And that is no energy, depression. Don't want to do

anything. Can't seem to get going in the morning. You want to go to bed at night. You're just worn out. Right?''

"I have been tired for a long time, yes."

"And Paula probably was worse than you, right?"

"I don't know."

"Well . . ."

"She wasn't in good shape."

Don leaned forward over the lectern, wishing he could be nose-to-nose with Robert for this. His voice rose and he brought out his cutting edge.

"If you weren't in good shape, then how come Tuesday, before the body was found, you and Paula had the best and longest-lasting sex you ever had?"

Robert sat frozen for what seemed like an hour. His face was expressionless, but the muscles in his jaw tensed. It seemed so long that Don began to think Robert wouldn't answer. Don finally decided the most dramatic thing to do was turn and walk away, leaving Robert staring blankly at his back. As Weber turned, Robert began to speak slowly and quietly, but emphatically.

"Let me tell you something. Sex can be a stress reliever. We loved each other very much. I was trying to comfort her. She was trying to comfort me. I believe in my wife. We tried to comfort each other."

Weber turned back toward the witness. That answer would not suffice. Don grew even more sarcastic, and lifted his voice into sing-song, mocking tone. "And it was the best and longest-lasting sex you ever had?"

"It was good."

"And this is right after . . ."

"It usually is."

More macho crap, right in the middle of the most important moment in his wife's life. Don felt the righteous anger rise.

He snapped, "Yeah. And this was right after your second baby, Heather, had been kidnapped and taken to parts unknown. And that's what you were doing and thinking about. Right?"

Robert's eyes squinted. "What are we supposed to do twenty-four hours a day?"

Don turned his back to the witness again and snarled, "No further questions." Don wanted his stride back to his seat to convey his confidence that he had destroyed the witness and any chance that anyone could believe him.

Groshong had no re-direct, surprising his opponent again. Weber wouldn't have let that last exchange ring in the jurors' ears overnight if he had been the defender. But he was relieved that Groshong chose that tactic.

Groshong and Williamson thought Weber's sex question was a mistake or, at the very least, a sword that could cut both ways. It was sarcastic, and they thought it might repulse the jury as a shameful attempt by the prosecutor to turn a tragic situation into something tawdry for the sake of sensationalism. To Groshong, the question had been character assassination of the worst kind. Weber had taken a cheap shot at a perfectly understandable, intimate act between a grieving wife and husband reaching out for comfort. Williamson knew that kind of risky tactic worked only if the jury was with the lawyer, and he thought it was too early for such an assessment. The verdict would determine who was right.

After almost five grueling hours on the stand, Robert slowly left the room. He didn't look at Paula, and her eyes did not follow him as he walked away.

The judge recessed court for the day. After the jury had left the room, Weber was mobbed by congratulations from his staff and police officers. Don turned for an appraisal from Ron Warren. Ron answered, "You ate him alive."

Weber felt exhuberant. He turned to Haine. "Get me a raw steak."

Circuit Judge John L. DeLaurenti, who presided in Bond County next to Madison County, had watched Weber's cross-examination. He offered the most colorful comment, comparing the last series of questions to the fireworks on the Fourth of July under the Gateway Arch in St. Louis.

But Don knew the next day would be the most challenging so far. He would face Paula Sims for the first time, and she now was warned about his theories and his case. She wouldn't be as easy to box in as Robert had been.

It was time for a couple of beers, and to turn in early.

In a holding cell in the Peoria County Jail across town, Paula's guards thought she looked angry that night.

Chapter 25

Paula Sims had three choices when she looked into the jurors' faces from the witness stand on Wednesday, January 25.

She could hang resolutely to her story about the kidnappings by "masked banditos."

She could change her story somehow to try to account for the glaring weaknesses and various contradictions that plagued it.

Or, she could take the Fifth and refuse to testify. As she sat silently, her attorney could argue that the state had not proven the elements of the charges beyond a reasonable doubt. The bandito could have taken the trash bag from her home, and the cops could have exaggerated, or simply misunderstood, what she had said about her head wound and some of the other pieces of her story. After all, no one had seen Paula do anything.

That was the course that would have been chosen by the prosecutor, if he had been in the seat across the table. It was risky, and Weber thought silence from the woman portraying herself as a hapless victim in these bizarre crimes surely would be renounced by the jury with a conviction.

So, when "the day that everyone had waited for" finally arrived, Weber would find out what course Paula would choose. Many of those who had followed the case closely, even Kit Morrissey and others among the prosecutor's staff, had never heard Paula's voice. Weber hadn't lost his grip on reality, but he still allowed himself to fantasize about a witness-stand confession from Paula. Ventimiglia had promised to pay the expense of a voyage to England, and serve as Don's personal valet, if that dream came true.

As they had the day before, the spectators began lining up early for a chance to hear Paula. The courtroom was jammed by the time one reporter arrived late, and his successful effort to squeeze into a seat close to the front was greeted with complaints that grew into boos from the cheap seats.

At 9:33 A.M., Don Groshong called his client, and the frail, brittle-looking woman took the stand. She seemed to lose weight daily, her ill-fitting clothes accentuating her bony frame. For the biggest day of her life, Paula again wore the knit, blue-and-white striped blouse and blue slacks. Kit Morrissey wondered why the defense attorneys had made no effort to soften Paula's stark appearance. A little makeup. A simple dress. A more appealing hairstyle. Anything would have helped. If they were hoping to portray her as the downtrodden, emotionally devastated victim in this, it wasn't working to her advantage. She still looked like the tough, scrappy, "butch" girls Kit had feared and avoided in high school.

So it came as a shock when Paula began to speak in a soft, feminine voice. Those who had heard her before noticed that her Missouri twang was suppressed a bit, but it still was there.

Groshong assumed a tone with Paula that seemed almost paternal. He wanted the jurors to know that he liked her, and that this woman who had been described to them as some kind of three-headed monster was just a regular girl from a simple family. Behind a kind and genuine smile, Groshong began a long day of testimony from his client.

"State your name, please."

"Paula Marie Sims." The quiver in her voice betrayed a nervousness that some might have found surprising. She stared intently at Groshong, seeming to cling to him with her eyes, as if he alone could protect her in this roomful of hostile stares.

"Paula, how old are you?"

"I'm thirty."

Groshong smiled reassuringly at her. "Are you nervous?"

She nodded slightly, but did not return the smile. "A little."

In just a few questions, Groshong led Paula on a brief journey through her childhood to her marriage to Robert Sims. They saved their money until they had enough to start their family—one boy and one girl. For the girl, she picked the names of Loralei, because it was pretty, and Marie, because it was the middle name shared by three generations—Paula, her mother, and her grandmother.

With the next series of questions, an amazing thing happened in the courtroom. Paula Sims began to resemble a human being.

"From your childhood, did you save anything?"

"Yes, I did. I saved my dolls. I saved a dress that I wore when I was fifteen months old. I have a picture of myself in the dress. My parents had taken me to get my picture taken, and I had saved that for my little girl, if I had a little girl some day."

Even in Weber's heart, Paula's quiet story about planning for a daughter felt real. Surely little girls, dressing and undressing their dolls, would wonder about the day when they would have real daughters of their own. Even if Paula still showed little emotion about it, Don believed it was as true as anything Paula would say from that witness stand. It was another face he hadn't seen before. Paula always would be an enigma.

Groshong showed Paula a fragile, off-white dress, and a photograph. It was her little dress and the picture of the toddler Paula. He passed the items among the jurors.

"Why did you save that dress?"

"I saved it for my daughter some day."

To Weber's surprise, Paula was proving herself an effective witness, and it had to have some effect on the jury. It certainly disturbed him, smudging the edges of the comfortably villainous portrait he had painted of Paula for himself. This Paula Sims was going to be a formidable witness, much more so than her colorless husband had been twenty-four hours ago.

Groshong produced a shoe box, and withdrew from it something undeniably pure and wholesome.

"This is my Barbie doll that I saved from when I was a little girl."

"Who did you save it for?"

"I saved it for my daughter some day. And these are

some dresses my mother made for my Barbie doll and a pillow for the Barbie doll.''

All of this Barbie doll stuff seemed effective to many of the male observers, Don included. But Kit Morrissey and DeeDee Duburow weren't buying it. They had been proficient in "Barbie" as girls, and this was not the way the premier symbol of fashion and style for America's female adolescents would have been preserved and presented years later. Barbie would not have been kept in a ratty shoe box. And this Barbie's hair was disgracefully uncombed and her clothes were unforgivably shabby. This was not the way that a girl preserved Barbie for her daughter "some day."

But it seemed to be playing well in the courtroom, where most others seemed to judge it as the real thing.

Another doll, Sally, was introduced to the jury next, also saved for Paula's daughter "some day."

Groshong left the dolls in plain sight for the jury as he moved on to Loralei's birth. Paula had wanted to give Robert a son—"Every man wants a son"—and she was a little upset that she had not done that. Her call from the hospital was an apology that her husband had said was unnecessary.

When they brought the baby home, Paula explained, they had stayed in the basement because it was cooler. The basement had a family room, bedroom, and half-bath. Paula said she was a good housekeeper and agreed with her attorney that some might call her a "neatnik."

"I like things clean and orderly," she said flatly. Robert did, too.

Life was great then. "We couldn't have been happier." Robert returned to work. But their world caved in on June 17 when a masked man came down the basement steps.

"He pointed a gun at me and told me to get on the floor—lay there for ten minutes or he would kill me."

"What went through your mind then?"

"I was scared. I was scared to death." Again, there seemed to be no real emotion behind her memory. The words came out, but they were hollow.

When she heard the door upstairs slam, after maybe

five minutes, she got up to check on Loralei before chasing the gunman.

"I looked in the bassinet, and she wasn't there."

For the first time, Paula Sims' voice trembled and her
face took on a pained expression. She shook her head.

"I lifted up the blanket, and she wasn't there. So I ran
up the stairs as fast as I could, and I was yelling her
name. Loralei."

Not genuine, Don thought. It had been another performance from an accomplished actress. There hadn't
been a tear; they're harder to do than a wavering voice.

Paula's description of her pursuit of the kidnapper
added a couple of new wrinkles—she had paused to put
on a pair of thongs at the top of the stairs, and she had
hesitated again outside to look toward the pond and the
road, and to listen for sounds of the fleeing kidnapper.
And she claimed now that she had neither heard nor seen
anything.

Weber could see that Paula was beginning to shade her
testimony to rebut some of his major points. She had
poised herself to deny the cops' claims that she had heard
the kidnapper in the driveway gravel and that she had
seen "a shadowy figure."

But she stumbled verbally right after that by claiming
that she was yelling "Loralei" as she ran down the driveway. The Grays already had told the jury that there had
been no sounds in that summer night.

Paula tried to explain away her comment to Wayne
Watson by saying one of the officers had upset her by
saying her baby could be in the lake. "I told them, if she
was in the lake, that I wanted to be there when she was
brought up."

Don knew why Paula had slipped through the authorities' fingers three years ago. She could turn on the faucet
for the appropriate emotion, and for the jurors' benefits,
and she had offered subtle changes in her story to fit the
newest revelations in the facts. She was very good.

Paula never looked away from her attorney. Her eyes
never left his face; she never looked at the jurors. But
they never took their eyes off of her. Weber watched for
reaction, and was impressed that the jurors were trying

to remain inscrutable. They were almost as deadpan as the master on the witness stand.

Paula's face still was stern as Groshong shifted to June 24, and the discovery of Loralei's body. She had heard the news from Yocom.

"I . . . It almost. . . . It almost knocked me down. It put me in total shock." Again, there were no tears, but her face was strained.

"What did you think then? What was going through your mind?"

"I didn't know . . . I didn't want to believe that it could be possible that it would be our baby, because she was missing. And then, they come and tell you that they found skeletal remains of a baby behind your house in the woods."

The tightness stayed in her face as she told Groshong that the accusations by the police against her and Robert had continued after that. Without mentioning the card shop testimony, Paula explained that she had picked up cards for Father's Day for her husband and her father at the grocery store before she went into the hospital. Weber still couldn't figure out why the Simses were so adamant that they had not been at the card shop in Jerseyville. It would become surprisingly clear the next day.

Don was pleased with Paula's account of the decision to buy the house on Washington Avenue in 1987. Whose idea was it? "Both of ours." Paula Sims was no docile puppet manipulated into murder by someone else.

When Paula was pregnant for the third time, the Simses wanted a girl again. "I always wanted a daughter, especially after our first daughter . . ." She hesitated, leaving the thought unspoken. "We didn't have anymore. I wanted one even more." When Heather was born, "I said, 'Oh, thank God.' I was very happy."

Groshong and Paula dismissed Stephanie Werner-Cook with a few quick denials. While testifying about the preadmission procedure at the hospital, Paula mentioned her refusal to take a chest X-ray or allow one of her broken foot "because I didn't want it to hurt my unborn child."

The considerate mother role didn't seem to fit.

Groshong went back to Stephanie Werner-Cook. Paula said she mostly had listened during their conversations, since her roommate was "quite a chatterbox." Paula slipped in that Stephanie had mentioned "previous miscarriages and abortions that she had."

Weber was furious. Paula had just misled the jury and slandered Stephanie, all in one breath. Stephanie's medical records indeed showed that she had suffered miscarriages, referring to them in medical terms as "spontaneous abortions." But Stephanie had not had any clinical abortions, and Paula knew it. That spiteful jab was the first time Paula had shown a vicious streak from the stand. And Stephanie was being maligned by a woman who had ruthlessly and systematically murdered her own daughters as they lay sleeping in their cribs. Although Don's first reaction was to hammer Paula on the point during cross-examination, he decided against it. It was better not to draw any more attention that might strengthen the lie. He would let it drop.

Paula insisted that she had told Stephanie only that a masked gunman had taken Loralei from their home in Brighton three years earlier. Stephanie had asked a lot of questions about it, but Paula had refused to discuss it any more because it upset her.

Finally, Paula arrived at April 29. She said she had straightened up around the house and put some trash in an empty bag from the Venture store sometime after 10:30. There it was again; she was beginning to shade this story a bit to reduce the time she was unconscious.

When she was confronted by the masked man and his "big black gun," she thought about her gun in the house.

"Did you think about anything else?"

"Yes, I did. I thought about my children, because it looked like the same man that had taken Loralei in 1986."

Don, and nearly everyone else in the courtroom, looked up. Had Paula really said it was the same guy who had taken Loralei? Had she waited until today to spring this new and explosive detail? Surely a dozen well-trained cops and FBI agents hadn't failed to write down that Paula had said that Bandito Number One was the

same as Bandito Number Two. But Groshong let it drop
and Paula moved calmly through the rest of her story.

"What happened next?"

"I felt a blow to the back of my head, and that's all I
remember."

That was plenty for Weber. She was sticking with her
story that she remembered the blow, despite Dr. Case's
unequivocal testimony that Paula could not remember
that. Maybe Paula should have stayed in the courtroom
to hear the doc. Don scribbled "I felt a blow . . ." on
his pad, and drew a large black arrow.

"What's the next thing you remember?"

"I remember someone saying my name. 'Paula, Paula.
Are you all right?' Something like that."

"What's the next thing you remember?"

"The next thing I remember is my husband helping
me up."

Keep remembering, Don thought.

"I went and I looked in the bassinet myself, and she
wasn't in the bassinet." Her voice cracked again, just as
it had at the same point in Loralei's story. Was it the
emotion of this identical, heartbreaking memory? Or was
it just a good place to kick in some emotion, finally?

"What went through your mind then?"

"Randy."

"What did you do next?"

"Went up the stairs and checked on Randy."

Paula was frank in her admission that she had offered
few details about the kidnapper's description to Patrolman Eichen. But she began to hedge about her injuries,
and created more discrepancies than she cleared. She had
a terrible headache, and a sore neck and shoulder. She
felt dizzy. She hadn't wanted to go to the hospital, but
agreed reluctantly. She had read the release form carefully, to be sure it was what Dooley said it was.

Groshong nodded. "You had some experience with the
police before, hadn't you?"

Paula nodded. "Yes, I have," she answered with dis-
taste.

Paula seemed astounded about an exchange she said
she had with the cops when they asked if she ever spanked
or abused Heather.

"I couldn't believe it. You don't whip a six-week-old baby. They don't do anything wrong."

It was Don's turn to be incredulous. The courtroom had just been lectured on the proper disciplinary attitude for parents by a woman who had smothered her babies for the offense of being female.

Paula shaded the point again when Groshong asked how long she had been knocked out. She said she had looked at the clock last at 10:30, but she had done some more cleaning after that. "It could have been quarter to eleven, eleven," she said. "I know it was before my husband got home. That's all I know."

That was new, and it obviously was in response to Dr. Case's testimony. Paula was decreasing the amount of time she might have been unconscious to lessen the impact of the doctor's conclusion.

When Paula recounted the search by the police, she spoke a line with more emotion and sincerity than she had at any other time during her testimony. Groshong asked what the police had taken from the house.

"They took my mop," Paula blurted out. She was genuinely peeved by that. She seemed more upset about the absent mop than she was about her missing daughter. *A homicidal neatnik who is pushed to the edge by the confiscation of her mop,* Don thought. *How many more goofy twists can this case produce?*

Then Groshong served up another minor surprise. Paula testified that she kept a few trash bags behind the bread box on the kitchen counter. A kidnapper easily could grab a bag there, without having to find the roll tucked away on the shelves in the basement stairwell. Pretty good, Weber admitted.

The defense turned to the damage inflicted by one of its own—Linda Condray. About eight o'clock Sunday morning, Paula had packed up Randy and had driven directly to the Condrays' house. Herb and his son had been there when she arrived.

"Was Linda there?"

"No, she wasn't. I passed her on the road. She was going to our house."

Groshong moved his hands in opposite directions past each other. "One of these deals where you go like this?"

"I passed her about where Gordon Moore Park is. I don't know if she saw me, but I saw her."

"Did you go to your mom's house?"

"No," Paula said quickly. "I had no reason to go to my parents' house. They weren't home."

"You had a key to it?"

"Sure. I've always had a key to my parents' home."

"And, when you got to Herb's house, did you stay there?"

"Yes, I did. The whole afternoon . . ." She corrected herself quickly. "Whole morning and afternoon."

"Did you hear Linda Condray testify a day or two ago?"

"Yes, I did."

"Did you hear her the same way I did? Did she say you didn't get to her house until three o'clock, something like that?"

"Yes, I believe that's what she said," Paula responded with a hint of disapproval.

"What about that?"

"Well, she wouldn't know because she wasn't there." Paula said it as if it settled any possible dispute.

Don leaned back in his chair. The tedious but careful questioning before the grand jury last June was paying enormous dividends now. But Don had to tip his hat. The embellished description of Paula and Linda as two ships passing in the morning was a nice touch.

Groshong gave Paula another chance.

"Are you sure you went over to Herb's?"

"I'm positive."

"If Linda says to the contrary, is she mistaken?"

"Yes, she is. She wouldn't know. She wasn't there."

Weber knew Herb Condray had said that Paula arrived in the afternoon. Weber considered calling Herb to the stand, but decided he was a loose cannon who might say anything in front of the jury. Weber assumed the defense was taking the same position.

In Paula's version, the press had followed her to the Condrays' that morning and back to their home that night. "I don't know why they were following me around when they should have been out doing other things."

Weber knew that this close analysis of the media's

whereabouts had shown they had not begun the surveillance of the Simses that Sunday. There may have been some brief attempts by reporters to get an answer at the Sims house and some walks up and down Washington Avenue. But there was no camping out at the house yet. That didn't really begin until after the body was found.

Groshong turned to the day Heather's body was dumped.

"Where were you on May 3 between 10:30 in the morning and 3:00 in the afternoon?"

"I was at home."

"Where was Bob?"

"I believe he was at home."

"Where was Randy?"

"He was at home, of course. I fed him lunch at the usual time, 11:30. He was taking his nap."

"You weren't in West Alton, Missouri, at that time, were you?"

"No. I haven't been to West Alton for quite a while."

"Your car never left the house that day?"

"No."

Paula's only alibi for Wednesday morning was Robert. Would the jury believe him?

Groshong asked if Paula had done any housecleaning between Saturday night and Wednesday, and spoke of cleaning up the mess left by the police—black fingerprinting powder all over the place. And she came back to that mop. "I didn't have my mop," she said with exasperation. "So I cleaned it up with a rag. The floor, I mopped the floor with a rag." She seemed frustrated about using the wrong tool for the job.

Her father had picked her up about 10:30 that Wednesday night to take her to the safety and consolation of the Blews' home as the whole world was hearing the news of the little body in the barrel. Groshong asked how Paula had learned about the discovery. Paula spat out, "From the news," her voice louder than usual. As Robert had been, Paula too feigned anger at McCain for not breaking the news to them personally.

The Sims family never spent another night at 1053 Washington Avenue—just as they had left the house in Brighton.

After lunch, Groshong steered Paula quickly to a recounting of the events the night of May 4 and early the next day, when Robert had submitted to more interviews with the police. Paula said Robert had returned home to accuse her of lying and to ask her to talk to the police again.

" 'And if you don't, they're going to take Randy away,' " she quoted her husband as saying.

"Was this a nice, quiet little chat at the table?"

"No, it wasn't. It started out, but ended up not."

"What happened?"

"I told him to get out," Paula said with an edge of anger.

That was the Paula that Weber had waited for. She was her own woman. She had defied Robert. No one could believe now that Paula had been brainwashed into committing those murders. She was a strong-willed woman who could solve her own problems.

As Groshong appeared to be headed toward the end of Paula's direct, he asked a curious question. He drew from Paula that she had undergone a tubal ligation, sterilizing her, when Heather was delivered. Weber wondered why that was brought out. Was it an attempt to establish some mitigation at the death penalty phase? After all, if she couldn't have any more children, she couldn't kill any more.

Paula had agreed with most of Robert's rules, such as guests taking off their shoes, washing their hands before holding the baby or staying away from the baby if they had colds. But she admitted the rules had caused a little trouble. She didn't elaborate.

Her attorney turned to the "kidnappers."

"I want to talk to you about the fellow you saw standing on the stairs in 1986, and the fellow you saw in your backyard in 1989. Did you see any similarities in those two people?"

"Definitely. It was the same guy." she answered with absolute certainty.

Her answer rocked the courtroom, creating almost as much stir as Dr. Case's surprise conclusion the week before. Weber was stunned; the reporters scribbled fiercely in their notebooks. Was Paula being audacious again, or simply stupid?

"How do you know that?"

"I know that, especially from his voice. I remember that voice. If I heard it today, I could recognize that voice."

Another shock wave ran through Weber. More great evidence that she forgot to mention to the cops? She would recognize the voice that she was unable to describe either time?

Groshong straightened himself for the final strafing of rapid-fire questions.

"On May 3, did you go over to West Alton and hide your daughter's body in a trash barrel?"

Paula's face tightened and her eyes narrowed. She said calmly and with rock-solid conviction, "No, I did not."

"Did Bob do anything in that regard?"

"No."

"Did you lie to the police about this?"

"No, I have not."

"I mean, in 1986 and in 1989."

"No I told them the truth."

"Did you kill either one of your daughters?"

"No. I did not." She didn't hesitate. "I loved my daughters, and I still do."

Groshong's voice softened. "Did you have plans for your daughters?"

"Yes, I had a lot of plans." Her voice trembled again, and her face clouded over. "But they're all gone now."

"What kind of plans did you have?"

She looked down. "I really don't want to talk about the plans I had, because I no longer have any plans any more."

Paula rested her case.

At a break earlier in the day, Weber had interviewed Gisella Rasp briefly to confirm what she had told the police about seeing the woman carrying the quiet baby in the card shop the day before Father's Day. Gisella Rasp was nervous about testifying, but Don needed her for his rebuttal case. In her thick German accent, she told Weber the same story as he had read in the reports. Then, standing in the narrow hallway behind the courtroom, she

added some startling details. After the woman Gisella
later recognized as Paula left the store, she stopped in
front of the window and a bearded man walked over and
put his arm around her. Gisella recognized the man later
as Robert. *Great,* Weber thought. *That puts Robert right
in the middle of it, too.*

But Gisella wasn't finished. Weber still was leaning
one shoulder against the wall as his witness described
the baby again.

"She was very still, and her eyes were only half-open.
When I moved the blanket to look at her, the baby didn't
move. She didn't blink or move her eyes or anything."

Weber straightened up, and he listened keenly.

"Mr. Weber, do you understand what I'm telling you?"
she asked in that accent. "Mr. Weber, that baby was dead."

Don was flabbergasted, and he felt the hair on his arms
stand up. "Are you sure? I mean, are you saying that
Loralei was not alive in the store?"

"That's what I mean. I was sure when I saw her. Her
face just wasn't right. I thought she was dead."

Don turned and looked at Kit Morrissey's face. She
was as stunned as he was. Did they finally have the explanation for the Simses' absolute denial of the card-shop
story and for the incident on Father's Day? Could it be
that Paula had taken the already-dead Loralei into the
store to set up an alibi for Saturday, so Robert could be
at work when the "kidnapper" struck three days later?

Don decided that he would take a risk and dig into Paula
on this point on cross-examination. On this chilling point,
the risk might be worth it.

Weber had polled several people at lunch, and they had
thought Paula had been an effective witness in her own
defense. Several suggested that Paula actually had seemed
sympathetic, and might be drawing some positive emotional reaction from the jury. One television reporter offered that Paula might have created enough reasonable
doubt about her ability to commit two cold-blooded murders—especially of her own daughters—to be acquitted.

Don agreed that she had shown a more human side
than he expected, but he rejected the views that Paula
had transformed herself into another Mother Theresa. His

biggest concern for cross-examination was avoiding anything that could give her an excuse to cry. Agent Diana Sievers had warned Weber a couple of nights earlier that Paula could turn the tears on and off at will. And Don knew that a male prosecutor badgering a woman witness into tears might do the case more harm than anything else Weber could do right then. It would be a delicate balance.

Don started with a line of questioning he knew would draw out a tough and aggressive Paula as she defended her brother, Dennis. She denied immediately that she and Robert had waited to have children because of his concern over Dennis' seizures.

But she balked when Weber persisted in asking if Robert had put a condition on the marriage concerning Dennis.

"I really don't understand your question, what you mean by condition." She was stalling for time to consider her answer.

"Well, you didn't seem to have any trouble understanding Mr. Groshong's questions, did you?"

Paula snapped, "Your questions don't make any sense."

Don thought that would suffice. She had stood up and faced him, and it would be difficult for her to melt into tears now. It was time to set the stage for the device that Don hoped would smash Paula's defense.

He began to spar with Paula over Jeff Reed as she denied telling her coworker that she didn't want to have kids.

"He's made a terrible mistake," she said, shaking her head.

Great answer, Don thought. He knew he couldn't have written the response any better for his purposes.

He asked about her first roommate's memory of the tearful phone call.

"Did she make a terrible mistake, too?"

"Yes."

Don moved on to Father's Day, and edged toward the information he would draw from Gisella Rasp in his rebuttal case. Paula denied taking Loralei out of the house, and said the trip to the Blews' for Father's Day was canceled because it was too hot. She had been upset and had cried when she called her mother to tell her; she knew she had disappointed her parents. But she had never heard of Gisella Rasp or the card shop, and had never been there.

"Your baby wasn't dead on Saturday, and you didn't take her to the card shop to set up an alibi for Robert?"

Paula was stone cold. "No."

Don asked about "postpartum depression," and Paula said she may have experienced a little with Randy, but not with the other two children. Good. That should remove any sympathy for a "depression" defense.

Don reminded Paula that Linda Heistand had quoted her as saying she was worried about Loralei being kidnapped before she disappeared.

"No, she's mistaken. I'm sure."

Don had been waiting for that. "Another mistake by another witness?"

"Yes."

Don trotted out Minnie Gray's neat little surprise.

"Didn't you tell Minnie Gray that you felt safe back there because your dog hears everything?"

"I don't believe I said 'hears everything.' She sleeps 80 percent of the time."

"Another witness made another mistake in this case?"

Groshong had finally had enough and objected; Matoesian sustained the objection and told Weber not to compare witnesses' answers.

Weber hoped he had made his point by walloping Paula four times with the "mistaken witness" line. He hoped the jurors would make the comparison for him each time he brought out another contradiction later.

Don hammered Paula about the "shadowy figure." She couldn't describe it or say where it was. And she resisted Weber's effort to get her to agree that she had told Morgan and Sievers that she had heard the man running in the driveway gravel. All she would admit was that she had heard footsteps in gravel somewhere.

"And it was the same guy that hit your house three years later, you say?"

"Yes, it was."

"Then, why didn't you tell the police the second man was a white man?"

"Because I wasn't sure, except for the voice."

"When did you become sure? Was it during the trial?"

"During the what?"

"This trial. After you heard the evidence. Is that when you became sure?"

"No."

"When did you become sure?"

"I think I told the officer that night that I thought it was the same man that had taken Loralei."

Weber would shred that answer in his rebuttal case.

He shifted back to Paula's comment to Wayne Watson. She was surprisingly agreeable, admitting that she had said just about what Watson had related. But she had meant that she didn't want to believe that her baby was in the lake "I believed she was still alive, and we were going to get her back."

Don jumped forward to the purchase of the house on Washington Avenue, getting Paula to agree this time that all of the changes they made on the property had been decided by both of them.

"Robert doesn't make all the decisions in the family, does he?"

"No, he doesn't," she said flatly. Don had his answer, and the jury was learning fast that Paula was not docile and passive.

Weber wanted to establish that the sonograms before the girls' births had failed to predict their gender, removing the argument that Paula could have had an abortion if she really didn't want daughters. As he raised the issue, Paula was offended.

She responded haughtily, "I would never have an abortion. I am totally against abortion."

Don was struck dumb again. She murdered her daughters shortly after their births, but she expected the jurors to be impressed by antiabortion sentiment.

It was time to shake things up a bit, and Weber started coming on stronger. Paula had been pugnacious and combative; there was little chance she suddenly would turn to tears in defense. He bore in repeatedly on what time she had gone outside. She said it was about 10:30, perhaps 10:45. She was unsure.

But Don hammered away at her claim that she had done some more house cleaning after she looked at the clock at 10:30. She insisted she had told the police that, and she took advantage of the failed tape recorder by suggesting that she might have said it to McCain. *Brazen and clever*, Don thought.

He skipped back to Paula's announcement that a single abductor had taken both Sims girls, asking why she hadn't told the police that the second abductor was a white man, as she had said in the first case.

She fumbled that one. "Because I wasn't positive. They wanted me to give them . . . to tell them if he was white or black, and I was not positive. So, I don't tell someone something unless I'm positive."

How would the jury read that. It was definitely the same guy because of his voice, but she wasn't sure.

And the exchange over that had rattled Paula. Her eyes had fluttered as she was answering, the first sign Don had seen that she was feeling the pressure.

Why hadn't she slammed the new steel door on the gunman as he walked into the kitchen? He was too close, Paula said. Why hadn't she mentioned that before? No one had asked. "You have to ask," she instructed him.

"Were there any obstacles you had to get over, or could you have made a dash for the gun? Anything on the floor?"

"No, nothing on the floor." There was that too-remarkable memory again.

"So, that wasn't memory you were just showing the jury?"

Paula protested angrily, "You're trying to put words into my mouth."

"I'm just asking you questions."

"No, you're not," she shot back. "You're trying to put words in my mouth."

"Well, here's a word you used. You said you felt the blow to the back of your neck."

"Yes, I did."

"What did it feel like?"

"Like I told the other officer that night, it felt like a hit. And he said, 'What kind of hit?' And I told him, 'Something like a karate chop.' "

"So, you have a memory of the blow and what it felt like. Is that correct?"

"I was trying to describe it to them."

"Well, you described it to Mr. Groshong, and twice you said, 'I felt a blow on the back of my neck.' You remember feeling the blow?"

"Yes, I do."

"And you remember what the blow felt like, right?"

392 Don W. Weber and Charles Bosworth, Jr.

"Yes."

He asked again.

"Yes, I remember getting hit."

Don wondered if she would 'remember' that answer as the moment she got hit again.

When Don swung the questioning around to what had happened after she awoke, Paula seemed to be catching on. She started hedging, fuzzying things up a little. But he wouldn't allow it.

"You knew who Heather was?"

"Yes."

"You knew where you had left her?"

"Yes."

"That was in the bassinet, right?"

"Yes."

"You knew what room the bassinet was in?"

"Of course."

Don led Paula on the chase through the house after she and Robert realized Heather was gone. Paula tried to slow the pace a little, saying she had felt dizzy and had leaned on the walls.

Don asked if Paula had experienced any memory problems while giving a statement to McCain and Dooley at the station. Paula responded, "That's when they were going to tape it, and I thought they were taping it. I wish they would have—that the tape recorder would have been working." She was pressing that one advantage well.

Don nodded and said quietly, "Yeah, me too."

Paula agreed. "Yeah."

Judge Matoesian called the afternoon recess at 2:45. When Paula resumed her testimony at 3:10, her voice was noticeably weaker.

Don began his charge for the finish line. He had to set up the last three points on his agenda—the sex line, Sunday morning, and Wednesday morning.

"Every night since Heather was gone, the sleeping arrangements changed back to you being upstairs?"

"Yes."

"How were you feeling around this time that Heather was gone—April 29 and 30, May 1, 2, and 3?"

"Terrible," Paula lamented.

"Depressed?"

"Yes."

"Sobbing?"

"Yes."

"Tired and worn out?"

"Yes."

"No energy?"

"I had some energy, of course."

"A little energy?"

"Yes."

"No appetite?"

"Not much."

The tease had perked everyone up, pulling them to the edge of their seats as they anticipated the "sex" question. But Don wasn't ready to spring it yet. He backed off and switched to Sunday morning. Paula had known about her parents' trip for a few days, and she had a key to the house. But she had gone to the Condrays' that Sunday morning. Don asked repeatedly why Robert hadn't driven his emotionally distraught wife and sole surviving child over to their relatives, rather than let her drive. Paula had no answer, except that Robert was staying at the house with the police.

"But you really didn't need any help, did you?"

"I guess I didn't."

Don moved to the big question.

"That Tuesday night, did you and your husband have the best and longest-lasting sex you ever had?"

The voices came forth in unison: As Paula snapped angrily, "No, we did not," Groshong protested, "I'm going to object. This is irrelevant to this case."

Matoesian nodded. "I don't see the relevancy. Sustain the objection."

It was too late. She had answered, and she had directly contradicted the portrait painted by her husband of a tender interlude by a loving couple seeking refuge from a world of grief. It may have been good for the gander, but it wasn't for the goose.

The prosecutor moved on to Wednesday morning. Paula had fed Randy and occupied herself with normal duties. It was time for Don to tell everyone where Heather had been while Randy was being fed in the kitchen.

"Were you worrying about the police coming back and looking in the refrigerator?"

"No, not at all." Paula was dismissing Don again. "It didn't even enter my mind. They had already looked in the refrigerator that night."

Don reminded her that the police left Sunday, and had not been back inside the house again, especially before the Blews returned home from Peculiar. "I do not know. I was not there," she said.

One last round of questions, starting with the simple queries he hoped would neutralize Groshong's venue issue.

"Now, from the time that you reported Heather disappeared until the time the baby was found, did you ever leave Madison County?"

"No, I did not."

"Did Robert Sims ever leave Madison County?"

"Not that I know of."

"So, when you went from your house to Cottage Hills, and wherever else you went, everything you did from April 29 to when the body was found was in Madison County, right?"

"Yes, it was."

Don pointed out that Robert had "a rock-solid alibi" for each of the times when his daughters disappeared. But Robert had no alibi for the weekend before he returned to work in 1986.

"Before Loralei was supposedly kidnapped," he added.

"She was kidnapped. There's is no supposing to it."

"And that's what you were doing in the card shop, Gisella Rasp's card shop. You set up an alibi for that dead baby."

Paula was angry again, and the hint of the hills was more obvious in her voice. She was slipping out of that carefully manicured testimony. "I wasn't in no card shop. I have never been to a card shop in Jerseyville. I don't even know of a card shop. I don't do shopping in Jerseyville. I already had Father's Day cards before Loralei was born."

"What did you do over at the Blews' house when you went over there?"

"When?"

"Sunday, April 30, between eight o'clock and two o'clock."

"I did not go to my parents' house. I went to Linda and Herb's."

Weber let his outrage flare as he spat out, "You went to your parents' house and you got that baby, and you brought it back to your house, didn't you?"

"No. I did not."

Weber slapped the cover on his file folder shut, spun quickly on his heel and walked toward his seat. "No further questions."

As Groshong told the judge he had no more questions, Kit leaned over to Don and whispered, "Good job."

Don took a deep breath. In three hours and forty-five minutes on the stand, Paula had not cried. And Don thought she had come off as a woman cold enough to take those babies' lives. But what had the jury seen in this woman?

Groshong rested his case as Paula, his thirtieth witness, slipped quietly off the stand and returned to a stiff posture in her seat at the defense table.

Judge Matoesian promptly followed Paula's testimony with rulings that prohibited Don from calling three rebuttal witnesses—Frank Yocom, former state's attorney Lee Plummer, and Bill Bailey, the man brought in after a two-state search. Yocom would have disputed Robert's claim to have suggested searching the woods behind the house in Brighton. Plummer would recount how Robert had warned him not to go into the woods because of the poison ivy. And Bailey would testify about Robert's comment that he had barred the "retarded" Dennis from the Sims property as a condition on Robert and Paula's marriage.

Groshong argued that those witnesses were being called to rebut testimony from Robert, not the defendant; Matoesian agreed. Weber felt the judge had just given the defense witnesses a license to lie with impunity. Weber stood against the empty jury box, and everyone in the courtroom could read his reaction on his face.

Gisella Rasp took the stand and looked nervously at Weber. She held her mouth so close to the microphone that her accented voice boomed through the room as it carried her chilling story. When she finished, Groshong had no questions.

Chapter 26

When Thursday morning dawned in Peoria, the January weather had taken a nasty turn. Snow was swirling along the windy streets and each weather forecast raised the expected accumulation and dropped the predicted temperature. The good-weather fortune of those attending the trial had just ended.

But in Courtroom C, preparations for the final day of evidence and the closing arguments were under way. A large crowd had gathered again, and several new reporters had arrived to cover the end of the trial.

Weber was making final arrangements for his rebuttal case. He had intended to call Robert's father, Troy Sims. But Weber talked to him first, only to learn he was backing off his statement that Robert had delayed having children because of Dennis Blew's condition. As Don left the interview room, he turned to Ventimiglia and announced loudly, "Take Troy Sims out and shoot him." The sergeant snapped to attention and said, "Right away." A local reporter who didn't know the pair very well stood nearby with a most puzzled look on his face.

During the break, Weber also received a message from the FBI in St. Louis. The weather had grounded Schultz's airplane, and the agent would not be able to fly in to testify that day. Perfect.

When Don returned to the courtroom, he announced that he was withdrawing Troy Sims as a witness. Weber snarled petulantly, "He's lying. I just talked to him."

At 10:47, Matoesian called in the jury to announce there would be no court Friday, and that they should bring a suitcase Monday on the chance that their deliberations required a hotel stay.

Weber called Rick McCain and Mick Dooley back to

the stand to rebut Paula's claim of cleaning the house after 10:30, before she took out the trash. When Groshong cross-examined them, he unsheathed a sharp, new edge in his tone. He reminded McCain that the time element had been discussed in the interview where the tape recorder had not worked, and no signed statement had been produced. What was McCain's proof of what Paula had said?

"Just my word," Rick responded.

Groshong got Dooley to admit that Paula never said which television station she had been watching. Groshong noted that news was aired on the Cable News Network all the time, so Paula might have seen a report on the baby food at almost any time.

Weber thought Groshong had finally put some sizzle in his cross-examination of McCain and Dooley. It had been short and to the point, and had packed a pretty good punch.

It had been a turbulent morning in court, and the jury was sent home for the day, out into the blizzard. But the folks from Madison County found themselves stranded in Peoria Thursday night. The roads across central Illinois were snow packed, and many near Peoria were impassable. It was midday Friday before most of the participants could head south for home.

On the drive, Weber thought through several ideas for his closing argument. How could he convey the emotional impact of this case to the jury? Finally, the definitive line came to him, and it hit him so hard that he felt the tears in his eyes. It would be his last comment to the jury before they retired to decide Paula's guilt or innocence.

Don also struck on a device to demonstrate Paula's shifting of the body from freezer to freezer. When he returned to Peoria Sunday night and met the group in the hotel lounge, he passed out English walnuts. Without divulging the surprise, Weber suggested that everyone might want to save a shell as a souvenir.

Special Agent Carl Schultz arrived early Monday on an airplane procured by the FBI to handle the wheelchair he needed because of his serious leg wound. Groshong

objected to Schultz's appearance in court in the wheelchair, fearing it would create immediate credibility and
sympathy for a stricken hero. But Matoesian agreed with
Weber that Schultz's injury left no alternative.

Schultz was rolled into the room and his wheelchair
was stopped in front of the witness stand. Don was reminded of a movie scene with the community gathering
on July Fourth to honor a war hero. At Weber's request,
Schultz explained how he and two other agents had been
attempting to serve a search warrant in a bank-robbery
case ten days earlier. As the agents entered the house in
south St. Louis County, the suspect opened fire, killing
Schultz's longtime partner and wounding Carl. He and
the third agent then returned fire, killing the suspect.

In his clipped, professional manner, Schultz firmly denied lying to Robert Sims about evidence in an attempt
to crack a confession out of him. Schultz had told Robert
the truth, including the agent's assessment that "no jury
in its right mind" would believe the Simses' stories.
Groshong insisted that Schultz had used misleading information about the evidence to plant the seed that would
cause Robert to doubt Paula. Schultz said he hoped Robert would convince Paula to confess, but the agent had
not deceived Robert to accomplish that.

Groshong's surrebuttal was brief. Linda and Dave Heistand testified that they had called Robert at his home in
Brighton on Monday, June 16, to deliver a belated birthday wish to him. They had heard Loralei crying in the
background, implying she had been alive two days after
Gisella Rasp claimed to have seen the deathly still baby.
That shook Weber. He had been burned by climbing out
on a limb with Gisella's testimony.

Robert's friend, John Miles, said he had visited the
Sims house in Alton on Friday, April 28, to see Robert
and Heather. That baby was alive then, too.

With all the evidence in, the defense renewed its motion for the judge to acquit Paula. Denied.

It was time for the all-important closing arguments,
where a circumstantial case could be won or lost.

Standing calmly behind the lectern, Weber would talk
for an hour and forty minutes, the first of two chances
he had to address the jurors. Don wasted no time in ex-

horting them to convict Paula Sims on a mountain of evidence and the depths of her own lies. Reject the plea for sympathy carried by the dolls, he pleaded. Calmly, he added, "And I would ask you not to have sympathy for Paula Sims or the act that she committed, just because she was once a little girl. Remember what that little girl grew up to be."

He pulled the jurors into the eye of the hurricane. "I would submit to you that I now have twelve eyewitnesses that Paula Sims is guilty of murder, because when Paula Sims told you that she felt the blow on the back of her neck, and when Dr. Case told you that was impossible, Paula Sims created twelve eyewitnesses to the fact that she murdered her daughter."

Pointing at Paula often during his remarks, Don tried to distill the case to an easy choice. "She has narrowed this case down to a simple proposition. If you believe that her story about the imaginary bandito is reasonable, then you should acquit her. If, on the other hand, you believe that her story is preposterous, unreasonable and, in fact, impossible, then you have to convict her."

Weber recounted the infamous story he had heard from Williamson about the lawyer in Madison County who once wrote a letter to a client saying, "Please don't discuss the facts of your case with anyone because the facts of your case may change." As the jury chuckled, Don added, "Well, that's exactly what happens in this situation. Every time we prove that Paula Sims's story is impossible, she has a real good answer—the facts change."

Don mocked Paula's story about the "shadowy figure," letting his voice slide into an exaggerated drawl and pointing toward a sketch of the Sims property in Brighton.

"He's running, probably with a gun in one hand and a communicator in the other hand, saying, 'Scottie, beam me up,' because that's the only explanation we've got for this man disappearing at the end of the road."

What about a motive?

"Ladies and gentlemen, I have to confess to you, I can't tell you why this happened. I can tell you a few things I know. Paula Sims didn't like little girls. Paula Sims didn't like the sleeping arrangements. Paula Sims,

the neatnik, didn't like Heather making a mess in her
house. I mean, someone who's going to worry about the
police taking her mop is going to get upset about other
minor things. Probably, if you took all the psychiatrists
in the world and interviewed this woman, you would
never figure out exactly why she did this.''

Don addressed his misstep on the card shop testimony
by calling it unimportant. What was important was that
Gisella Rasp had identified the Simses positively, and
that, for some unexplained reason, they were lying about
being in the shop.

He recalled the chilling story told by Stephanie Werner-
Cook, and buttressed it by quoting her mother: ''It's
Stephanie's roommate, and she was taking out the trash
again.''

No one could doubt that the trash bag that held Heather's body had come off the roll at the Simses' house. Don
shook off the ''burglar's pillowcase'' theory as too absurd.

Dr. Case. Ah, yes. Even Groshong had recognized her
expertise by refusing to challenge her testimony that
proved conclusively that Paula Sims' story was medically
impossible.

''And you twelve people heard it yourselves. You heard
her lie to your faces. You heard her tell that story. Just
on that evidence alone you have to find her guilty of
murder beyond any doubt whatsoever.''

What about Paula herself? ''They called some of her
girlfriends, and her girlfriends testified as to one of the
many faces of Paula Sims. The one they saw was the
loving mother. You saw some other faces of her. You saw
the emotionless, cold-blooded face when the barrel that
her baby was found in and the bassinet the baby was
supposedly taken from were brought into the courtroom.
Stoic. No response. You saw the robotic face of Paula
Sims as she routinely answered her own lawyer's questions. And you saw the smart, tough, cunning face of
Paula Sims when she answered my questions. I would
submit to you that, of the two strange people that we have
in this case, Robert and Paula Sims, Paula is the smarter
and the more cunning, and more cold-blooded than Robert.''

Don wondered aloud why Paula had answered his questions with "I don't know" sixty-four times if she wasn't being evasive and trying to cover up the murderous truth.

After all these months, the moment finally arrived for Don to lay out his freezer theory in plain language—as the "shell game" it had been.

He placed three photographs on the railing of the jury box—the Blews' freezer, the Simses' kitchen refrigerator and the Simses' freezer in the basement. On each picture, he set half of an English walnut shell. Some of the jurors in the back row stood up to see.

"Now, on April 29, when Paula murdered Heather, the Blews weren't home. She went over to the Blews' freezer, and she put the baby in the freezer." Don slipped the pea under the shell on that photo.

"And then, an unfortunate thing happened—not planned. Robert called the Blews. Of all the conversations of great interest in this case, probably the best one was when Robert said, 'By the way, Orville is coming back.' And Paula Sims said, 'What a mess you've gotten us into now. That's where the baby is.' That's why, at eight o'clock on Sunday morning, Robert wants Paula to go to the Blews.

"Now, when we were at the Simses' house, there is no baby there."

He lifted the empty shells on the two photos of the Simses' freezers. "April 29, April 30. There is no baby here. We checked it. Nothing.

"But on April 30 when we leave at ten o'clock in the morning, and she gets over to the Blews' house . . ." He slipped the pea out from under that shell.

". . . puts the baby back in her own freezer." As he spoke, he tucked the pea under the shell on the picture of the Simses' refrigerator.

"And then, when the Blews get home, no baby." He picked up the empty shell to illustrate the point.

"Paula was nervous until May 3, when she dumped the body, and then we have no baby." He slipped the pea out from under the last shell, and hid it in his palm.

"As you can see, what she was doing was the old shell

game, only with a tragic and grim twist. She's moving a dead baby in order to cover up her murderous acts.''

Don showed the jurors the photograph of Loralei's bassinet, noting the neatly folded blanket, and reminded them that nothing else in the Simses' houses had been disturbed.

''Well, I guess this bandito must have been a neatnik. Well, who do we know in the courtroom who's a neatnik? Paula Sims.''

Don shifted to Robert, trying to assuage the concerns of any of the jurors that Robert was involved and might escape justice. ''I think you are going to have to trust the system, the prosecution, and the police to see that the right people are fully prosecuted for their involvement in this crime.''

Don referred once more to Robert's ''great sex'' line.

''I would submit to you, tragically, that it was much more like a celebration than a consolation prize.''

Don looked back at Paula. Still sitting there like a statue. Not a flicker of feeling on her face as he slashed away at her.

He explained the law on the theory of accountability, as the judge would again later. Simply put, even if Robert killed Heather and Paula only helped plan it or carry it out, she still was guilty of murder.

Don turned to a list he had written out on a large sheet on an easel—''The Roll Call of the Defendant's Guilt.'' There were twenty-five names in two columns. To acquit Paula, the jury had to believe her fantastic story and accept all its contradictions, and reject the testimony of the others.

''Twenty-five witnesses are wrong, and Paula Sims and this preposterous story that she tells you are right? Is that reasonable?''

Don charged on for another thirty minutes, pounding away on the evidence, on Paula's stories, on the contradictions. He pulled to a halt at 12:17 P.M., by asking the jury to require Groshong to look at the evidence when he spoke to them after lunch.

''I don't think he wants to do that very much because, in the noonday sun, a shadowy figure on the driveway vanishes to nothing. And that's exactly what the defense is—an impossible story under implausible circumstances. And that's why you should convict Paula Sims of murder.''

As Don walked back to his seat, he thought ahead eagerly to his rebuttal closing. That was when the defense had to sit quietly, while the prosecution let it all out. Rebuttal always was more fun.

After lunch, Groshong took his only shot at swaying the jury. He urged the jurors to think of his responses for him when they heard from the prosecutor again later. He agreed that the deaths of those infants were terrible tragedies, and he called both cases unsolved murders.

''Now, there is another tragedy here, too. And its that this woman had been charged and put through this. And she has been put through this on something like a shell game, like the game that was played on the bench here today. There have been several games played here, several lawyer's stunts and tricks.''

''The state said in its opening statement, 'Paula's account is preposterous. It's unbelievable, ridiculous, and imaginary.' I ask you to judge the state's case against her by the same standard. Is their case preposterous, unbelievable, ridiculous, impossible, and imaginary? I think you are going to find it is.''

What about venue? ''There isn't the slightest evidence here that this death occurred in Illinois. Could it have? Sure. The answer is, we don't know.''

What about the forty-five-minute knockout? Paula never said it was forty-five minutes. That had come from Dooley, who had added big assumptions to estimated times to reach a questionable sum.

Groshong argued that there was no way Robert or Paula could have hidden the body Wednesday morning because they were being watched by the cops and the press. And he ridiculed the notion that Paula was a schooled schemer.

''She formulates a plan where she will have to move the body over and over and over. Boy, that's brilliant.''

Groshong set the prosecution's case on six cornerstones, and then set about kicking over each of them.

Motive. Wasn't that based on her comment about not having children, which she supposedly said when she was

single? Groshong added that he didn't want kids when he
was single, either. Robert wanted a son first; so did Groshong. The sleeping arrangements? What was so strange
and incriminating about a woman sleeping downstairs
with her new baby so she wouldn't have to climb the
stairs?

The evidence to disprove the supposed motive had
come from the defense. Pictures of a loving and joyful
young family. "And, boy, photos don't lie . . . The look
on these faces tell you more than any lawyer can tell you.
Those people loved that baby."

Groshong trotted out the reminders from Paula's childhood—her dolls and her baby dress. "What else could
you bring in to prove you loved your children if they say
you didn't? You could bring in things like this."

Would a mother planning her daughter's murder take
the baby to the doctor for diarrhea a week earlier? Would
a homicidal mother refrain from taking X-rays to protect
an unborn baby she might murder later? No insurance;
no motive there. The tender sentiments written on the
calendar show the real feelings of these parents.

Why would a kidnapper kill his victim? "There are a
lot of Charles Manson-type lunatics out there. And we
don't know why they do what they do, but this is a situation like that."

The second cornerstone was Stephanie Werner-Cook.
The defense attorney shook his head. Here was a story
that was incredible. No one could believe that Paula Sims
had plotted the murder of her daughter the day of her
birth, and then had disclosed the details of the coverup
story to a complete stranger? And, beyond that, there
was Stephanie's credibility problem over the room brou-
haha.

"The state says there are no signs of a struggle, no
signs of kidnapping? What evidence do you think there
would be of a kidnapping? Stop and think about that. If
I come in the house and take your child, and I have gloves
on, I'm not going to leave fingerprints. I walk in and pick
up your child. What's the evidence? What would you expect to find?"

Groshong disagreed with Weber about the canine
searches. Donovan's dog had hit on a scent by the pond.

And it was absurd to believe that the dogs hadn't smelled a decaying body in 100-degree temperatures for a week. Didn't that suggest that the kidnapper had returned the body to the scene later to throw off the cops? Groshong's conclusion was that the dogs weren't as accurate as their handlers wanted everyone to believe.

The reenactment also came in for some brutal criticism—evidence manufactured by the prosecutors and the police, using officers who hadn't just had a baby, taped at a different time of day and year to support the theory of the state.

The defender rose to the occasion as he turned to the trash-bag evidence, the third cornerstone. He agreed that the bag with Heather's body had come from the roll at the Sims house. He noted that the police had confiscated two bags of trash on May 10, six days after the roll of bags was seized by the police in an earlier search. Those two bags also came from the same roll, according to the FBI. How was that possible if the police already had it by then? The answer was that Robert Sims always pulled several bags off the roll at a time and stashed them behind the bread box in the kitchen. It was handier than the shelves in the basement stairwell. The kidnapper took one, maybe more, of those bags as he escaped. But he left behind some that the Simses used later for their trash.

Weber was impressed. That was a pretty good explanation for why alternating bags from the roll were missing, and it got some loose bags to a more convenient place for the phantom kidnapper to find them. A good lawyer will try to explain what he knows the jury believes, and Groshong was a very good lawyer.

But his next hypothesis seemed so silly that Weber thought his opponent had lost the progress made with the bag explanation. Groshong suggested that if he were the kidnapper he would have used the bag to carry the baby out of the house.

"Nobody thinks anything about a trash bag. So their trash bag goes out with the child, and that's why I told you in my opening statement that the bag is my pillowcase."

The fourth major point was Paula's blow on the head. Dr. Case's testimony was just another stunt pulled by the prosecutor. She never even worked on living patients, and her conclusion about Paula's injury was based solely on what the prosecution had told her, not any medical information from Paula.

Then he delivered a pretty good counterpunch.

"Anybody on this jury that's ever watched boxing on television knows people get knocked out. They get up; they finish the fight without a mark on them. You also know that sometimes a guy gets knocked out in the ring, and that's the end of the fight. They interview him after the fight is over, and he can describe the punch. He can describe everything that happened in the whole round. 'Should have ducked here; he got me with a good one.' Here's a guy that had been knocked out."

Point five was the coincidence of two similar kidnappings. Groshong argued that lightning can strike twice. The similarities in both cases could prove the existence of a single kidnapper more readily than Paula's guilt. Was it possible that the kidnapper had arranged the discoveries of the bodies, when the Simses could have hidden them permanently without much effort?

"Is it unbelievable? No. Is it bizarre? Yes. Is it unusual? Yes. The fact that Bobby and Jack Kennedy both got assassinated is a coincidence, and that's odd and unusual, too."

What was unbelievable, the attorney argued, was that the police had failed to put the Simses under surveillance when they were using FBI psychological tactics to pressure them, and the idea that Paula was so smart that she put the body where it could be found and traced back to her. What was unbelievable was that Paula would devise a plan that would force her to ferry a frozen body around town while being watched by the press every minute, and eventually bring it back to her house where the police might find it at any second.

The state had resorted to character assassination, in the absence of real evidence. "Let's talk about your sex life, you know. Your child was gone, and a few days later, you seek each other's comfort. That's understandable. Let's bring that up in the courtroom and talk about it like you're sick or something."

The sixth point was Gisella Rasp, a woman who could

ID a tiny baby in a picture from a four-second glance days earlier. If her story were true, Paula easily could have admitted it without damaging herself.

What about that stone face?

"The prosecutor tries to paint a picture of Paula. She's an actress. She's a person of many faces. I'll tell you what she is, ladies and gentleman. She's a woman who has lost two children. That's a hard loss. And you can cry, and you can hurt inside for a long time. And then you can add insult to injury when they accuse you of doing it. And that can go on and on. And, after a while, it's hard to cry anymore, and it's hard to have any emotion anymore because you're drained. You don't have any more. A person can only take so much."

Groshong rejected Weber's "roll call" of witnesses, and, one by one, offered his explanation of misunderstood evidence or innocent differences of opinions.

The defender's finale was simple. There was no evidence she did any of the things for which she was charged.

"And, after you think about this, I would ask you to return a verdict of not guilty on everything. This woman is innocent."

During a fifteen-minute recess, Weber prepared the courtroom for his rebuttal argument. He placed the trash barrel—with its scratched-up, silver paint job and the opening still covered by cellophane—in front of the jury box at just the right angle. When the jurors looked at the barrel, they would see Paula sitting right behind it.

Don placed the bassinet on the floor near the opposite end of the jury box, about eight feet away from the barrel.

Groshong purposefully had left Paula's Barbie doll and the Sims family photos on display on the jury-box railing. Weber put the puzzling photographs away, and gently laid the Barbie doll in the bassinet.

When it was time for Don to have the last word, his voice came out in a tone of indignation and with a cutting edge he had not used in the trial before. He sliced into Groshong's points, one by one. Why had Paula made the careless comments to Stephanie? Perhaps the painkilling drugs fed into Paula's arm by the intravenous device she controlled with a button had loosened her tongue.

Did Groshong really think a man carrying a trash bag with a wiggling and crying baby inside wouldn't be suspicious?

Why hadn't the defense asked Dr. Case to explain boxers who remembered punches? Was the defense afraid of the answers? Why weren't some boxers called to the stand?

But none of Don's comments hit as hard as his final words as he stood between the bassinet on his left and the trash barrel on his right.

"Mr. Groshong has repeatedly showed you the dolls, and I would tell you that it's unfortunate that she didn't take as good care of her baby as she did these dolls. At least this Barbie doll got a shoe box and not a trash bag. It's unfortunate that the people who weep in this case for baby Heather are the people of the State of Illinois. I was wondering, when I heard one piece of evidence—when Paula Sims was smothering that baby, and its chest was burning and it was flailing its hands and kicking its legs for two minutes before it went unconscious . . ."

Don's voice was growing louder and angrier.

". . . I wondered if Paula Sims counted every precious little finger and every precious little toe when she was doing that to her. She didn't," he scowled.

He had reached a new level of outrage, and the first angry passion shown by anyone in the courtroom rolled out and over the audience in a wrathful voice.

"A baby is a precious gift from God, not a piece of garbage. And I weep for that child who never went to school the first day. She never had her first boyfriend. She never had her first date. She never grew up. She never had a birthday, and never saw a Christmas. The people of the State of Illinois cry for this, and Heather cries out right now for justice."

"Now, I don't want you to convict Paula Sims on passion or prejudice. That's not right. And I don't want you to convict her because the people in my county are outraged at what she did. I want you to convict her because there is no reasonable doubt about her guilt; because what she did in her murderous, malignant heart is beyond statement."

Don looked down at Barbie in the bassinet.

"And I want you convict her because a baby belongs in a bassinet . . ."

He leaned over and tenderly picked up the doll, and then wheeled around quickly and dropped it onto the cellophane covering the barrel.

". . . and not in a trash barrel."

As he spoke, he kicked the barrel in disgust. The sound rang through the stunned courtroom.

"And you should convict her, and it is your solemn duty to convict her, because she doesn't know the difference."

The words reverberated through the courtroom, an appropriate echo to the sound from the barrel. He returned to his seat. The anger still showed on his face. The courtroom fell silent.

The jury retired to the room just off the courtroom to begin deliberations at 5:25 P.M., and Weber walked the two blocks back to his hotel. Now it was in the hands of twelve good and true men and women from Peoria County.

He went to his room, and went right to sleep. The cross-examination of Robert and Paula in the days before and the closing arguments had left him exhausted. The nap felt good. At eight o'clock he switched the television to a basketball game with the Fighting Illini. When the game had been lost, Don returned to the courthouse, where the vigil awaiting the verdict was well under way.

Around the corner from the courthouse the media had set up its waiting room—at Sully's Bar. But this night was different, for the press was joined by Groshong and Williamson. For the first time, the defense attorneys felt free to let their guard down a bit with the reporters they mostly had shunned during the trial. It became a jovial session, with many of the reporters who didn't know the two lawyers discovering what fascinating men and great conversationalists they were. And Williamson's generous habit of picking up the check ingratiated him that much more.

The jurors had eaten dinner shortly after beginning their deliberations. The eight men and four women had become relatively good friends throughout the weeks, and

Juror 4, Mr. Ryan, was elected foreman, as everyone had predicted. The deliberations began on good terms among the twelve calm people.

It wasn't long before the jury sent a note to the judge asking, "What does two (underlined) counts of First-Degree Murder mean? We are confused on the 'two.' " Weber had wondered if he should have dismissed one of those counts to keep it simple. Now, he wished he had. It really wasn't that complicated. The first count referred to a killing done intentionally. The second referred to acts the person should have known would cause death.

Judge Matoesian responded quickly with a note. "The 'Counts' refer to two theories. The defendant can be found guilty or not guilty of only one murder." That cleared up any confusion over whether the charges referred to Heather and Loralei, or just Heather.

Not long after that, another note with a common question asked by juries arrived. "Do we get a copy of the transcript?" The judge said no. A transcript would take months to prepare.

For those outside the jury room, the wait was becoming increasingly tense. Especially for Tony Ventimiglia. He had waited out juries before, and he didn't like his gut feeling this time. Weber had his own timetable, and wouldn't allow himself to get concerned until after 10:30. At that point, experience had taught him, juries could become unpredictable. Four hours of deliberations was average in a murder case.

In his chambers, the judge and the attorneys were deciding when to call it a night. The judge thought he would send the panel to a hotel about 11:30; Weber wanted him to wait later. At 11:15, the jury sent out a note asking to break for the night.

Ventimiglia called McCain, who was waiting anxiously in Alton. McCain's opinion, shared by everyone at the station, was that the lengthy deliberations meant the case had gone down the toilet; there should have been a conviction by then. Ventimiglia was standing on the darkened balcony outside the courtroom hallway when Wayne Watson brought him the news that the jury was heading for the hotel. Ventimiglia's face fell, and he shook his head. "That's it. It's over. We're dead. It's down the toilet now," he said, disgusted.

His opinion had upset Weber. This was no time for faint hearts. The prosecutor still was optimistic, but he had started to worry. Had Groshong injected enough doubt to sway the jurors? Could they accept the horrible notion that a mother had murdered her young, or would they reject it because it was just too painful to believe?

Don called his wife, who told him that the three major television stations in St. Louis had been going crazy with regular bulletins all evening, each of them pledging to be first with the news of the verdict.

Virginia had been through all of her husband's trials with him for fifteen years, and had become an uncanny prognosticator. She reassured Don that the jury was just being careful, going over the voluminous evidence from a very long trial; there was no problem. Bolstered by Virginia's confidence, Don went to bed. It was a restless night.

The congregation returned in full early Tuesday morning. Don already was in the courthouse when the jurors arrived after a walk from their hotel that delighted the TV crews. He couldn't read their faces; they still were inscrutable. But they also still were friendly with each other, an indication that there was no serious battling going on. They filed quickly into the deliberation room, and the vigil resumed. The hours dragged by, and as noon arrived, Don's confidence began to weaken. The longer jurors batted around a case based on circumstantial evidence, the greater the chance they would begin to lose sight of the obvious, to lose their perspective.

Just about twelve o'clock, the jury tried again to get an answer on the "two theories" question. The note read, "What are the two theories in reference to the two counts of First Degree Murder?" This was getting serious, Weber feared. Matoesian's pointed answer to the jury was, "You have been instructed as to the law by the Court, and I cannot supplement the instructions."

Shortly before 1:30, a fourth note was sent out, asking bluntly if they could convict Paula even if some of them felt someone else actually had killed Heather.

Weber argued loudly that Matoesian could send the

jurors a brief explanation. Groshong disagreed. Weber asked Kit Morrissey to research the point in the law library down the hall as the judge sent a note back telling the jurors that he already had given them the applicable law.

Within minutes, the jury had a verdict. Bill Portell told the reporters in the hall there was a verdict, but the jurors wanted to finish their lunches before returning their decision. Everyone began to assemble in the courtroom. Paula had been waiting in a conference room behind the courtroom, and was whisked quickly to her seat at 2:02. She was wearing an off-white sweater and brown slacks, and she looked haggard.

A bailiff asked Weber where Kit was. Weber, flustered and befuddled from the rush and an onset of last-minute jitters, drew a blank. He responded with an off-handed comment he would regret.

"I dunno. She's probably shopping or something."

The jurors filed across the courtroom in the most excruciatingly long thirty seconds Weber ever had experienced; those seconds before the verdict always were painfully long.

In a rare show of concern, Paula anxiously searched the jurors' faces for some sign. But they weren't looking at her. Jurors who were acquitting usually looked at the person they were about to set free. The reverse signal from this jury wasn't lost on the defense attorney, and his face sagged in resignation.

As the jurors took their seats, Juror Number One, Lisa Randle, looked at Don, smiled, and winked. The terrible uneasiness lifted immediately. The foreman solemnly handed the folded verdict forms to Portell, and he handed them to Matoesian. The courtroom was deathly silent, but the air was charged. The judge tilted his head down to read through his half-lens glasses.

"The verdict forms read as follows: We, the jury, find the defendant, Paula Sims, guilty of first-degree murder."

Paula shook her head, and dropped her eyes toward her lap. Groshong pursed his lips and gazed passively at the jury.

A restrained buzz of whispers ran through the courtroom, and the reporters glanced sideways at each other as they scribbled.

Guilty. The sound of the word from the bench sunk in on Don. After all those months, guilty. Now, it was worth all the effort, all the worrying. Even though there remained the challenging and emotionally demanding hearings on the death penalty, Don could breathe easier. Finally, Paula Sims's guilt had been established in a court of law. She would answer for Heather's murder, whether it was with death, or long years in prison. Justice had been done.

The judge announced the other three verdicts individually, each with the same result. "Guilty, guilty, guilty" on two counts of obstructing justice and one count of concealment of a homicidal death.

The doors of the courtroom exploded out into the hallway with a shattering din as they were hit by the force of the scrambling reporters. The television and radio reporters raced down the hall to see who would be able to claim the "promo" bragging rights as first to announce the verdict "live from Peoria." Their newspaper colleagues were left in the courtroom to watch in amusement and embarrassment. Weber was jolted by the unexpected eruption at the rear of the room, and even Judge Matoesian seemed shocked. Neither of those experienced courtroom participants had ever seen anything like that. It played like a scene from the Scopes Monkey Trial in one of Don's favorite movies, *Inherit the Wind.* What rabble.

Kit was seated awkwardly on a small step stool in the library, with several law books spread open at her feet, when she heard the commotion in the hallway. She heard a reporter yell, "Guilty on all counts." She darted down the back hall. "Surely that's not our case. Don wouldn't let me miss the verdict after all of this."

Groshong asked that the jurors be polled, and each of them confirmed their guilty votes. They revealed little of what was going on in their minds. They had become very good at holding back their thoughts. But the hunting-dog owner in the back row seemed shaken, relieved that at least that much of it finally was over. He leaned his head back against the wall, rubbed his red eyes and then squeezed them closed tightly.

Paula crossed her legs and stared sullenly at the floor.

As the poll was under way, Kit came into the courtroom with a puzzled look on her face. As she slipped into her seat beside Don, he looked sheepishly at her and said, "I'm sorry. I couldn't remember where you were. I told the bailiff you probably were shopping. I'm really sorry." Kit smiled and whispered, "I'll never forgive you for this." But she understood the crush of a moment like that.

Judge Matoesian denied Groshong's motion to sequester the jurors for the punishment phase. The judge told them to report back to the courtroom at 9:00 A.M., the next day.

Paula was escorted from the room. She looked drained, in shock. Within seconds of entering the conference room where she had awaited the verdict, Paula Sims broke into uncontrollable sobs and cried. Bill Portell could hear Paula's collapse from the hallway. It was the first time he had known any human reaction from the woman. Robert Sims went into the room briefly, and then slipped out through a back door without speaking to anyone.

Weber's friend and opponent at the defense table was taking the verdict hard. It had been a tough loss in a case Groshong genuinely thought he could, and would, win.

In stark contrast, Weber was surrounded by well-wishers. But his thoughts turned to all the doubts that had been expressed so freely by so many others, especially the packs of defense lawyers who loved to nip at his heels.

Don took Groshong aside once they could be alone, and shook hands with him.

"You did a great job. You did the best you could with Paula's story. You were stuck with it, and there was nothing you could do. Once I got the evidence on Loralei in, there wasn't anything you could do."

Groshong nodded. "That's the story she told, so . . ." But in his heart, he still felt there hadn't been enough evidence for the jury to return that verdict. He couldn't help but feel that it had been based on an emotional response to a bizarre situation, not on the evidence.

Weber slipped into the judge's chambers for a few minutes to collect himself and discuss the stunning climax with Matoesian, one of the people whose opinion Don respected most. When Don felt ready to face the press, he walked back into the courtroom where the reporters were waiting. He spoke from his heart.

"Don Groshong is the best defense lawyer in the State of Illinois and he made me a better prosecutor. I knew that, if I made a mistake, he would drive a Mack truck through it."

The press also was waiting for Groshong when he left the hallway. Despite the questions thrown at him, his only response was, "More work to do."

Alone in the hallway, Tony Ventimiglia paced slowly back and forth. When he was asked for a comment by a reporter or two, he said only that there were a lot of officers back in Alton who deserved to share in this moment. They had worked hard, and had never lost faith in what was right.

The next day, Steve Arnie of the Edwardsville *Intelligencer* ran a sidebar story about Ventimiglia, calling him the "quiet man in the modest suit" who had been in the middle of the case, but had stood unobtrusively off to the side when it was all over. Tony liked that description; it fit him like the modest suit.

The prosecutor could relax a bit that evening and enjoy the moment in the hotel lounge with his cohorts. He already had set up the jury for most of the aspects of the penalty hearings with his use of words such as, "cold-blooded and merciless." He didn't need lengthy preparation for the next day.

His evening was tempered, however, with strange, mixed feelings. He was glad to be part of the effort to bring Paula Sims to justice. But, unlike his successful efforts to bring down the death penalty over the years on vicious murderers, and even a serial killer, this one felt different. He wasn't sure his heart was in it. And now, even more than in the past, Don's thoughts turned to Loralei and Heather. God knew they shouldn't be forgotten in the middle of all of this, especially this self-conscious celebration over Paula's conviction. Their short lives and brutal deaths had led to this, and nothing could bring them back. Not even the ultimate penalty inflicted on their killer.

Chapter 27

Even before court resumed Wednesday for the jury to decide whether Paula Sims should lose her life, a new controversy over her fate had arisen. In St. Louis the night before, Channel 2 had sparked its newscast about Paula's conviction by announcing a telephone poll for viewers to vote on whether Paula should die. "Well, what do you think? Should Paula Sims get the death penalty?" the anchorman had inquired. "Tonight, *you* have a chance to be the jury."

When other members of the press learned of the effort the next morning, most of them were horrified and repulsed at the idea of making a fifty-cent phone call to reach out and kill someone. What was the phone number? 1-900-FRY-PAULA?

When Bill Haine was informed of the blood-thirsty gambit for higher ratings, he flew into a rage. He learned a few minutes later that the Peoria *Journal-Star* was running an identical call-in poll in its morning edition, right there in the town where the jury was about to make the life-and-death decision.

Haine called the reporters together in the courtroom before court opened, and ripped into the callous promotions for creating "a vicarious, lynch-mob atmosphere" with tactics from "the Roman coliseum in the Second Century, B.C. Thumbs up or thumbs down."

He called on the news organizations to withdraw their polls. Editors at both operations defended their actions as encouraging public debate on an important issue. But they agreed to withhold the results until the jury had made its decision. In the end, both polls showed overwhelming support for executing Paula Sims.

* * *

Haine's tirade had been good cover for an unexpected and secret development in the corridors behind the courtroom. Groshong had surprised Weber with a question: "How much would you give to know the truth?"

Weber leaped at the opportunity. "I would give a lot, if it's the truth." Was this the day he had been waiting for?

"Do you want to talk to her?"

"Yes, I do."

"Okay, but we've got to establish some ground rules. You cannot divulge ever, to anybody under any circumstances, what Paula tells you, unless we make some sort of agreement."

"Okay, that's the agreement."

The two Dons and Paula sat in a conference room and talked for about ninety minutes. The rumor began to circulate among the press that Weber was talking to Paula, and some sort of deal was impending.

Don had promised his friend and his colleague that the content of the conversation never would be divulged. But what Don experienced was another of the many faces of Paula Sims—only this time, it was a desperate face.

Paula obviously had been crying when she was brought into court at 11:40 that morning; her eyes were red and swollen. As the jury was seated, the foreman looked directly at Paula for several seconds. His face gave no hint of what the stare meant.

Weber was joined at the table by Assistant State's Attorney Todd Taplin, replacing Kit Morrissey, who had returned to Madison County to get some other cases going.

But Groshong was alone. Williamson and his other partners, several of whom had attended the trial at different times, had returned to Madison County to resume their duties. Groshong understood that, and he appreciated their assistance up to that point.

There would be no witnesses this time, just arguments from the attorneys. Weber was first.

He explained to the jurors that the day's business would be rather mechanical. They would decide only if Paula Sims was eligible for the death penalty, not whether she should be sentenced to death. If they found her eligible, the final question would be taken up the next day. Don explained that eligibility hinged on two points. First, was she eighteen when she committed the crime. No question about that; she had been twenty-nine.

The second was whether any of the aggravating factors in the death penalty statute applied to this crime. Was the victim under twelve? No doubt about that. Did the death result from exceptionally brutal or heinous behavior, indicative of wanton cruelty? Was it premeditated, prolonged, or torturous? Don had been using precisely those words since the first day of jury selection.

"The burial cloth of Heather Sims was a half-cent trash bag bought at a blue-light special," Don said solemnly. "Heather's trash bag—I can hardly say that—the trash bag for his poor little girl, was the first bag off the roll."

Then Weber announced his next dramatic demonstration.

"Let's take two minutes and see how long it took Paula Sims to murder her child."

"I object," Groshong interrupted angrily. "This is another courtroom stunt."

"Overruled."

Weber turned back to the jurors. "Let's take two minutes." He looked at his watch.

As the seconds slowly ticked by, the jurors stared self-consciously at the notebooks in their laps. The foreman kept looking up at Paula, waiting for . . . what? Some glimpse of pain, or humanity or sorrow? Any sign? Groshong tilted his chair back and sat there with a disgusted look on his face.

Weber stood at the lectern. After what seemed like a long time, he glanced at his watch. Thirty seconds had gone by. That's all? Surely it had to be more. He glanced at the jurors, but they all were looking down. The seconds dragged by. Weber never had felt time moving so oppressively. He looked at his watch again. Barely more than a minute had elapsed. He looked across the jurors' faces again. This time the jovial woman Don had dubbed "the social director" was staring bullets at Paula. Don hadn't seen that kind of look on her face before.

* * *

How long can two minutes be when you are thinking about the suffocation of a helpless infant? Take two minutes now.

The audience had begun to fidget and the jury had begun to squirm. When Don's watch registered a minute and forty-two seconds, he couldn't bear it any more. And he knew he had proved his point. He broke the silence.

"This is a crime that was grossly ruthless. It was devoid of mercy or compassion, and it was ruthless and cold-blooded. And I believe you should find that Paula Sims qualifies for the death penalty."

The Groshong swagger was gone, but there was some defiance as he told the jurors that Paula still maintained her innocence.

He argued that not all murders deserved the death penalty, and that it had to be obvious that Heather's killing had not been carefully planned. He said the jurors should not find Paula eligible for the death penalty if they believed someone else had killed Heather—or if they wondered if Bob Sims had done it.

Groshong admitted, "It was a dramatic thing for the prosecutor to do, to stand here and let you wait for two minutes." But it was another stunt, not evidence. He proposed that death by smothering was not as heinous as other kinds of murder, not as brutal as some other things "in this pecking order of evil."

Weber came back for rebuttal with more fire than before.

"Paula Sims chose the way of death—not the judge, not me, not the police, and not you twelve people. What I'm asking you to do is to stand up for society and for society's right to self-defense. I am asking for a reaffirmation by you of the sanctity of Heather Sims's life.

The jury was out for two hours, including time for lunch, and returned with its decision at 2:40 P.M. Judge Matoesian read the form again.

"We, the jury, unanimously find, beyond a reasonable doubt, that the defendant, Paula Marie Sims, is eligible for a death sentence under the law."

The television and radio reporters blasted through the back doors again and scattered down the hall.

Paula looked stricken, but she didn't move a muscle. Groshong looked devastated. As the judge dismissed the jury until 9:00 A.M. the next day, a bailiff walked over to escort Paula from the room. But she just sat there, her jaw almost slack. Groshong leaned over Paula's shoulder and whispered into her ear briefly, and she stood up and started to walk out of the room. As she walked by the prosecutors' table, she gave a rare glance at Weber and Haine. They did not see her or return the look.

No one would know until the next morning that Paula Sims had misunderstood. She thought she had just been sentenced to death.

Weber felt even worse for his friend that day. Don called Groshong's office and exhorted his partners to give their colleague some support for the last day. Don had begun to believe that the jury just might sentence Paula to death, and he didn't want to see Groshong take that decision by himself. He didn't think Groshong should have to feel that he alone stood between his client and her death. Weber would learn later that Groshong's partners had offered to come back, but Groshong bravely declined.

Weber went to Groshong's hotel room Wednesday night for a friendly conversation about the next day's events. It struck Don as a meeting between brothers during the Civil War—one a Yank, the other a Reb—on the night before the climactic battle.

There was one last blow to what was left of Paula's humanity and dignity on the last day of her trial, Thursday, February 1. The sheriff of Peoria County agreed to requests from several cameramen and reporters from television stations to walk Paula into the courthouse so they could get some fresh footage of her. One pool cameraman for television and one photographer would be allowed.

So the handcuffed Paula was paraded some twenty feet into the building on what could be the day she would be sentenced to death. It was obvious to Paula why she was taking the little walk. But Groshong learned of the affront only when he arrived to talk to her that morning; he was outraged.

And it was only then that Groshong learned that she had spent the night assuming she had been sentenced to die. But that was not all she told her attorney that morning.

Before the jury was called in that morning, Groshong

surprised the small crowd in the courtroom by announcing that Paula Sims had again waived her right to be present, and he asked Matoesian to conduct a hearing on her fitness to be sentenced.

"The defendant has told me that she wants to be sentenced to death and, as a result of that, I believe she is unable to assist in her defense."

In response to opposition from Weber, Groshong added, "She couldn't care less what the jury does. She is of the opinion that it doesn't make any difference, that it was all decided before she arrived here."

Matoesian denied the motion, saying it was not unusual for a defendant in a murder trial to feel that way— even asking for death. That didn't make her incompetent. But the judge did grant Groshong's request to make the first and last arguments to the jury. "He's fighting for his client's life," Matoesian told the lawyers. "He deserves the last word."

Paula looked ghostly and gaunt as she entered the courtroom. She wore maroon slacks and a gray and maroon striped sweater with a white blouse underneath.

The jurors' final decree of life or death would turn on whether there were mitigating factors sufficient to preclude the death penalty. They included lack of a criminal record, rehabilitative potential, extreme mental or emotional disturbance, whether mercy would be appropriate and whether there had been marital pressure to commit the crime.

Groshong's opening statement was his most effective, and emotionally persuasive, moment before the jurors. In somber tones, he asked them to think about some weighty questions.

"Is life sacred? Can people be rehabilitated? Is the death penalty purely retributive? Is that what it is? Is life imprisonment more severe than the death penalty? Are you the same person now that you were when you were twenty? Is punishment by imprisonment a situation where you are punished everyday?

"Are there good things in everybody, even the worst of us?"

The defender admonished the jurors, "Killing Paula will not bring back life. Killing Paula will not make anything right. If she lives, maybe somebody can learn from

422   *Don W. Weber and Charles Bosworth, Jr.*

her. If Paula killed for little or no reason, there is something wrong with her . . . Killing a baby is an irrational
act, an insane act.''

Weber responded that the answers to some of those
questions did not allow mercy for Paula. He asked for
the death penalty, and reminded the jurors, ''You reflect
the conscience of the community of Madison County, the
State of Illinois, and, probably, the country.''

Paula sat with a continuous look of pain on her face.
It was the most emotion that had come through her eyes
in months.

Groshong was allowed to call witnesses, and Nylene
Blew was first. The slim, dark-haired woman seemed almost paralyzingly nervous as she took the stand. Paula
swallowed hard as Nylene looked at her and told the jury,
''I'm her mother.'' It was the first time Paula had reacted
to a family member on the stand. Clearly, the verdicts of
the last two days had cracked that facade.

Nylene told a little about the family's background, and
explained that Paula seldom showed any emotion to others.
Nylene mentioned sadly that her sixty-fourth birthday and
her husband's sixty-first had been in January, while their
daughter was on trial for murdering their granddaughter.

Groshong smiled faintly. ''Do you love your daughter?''

''Yes, I do, very much. And I'm very proud of her.''

The last comment struck Weber like a sharp pain. Of
all the things the mother of Paula Sims might say, that
seemed the most unlikely and, to Don, the most inappropriate. But he would ask no questions of Nylene Blew
today. She had been through enough.

Orville Blew crossed the courtroom again and took the
stand to offer what would be a surprisingly candid and
revealing look at the marriage between Robert and Paula
Sims. It was a story of a daughter torn between love for
her parents and brother, and a desire to satisfy the peculiar
edicts and habits of her new husband. Robert's ways had
been different from the way Paula had been raised. The
Blews wanted to share their lives, but Robert tried to shut
them out. Paula was pulled in two directions.

Orville looked down at his rough hands folded in his lap.
''Even while she was out here, she called me on my birth-

day and sang Happy Birthday to me.'' A tender memory shared by a wounded father and his imprisoned daughter.

What a pity, Don thought to himself. The Blew family should have been part of the heartland. Instead, it had been ravaged and left shattered. No questions for Orville. He too had been through enough.

At the recess, Orville and Nylene left the courthouse, followed closely by Robert, with his Bible tucked under his arm. As the photographers and reporters swarmed around them, Orville held Nylene tightly by the arm. Paula was left alone to face her fate.

In closing arguments, Groshong asked the jury to ponder whether this crime was committed under an extreme mental disturbance that could have resulted from her childhood tragedies or her unhappy and strained marriage.

One last appeal. ''Heather's life was sacred. Mr. Weber was right about that.'' This time, it was Groshong who pointed at Paula. ''And so is hers . . . To thine own self be true . . . Do what your heart tells you that you ought to do.''

Weber thought Groshong had been eloquent, and had delivered the most touching and articulate closing argument in any of the death penalty cases Don had handled. It may have been Groshong's finest hour, Don thought, but it may have come too late.

He looked at the woman he was about to ask the jury to send to her death. And he was wounded by what he saw. She was no longer the evil, ruthless baby killer he had watched for months and had prosecuted so vigorously. She was not the scheming, heartless demon who had snuffed the life from her daughters for some unfathomable reason. Now, she was a devastated shell of a human disaster. He could see, for the first time, a human being in there somewhere, behind the sunken eyes. She had been swallowed whole by some inexplicable pathology, and it had devoured everything she might have worshipped under different circumstances. In her face, Don could almost read the confusion about how she had come to this day. The mask was off now.

Don couldn't find the fire this time. He couldn't find the justice in death for this pitiful creature. He would do his job, but his heart wasn't in it. He had developed great respect for these jurors. He would give them the facts, and accept their decision without hesitation.

Don's change of heart was obvious when he addressed the jury for the last time. The words were there, but the soul of Weber the prosecutor was not behind them anymore. He asked for death for Paula Sims. "The enormity of the criminal conduct, the cruelty and cold-bloodedness of this crime—that is sufficient to warrant the death penalty."

The judge instructed the jury on the law and the list of mitigating factors. They were defined as "reason to punish the defendant with a sentence less than death."

The jurors went out at seventeen minutes past noon, and the attorneys retired to the judge's chambers to discuss the various options for sentencing. Judge Matoesian was insistent that, if the jury spared Paula's life, he had the authority to hand down his sentence on the spot. Groshong was just as sure that the judge had to conduct a sentencing hearing later. Weber was unsure, but said he would go with the judge's decision.

The verdict came at 2:40, just as it had the day before. Before the panel came back into the courtroom, Groshong brought Paula before Judge Matoesian. Again, she waived her presence for the verdict and left the room.

As the jurors filed into the box this time, Juror Number One didn't look at Don. He knew what that meant, but he still felt justice had been served.

As the form was handed to the judge, he asked the media to refrain from the thundering display of the last two days as they bolted from the room. Then he read the form.

"We, the jury, do not unanimously find that there are no mitigating factors sufficient to preclude imposition of the death penalty. The court shall not sentence the defendant, Paula Marie Sims, to death."

The reporters crashed through the doors again, and the small crowd of spectators, even the judge, laughed.

Don looked at Paula's empty chair. It was the only time she had won in this case, and she wasn't there to experience it. *Kind of the story of her life,* he thought.

Matoesian thanked the jurors profusely for their long and dedicated service, calling them "excellent jurors." And then he released them. As they came out of the jury room with their coats, many of them stopped to shake hands with Weber and Groshong, and most of them remained in the courtroom to await the end of the story.

Paula was brought before the bench one more time. Groshong announced that she would have no statement before sentencing. But he asked for punishment that would give her "some light at the end of the tunnel."

Weber allowed Bill Haine to speak for the people of the State of Illinois. "Your honor, the people recommend natural life in prison."

Matoesian looked down over the edge of the bench. "It is the judgement of this court, Mrs. Sims, that you be sentenced to the Department of Corrections for the rest of your natural life. The court agrees with the jury that this first-degree murder was accompanied by exceptionally brutal and heinous behavior, indicative of wanton cruelty. In plain English, it means you are not eligible for parole. You may understand that, and you may not."

Paula had no reaction to the last event in that courtroom, just as she passively had accepted all the other blows there over the last four weeks.

She was spared death, and sentenced to life, all on the second birthday of her sole surviving child, Randy. Somewhere, a little boy who had no idea what had been happening in his life, was turning two years old.

As Paula was escorted from the room, her face still blank, many of the jurors gathered around Weber. Juror Number Two, John Joplin, asked for Don's autograph.

Groshong's only comment to the press was that the verdict and sentence would be appealed. "You win some, you lose some," he shrugged without much expression.

The jurors were asked by the reporters to go to the lobby, where a lectern had been set up in front of a battery of television cameras. Only three jurors agreed to talk. Harold Ryan, Jr., the foreman, was the spokesman, and he was joined by Joplin, a truck driver, and Juror Number Nine, Eugene Farris, a music teacher. They were met in the lobby by a scene out of a movie. Nearly two dozen reporters, waiting eagerly in the glare of the television lights, formed a semicircle around the lectern, where several microphones and tape recorders were set up. Behind the reporters and around the balcony

426   Don W. Weber and Charles Bosworth, Jr.

railing above, dozens of spectators gathered to watch the scene as the news conference unfolded.

Ryan seemed a natural for the role. He spoke articulately and cautiously, answering each question precisely, or, in some cases, refusing to violate the jurors' privacy by answering a probing question. The jurors had been unanimous from the beginning, in general agreement about Paula's guilt as soon as they began talking. But they had decided to go through each piece of evidence and their notes.

They quickly had rejected as unbelievable Paula's stories about a masked gunman, and they had believed Stephanie Werner-Cook's testimony. They had been impressed by Dr. Cases's testimony and the FBI's evidence about the trash bag.

Weber stood off to the side, drinking in the scene.

The jurors had voted only once at the end of each phase, always getting a unanimous result. Their decision not to impose death had been affected by a couple of mitigating factors, including concerns about whether Robert had been involved and whether Paula had suffered from some mental disturbance. They all had wished some of those questions could have been answered. And Ryan said it would have been nice to have had a "smoking gun."

Joplin and Farris agreed with Ryan's comments down the line. Joplin was frank about Paula's kidnapper story. "It's a fairy tale—a lie." He said the jurors had hoped a life sentence would spur further investigation to determine Robert's role. A death sentence might have closed the book on the case, the group had feared.

Weber and Haine took their turns before the microphones. Weber had been interviewed before, but he never had experienced anything like that. He and Haine told the reporters that Robert could face charges in the near future, some of them based on his testimony at the trial.

In the middle of the tumultuous aftermath of the trial and conviction, Don looked at the incredible scene and reminded himself, *All glory is fleeting.*

Epilogue

Paula Sims cried nonstop in the backseat of the car as Deputy Jim Neumann drove her back to jail in Madison County on Friday. After nearly ninety minutes on the road, they passed the city-limits sign at Springfield. She was startled when she saw the sign and asked Neumann in surprise, "Where are we going?"

"We're going back to the county jail in Edwardsville."

Paula stopped crying. "Oh, I thought I was going to the prison in Dwight." There was not another tear the rest of the way.

Because of her comments to Groshong after the verdict, and similar comments to guards in Peoria, Paula was placed on a suicide watch when she reached the jail in Edwardsville.

A snitch later told Weber that Paula began to sob so hard when she was placed in her cell that she was unable to make up her bunk. She sat on the edge of the bed and wept, "It's my husband. It's my husband. It's all his fault. He's as guilty as I am."

The paperwork for Paula's transfer to state custody was completed in a few days, and she was shipped out to the women's prison on February 7. This time, Neumann did drive Paula north to Dwight. Her parting comment to cellmate Kathy Gaultney was, "See ya' in Dwight."

The defense wasted no time in its posttrial assault. On February 9, Groshong filed a motion listing one hundred and eleven reasons why Paula should get a new trial. The major point was Matoesian's decision to allow the evidence about Loralei into the trial about Heather. But Groshong also complained about Dr. Case's surprise testimony as an expert on head injuries.

Paula was back in Edwardsville in March, when Matoesian levied meaningless, five-year sentences against her for the convictions on obstructing justice and concealing a homicide. Matoesian denied the posttrial motion in April, and Groshong filed his notice of appeal to the Appellate Court at Ottawa. It will be a lengthy process.

In an effort to convince the police of his innocence, Robert agreed to take a polygraph test in February. He rode to Springfield with Ventimiglia and Groshong, and took the test from an expert with the Illinois State Police. The conclusion was that Robert had knowledge of the murders, and probably had participated in at least the concealment of the bodies. But the expert was unable to conclude that Robert had been involved directly in the murders.

On April 23, Robert won a round in court. Judge Duffwilliams gave him permanent custody of Randy after a hearing in juvenile court in which she ruled that there was not enough evidence to believe the boy would be in danger from his father.

No charges were filed against Robert, despite persistent rumors that Robert would be indicted at almost any moment. In April, Weber cited personal reasons and stepped down from the investigation of Robert. It was handed off to the "old pro," Robert Trone, and still is pending.

Although Rick Ringhausen and Sheriff Yocom had said Paula could face murder charges in Loralei's death because of evidence presented at the trial, a surprising deal worked out on May 1 ended that possibility. Ringhausen agreed never to charge Paula with murder in exchange for her guilty plea to two counts of obstructing justice; she was sentenced to five years, concurrent to her previous sentences. For Groshong and Paula, it was too good to pass up. She entered an "Alford plea," in which she did not admit guilt but agreed that the prosecution had enough evidence to win a conviction at trial. She will satisfy the sentence by the time her appeal in Heather's case is decided. If she wins a reversal of that conviction, she will be free, and never can be prosecuted for Loralei's death.

Weber went on to other cases. Two weeks after Paula's trial, he won his seventh murder case. It took a jury just forty-two minutes to convict Kathy Gaultney of killing her husband. She was sentenced to forty-five years in prison, at Dwight, where she hooked up again with her old friend from the county jail, Paula Sims. "See ya' in Dwight" was indeed prophetic.

While Don was trying Gaultney, he got a call from Sims Juror Number Ten, Edward Gilles, who wanted to know if it was all right for the group to meet with Groshong. He had invited them for drinks at the Holiday Inn in Peoria to discuss the case. Don told Gilles to go and enjoy himself.

But Gilles also offered some more insight into the jurors' deliberations. They could have convicted Paula in five minutes, but had combed the record, searching for something even approaching a reasonable doubt. They had found nothing.

Weber also asked about Gilles' reaction to Paula's testimony. Don had been told by some reporters that Gilles had grimaced when the prosecutor's questions got tough. Apparently, Don learned, those grimaces had been in response to Paula's answers. Gilles said he had listened to Paula's testimony and wondered, *Why are you lying to me?* What about the body in the freezers? "I thought that baby was right where you said it was," Gilles told Don.

Groshong met with a few of the jurors and came away convinced that he would have had a chance to win if he could have presented some of the evidence barred by Matoesian. A couple of jurors told Groshong they may not have voted for conviction if they had heard about the exchange of the bundle in Alton or the unidentified footprints near the barrel. Weber shrugged that off. They had told Groshong what they knew he wanted to hear. They could afford to be gracious then.

In July 1990, Robert visited Paula at Dwight to break the news that he wanted a divorce. And he wanted Paula's name taken off their daughters' headstone below the banner that proclaimed, "Together Eternally in Love, Mom and Dad." Paula was shattered, and cried for hours after Robert left.

Robert was linked to another woman, incredibly also named Paula. That woman denied that there was anything but friendship between Robert and her. She said she had felt sorry for Robert and befriended him after becoming a babysitter for little Randy.

But to complete the bizarre coincidence, this second Paula pleaded guilty to a misdemeanor charge of battering her ten-year-old daughter. The woman was placed on court supervision and, as a precaution, the judge ordered the girl kept away from Robert Sims. The state is still trying to get supervision of the girl as an abused and neglected minor.

Associate Judge Ellar Duff (formerly Duff Williams) ordered the Simses' divorce file sealed. But in January 1991, Paula and Robert met behind closed courtroom doors for a secret hearing, at which Paula asked for visitation rights with Randy and complained about the newest of "Robert's Rules of Order"—during Paula's calls home from prison, Robert would not allow her to tell Randy that she was his mother. Paula appeared to have been crying when she left the hearing, but none of the parties would discuss what had happened.

With the marriage in ruins, some of the police officers close to the case have let themselves hope that a betrayed Paula would turn on Robert and implicate him. Weber is not so sure that will happen. Paula is an inveterate and practiced liar; having cried "bandito" twice, who could believe her now?

For Don Weber, there never would be any doubt that Paula Marie Sims murdered both of her baby daughters. She smothered them with her own hands. Why she did it, and how she pulled it all off, may remain subjects for some speculation. But the evidence had drawn Weber to several unavoidable conclusions, and a few gut-level conjectures.

Paula had been crushed by the tragedy of her brother's death, and perhaps by a relationship with him that was too close. She had felt guilty, as if she had caused his death and inflicted that horrible pain on her long-suffering parents. Carrying all of that around, Paula probably had felt, as Jeff Reed had said, that she never wanted children, especially little girls. It seemed their only purpose was to cause grief.

Despite that, from looking at those astonishing Sims family photographs, Don believed Paula probably had felt normal, maternal love for her little girls. But her own pathology, and her ability to cross the line into violence, could have been triggered if she was subjected to extreme and unrelenting pressure by Robert. If he had disliked little girls to an extreme, set off against his adoration of little boys, Robert could have brought incredible pressures to bear on Paula, including his absence from the marriage bed. She could have buckled under the strain.

She had no self-esteem, no reservoir of inner strength if Robert bore down on her. If she had married someone else, without his own bizarre pathology, Paula may never have harmed her children.

But, as Bivens had asked, "What brought Bonnie and Clyde together?"

Don was convinced that Paula had planned the killings carefully, and had carried them out ruthlessly and mercilessly. As a cat might lay its small prey at the master's door, had Paula neatly folded the blanket over the edge of the bassinet as evidence that her master's bidding had been done, each time? A gift to him?

She may have regretted it, but not enough to keep her from sitting in the house while Loralei's body rotted in the woods a hundred feet away, probably in a shallow grave invaded by small animals. And not enough to keep her from carting Heather's frozen body around town until it was time to stuff it into a trash bag and dump it in a convenient trash barrel.

Don believed Stephanie Werner-Cook completely. Paula had planned the murder of her newborn daughter from her hospital bed, and had tripped over her own tongue when she let her chatty roommate in on the unspeakable secret.

Paula Sims remains an enigma—an aberration of motherhood, a riddle with no answer. All that is known is that she murdered both of her infant daughters ruthlessly and without mercy.

Babies belong in bassinets, not in trash barrels. And Paula Sims didn't know the difference.